HARD MARCHING EVERY DAY

D1236713

Wilbur Fisk, Second Vermont Volunteers

HARD MARCHING EVERY DAY

*The Civil War Letters of
Private Wilbur Fisk, 1861–1865*

Foreword by Reid Mitchell

Edited by Emil and Ruth Rosenblatt

UNIVERSITY PRESS OF KANSAS

MODERN WAR STUDIES

Theodore A. Wilson
General Editor

Raymond A. Callahan
J. Garry Clifford
Jacob W. Kipp
Jay Luvaas
Allan R. Millett
Series Editors

©1983, 1992 by Emil Rosenblatt
All rights reserved

Published by the University Press of Kansas (Lawrence, Kansas 66049), which was organized by the Kansas Board of Regents and is operated and funded by Emporia State University, Fort Hays State University, Kansas State University, Pittsburg State University, the University of Kansas, and Wichita State University

Library of Congress Cataloging-in-Publication Data

Fisk, Wilbur, 1839–1914.
    [Anti-rebel]
    Hard marching every day : the Civil War letters of private Wilbur Fisk, 1861–1865 / foreword by Reid Mitchell ; edited by Emil and Ruth Rosenblatt.
        p.   cm. — (Modern war studies)
        Reprint with new introd. Originally published: Anti-rebel. Croton-on-Hudson, N.Y. : Rosenblatt, 1983.
        Includes index.
        ISBN 0-7006-0529-0 (cloth) ISBN 0-7006-0681-5 (pbk.)
        1. Fisk, Wilbur. 1839–1914. 2. United States. Army. Vermont Infantry Regiment, 2nd (1861–1865)—Biography. 3. United States—History—Civil War, 1861–1865—Personal narratives. 4. Soldiers—Vermont—Biography. I. Rosenblatt, Emil. II. Rosenblatt, Ruth. III. Title. IV. Series
E533.5 2nd.F57 1992
973.7'443'092—dc20
[B]   91-46739

British Library Cataloguing in Publication Data is available.

Printed in the United States of America
10 9 8 7 6 5 4 3 2

The paper used in this publication meets the minimum requirements of the American National Standard for Permanence of Paper for Printed Library Materials Z 39.48-1984

CONTENTS

For their help, we sincerely thank:

Mildred A. Christianson, Wilbur Fisk's granddaughter,
who generously shared family papers and photographs with us

Rose Anne Burstein, Director of Libraries, Sarah Lawrence College,
who provided information and encouragement

Euclid Farnham, President of the Tunbridge Historical Society

Philip F. Elwert, Deputy Director and Curator, Vermont Historical Society,
who helped us find the Civil War button
adapted on the title page

The cooperative librarians at the Vermont State Library
and the Vermont Historical Society

Marie T. Capps, Maps and Manuscript Librarian,
United States Military Academy

FOREWORD
Wilbur Fisk, Public and Private

Private Wilbur Fisk's letters to a newspaper back home in Vermont make up one of the richest collections of Civil War letters I have seen. I doubt that any collection surpasses it. Fisk is intelligent and thoughtful. He writes well and the prose is still accessible to the modern reader. He successfully presents the minutiae of soldier life—marching, food, picketing, pay, battles—while also explicating the issues behind the war. The collection is also chockfull of good stories. It's not surprising that his hometown newspaper encouraged him to keep sending these letters—Fisk's letters are exceptional. However, while he was more articulate than most soldiers, I don't think that he is unrepresentative of large portions of the Union army. He possessed, in large measure, the ability to articulate the beliefs of his fellow soldiers; he had the same gift of expression, to a lesser degree, that helped make Abraham Lincoln such an effective war president.

Ideology helped motivate Fisk. He interpreted the war as one of freedom against slavery and of democracy against aristocracy. He believed that the slaveowners of the South developed tyrannical tendencies because their lives were rooted in the tyranny of slavery and that their mastery of slaves made them desire to rule or ruin the Union itself. These were points his letters kept before the citizens of Vermont. Insofar as his letters were designed to encourage a Republican understanding of the war, he considered them part of his service to the country. This war required not just live bodies and higher taxes but ideological commitment from soldiers and civilians alike. "Anti-Rebel" meant to keep that commitment strong. Fisk labored over his "Anti-Rebel" pieces. He noted in February 1863 that writing a letter while in the convalescent camp "took me nearly two days to fix it up to suit me though I did not feel inclined to spend more than an hour or two in writing at a time."

In the letters Wilbur Fisk presented himself as he wanted to be seen. Behind these public letters stood the more complicated private man. The confident young voice which emerges from the public letters suggests a confident young man—humorous, patriotic, full of common sense. That Wilbur Fisk wanted to be that young man is clear. It is also clear that he often failed to maintain that confidence and good cheer. From January 1863 to October 1864, Wilbur Fisk kept a diary; a typescript of it is on deposit at the Library of Congress. The man revealed in the diary was more troubled than the man presented in the letters.

For example, a gap between his public persona and his private self appeared in his religious considerations. Publicly, he spoke with confidence, linking the justice of God to the righteousness of the Union cause and the inevitability of Union victory and the destruction of slavery. Privately, he had doubts—not about God's grandeur or the Christian scheme of salvation, but about himself. On April 5, 1863, Fisk wrote the following in his diary: "Was much impressed by reading a tract on surrendering all for Christ. Am I willing to do that? Are there not some secret sins that I am cherishing and which prevent me from approaching God in faith?" He feared that he, like St. Paul, suffered from "a weakness . . . which God has ordained to humble my pride and keep me weaned from the world." If he was truly a Christian, he asked himself, "Where are the fruits of my Christianity?" He worried also about the soldiers around him, who judged him a Christian and who themselves had "serious thoughts for their own soul's welfare. . . . Could I take such by the hand and with confidence in my Redeemer point them to the Savior? No, I could not." Fisk was troubled because his faith did not seem to propel him to witness. This was the concern that led Fisk, a decade later, to become a preacher.

There were other discrepancies. In reality, Fisk worried far more about money than one would have guessed from his letters. He worked various schemes for making money, such as selling pens and paper to his fellow soldiers. When he reenlisted, he confessed that "I have never earned money easier all things considered than I have here in the army." Yet he knew that others considered him too grasping; he made excuses for himself to himself and kept his money-making out of his letters to the newspapers.

Then there was the story of his marriage. During the winter of 1862/63, Fisk temporarily left his regiment. He was in a convalescent camp outside of Washington—the story of how he got there is in the letters. By New Year's he was recovered: "I can report tolerable good health to commence the year with. Am still somewhat troubled with the diarrhea but not seriously." He served as a guard at the camp. When he went to draw his pay, he discovered that for some reason he was marked down as having deserted his regiment. A friend told him he had better get back to the regiment as soon as he could and clear matters up.

Still Fisk lingered. Indeed, when a party of Vermonters started for home, Fisk accompanied them—going in a direction opposite from the one he should have picked. He spent a month in camp at Brattleboro. Then he went home "on a French furlough." There he visited friends and family; but he spent much of this time in Lowell, paying court to Angelina Drew.

It was in the midst of this—while he was listed as a deserter, while he waited for Angelina's decision, and while he felt unworthy of the woman he wanted to marry—that Fisk expressed many of the doubts he had about his own morality. On February

25, he confided to his diary that "the wear and tear of my nervous system in consequence of my dangerous position as a deserter and my anxiety and wakefulness which I cannot overcome is making sad havoc with spirits and feelings and physical enjoyment." He also worried that "should Angie accept me as her husband she will be surprised to find what a weak affair I am." His hope was that "if God will grant me the full restoration of my health and physical vigor perhaps I can show myself more of a man than she had known me yet." He was still recuperating from illness, in love with a woman whom he believed too good for him but whom he was pressing to marry him, and he was regarded as a deserter from his regiment—although he planned on returning. He was in a funk, unable to act. Fortunately for him, Angie agreed to marry him. That lifted the funk at least enough for Fisk to act—or perhaps Angie provided the common sense that got Fisk moving. The wedding took place on either February 27 or 28; on March 2, Fisk reported to the camp in Brattleboro and was placed in the guard-house; on March 4 he was enroute to his regiment; he reached it March 8—over two months from the day he went to the paymaster in Washington and found out he was marked down as a deserter.

What saved Fisk from the consequences he might have expected from being AWOL was his status as a newspaper correspondent. After his return to his regiment, his superior officer—who had political ambitions which depended on newspaper support back home in Vermont—decided to overlook Fisk's absence. If there was an implicit bargain, Fisk was true to his (unspoken) word—none of this showed up in his letters to the *Freeman*. But none of this would have made Fisk look very good either. If he had told the story, it's hard to guess what his readers would have made of it. Would they have dismissed his long absence as trivial? After all, the Second Vermont spent that time in camp, not on active operations. Would they have recoiled from Fisk as an immoral deserter, embraced him as a passionate wooer, or laughed with him as a scamp? Or would they have seen that Wilbur Fisk had succumbed to depression—Lincoln suffered also from what they would have called melancholy— and had what we would call a nervous breakdown? Fisk's decision not to tell this particular tale is understandable, but I wish he had attempted to present Vermont citizens with yet another one of war's unpleasant truths.

Did Fisk sometimes conceal other unpleasant stories that might have hurt the war effort, diminished the reputation of Union soldiers, or embarrassed himself? Generally speaking, no—he was an unusually honest reporter. His diary does tell of incidents that did not get into his public letters; for example, an incident in the Shenandoah Valley in which his forage party was arrested for stealing. He and the rest were let off but he noted in his diary that "it was rather mortifying though to have our names taken down at every headquarters as thieves and plunderers." Yet Fisk was willing to tell of five or six soldiers who "went out to a house near the picket line, for purposes too foul to mention"; he told of soldiers robbing sutlers—even ones who didn't deserve it; and he cheerfully told stories on how he himself had run from battle—his letters of May 19, 1863, and May 9, 1864, are two of the more insightful Civil War accounts of panic in battle. Fisk's letters are almost always more realistic than romantic.

But Fisk was always acutely aware that these letters were public, and he did allow that fact to shape what he wrote. This is made clear when we compare his diary and his letters during the summer of 1864 when so many soldiers of the Army of the Potomac were so demoralized by the bloodshed of Grant's Virginia campaign. In June, Fisk had to watch the soldiers in his company who had declined to reenlist go home. He noted in his diary that "for the first time I repented most bitterly having reenlisted." The Wilderness campaign and the slaughter at Cold Harbor had depressed him. He began to doubt the possibility of Union victory. "Men that fight as these Southerners do are not to be easily beaten." Watching the "old boys" go home and realizing that he had another term of service ahead, he wrote, "God forbid that the war should last three years longer."

A few weeks later, he wrote the *Freeman*, "God grant that it may not require another two years to subdue the rebellion." But writing for the public eye, he was more philosophic. "But to insure us victory, there must be more fighting and bloodshed. The rebels will fight as long as they can, and fight with all the energy of despair." And here he expressed no reservations about the inevitability of Union victory. "What the result will be, unless our national sins are past forgiveness, no one that believes in a God of justice, can for a moment doubt."

Does this make Fisk a hypocrite? Of course not. He was under no obligation to share his private doubts publicly—any more than Abraham Lincoln should have transformed his fears and apprehensions into statements of public policy, although he brooded long nights in the White House and sometimes feared that the war would be lost. Both in Lincoln's writings and in Fisk's letters, however, one can hear sometimes the resonance of their deliberation, a quality that enriches their hopefulness. In Lincoln one hears it most profoundly in his Second Inaugural. In Fisk, I hear it when he foreshadows the Second Inaugural in April 1863, saying, "The whole nation is involved, and deep grief and poignant sorrow must be borne by the North, to expiate the crimes of the South. The issue as yet seems uncertain; and yet it cannot remain uncertain so long as God is just. God does not love slavery; there is no slavery in Heaven. God does not love rebellion; rebellion could not live there. He hates oppression and oppressors. He loves liberty and a respectful obedience to just law." I hear it again a year later, in April 1864, when Fisk says, "Never in a war before did the rank and file feel a more resolute earnestness for a just cause, and a more invincible determination to succeed, than in this war; and what the rank and file are determined to do everybody knows will surely be done." Neither Lincoln nor Fisk were facile optimists; their convictions—and the language that expresses them—come out of their deepest feelings.

Wilbur Fisk survived his war, but he continued to reflect on his experience and its meaning. Included in this volume are three talks—Fisk preferred they not be called "orations"—which Private Fisk, by then the Reverend Fisk, made in the 1890s when the young man of the 1860s was in his fifties. These talks give us the chance to compare how the young man fighting the war understood the conflict to the way in which the older man remembered it.

Perhaps the most surprising thing is how little Fisk had changed his mind. True, occasionally he lapsed into old soldiers' stories that make the war sound like more fun than it was—but his audience included veterans who liked to tell such stories themselves and who knew better anyway. True, over the years he had gained more sympathy for the other side. And he came to hope that war itself would grow outdated. "Here is one party in line of battle and there is another in another line of battle and because they cannot settle their differences any other way they must shoot at one another until one side or the other cries Enough. Certainly Christian people ought to settle their disputes some other way. When they have done their killing there remains the question to be settled the same as before. They might as well have settled it before the shooting as afterwards." But he continued to believe that the war had to be fought, that slavery was at the heart of secession, and that underneath the terrible events God's will was working upon the American people. "Sin and wrong are always costly things in the end and it seems to be ordained that full and exact payments have to be made," Fisk said in 1894. "Every drop of blood taken from the back of a black man as Mr. Lincoln intimated in his inaugural had to be paid back by one drawn by the sword from the white man and all that was accumulated by those years of unrequited toil on the part of the slave was more than squandered during the war." The problem with just war, however, as both Lincoln and Fisk acknowledged, was that "it seems to be ordained that the innocent shall not only suffer with the guilty but often suffer for them."

It is all too easy when we look back on the era of the Civil War to imagine it as a more straightforward time. Then, we sometimes think, Americans were heroic and simple while we are vacillating and complex. I do not dispute the heroism of that generation but I do insist that they were just as troubled as we are and that they faced profoundly disturbing moral choices—which different Americans resolved in different ways. Reading Wilbur Fisk's letters shows us how one American understood the choices placed before the generation of 1861 and what burdens he bore by making the choices he did.

Reid Mitchell

INTRODUCTION

In July, 1976, we went to a meeting of the Tunbridge (Vermont) Historical Society. The president of the Society arrived a little late, explaining that the grocery carton he was carrying had been given to him just as he was preparing to leave for the meeting. The Domino Sugar box contained a collection of documents related to the Civil War. That summer we accessioned all of the papers and returned them to the Historical Society.

The next summer we examined the papers more closely. Everything was handwritten, and in different hands was written the history of Company E, Second Vermont Volunteers, organized in Tunbridge, May 21 (or May 22, depending on the source), 1861. Some of the papers were government forms, filled out on the battlefield by the officer in command. Many of these were signed by Orville Bixby, but in the Battle of the Wilderness, Captain Bixby fell, "hit by a minnie ball in the head."[1] At Captain Bixby's death, Lieutenant Henry Hayward of Tunbridge took command. It was Lieutenant Hayward who had saved these papers, and a relative of Lieutenant Hayward who had given them to the Historical Society. These papers recorded the ordinary details of an extraordinary time. In addition to the material of the war years, the box contained correspondence about a reunion planned for the twenty-third anniversary of the Battle of Antietam, on September 17, 1885. Among these letters were two signed by Wilbur Fisk that intrigued us because they were from the Pastor's Study of the Congregational Home Missionary for Freeborn, Hartland, Richmond and Lemond, Minnesota.

We had promised to talk to the Tunbridge Historical Society about the papers. Because we thought it would be interesting to tell of this Minnesota-Vermont connection, we wrote to the Freeborn Historical Society and to the Town Clerk asking for information, asking whether Wilbur Fisk had come from Vermont and whether any of his descendants remaining in the area could tell us more about him.

About a week after we wrote, we received a response from Mildred A. Christianson. "Your letter, addressed to the Town Clerk of Freeborn, Minnesota, was forwarded to me, a granddaughter." She included a paper about Wilbur Fisk written in 1932 by her grandfather's youngest brother, Pliny, and a phrase in that paper puzzled us. ". . . Fisk was a correspondent of

The Green Mountain Freeman, an influential newspaper published at Montpelier."² What did it mean? What kind of correspondent? Again, Mrs. Christianson provided clues. Through her, we learned that Wilbur Fisk had written letters regularly to *The Green Mountain Freeman* and had signed them Anti-Rebel.

We called the Vermont State Library and learned that the Library had a complete run of the Civil War issues of that newspaper. We went to Montpelier again and again, carefully turning the brittle pages of the bound volumes, looking for the letters. And we found them, from the first to the last, with a few numbers missing and a few numbers repeated, nearly one hundred letters, all signed Anti-Rebel.

Anti-Rebel was a citizen in uniform, consciously and deliberately dedicated to the cause of Union and freedom. As "Our War Correspondent" for *The Green Mountain Freeman* he wrote of slavery, of the Confederate States and the Copperheads, of battlefields, of the wounded and the slain. He examined military strategies, military formalities, military accommodations and military provisions.

In his first letter to *The Green Mountain Freeman* he mentioned his humble position. "By way of preface I ought to say that my rank here is that of a private, and privates are expected to know just enough to obey orders. Many of us have yet to learn even this." However, through the years his letters demonstrated that he did indeed know more than "just enough to obey orders."

He told of the rifleman's daily life, but because he often wrote days after the events, he attempted to see beyond the soldier in the threatened rifle pit or the lonely post on the picket line. Unlike the professional correspondents he met and read and heard about, he did not have access to rank and headquarters. But his vision of the Union inspired him to see and consider all the common experiences of march, skirmish, rest and play as parts of the effort to reunite the states. The Civil War experience became singularly his through his thinking, his phrasing, his language. In spite of frustration and tragedy, humor and irony are in his letters. At times, the humor is stark and cruel.

Pondering issues of secession and war and slavery, he believed that the war must end in Union victory, that democracy and freedom must triumph. With the triumph of the North, slavery must be eliminated. There must be no concession to the Confederate cause. Although for Wilbur Fisk the Civil War was primarily a war to preserve the Union, he could not and would not ignore the terrible conditions of a nation half slave and half free. Slavery for him was "a relic of the darkest ages."

Anti-Rebel's appreciation of man's sorrow and hardship is eloquently apparent in his letters. In his later letters there are expressions of war weariness, and mixed with a righteous appeal for some retributive justice is the recognition of the cosmic suffering in war.

Except for a brief period when he worked in the mills of Lowell, Massachusetts, Anti-Rebel spent the years before the Civil War in his native Vermont. He loved Vermont and the White River Valley. He felt keenly the separation from family and homeland. He was proud of being a Vermonter. Yet, in July, 1865, when the war was over and he returned to Vermont, he wrote that "they have closed the hills up nearer together and made them perhaps a little more steep and abrupt. We miss the large plains of Virginia." In his final letter, Anti-Rebel wrote that he felt as if he "had been through a long dark tunnel, and had just got into daylight once more."

Wilbur Fisk, Anti-Rebel, was born June 7, 1839, on a small farm in Sharon, Vermont, the third child of Joseph Morse Fisk and Phoebe Densmore Fisk. In the spring of 1852, the Fisks left their hilly and unproductive thirty acres for work in the woolen mills of Lowell, Massachusetts, but after two years they returned to Vermont and settled on a newly acquired farm in Tunbridge. After their return, Wilbur Fisk, who was mainly self-educated, taught in a rural school district for seven terms. Then in 1861, he enlisted in Company E, Second Vermont Volunteers. He believed he should regret it in after years if he did not defend his country.

In a speech delivered on Decoration Day, May 30, 1894, he remembered "the news . . . that came to the little town where I lived in Vermont. I was in the P.O. with some other young men to inquire for the news. The postmaster, an aged man, said almost with tears in his eyes, 'The war has begun. I was in hopes something could have been done to have prevented it' and he spoke as if he felt there was an awful calamity brooding over the nation. We boys who loved excitement did not take it so seriously as he did. We were ready to shout hurrah because now there would be a chance to teach the South a lesson, but we didn't realize how much it would cost us to teach it."

In 1932, his brother, Pliny, fifteen and a half years his junior, recollected that his parents grieved, "as they followed their soldier boy to our railroad station at South Royalton and saw the departure of the train that took him from their sight."

For four years Wilbur Fisk took part in the stubborn and slow and deadly warfare to capture Richmond and defeat the Confederacy. He found inspiration in his life in the Union Army, and this feeling of inspiration and idealism expressed itself in his loyalty as a soldier and in his dedication and ability as a correspondent. On one occasion his life as a correspondent gave him practical assistance in releasing him from the guardhouse.

From Pliny, we learned that, "In the fall and winter of 1862-1863 he was sent to the hospital of his regiment on account of sickness. While in the Brattleboro camp he managed to secure a brief leave of absence during which he first made a hurried visit to the home in Tunbridge, staying only two nights and the intervening day. He then returned to his quarters, as the people at home supposed. Later developments, however, revealed that instead of going back to his camp and reporting as a loyal soldier would normally do, he detoured to Lawrence, Massachusetts, some seventy miles from camp, where a young lady friend by the name of Miss Angelina Drew, a farmer's daughter whose father's farm joined the Fisk farm in Tunbridge, was employed in the large cotton mills. Together they crossed the state boundary to Nashua, New Hampshire, in which state previous announcement of intended marriage was not at that time required and were married. When he returned to camp, notwithstanding his captain had responded for him at roll call, a superior officer...having heard of Mr. Fisk's absence without formal leave, promptly locked him up in the guardhouse to await trial. The captain, a short time afterwards took occasion to suggest to the said superior officer that Fisk was a correspondent of *The Green Mountain Freeman,* an influential newspaper published at Montpelier...Being himself a Vermonter with certain political aspirations whose realization depended...on the support of that particular publication...he forthwith ordered the release of his prisoner."

During his four years as a soldier in Virginia, in Pennsylvania and in Maryland, involved in life-destroying encounters, Wilbur Fisk wrote his letters to *The Green Mountain Freeman.* From his first letter on December 11, 1861, from Fairfax County, Virginia, to his final letter on July 26, 1865, from Tunbridge, Vermont, he wrote about his thoughts on the war and his experiences in the war.

Before the war ended, the Fisk family had moved to frontier Kansas, and after his discharge, Wilbur and Angelina Fisk followed them. For nearly ten years they worked hard on their quarter section in Geneva, Kansas, and then in 1874, Wilbur Fisk began conducting meetings and religious services. His brother wrote, "While laboring on his farm, something stirred in the heart of this man...He became conscious...of an urge to be about his Father's business in a more comprehensive field than the few acres to which he held title."

His efforts were encouraged by his pastor and in the summer of 1874 Wilbur Fisk asked the Association of Congregational Churches of Kansas for a license to preach. This request granted, his life changed. With the help of his wife's brother, Reverend Stephen Drew of Albert Lea, Minnesota, he found a place in a church at Freeborn, Minnesota. In the spring of 1875, he and his family moved to Freeborn where he served as "a humble, faithful and tireless worker" for thirty-four years. During this time, he wrote sermons and delivered orations on Memorial Days and at G.A.R. meetings. He continued to reveal the wit, sympathy and social and historical awareness manifest in his Civil War letters.

In 1898 he visited California and touched the western boundary of a Union that had grown and become more unified. And in 1901 he traveled and visited Rome, Naples, Athens and the Holy Land, the world of Anti-Rebel's frequent and relevant Biblical references and metaphors.

Wilbur Fisk retired September 12, 1909. *The Congregational Work of Minnesota 1832-1920* states that Wilbur Fisk's was "the longest Congregational pastorate in this state." He spent more than forty years as teacher, soldier and pastor. In more than forty years of his life he was actively concerned with the political and moral issues in American life.

On March 12, 1914, Wilbur Fisk died in Geneva, Kansas. He is buried in Freeborn, Minnesota. His name is on a bronze plaque imbedded in a granite boulder in Freeborn, and his name is on the soldiers' and sailors' monument in Tunbridge, and, as Anti-Rebel, his name is on each of these letters describing his Civil War world.

Ruth and Emil Rosenblatt
Croton-on-Hudson, N.Y.

THE CIVIL WAR LETTERS OF WILBUR FISK

From the Second Vermont Regiment[3]
Camp Griffin[4]
Fairfax County, Va.
Dec. 11, 1861

By way of preface I ought to say that my rank here is that of a private, and privates are expected to know just enough to obey orders. Many of us have yet to learn even this. As for the plans our superiors are laying out for us to execute we know as little as a horse knows of the plans of his driver. The answer we are obliged to give to all inquirers, is one that would be perfectly familiar to those who belonged to a certain secret political organization noted chiefly for its hostility to foreigners.

This regiment would relish a fight now extremely well. When that event takes place you may be assured the Vermont Second will do their share to wipe out the stigma upon our arms, which they have coveted the privilege of doing ever since the Bull Run disaster.[5]

Since the boys here have received their new clothes, they have been able to keep themselves tolerably comfortable. Before this they had just cause for complaint. I cannot very highly recommend some of the clothing they have given us. I have seen some of these blue pants after a fortnight's service, so far gone as to be actually indecent to wear. Some of the boys have no rubber blanket, nor bed-tick, nothing but the ground to lie on. These articles are very necessary,—almost indispensable. Many of the soldiers would gladly accept an extra woolen blanket these cold nights. In other respects we are as comfortably provided for as our circumstances will allow. You must bear in mind, however, that I lay no claim to any extended observation.

Most of the large tents have small stoves in them made especially for this business. The boys procured them on their own hook. They are bound to keep warm if possible. The tent I occupy is the smallest-sized army tent. To call these tents *contemptible* is using the mildest term that will apply to them. I don't

---

Occasional lapses of grammar, variant spellings, capitalization, and punctuation are as they were in the printed letters. We have corrected only those errors (e.g., repeated words or obviously omitted letters) that must have been typographical.

know their exact dimensions in feet and inches, but a man any above the medium height, lying down, can touch the opposite sides of one of these tents with his head and feet at the same time, and the united breadth of five ordinary men will cover its entire length. Three others with myself make one of these our temporary home. When we are all in the tent, together with our bed blankets, overcoats, knapsacks, haversacks, canteens, guns and equipments, besides having a fire-place and generally as much as a half cord of wood on hand seasoning for use you may imagine that there is but little room to spare. This is no Gulliver tale. We contrived to make so much of so little room by digging down and settling the floor (i.e. the ground) of our tent about two feet and then building up around this excavation with logs in regular Tippecanoe style about two feet more and over the whole placing our cloth tent. This basement protects us securely from the wind, is quite warm, and affords us a chance to stand erect anywhere within our circumscribed limits while before we could do so only along the middle of the tent. We made a sort of platform for a bed on each end of the tent which gives us room, underneath for our wood, &c. On one side we excavated a fire-place with an opening to the surface of the ground outside the tent around which we built a chimney. The soil here is of a peculiar kind of clay indigenous to this locality and when heated by fire it becomes firm as a rock. Two of our number sleep on the ground with their feet in pretty close proximity to this fire-place. Neglecting to place a big stone before it one night to protect them nearly cost us our lives. A woolen blanket took fire, and before we awoke we were nearly suffocated with smoke.

The Vermont M.C.'s made us a visit last Saturday, and out of curiosity peeped into this tent. They admired our ingenuity, but were apprehensive that living below the surface of the ground was prejudicial to health. Our experience however fails to corroborate this view. To our anxious friends at home, I beg leave to say that the fire in our rude fire-place *draws* remarkably well, and we find no difficulty in keeping ourselves warm by it this cold weather. There are other tents fitted up in a manner similar to ours, and some of the boys have built regular log huts.

But my letter is swelling far beyond the dimensions intended. That we may prove ourselves worthy sons of Vermont, and inherit the title of Green Mountain Boys, with all its historic luster, is the firm determination of every brave heart, and their number is not few.

Picketing
Camp Griffin, Va.
Feb. 12, 1862

I have just returned from picketing, and being granted a brief time to rest, I feel strongly inclined to write a description of my experience in this peculiar service. I presume abler pens than mine have given your readers full accounts of this duty, so that anything further on the subject is at the imminent risk of being consigned to ignominious oblivion, unless it be *very* interesting—a consideration entirely out of the question with anything I can write. But perhaps, Mr. Editor, among the multitude of young lads who read the *Freeman,* there may be some who do not have friends here to furnish them with letters from the war, to whom a few words from one in the ranks would not be wholly uninteresting. If you have given our superiors room in your columns to tell their story, on behalf of the privates, I plead the privilege of telling mine. I think the privates ought to be represented in the press even if the representation be a poor one, because we are largely in the majority and have the burden of the work to do.

Of all the duties required of us, picketing is considered among the least desirable, especially so if the nights are cold and stormy. The pickets are posted along in a line about a mile in front of the Federal camps, and extending, for ought I know, from the Atlantic to the Mississippi. A certain portion of this "line" is assigned to the Vermont brigade, each regiment taking their turn in guarding it. There are five regiments in our brigade, consequently each one's turn comes once in five nights. (We always use the term *nights,* because the most unwelcome portion of this duty is in the night, but we *mean* twenty-four hours.) The number detailed each time is two hundred, making twenty to each company. If a company has forty able men not otherwise detailed, it has enough for two installments, and hence each individual's turn will be once in ten nights, which is about the average. This detail is read to us the night beforehand at tattoo, by the orderly sergeant, so that each man detailed may be ready at the appointed moment, armed and equipped for the service. In the morning the camp presents an unusually brisk appearance. Reveille is beat sooner than usual. The cooks are busy preparing us something good for our rations. We generally get a generous handful of doughnuts, which, considering the limited resources of our cooking department, I may safely set down as first-rate. This, with the usual "regimental" bread and "salt junk," is amply sufficient to satisfy the inner man.

The pickets are busy, too, in getting their equipments on, their haversacks filled, and their blankets shouldered. Soon the order is heard, "pickets fall in." Each orderly sergeant then forms his men into a line, and calls the roll to see that all are on hand, and then we march out and form into one company or battalion. If a fellow is behind the time, as I was once, owing to my overweening anxiety to get a letter into the office before I started, he must fall to the rear and be among strangers all day. We are then marched (there is a special propriety in using the passive verb here) the best part of a mile out of our way, to the General's headquarters, to go through a performance, the practical utility of which it would be out of place in me to question, though I confess I am too obtuse to fully understand it, called "guard mounting." This is a new "General Order," the "No." of which I have forgotten. It is exceedingly unpopular with the boys. We are drawn up in a line before the General's tent, and ordered to stand at *attention*, under pain of being detailed for picket every five nights in succession. To stand with the heels apart, or to scratch an itching nose, is a violation of the order, and subjects the offender to the above mentioned penalty. Commissioned officers are then ordered a certain number of paces to the front, and non-commissioned officers half as many, and certain other officers are assigned certain other positions, which a Philadelphia lawyer would be puzzled to understand. The officers seem to need *one* more lesson judging from their perplexity and awkwardness. However, after considerable extra maneuvering, and no small amount of gratuitous instruction by the General's aid, who is appointed chief organizer, and who exhibits an amount of patience on these occasions truly commendable, they finally assume their proper positions, when the order is given to *about face, inspect your guard, march.* They then pass by each one of us, and taking our muskets, which are held up to them according to the manner prescribed in _____ Tactics, pretend to examine them. Of course they are all right. The farce of examining our cartridge-boxes is next enacted. After sundry other preliminaries, the final order, *to your posts, march,* is given. We march a long mile, such miles as are peculiar to Virginia, through mud such as no other state can produce, to the "Big Reserve." This was formerly posted in a prostrate woodlot, where there was plenty of wood for picket fires, but no shelter. Lately this reserve has been removed to a large dwelling house in Lewinsville. Here we are divided into two reliefs, or wings; the right wing going forward and taking their post four hours, the left remaining at the reserve. It is now supposed to be nine o'clock. I find myself counted with the left wing. Each wing is divided into three supports, right support, left support and center support. The right support has in charge the right end of the line meeting Gen. Hancock's pickets, the left taking position on the left end of the line joining the New York pickets, the center that portion between. There is a small reserve at each of these supports. At these reserves the supports are divided into two other reliefs, the first taking their post, the second remaining at the reserve. In two hours they exchange places. Thus it will be seen that we are actually on our posts but six hours out of twenty-four.

The different supports at the big reserve stack their arms together, where they remain until one o'clock in the afternoon. Meantime we are at liberty to amuse ourselves in a way each one deems expedient, provided we remain in certain prescribed limits. Here may be found young men of every grade of character, some grouped together discussing the news of the day, some playing cards, some whittling out wooden pipes, *a la Yankee,* some reading newspapers, or what is better, reading tender epistles from the dear ones at home, and others are wrestling or knocking off caps, or boxing, giving vent to the overflow of their animal spirits by mingling their sports with loud peals of laughter, as some unlucky champion gets thrown or bruised. Here are many, alas, too many, to whom you would have to listen long before you would hear a single manly thought expressed, or a single ennobling sentiment uttered. Their conversation is copiously interlarded with oaths and blasphemy, and their coarse jokes and vulgar obscenity is loathsome in the extreme. But there are others that are far different, sober, thoughtful young men who have come here for the sole purpose of putting down the rebellion, and they would rather let their life's blood moisten the soil, than return to their homes leaving their insolent foes unhumbled and masters of the field. Here are others, too, that differ from either of the above. Externally they are rough, but at heart honorable. They have seen hardship in every clime, on land and water, and their interesting yarns and thrilling accounts of personal adventures serve to while away many a weary hour at the reserve. There are still others who are mere boys in experience. Innocent and unsuspecting, they are too ready to yield to the seductive flatteries of vice.

A few minutes before one the order to "fall in" is heard. The different supports then march to their respective small reserves. My lot happens at this time to be with the left support. The reserve here is in a thick undergrowth of pines where a little clearing has been made and the brush fixed up shed-like on three sides to keep off the wind. On reaching this place, we are divided into two reliefs, and I find myself with the first. We march immediately to our post, relieving the first wing, who now go back and form the big reserve. We are posted along at distances of from ten to twenty rods apart, this distance between the pickets comprising each one's beat. Our instructions are to signal any one that approaches from outside the line, and if he answers it correctly permit him to approach, if not, and he be unarmed, take him prisoner. If armed, he is to be shot or taken prisoner, according to circumstances. We are allowed some discretion here. If a man approaches from the inside, and has a pass signed by certain high authorities, he can be permitted to go along about his business; otherwise, he must be detained till the officer of the day comes round, who can dispose of him as he sees fit. At night no one can pass either way without the countersign. Walking back and forth on a beat alone, as we are strictly required to do, is by no means an expeditious method of killing time. We are left to commune with ourselves. We can look off on the hills that overlook Washington, and though we cannot quite see the city, we can contemplate the wisdom gathered there.

There the sages of the Capital are convened, transacting business which engages the attention of every man, woman and child, capable of reflection, throughout the entire nation. And not only that, but the destinies of unborn generations are to be affected by the deliberations of that august body at this critical time. What grave responsibilities for frail men. The citizens here have told me that Washington has become a changed city, changed in appearance, but changed more in sentiment. Anti-slavery lectures are now delivered there and applauded, which before would not have been thought of, much less tolerated. Let the friends of Freedom rejoice at the auspicious omen. Although we are within a few hours' walk of the city, it is only a few lucky ones that get a chance to go. I tried hard to go at the time Horace Greeley lectured there, but the Colonel not appreciating my literary taste refused to grant me a pass. I was sorely disappointed. I have long wished to see and hear the Editorial Philosopher, and I could hardly reconcile myself to the discipline which made me when living so near this great nation's Capital, practically farther from it than ever before. I certainly should rather have lost a month's pay, such was my infatuation. But pardon this digression.

At precisely three o'clock we are relieved, when we go to the small reserve and stop at a comfortable fire for the next two hours. We had tea and sugar and tin cups in our haversacks, and we here prepared ourselves an excellent beverage to drink with our cold lunch. Thus eating, drinking and chatting, we spent the next two hours quite pleasantly, when we were relieved at five o'clock by the first wing from the big reserve. As soon as those on post come in, we march to the big reserve to remain the next four hours. Here a few can get a seat near the fire, but the remainder have to stand back and shiver in the cold, or devise some other method for keeping warm. Some of the boys, during the night, would wrap themselves up in their blankets and lie down and try to catch a little sleep. As surely as they succeeded they would soon awake, chilled through and trembling with the cold.

The house where this reserve is posted is already reduced to a mere shell, a sad wreck of its former beauty. The doors and windows have been broken to pieces, and whole partitions used for fuel. During the night of which I am speaking, a staircase and a partition between two rooms were smashed down and burned. Another visit from the Vermont Second and its ruin will be completed.

At nine o'clock we again fall in and march to our former post. The veil of night has now shrouded everything in gloom. No sound charms the ear, nor sight greets the eye—nothing but dull vacancy. The moments seem oppressively long, and the pickets wear long faces. Merriment seems sadly out of place, like laughter at a funeral. At such a time how natural for the mind to revert back to the pleasant homes we have left behind. We almost fancy we can see the family circle gathered around the fireside, and hear them speaking of the absent one, and wondering if he is picketing this cold night. It may be a weakness unbecoming to a soldier, and if so we will forfeit all claim to being strong, but in these moments of loneliness, in spite of us, thoughts of parents, brothers and sisters, and kind friends at home, will throng upon our memory, and picture glowing anticipations of the time when the rebellion shall be crushed, and we be permitted to return home and greet them face to face.

> "And when our battles all are o'er,
>   And all our victories won,
> Then, O, my Country, I implore
>   To give me back my son."

Such were the lines received over the signature "Mother," and to that prayer we could respond a hearty amen.

Thus musing, time passes away almost unheeded, and before we are hardly aware of it, the agreeable intelligence "relief's coming" is passed from lip to lip along the line. We gather up our things and as soon as relieved start for the small reserve. It is now eleven o'clock. At one we march to the big reserve again. Finding a seat by a fire, I lean my head on a comrade's shoulder and pass the time in not the very best of slumber, but much better than none. At five o'clock in the morning we march to our post again. It is still dark, but it is hard to realize it is the same night we were on post before. When we reflect that we are standing on the outer verge of all that is left of the American Union, and nothing but darkness and rebellion is beyond, and that we are actually guarding our own homes and firesides from treason's usurpations, we feel a thrill of pride that we are permitted to bear a part in maintaining our beloved Government.

At nine o'clock we are relieved by the Third boys and permitted to march back to camp, which we reach about ten o'clock. Till noon we can rest, but after noon we are liable to duty. I have been somewhat minute in this account, but I have endeavored to give just such information as my own curiosity chafed exceedingly to know before I enlisted. This is a fair description, as well as I could give it, of what is done here in the "Army of the Potomac," every day and night.

Camp Griffin, Va.
Feb. 25, 1862

Yesterday we were visited by the severest wind that we have experienced since we have been in camp. It blew a perfect gale the greater part of the day, making sad havoc with our tents, and prostrating most of the remaining trees. In the morning the sky was lowering, and the hills were crowned with fog. About nine o'clock the fog lifted, and the sky brightened up with every appearance of fair weather. A little later, an ominous black looking cloud of huge dimensions loomed up from the Southwest. It had a dark and angry appearance. Perhaps it reflected the political condition of the country over which it had just passed. It was fiercely charged with wind and rain, with a large preponderance of the former. As the tempest closed upon us, it proved to be all that it had threatened. The rain poured in torrents, and the wind defied everything before it. Men hitherto of reputed sobriety, as they passed by the rows of tents among the shifting gusts of wind, reeled and staggered in a manner that in ordinary times would have excited grave suspicion. The rain was soon over, but the wind prolonged its stay much longer than was desirable.

Probably you are aware that this regiment is encamped in the woods, part of which is second growth pine, and the remainder chestnut and oak. The trees outside of the camp have all been cut and used up long ago, and since fuel has become scarce, so scarce that hardly a sound stump can be found in this vicinity which has not been chipped off close to the ground, we have been permitted, in anticipation, I suppose, of warmer and calmer weather, to cut some of the trees inside the camp ground, especially the oak and chestnut. These encroachments upon our natural protection have left the western portion of the tents naked to the wind, and the eastern part where the slender pines stand—or stood, rather, for but few of them are left—was but little better protected, for these bushy-topped trees having but a feeble hold upon the soft, miry soil yielded like a reed before the immense pressure. Thus the whole camp, which is situated on an eminence, was peculiarly exposed to the aerial forces and they raked us with an energy and effect that Jeff. Davis may despair of ever imitating. Many of the tents were blown down and some were torn in shreds, and a few manfully stood their ground. The trees were being prostrated in all directions, and only by extraordinary exertions were many prevented from crushing the tents in their fall. A heavy army wagon, standing on level ground, was upset as easily as if it were a thing without weight.

Night set in intensely cold. We had hoped that at sundown the wind would abate its fury, but in this we were disappointed. Many of us had no tents, and many of the tents had become so torn that their protection was insignificant. Those that were destitute huddled around their fires and made themselves as comfortable as possible till morning, and those that had tents retired as usual, but not without serious apprehension that some unlucky gust might suddenly reveal to them the unpleasant fact that they were sleeping out in open air. The wind raged till midnight when it became more calm.

I hear of no serious accident to life or limb in our regiment, but in one of the Pennsylvania regiments it is said three men were killed by a tree falling on and crushing the tent while they were in it. Some of our tentless outcasts have provided them a temporary home in the old hospital tent.

The weather today has been fine with a cool Northwest breeze. We have had an excellent brigade drill, the first one for a long time, the ground being frozen very hard. It was quite a treat to get on solid terra firma once more.

———————

Camp Griffin, Va.
March 8, 1862

I frequently receive letters inquiring how we live here in camp, and what we have to eat, &c. I suppose our kind friends in Vermont have some anxiety as well as curiosity to prompt these inquiries, and if it be no intrusion I will, through your columns, give a kind of wholesale reply to them, in my rough way.

First, then, on the list of edibles, stands wheat bread, sometimes sour, but nevertheless containing the principal element of nutrition. Of course it is wholly unadulterated by milk, lard, cream, or any superfluities of that kind. To eat with this, we have sometimes fresh meat, but most generally boiled salt meat; the boys call it *"salt hoss,"* and I am not inclined to risk my reputation for veracity by disputing its merit to that title. The want of no one thing is felt so much as the lack of butter, or its substitutes, in our rations. The sutlers furnish butter for thirty cents per pound, and the boys generally supply themselves with it while they have plenty of money, but when that is gone they must go without, unless their more prudent comrades are willing to lend to them, for getting trusted at the sutlers is "played out." Meat and bread, or, for a change, bread and meat, with a cup of coffee forms the principal staple of fodder for all except the officers. Potatoes are sometimes furnished us, but their cost and the trouble of transporting them, makes it too expensive for Uncle Sam to indulge us in this luxury to any great extent. Beans we have occasionally, say once a week. Peas, semi-occasionally. Boiled rice and hominy are thrown in as incidentals. The hominy being made of coarse white Southern corn does not taste bad, from the fact that it requires a pretty hungry man to perceive that it has any taste at all. A plate of soup, twice as greasy as any dishwater ought to be, is sometimes served to each of us, and it relishes first-rate. On a march we take hard crackers exclusively, because they are light and occupy but little space. A man with poor teeth is certainly an object of pity on these occasions.

When the drum beats, or the cooks halloo, "Company _____ fall in" for breakfast, dinner, or supper, as the case may be, we all rush pell-mell for the cook's stand, which is a log shanty or a tent, or both, and crowding our way up to the door receive our bread and meat and cup of coffee. Now if we can back out without having our coffee spilled, and our bread knocked out of our hands, why, all right;   if not, a volley of oaths and threats are pretty apt to be the consequence. Those that have fire-places in their tents can improve the flavor of their bread by toasting it before the fire. Toasting-sticks are the most important culinary utensils that we use. Most of us have frying pans, and we hash up our meat and bread together and make it quite palatable. As regards etiquette and politeness we are not one whit behind the most fashionable of swine.

Let it not be understood that I write this in a complaining mood. On the contrary, our fare, though plain, is wholesome and amply sufficient to supply our wants. Some of our good friends at home entertain the idea that we suffer greatly in this respect, but it is not necessarily so. True, our supplies may sometimes be short owing to unforeseen and unavoidable circumstances, and it may happen just as we are about to march, or do some other severe duty, but these exceptions ought not to be made the basis of such sweeping comments as many of the boys love to indulge in, in their letters to their friends. As a general rule more rations are allowed us than we can possibly eat.

The privates in this regiment have presented their Colonel with a sword and accoutrements costing nearly four hundred dollars, and he made a fine appearance in his new dress at our usual inspection this morning. Col. Whiting[6] is much more popular with his command now than formerly. Strict discipline, faithfully enforced, though it may engender bitter and angry feelings for the time, is sure, in the end, to command respect. A man with unyielding principles and firm resolution, blended with judgement and kindness, if clothed with authority will make a good disciplinarian and one that will be respected. That our Colonel possesses these high qualities and many others, is abundantly proved by this token and manifestation of regard from the men under him. Col. Whiting is a praying man and a consistent Christian, which, though a rare, is in no sense a mean commendation for an officer in the American army.

The ground is rapidly drying up, and *mud* cannot much longer be pleaded in justification of the "masterly inactivity" of the "Army of the Potomac."

Camp near Cloud's Mill
March 20, 1862

We are having our equinoctial storm here now, and of course drilling is out of the question, so to prevent the horrors of ennui from finding a lodgment in my idle brain, I propose to weary your patience with another letter.

Gen. McClellan's army has at last made an advance, as almost every man in the Union knows by this time. Monday morning, the 10th inst., at two o'clock, orders came to Camp Griffin to have the cooks prepare a day's rations for the regiment, and I suppose every regiment received the same order, for in two hours we were to march. We had before this frequently been ordered to get ready, but there it ended. There was no mistaking the import of *this* order. But very few believed that it would result in mere preparation as heretofore.

Before daylight the drum beat to fall in, and, bidding adieu to our winter's home with many feelings of regret, we obeyed the summons, and marched out to the road, and waited for the other portions of the army to get their proper places. We were in "light marching order," that is, we were allowed to take our rubber blanket and overcoat, but no more. Our knapsacks, and the remainder of our clothes such as could not absolutely be dispensed with, were afterwards sent to us. Most of our little valuables were left behind, with all our surplus stock of clothing, &c. Regiment after regiment, and brigades, and divisions, with miles of artillery and cavalry passed us as we stood there awaiting our turn to fall in with the onward, surging tide of humanity. It was an animating spectacle. If the men had just been freed from prison their countenances would hardly have worn a more gleeful expression. Long trains of army wagons, covered with black rubber cloth, on which was printed in large snow white letters, "ammunition," followed by another train of sombre-looking ambulances, told plainly of serious work in contemplation. About this time it commenced raining. The boys that have been with this regiment from the beginning, say that they have never yet made a permanent move without being followed by a rainstorm. Whether these singular coincidences can be accounted for in the ordinary relations of cause and effect, remains a problem. Some of the trains returned as it began to rain, and the rumor was started, "orders countermanded." Expressions of disappointment were freely exchanged at this new aspect of affairs, but all apprehensions were soon relieved by the order, Forward march. As we passed the line of pickets, we noticed every post was deserted, which gave them a singular and lonesome appearance. We marched a dozen miles or so, through the mud and rain, and halted about noon near Flint Hill, an eminence not at all commensurate with so dignified a title. Here, on ground so thoroughly saturated with water, that much of it was standing on the surface, we pitched our tents for the night.

The tents we use in this campaign are nothing more than pieces of flax cloth, about a yard and a half square, with buttons and buttonholes on three sides, and can be carried in our knapsacks. Two of these buttoned together and suspended over a pole or held up by two bayonets makes a tent somewhat resembling a certain description of a hencoop with the ends open. Any number of these can be buttoned together, if we choose. The wind was changing to the Northwest, growing colder every minute, making the prospect for a night's rest, in that place, anything but inviting. We repaired *en masse* to the pine woods near by and collected large quantities of boughs for a carpeting to our tents, determined to make ourselves as comfortable as possible. But notwithstanding our efforts, only a few of us could endure to lie in so chilly a place more than an hour or two at a time before the cold would compel us to "evacuate" and warm ourselves by the fire or by stirring about. In one of these nocturnal rambles to get warm, I visited Flint Hill, from the top of which, as far as the eye could reach, every clearing was thickly dotted with the bright camp-fires of the newly arrived multitude. It was quite an imposing spectacle; so many brilliant lights emitting heat and comfort to thousands of armed men quietly sleeping (?) near, ready at any moment at the word of their gallant Commander to move forward and give the rebels particular fits in their own strongholds, or wherever they have a mind to meet us and give us a chance for a fight.

Long before morning the whole regiment had "fell back" to the woods, where we built innumerable fires and kept them pretty well surrounded till daylight. In the morning we moved our tents to a dryer locality. We were not long in making ourselves familiar with our new situation. The orders at dress parade gave us to understand that stealing, plundering private dwellings, house burning, and such unsoldierlike depredations would be visited by severe and speedy punishment. The limits of our encampment were drawn pretty close, and any one found beyond them, without permission, would be held to a strict account. The Colonel told us that, if necessary to enforce these restrictions, he would establish a line of pickets around the entire camp. It was evident that the lawlessness of the men, which characterized last summer's campaign, was to find no counterpart in this.

That night I was placed on guard, though I felt sorely in need of a little sleep. Thursday we were reviewed by Gen. McClellan. As the General rode around the square formed by this Division the men everywhere cheered him as he passed them, with the intensest enthusiasm. His very looks, with his lofty and gentlemanly bearing, are sufficient to enkindle a spirit of energy and bravery in the hearts of the troops under his command. All the men place the most unbounded confidence in their General.

Saturday, at 6 o'clock, we packed our knapsacks and resumed our march. Before we reached Fairfax Court House it commenced raining in good earnest. From Fairfax we took the road to Alexandria, and after marching some seven or eight miles we halted in a pine woods, a little distance from the road on the right. The rain had been pouring in torrents for the last two or three hours, which made it very tedious marching, from the accumulating mud under our feet and the fast increasing weight of our clothes. Some of the weaker ones fell out of the ranks, and others threw away their knapsacks containing their blankets and all of their extra clothes. The officers kindly assisted us every way in their power, often taking the gun or knapsack of some lagging soldier and carrying it themselves.

We put up our miniature tents this time on an improved plan, by elevating the ridge pole and leaving one side nearly open. We formed them in a sort of a circle, and built up a rousing fire in the midst. We were thoroughly drenched to the skin, but still it rained. Some of the boys stood around their fires nearly the whole night; others piled large quantities of pine boughs in their tents, and spreading their blankets on this for a bed, ventured to lie down in their wet clothes, while directly under them the water was running at the rate—I had almost said—of a barrel per minute. It is no disparagement to the boys to say that they "steamed" that night in the most literal sense of the word,—the warmth of their bodies in contact with their wet clothes, produced this effect. I fancy those that went to sleep in that situation must have dreamed of Paradise and downy beds. For my part, I lay shivering most of the time in the sublimest misery. At midnight it ceased raining, and Sunday was a tolerably fair day.

I hear of no one's taking cold in consequence of their exposures, nor suffering in any way worth mentioning. The next morning we moved to a more pleasant locality. It sprinkled a little as we started, but the distance was short and the rain was soon over. We are now encamped on the slope of a hill bordering a small pebbly stream of pure water, where there is plenty of oak timber, and where the ground is less muddy than the place we left. Just in front of our encampment, at the top of the hill, is a level plat of ground stretching out to the West, and hemmed in on all sides by the thick woods. It makes us a beautiful parade ground and an excellent place for drilling. We have several drills in the bayonet exercise each day when the weather will permit. Proficiency in this drill must give one great confidence in a bayonet charge, being conscious of the ability to parry a thrust from an adversary.

So much for a week at soldiering.

———————

Warwick County, Va.
April 6, 1862

Gen. McClellan is now verifying his promise to bring us face to face with the rebels.[7] We are now close upon the rebel fortifications and while I am writing their heavy artillery can occasionally be heard with the prompt reply from our own batteries. The rebels are occupying a strong fortification on James river on the opposite side of the Peninsula from Yorktown and about eight miles from that place. There is a line of fortifications, connecting these two places and probably defended by the Manassas army. The rebels consider this position impregnable according to the testimony of a number of prisoners that we have taken. Perhaps a brief description of some of the incidents connected with our journey here may be interesting to the reader.

We left our pleasant camp near Cloud's Mill the 23rd ult., and a little after sundown we were anchored in the middle of the Potomac some 7 or 8 miles below Alexandria on the steamboat Vanderbilt. Although we had no opportunity to know what disposal was to be made of us in the impending campaign so many rumors of marvellous numbers of troops being daily transported from Alexandria to Fortress Monroe had been afloat in camp that the order to have our things packed and be ready to march Sunday morning did not take us by surprise, nor were we at all disappointed at seeing the head of the long column take the road in the direction of Alexandria. Alexandria is considered a very handsome city, and perhaps the reputation is deserved, but in passing through it I saw no beauties there surpassing those of which almost any New England city can boast. Perhaps the distracted condition of her political affairs may account for the vacant look everywhere apparent; otherwise I should consider it a decidedly stupid city. Of course, my observation was limited.

While waiting at the wharf to take our turn in going aboard some one of the numerous steamboats there in readiness, I had a golden opportunity to feast my eyes with beholding the surrounding objects, a description of which would not be interesting to the common reader perhaps though they were deeply so to a verdant Green Mountain youth like myself. So, without noticing particularly the giant steamboats that were moving hither and thither receiving their quota of soldiers with remarkable business-like rapidity, or the enlivening strains of music played by the several regimental bands from their positions on almost every boat, for a parting salute as they steamed away down the river, or the hearty cheers which the ladies and gentlemen gave us from the regular passenger boat between that city and Washington, as a token of their loyalty to and appreciation for the cause in which we are engaged, ere I proceed further I would like to remind the reader that, if he has never stood on the wharf at Alexandria, and had a view of Washington and its public buildings from that stand point, just as the sun was shedding his last rays, he has failed to witness one of the most prominent beauties of art of which our country can boast. The noble old Capitol, towering far above all the rest, the white marble reflecting the lingering rays of the sun, and its lofty dome pointing heavenward, as if proudly conscious of being the seat of power for a great and—yes I will say it—free nation, loses none of its beauty though seen at a distance of eight miles. A view of these enkindled my patriotism more than the best peroration on the Union could have done, though delivered with the most impassioned eloquence. Who would not fight, desperately if need be, rather than have this monument of our National greatness fall into the hands of an insurgent power? and who would not almost blush to acknowledge himself an American citizen, should such a catastrophe occur.

The next day we steamed down to Fortress Monroe, and slept that night on the sandy beach, with no protection from the chilly night air except what our blankets afforded. The following day we moved on several miles farther by land, passing the town of Hampton, which the rebels burned to the ground last Summer. This village, or city was built of brick, and must have been a very elegant place, judging from the magnificence of its ruins. Nothing now remains but the blackened crumbling walls—a sad commentary on the ravages of war.

Thursday the 27th we made a reconnoissance in force toward Big Bethel, and succeeded in driving in the enemy's pickets. We held possession of the ground that night, throwing out one company for picket guard. In the morning we "fell back" and encamped near Newport News. We had started out with the firm belief that we were marching forward to meet the enemy, and we confidently expected victory, and *falling back* was the very last thing that we desired to do. "Twenty thousand men drive in a few rebel pickets and then fall back! Is this war?" No wonder the boys grumbled, and this mortification was not a little increased by the rumor that the rebels had retaken Big Bethel, and were close upon our heels. That night two companies of our regiment were stationed out as pickets. Picketing here in the face of a hardly pressed and malignant foe, has but little of romance about it, and since we have approached the enemy again, picket firing is kept up with most harassing constancy. By a gross mistake a line of pickets was placed that night inside of ours, and had we been driven in or forced to alarm the camp a mortifying and terrible disaster must have occurred.

April 3rd, we received orders to be ready again to march at early dawn. The Colonel prefaced the order by giving us some advice, physiological as well as military, and told us that in all probability before the morrow's sun should set we should see the enemy. The boys all received the order with evident satisfaction, not because we have any particular relish for the carnage of the battle-field—but being anxious to see the work done we have no desire to have it postponed. The next day we were promptly on our way. Skirmishers were thrown out each side of the road as soon as we passed our line of pickets. The position of a skirmisher is anything but enviable. They deploy something in this way: For instance, if we are to deploy five paces apart the first man marches within five paces of the road and the next man within five paces of him and ten paces from the road, and so on, stretching out sometimes as far as a whole regiment will reach. To march across fields, over fences, ditches, bogholes, creeks, and through swamps and almost impenetrable thickets with a heavy knapsack strapped to one's back, besides his haversack containing two days' rations, a canteen of water, equipments with forty rounds of cartridges and withal carrying a loaded gun, bayonet fixed, is no easy task. The skirmisher is the first to meet the enemy and receive his fire.

We drove the enemy from a position they had fortified without any fighting, and that night we occupied the place ourselves. The rebels left quite a village of huts or barracks, and from appearances they had enjoyed much more comfortable quarters during the winter than we had ourselves.

By two o'clock next day our artillery had felt their way to the enemy's stronghold and had commenced exchanging shots with them. We were marched into an interminable woodland swamp, picking our way through brush, briers, and all manner of bogholes. Sometimes our knapsacks would get entangled in the thicket and bring us to a sudden halt at the imminent risk of a dangerous collision with the next man's bayonet,—but on we marched, filing right and filing left, until not one in a hundred could tell the points of compass or where we were any more than if we had fetched up in the interior of Africa. We made the wet ground our bed that night. Several of the wounded skirmishers were brought in and cared for just before dark. After dark the firing ceased but was resumed in the morning at intervals.

It has been more than a week since I commenced writing this letter, but we have been so constantly moving about that I have not yet found opportunity to finish it. The prospect for a fight seems to grow "beautifully less" every day. Our regiment has been doing service picketing the past week, one half remaining in camp as a reserve while the other half takes their turn by companies to go out on post. The rule was somewhat modified last night, and several of our companies were on post and close to the enemy's lines. We could hear their conversation, but not distinguish what they said. We were posted, or rather we had posted ourselves in the edge of the woods bordering the rebel clearing, calculating to screen ourselves from their view, while we could observe their movements at our leisure. They evidently were not ignorant of our whereabouts, for two of their number, creeping up behind the chimney of a dwelling that had been burned, fired at some of our men. The ball struck the tree that protected them just above their heads. From appearances it was thought that they were Minie bullets from a Belgian rifle. Other bullets occasionally whistle through the tree-tops over our heads, and sometimes one would strike in the mud very near us. Our men all remained firm at their posts without returning a single shot. The Vermont Second has never yet flinched on picket, and they have never been frightened into camp by a false alarm. The attempt to relieve the men at midnight had well nigh proved abortive and would never have succeeded had not one of the pickets themselves acted as guide, for no officer unacquainted with the locality could ever have picked his way through that almost impenetrable woodlot and found all his men, for the pickets took good care to make as little noise as possible during the night. But I fear this letter will spoil of old age, and I bring it to a close in season to "fall in" for I am one of the night relief.

Written in the woods at our big reserve by your humble servant.

P.S. Since writing the above, an alarm was sent in to our reserve post haste, and some fifteen of us were ordered out to repel an attack of two rebel companies, probably sharp-shooters, who were skulking about trying to pick off our sentinels. You may be sure we were not long in getting ready, and starting off double-quick, we were soon at the scene of action. The pickets had fallen back a few paces, as only nine were stationed at the exposed point, but they immediately rallied, and securing ourselves in as good positions as we could, we were prepared to give them as good as they sent. As surely as one of them showed his head from behind his concealment, just so surely would he receive a bullet in pretty close proximity to it. And the same was true of us. One of our boys exposed himself by jumping from one tree to another; the rebels to compliment him for his daring, sent a bullet which struck the tree protecting him nearly breast high. This is pretty accurate shooting, considering the distance, about six hundred yards as near as I could estimate by the range of my Springfield rifle. We contested the ground warmly for fifteen or twenty minutes, when we had the satisfaction of seeing them scud for the woods. It was worth a week at picketing to see them "hi-cah,"—so the boys said. After this, they tried to vent their impotent spleen by throwing shells at us, but their sober second thought convinced them that this was not the best part of valor. It is hardly possible for these two armies to shake their fists in each other's faces much longer, without a more important collision. I hear of no one being hurt on our side on this occasion.

Camp before Lee's
Mill
April 24, 1862

I believe if there is anybody in the world that fulfils the Apostle's injunction, "beareth all things," and "endureth all things," it is the soldier. All night, perhaps, we are employed in digging rifle-pits in the rain and mud, and the following night on picket, and then should a night occur with no duty for us to do, ten chances to one if we are not called into line at the alarm of the pickets, to repel the enemy. Hard crackers and occasionally a little meat are our only diet. However, there is but little complaint, and I have no desire to be the first one to grumble.

The army here is not without its "special correspondents," and as they have free access to the highest authority, and enjoy the widest range of observation, anything from a common soldier confined to the strict limits of his own sphere of duties, must be stale and insipid in comparison. Of course it would be outside of Vermont, but in writing to our friends we have the vanity to believe that soldiers' letters are not wholly without interest. The snow, according to our latest advices, still tenaciously holds supremacy over the struggling approach of Spring in your climate, and I can almost sympathize with its reluctance to leave; but here the weather is often so warm as renders shade an agreeable protection. As long ago as the 4th inst., the boys went swimming in James river. The trees are beginning to put out their foliage, and the grass is starting up all about.

Wednesday, the 16th, was a bloody day for a part of the Vermont brigade, and one which will be remembered with pride and satisfaction by all. There had been a disturbance with our pickets the night previous, and early in the morning we were ordered out, and about eight o'clock our artillery opened fire on the rebels from the very place where we were fired upon while on picket duty the Sunday before, as described in my last. The enemy had the range exactly, one of their shells bursting precisely over one of our guns, effectually clearing it of its men, killing three and wounding four. Our men were not long in returning the compliment, and with similar effect. We were stationed in the rear of the battery, ready at any moment to storm the enemy's works if called upon. The battle-field was in an opening surrounded by woods composed mostly of pine. The rebel fort was on the west side of this clearing, situated back in a kind of a bay formed by the trees, and in front of it was a creek with a wide dam, which drank the blood of many of our men in one brief hour.

The Second regiment, which during the afternoon, had been marching hither and thither, in the woods towards the right, without, as it seemed to us, any definite purpose in view, received orders about three o'clock to march—somewhere, double-quick, to support the Third. As we emerged into the clearing, the smoke of the battle was rolling up in dense clouds, growing thicker and thicker every moment as our batteries vomited forth from their brazen throats their death dealing missiles to the accursed minions of slavery. We rushed past the batteries in their rear to the left, losing but one man killed, and one wounded by a piece of shell from the enemy. We quickly formed in line of battle, sheltered by a piece of pine woods bordering on the creek which separated us from the enemy. There were other regiments ahead of us, and we were to be their support in case they attempted to charge across the creek. The rebels had ceased firing, and it was unknown whether they were evacuating or playing possum. As the Third and Sixth attempted to cross, they found to their cost that the enemy had a stronghold there, and were determined to hold it. The water, supposed to be about knee deep, was found to be much deeper, and it is thought that the rebels had some way to let in water at will; many of the boys who crossed at the time have assured me that they found the water had quite perceptibly increased in depth when they returned. When they were in the worst possible situation, the rebels opened fire on them from their rifle-pits, with terrible effect. From where our regiment stood, we could hear the musketry, but could not witness the strife. Our artillery at this juncture opened on them with redoubled fury, and for a few minutes the ground fairly trembled under our feet. Our suspense was painful. In a few minutes squads of men were seen emerging from the woods with their wounded comrades, carrying some of them on their backs, some on stretchers, and others were assisted hobbling along the best way they could; and many, alas! were left that could not be recovered. This confirmed our worst apprehensions. The men were wet to their waists, and of course every cartridge was soaked, and rendered for the time worthless. The dead were not recovered till Saturday, under a flag of truce.

The Fourth also participated actively in the fight. Part of them, headed by Col. Stoughton, had advanced to the creek on the right, and when the Third and Sixth retreated, the enemy's attention was directed to the Fourth, and they were in a most critical position with nothing to cover their retreat. While they lay on the ground they were comparatively safe, but the moment one attempted to rise he did it at the imminent risk of his life. By jumping up and running a few steps and then throwing themselves flat on the ground again, they managed, in this way, to work their way back to the woods. They presented a singular and almost ludicrous appearance in their dangerous retreat. Nearly twenty of their number were either killed or wounded.

There are many incidents connected with this day's work, which are worth relating, but doubtless you will receive full and accurate descriptions of them long before this letter reaches you, and even now it is more than probable that your readers are acquainted with all its details; besides, perhaps those regiments the most engaged would prefer to tell their own story.

That night I was on picket. All was comparatively quiet, except the semi-hourly gun which we fired at the enemy to remind them that we were still living, and to prevent them from repairing their damaged works. The next night I was on picket again, but this time there was more picket firing. We were stationed down the moderate descent close to the dam and directly in front of the rebel rifle-pits. Just after midnight, for some cause, the rebels took alarm and fired volley after volley, keeping up a continual roar of musketry for a number of minutes. The sound of so many hostile guns, as the echo reverberated through the woods at that silent hour of the night, enkindled a feeling of awe and sublimity, such as I had never before experienced. The bullets whistled about our ears in the wildest irregularity, but we lay low and escaped harm. A few shells from our battery, sent with remarkable precision, put a stop to their noisy demonstrations almost instantly. The boys could hardly withhold from shouting in triumph at their sudden defeat, but as silence had been strictly enjoined upon us, we refrained from mocking them in their misery. At daylight we withdrew further back into the woods. During the following day, and almost every day since, quite a number of shots were exchanged, and at times the firing was considerable brisk. It was almost certain death for any one to expose himself to view. Occasionally a secesh could be seen scampering over their works as if on an errand of life and death, and I have no doubt they were. My nearest comrade, noticing one bold fellow walking leisurely along in open defiance of our bullets, drew up his faithful Springfield and taking deliberate aim—I fear with malice aforethought and intent to kill—fired. My friend is a good marksman, and as secesh was not seen afterwards, the presumption is that he had an extra hole made through his body. Our vindictiveness had been aroused to an uncommon degree that morning, by the loss of one of our number. A fellow from Co. B, who came out to the reserve to bring some hot coffee, &c., to us, out of curiosity, ventured out to look at the works our men had been erecting during the night, and in less than ten minutes he was brought back a corpse. A ball had passed through his breast near his heart. His name was John Savery, and he was universally esteemed by his associates.

Such are the horrors of war. Saturday night we were alarmed again by firing on our outposts and many of the pickets fled in terror to our camp. (It is needless to say those pickets did not belong to the Vermont brigade.) It was a stormy night and dark as inky blackness. It was impossible to distinguish friend or stranger. We were not permitted to talk aloud but a perfect buzz of whispering could be heard everywhere. "Who be you?" "What company is this?" "Where is John Smith?" and a host of similar inquiries were oftener made than answered. A Sergeant roughly seized the Colonel as he was passing along the line quietly giving his orders, supposing him to be some cowardly shirker and, severely threatening him, not very politely asked who he was. The Colonel did not show the slightest trepidation in giving his name and after duly apologizing Sullivan allowed him to proceed on his way. We formed in line of battle some little distance from camp and remained until the disturbance ceased and quiet was restored when we marched back to our quarters. I cannot tell how all the boys found their way back, but I know I found my way back by clinging fast to the coattail of my file leader. Our officers are very vigilant to prevent the Rebels from crossing over here and I have no doubt they are equally anxious to keep us from crossing the creek to them, especially by night. Apprehension of this was probably the cause of their firing.

The next day, or Monday, we all turned out and built a brush fence between us and the enemy, which though it may not suggest anything very formidable to anything of more consequence than a flock of sheep, yet we have so arranged that a row of fires can be built at a short notice in front of it, which reflects its whole light upon the fence, and, if a body of rebels should attempt the hazard of picking their way through it, a regiment standing back in the woods out of *their* sight could mow them down by scores.

Heavy details are made every night to dig rifle-pits and throw up breastworks for artillery, &c. The work seems to progress finely; let our friends have patience, the more we fortify the less will be the loss of life.

On the March
Camp near West Point
May 11, 1862

The duties of a soldier are very unequally divided in regard to time. Some days he may have nothing whatever to do but to pass the time as best he can; and then of a sudden he may be called upon to perform all that his physical powers can possibly accomplish, and often his power of endurance yields to exhaustion, and he is obliged to stop ere his task is completed. These extremes of physical exertion may not accord with the strictest rules of physiology, but they certainly do not conflict with the rules of military life.

Sunday, May 4th, was something after this sort; previously we had been doing but little, except such guard duty as was necessary, but this day we were called upon to march—not so great a distance, perhaps, as many have done, but added to our skirmishing it was far enough to severely test our capabilities for this department of a soldier's duty. We were preparing ourselves for our usual inspection, when the order came to fall in with arms. The rumor was in every one's mouth that the enemy were evacuating. We could hardly think it possible. We did not know whether it was a matter for congratulation or regret, for we had confidently believed that Gen. McClellan would, in the end, bag the whole of them, and we did not wish to have them escape. They had either deceived us or had become frightened at the magnitude of the operations that were being prepared for their destruction. This was a point that caused considerable animated discussion in the ranks, but which probably failed to bring out any very scientific strategical knowledge on either side. However, there was a great feeling of relief, and the boys cheered heartily as the news spread.

We marched out into the open field beyond our picket line, where it had been certain death for a man to show himself heretofore, and straight across the dam into the rebel works. Everywhere was apparent the terrible destructions our firing must have caused on the 16th ult. Trees were pierced through and broken down, branches were strewed about, and the ground was gouged and furrowed in all shapes and directions. Dead horses were laying half buried inside the fort, and other offensive matter scattered all about. The stench was intolerable, and must have bred a pestilence as hot weather comes on. After a short consultation among the officers, we were sent back after our knapsacks, tents, and rations. This we interpreted as meaning a march, and we were not disappointed. So, partaking heartily of some half-cooked beans that had been intended for dinner,—for we had no notion of losing the very best luxury our commissary department affords,—we prepared ourselves for our journey and started. We marched on through fields and woods, turning to the right and left, and marching sometimes in one direction and then in a direction nearly opposite. I verily believe if our course was all considered beforehand the man that planned it must be in league with some supernatural power. It was a very warm day, and the heat increased every hour as the sun mounted toward the zenith. Cold water was very much needed, but it was very difficult to obtain any fit to drink. A pure spring by the wayside would afford drink to but comparatively few; besides we had no time to stop. Our knapsacks grew heavy; many of the boys threw them away to relieve themselves of this tormenting burden.

From a negro it was found that some "horse troopers" had gone in a certain direction, and our regiment was deployed as skirmishers in pursuit. We soon came upon what appeared to be a burning bridge, and we hastened forward to save it if possible. It proved to be a mill that the rebels had set fire to, and they were just leaving. We pursued them, firing whenever we saw a good chance. They had made a bonfire of boxes of cartridges by the side of the road which cracked like a bunch of fire crackers on a Fourth of July. We marched in this way as skirmishers the greater part of the afternoon, when we were ordered to return as we came. At the burning mill we saw the owner, a negro, who was guarding his household goods which had all been carried out of his house. He said the rebels told him to burn his house and follow them, for the Yankees would destroy him, and all he had. They probably would have made his house share the fate of the mill had it not been for our timely arrival. He manifested as much inward satisfaction at seeing us, as if he had suddenly recognized an old friend.

The afternoon was fast waning when we got back to where we were first deployed as skirmishers, and being very tired as well as hungry, we expected this would be our camping place for the night,—the wish being father to the thought. Probably but few orders had been obeyed with greater promptness during the day than the command, Rest, was at this time. O, what relief a few minutes rest like this afforded! Surely they wouldn't be so unfeeling as to make us continue this weary march any further that night. But the stern, prompt order, Fall in, sounded the death knell to these pleasing illusions. We were soon on the way again. The Vermont Brigade was two miles further on, and we must overtake them. Could we accomplish this distance? Our shoulders ached under the galling knapsack straps which they had supported all day, and our feet were sore and blistered, but still the column moved on. Our two miles lengthened into four, but no signs of the Brigade yet. The Captain, leading the column, was often implored to halt and allow us a few minutes rest,—the Colonel having rode on some distance ahead. He yielded, but it was not in accordance with orders, and he was put under arrest, but subsequently was released.

We continued our march till about 9 o'clock, when we finally halted in a newly plowed field where we spent the night. We spread down our blankets on the moist, almost muddy ground, and laid down for a night's rest. The ominous haze that had been gathering around the sun in the afternoon, now thickened into a rain storm about midnight. Perhaps the reader can imagine the peculiarly pleasant sensation one feels sleeping in the open air with the gentle rain pattering constantly in his face, but I confess I lack the ability to describe it.

In the morning we found ourselves considerably refreshed, though we were wet and somewhat stiff and lame. After breakfast we were soon on our way again. We marched but a short distance and halted to support a battery. We remained in the edge of the woods during the battle of Monday and the succeeding night; we were a sort of picket reserve. The success of Gen. Hancock just at night was received with the most enthusiastic cheering. The woods fairly rung with their shouts. These cheers were so galling to the rebels that they sent several well directed shells to us, but this only increased the cause of their annoyance.

It rained till midnight. In the morning we moved and encamped in the woods near the battle-field. Till Friday we had but little to do again. Thursday, in company with a friend, I visited the battle-field where there were many of the dead still unburied. One can hardly refrain from shedding a silent tear over the last resting place of these brave men. I saw as many as a dozen buried side by side in one grave, all from one company. Perhaps in other places there were even more than that. Those that I noticed in particular were from the 1st regiment Excelsior Brigade. Like a band of brothers they had fought like the heroes they were, and perished, nobly contending for the cause of humanity against armed usurpation; and now a simple shingle with their name marked on it tells the traveler where they lie. But the saddest sight of all was to see wounded men still alive and uncared for. I saw a man wounded in the head, a clot of brains marking the spot where he was hit. He was leaning back against some logs, in a partially upright posture, still breathing, though apparently unconscious. I might multiply descriptions of these horrors if it were pleasant to write of them, but it is not.

Friday and Saturday we continued our march. On to Richmond has lost its unpopularity, and we have faith to believe we shall soon possess that city.

Vicinity of Richmond
Tuesday, May 20, 1862

It may occur to you that this is a novel place from which to date a letter, but it is the nearest approximation to accuracy that I can give. We are marching towards the rebel capital slowly but surely, the rebels retreating as we advance. A negro has just informed us that we are within sixteen miles of that city. According to his testimony, he has heard them express their determination to make a desperate stand at the Chickahominy river, five or six miles this side of Richmond, and fight us there till their last man is killed, if necessary, before they yield. This kind of talk is getting to be an old story; the same was said at Yorktown.

We left our pleasant camp near Williamsburg Friday morning, May 9th, at break of day, and, in the language of horse racers, made excellent time till the middle of the afternoon, when we halted for the night in a wheat field adjoining the road. Here we spread down our blankets for a bed in the open air and laid down to rest, the moon keeping vigil over our unconscious hours. I doubt if ever king in his royal palace enjoyed more refreshing repose than did we soldiers that night, fatigued as we were by the day's march. If a spectator had visited us at dead of night and heard the hoarse music that was discoursed in regular metre from a thousand pair of nostrils, he would need no further evidence that soldiers can sleep soundly enough in open air, and that soft beds and downy pillows are not indispensable to a good night's rest. We resumed our march early in the morning, and pushed on till afternoon, this time halting in the orchard of a staunch secessionist. Hungry and tired, it was a grateful privilege to rest, but our haversacks were a solemn mockery to our appetites. Hard crackers, and but a limited supply of them, were their sole contents. No meat, salt or fresh, and (of course) no butter or cheese to eat with them. I have noticed in some papers the tantalizing statement that abundant supplies of commissary and quartermaster stores have been furnished the army here; but if so we are quite frequently an uncomfortable exception in receiving this bountiful supply. It don't mend the matter to complain, so the boys patiently submit.

Those that had the materials made coffee in their tin cups to eat with their crackers, and bread and milk fashion such a dish relishes well, providing a fellow is sufficiently hungry. Under these circumstances, you will hardly blame the boys for being tempted to capture some of the "Virginia rabbits" that were squealing about in the woods near by, apparently common property. There were some good suppers eaten outside of the officers' tents that night, which may possibly diminish the inventory of property on the estate of this man, who, if I am correctly informed, has served in the rebel army. This "wanton destruction of property" was promptly checked as soon as it became known. A large patrol guard was established and heavy punishment threatened to every soldier caught in this business. Secesher's property was vigilantly protected. Not a rail was allowed to be touched, nor a hen insulted, that belonged to him. I hope he will be induced to reciprocate this unmerited kindness and take the oath of allegiance.

Sunday we had entirely to ourselves. No marches or fatigues are required of us on this day, unless absolutely necessary. Gen. McClellan respects the Lord's day, as do a large proportion of his men. Many of them respect it more because *he* does than from any other consideration. Divine services were held in our regiment, the first we have enjoyed the privilege of attending since we left Camp Griffin.

The next day we marched on to New Kent Court House, where part of our regiment was detailed for picket. We left our posts the following morning, falling into line as the remainder of the regiment came up, marched to Cumberland or Perham's Landing on the Pamunkey river. This was emphatically a crosslot march, and the distance, if counted by difficulties instead of miles would reach an enormous figure. The route lay through swamps and creeks and thick undergrowth woods—the most difficult place in the world to march. Marching in a column a mile or more in length is altogether a different thing from marching alone. If the head of the column comes to a place where but one can pass at a time, those in the rear are obliged to wait till all ahead of them have reached solid ground, so that whenever they have crossed the swamp, or creek, or whatever the obstruction may be, they are far behind and it takes a long time to get the ranks closed up. There is a general order issued to remedy this evil, but it can hardly be said to be effectual. This kind of marching, especially after a rain, may be considered the rule, while good marching on good solid ground is the exception. If some of the boys in Vermont, who think a soldier's life an easy one, had been in the ranks with us during our various marches, they would have found a practical logic in the reality to convince them that marching is fatiguing business, even for soldiers, these hot days—and rainy ones are no better.

The word "halt" is always an agreeable command, but there is always a great many annoying preliminaries to go through before we can take advantage of it to rest. Often just as we are about to release our aching shoulders from the galling knapsack strap, the order "attention" is given, and we are moved perhaps six inches and perhaps six rods when we halt again and wait for further orders. Some run the risk and sit down, others throw off their knapsacks, but the majority wait, expecting every minute to move to another position that will square more precisely with military exactness. Now while I am in a complaining mood and have the subject under consideration I will give one of a thousand instances, just for an illustration. I suppose it is understood that I am writing these letters for the exclusive benefit of the younger portion of your readers, who no doubt have a laudable curiosity to know everything that pertains to the army, and all others are requested to pass them by.

When we reached Perham's Landing, we stopped as usual, and of course went through the customary evolutions preliminary to a final halt. The word came at last and not doubting its good faith we eagerly threw off our burdensome knapsacks, hoping to have time to rest and partake of our rations. (I suppose "refreshments" is a word more in accordance with the refined use of language, but it does not at all accord with my present humor.) We had had no coffee that morning, many of us had eaten nothing since the afternoon previous, having come directly from the picket, and as it was close on to noon, we naturally began to feel the keen demands of appetite. One of our company happened to have a paper of tea which he generously distributed as far as it would go, and we repaired to the bushes near by and struck up a fire, and in a short time had it covered with cups of water for our tea. Just as it was beginning to simmer, and we were anticipating a decent breakfast after all, the everlasting order came for the fifth time I believe, to "fall in." We had no means of knowing whether we were to march ten miles or ten feet, but the old Colonel was coming and the order must be obeyed, and promptly too. So away went our tea into the fire, and with it all our labor and expectations, and many I fear lost their patience too in that unlucky moment, for their countenances, which a few minutes before were all aglow with animation, suddenly became darkened with angry scowls, and more than one fierce thunderbolt of wrath, in the shape of oaths and curses, was hurled forth from under that black cloud of frowns, but of no avail. Forward march was soon ordered. We go on 200 yards perhaps and halt, unsling knapsacks and sit down once more, but not long. "Fall in," was the order again and we marched straight back to the place where we were at first. "Such is life," soldiers' life at any rate. We have our vexations, trifles as well as stirring events.

The next day we marched up the river to the farm of Col. Robert, General of the rebel army near the White House, where we remained till morning. This was a very pleasant place. We had but very little to do except guard duty, but considerable of that as a guard was stationed around every regiment to keep us where we belong, The always expected, but never welcome detail for night fatigue that we had become accustomed to at Lee's Mill, did not trouble us here. We had nothing to do the principal part of the time but sit in our tents and discuss the events of the day.

The inevitable negro question would of course be the subject of the most animated conversation of anything we could bring up, for that inexhaustible subject claims preeminence in camp as well as court, and there are almost as many opinions expressed in regard to it in a tent's company as there are in Congress. The boys think it *their* duty to put down rebellion and nothing more, and they view the abolition of slavery in the present time as saddling so much additional labor upon them before the present great work is accomplished. Negro prejudice is as strong here as anywhere and most of the boys would think it a humiliating compromise to the dignity of their work to have it declared that the object of their services was to free the repulsive creatures from slavery, and raise the negro to an equality with themselves. I verily believe if such a declaration was made to-day a majority would be inclined to lay down their arms and quit the service in disgust. The most cordial reception by far that we have received since we left the free states, was tendered us by this sable species of human property. As we were passing by the premises of one of the more wealthy farmers on our way here, a group of negroes, a score or more composed of men, women and children of all ages, climbed upon the fence by the roadside and greeted us in in their earnest simple way "God bress you," "I's glad to see you," "I's glad you's come," "God bress you," and many similar exclamations as they bowed, and courtesied, and waved their hands to us, attesting their childish glee at seeing so many Union soldiers. They were dirty and ragged and probably as a perfectly natural result were ignorant and degraded, but they seemed to understand, as nearly all the negroes here do, that somehow all this commotion has a connection with them and will bring about their freedom in the end. They seem conscious of being at the the bottom of all this trouble, and all the deceptions their masters could invent have failed to rob them of this knowledge.

Monday the 19th we had orders to start on again. We were thoroughly rested and idleness was beginning to be as irksome as marching had been. It was actually a relief to be on the road once more. To-night we are encamped in an oak woods, whose rich foliage protects us overhead while huckle and blue berries just in full bloom make a beautiful carpet underneath. The whipowill is singing merrily on a branch over my head and as we are to start again in the morning at precisely four o'clock I am reminded that it is time to seek repose.

Across the Chickahominy, Va.
June 7, 1862

Day before yesterday we crossed the Chickahominy, but did not leave behind our knapsacks as per order a few days previous. Neither did we cross in front of our temporary encampment, as we had anticipated, but we marched down the stream and crossed on another bridge from that we had been engaged in building near the battle-field of Saturday and Sunday. For twelve days we had been encamped in the woods on the opposite side of the hill from the creek and about ten miles above the railroad bridge. From the brow of this not very high hill could be seen the eminence beyond which separated us from Richmond, said to be provided with powerful means for defensive warfare, while between lay the valley of the Chickahominy. Although the rebels are doubtless as thick as Egyptian frogs in the woods opposite, they manage to keep pretty well out of sight. Only now and then a stray horseman could be seen riding rapidly hither and thither, and always quickly disappearing from view in the woods, where probably they had their forces concealed.

While here we had but little to do but picket and build bridges. This creek, which is fast becoming famous, is the most unpromising stream I ever saw to bridge. Like a city, its suburbs extend far back into the country on each side, and the whole valley, or plain, is one endless swamp, in places overflowing with several feet of water, and generally covered with dense forest; for the trees here seem to have no objection to growing, even if their roots, and a considerable portion of the trunk, are buried under water. It can readily be conceived that to build a passable road across a place like this is more than ordinarily difficult, especially when there is a hostile army on the opposite side warily watching every movement we make. I will not attempt to describe the *modus operandi* of building these unique and singularly constructed bridges, for I am conscious you have other correspondents here who *know how*. All I can say about it is, the pioneers and others who are detailed for this purpose take their axes and wade in to the handiest trees and, after cutting them the right length, float them to where they are wanted, when other men take them and give to each log its proper position in the forthcoming bridge. An extra regiment goes with the workmen to protect them. Batteries, too, are stationed at every available point to command the bridge. Once, while our regiment was acting as guard, and when we were quietly passing away the time, as unconscious of danger and as unmindful of the presence of an enemy as if we had been playing with the kitten under the parental roof in old Vermont, we were suddenly startled into the liveliest activity by a well-directed cannon ball which passed just over our heads and planted itself in the ground a short distance from us, followed by the second and third shot in almost the same place. There was a lively bustling among the boys just then. The thread of many an animated discussion was suddenly broken; papers were thrown aside by those lucky enough to possess them; cards were rejected without the least regard for their loss,—for it is quite noticeable that card-players, gamblers especially, have an instinctive dread, a superstitious fear of cards in moments of alarm and peril,—all were quickly on their feet ready to run, or dodge, or look out for themselves the best way they could. Soldiers, when they are not in the ranks armed and equipped and under the influence of discipline, and not directly under the control of a leader, feel just as other people are supposed to in times of danger, and when one shot has barely missed them, and they have reason to believe another is about to be fired, with no chance on their part to return it, or for concerted action to resist the foe, it is the most natural thing in the world for even soldiers to feel inclined to run, and to any one who would attribute this inclination to cowardice, I would say it is a great pity, the Army of the Potomac should be deprived of *their* services. However, there was no running of any consequence here; many of the boys never so much as stirred out of their tracks. Our batteries promptly accepted the rebel challenge and silenced their saucy demonstrations in short metre. The workmen kept right on with their work, without scarcely deigning to notice anything but their own legitimate business. In due time, when all these bridges are finished, we expect the whole army to march across and either get terribly whipped or force our way into Richmond.

As I said, we had but little to do, but idleness is by no means the parent of contentment. If one's mind is unoccupied it will prey upon itself, or seek gratification in whatever comes in its way, no matter how unworthy; hence the tendency to evil in camp life. But, excepting a few grumblers, the boys have been in good spirits and have enjoyed themselves comparatively well, confident of being soon led on to victory by our almost idolized General. Hard crackers and meat are the sum total of our living, the visits of sutlers being almost as rare as those of angels. There is but little temptation to surfeit, to the detriment of health or comfort, on such fodder, and all attempts to modify the flavor of our plain fare—as, for instance, to warm over our meat in a spider and fry our crackers in the surplus fat—is promptly frowned down by the authorities that be. Doubtless these restrictions are made out of a wholesome solicitude for our physical welfare, so while we are all prohibited from making our rations more palatable—and I submit to you if the desire is not a laudable one under the circumstances—no doubt many of the more imprudent are prohibited from enjoying the luxury of a sick headache quite too often to make it profitable for Uncle Sam. The boys found a place a short distance outside of the camp, at a certain mill, where they could occasionally buy a cup of flour or meal, at a price which would render a common crop on an ordinary farm worth a fortune to its possessor, and out of this manufacture puddings or flapjacks in a style of simplicity such as only soldiers would think of adopting. I fancy our tidy New England housekeepers, who take honest pride in setting a well furnished table, would smile to see what splendid novices we are in the culinary art. But any young lady so foolish as to contemplate matrimony with such rugged specimens of humanity as we poor soldiers, if she be an indifferent cook, need not be unduly elated at this account, nor think her imperfections will be lightly overlooked, for these same boys, who out-Graham Sylvester Graham[8] himself, in his most radical ideas of simplicity in diet, would scorn to accept such food if served to them by their dearest beloved, of whom they will imagine angelic things. Coarse meal, cold water and salt have been the ingredients composing many a meal for us, which a thanksgiving supper, in other circumstances, will scarcely rival. Occasionally a sutler comes into camp, and forthwith a rush is made for their "goodies," regardless of the extravagant prices demanded. Cheese at fifty cents a chunk, said chunk supposed to weigh a pound, pies as large as a common saucer, and perhaps a little too thick to read *fine* print through, for a quarter, and other things accordingly. A hungry man could invest five dollars for a dinner at one of these establishments and scarcely do justice to his appetite. I suppose people of refinement would consider it in bad taste to have much to say on the mere matter of eating and drinking, but we plead for an exception in our case, for what can "the men" be expected to know of the common courtesies of life.

It seems, then, after much debating, that Congress has refused to pass the Emancipation act, but Provisional Governor Stanley of North Carolina, without stopping to debate at all, has *not* refused to close the schools in that State for colored children, nor to return runaway niggers to their masters, providing the master will take the oath of allegiance. Simplified to the comprehension of a soldier, it seems to amount to just this: if a man—a rebel, if you please—accustomed all his lifetime to swearing, is willing, in accordance with his profane habit, to again swear allegiance to the Government he has before sworn to maintain and since sworn to repudiate, he may take his human property wherever he can find it, with the pleasing consciousness that Lincoln's government is better able to protect the peculiar institution than that of his majesty, Jeff. Davis, and withal full as willing. So our deluded "Southern brethren" are to be conciliated after all by some sugar-plum policy, instead of being forced into obedience at the cannon's mouth. "But," says the slaveholder's apologist, "you are here to suppress rebellion and restore the laws as *they were,* State laws and all, without any distinction between slave and other local laws, and what are you going to do about it?" Of course we are cornered, and can only say, if we are here in Virginia fighting to restore the old slave code in this corrupt State, then in the name of consistency let it be so understood. They may fire upon our flag and trail the Stars and Stripes in the dust; they may send their murderous shells hissing through our ranks; they may fire upon our flags of truce and impose upon us by theirs; they may exhaust their ingenuity in inventing infernal machines for the downright murder of our troops, and perpetrate deeds of infamy and cruelty upon our wounded and prisoners that fall into their hands such as would make ordinary devils blush; but no matter, only swear allegiance when you are caught, dear rebels, and we will return you your niggers. Why won't the rebels appreciate the wondrous magnanimity of our government.

Well, I am sure we all want the war to close at the earliest possible moment, for we are anxious to return to our peaceful avocations at home as soon as possible, but it seems an insult to the dignity and patriotism of any soldier to ask him to fight for restoring slavery, already crippled by its own self-inflicted blows, to its former position of power and haughty defiance. And it is a most lame and impotent conclusion to suppose that to be the shortest road to permanent peace. If the Union is to be built up in this way I wish some one strong in the faith promulgated by such sheets as the New York *Herald* would estimate its value and tell how long it would last. Would it ever survive another change like the one from Buchanan's to Lincoln's administration in peace? We opine not, but should be pleased to be convinced to the contrary.

But my letter is long enough, plenty.

Yours Abruptly

Across the Chickahominy, Va.
June 15, 1862

Having visited nearly every tent in the Regiment in the hopeless search for something to read, and meeting everywhere the same inevitable negative, I have concluded as a *dernier resort* to kill time, to put your patience to the rack once more by attempting to manufacture another rambling epistle. So piling up all the knapsacks I can beg or borrow for a seat and writing desk under our excellent shelter-tent (or sunshade as they should be called, for being elevated a number of feet from the base to admit the cool air on all sides, while at the same time protecting our heads from the burning rays of the sun, they seem, by virtue of office, to merit that title), I have taken up my position and will endeavor, under the potent inspiration of innumerable voices talking all manner of sense and nonsense—"camp-talk,"—to present, if possible, a rough outline idea of how we live, and move, and have our being, here close up under the rebels' noses. To add to the special felicity of my position, I find it by no means invulnerable against the powerful caloric batteries of the sun, notwithstanding we have constructed quite an abattis of boughs, freshly imported from the woods, and an extra armor of blankets over the tent. Indeed, I consider it a mild expression to say that it is hotter here than in that place where we presume the rebels are booked to go as soon as we shoot them.

Last Tuesday was a cold, drizzling, rainy day, but ever since then it has been growing hotter and hotter, each day being about seven times hotter than the one preceding. That day and the night previous the old Second was on picket—part of us. In this place the two lines of pickets, ours and the "rebs," are close together, only an oat-field about sixty rods wide separating them. We are now encamped on what appears to me rather a worn-out farm, though of respectable dimensions, owned, of course, by a loyal secessionist. It is enclosed on all sides, as nearly all the farms here are, by woods, while on the North side flows the far famed Chickahominy. West of us there is a sort of ravine, the opposite side rising abruptly, and is covered with timber. Here we have our picket reserve. At the top of this bluff the table-land stretches off to the West, covered with as handsome a crop of oats as I ever saw wave before a passing breeze. Just beyond this oat-field, are woods again, in the edge of which are the rebel pickets, while we are stationed behind stumps and trees on this side. The rebels took occasion to fire at us whenever they fancied they saw a good opportunity, but we were not allowed to return the compliment. This prohibition rather crossed the grain of some of the boys who ached to teach them better manners; but no doubt the officers had good reasons for keeping silent, not apparent to us.

Not content with musket firing, the enemy opened on us from a battery of more formidable belligerent power, and threw shot and shell pretty freely through the woods where part of the line was stationed, but providentially no one was hit, nor did any of the boys skedaddle. Just after sundown and while those on the reserve were trying to get a little sleep, preparatory to going on post, the rebels saluted us again with their infernal shells, which seemed to burst almost in our ears, but doing no damage. The boys were all suddenly inspired with a desire to change their position, if not but a few feet, though it would be difficult to tell in what respect one place was more secure than another. The "rebs" have fired over into our camp several times, and in more than one instance with fatal effect. For a few days past they have been remarkably quiet, and the story goes that our sharpshooters have such command of their battery that they cannot work it. How true it is, I do not know, but I know that the men are ever ready to give prompt reasons for occurrences which Generals are often at a loss to account for.

During the night the rebels coolly advanced their line of pickets into the oat-field, so near that we could hear them cough, and even whisper,—they did not seem to think it prudent to talk aloud much. Some of the boys declare they heard them speak of their dangerous proximity to the *Vermonters*, who, they seemed to have discovered, occupied the line in their front. They commented upon our personal prowess in a way quite flattering to us, coming as it did, from such a source. They thought men of such gigantic proportions, carrying such long ranged rifles as we do, were opponents that would give them trouble to cope with.

One night we were aroused by sharp firing among the pickets. We hustled out of our tents, and in an incredible brief space of time, were in line of battle, ready to meet the enemy if attacked. The hurried order, "fall in,—wake up, boys,—wake up,—quick,—fall in," and the sharp crack, crack of musketry, with an occasional crash as part of a volley was fired, at that hour of the night, and foreboding, as it did, bloody, desperate consequences, had the effect to render the camp a scene unusually animated and exciting. The firing gradually ceased, and after remaining in line a short time without any alarm being given, we broke ranks and returned to our tents. As a compensation for this intrusion upon our slumbers, we had the privilege of seeing the moon completely veiled in the earth's shadow, for at that particular time the moon's eclipse was total.

Large details are made every day for fatigue duty. Bridges and roads are being built across the creek with all possible dispatch. Cutting pine logs for corduroy roads and bridges, is very pleasant business for an exchange, but some portions of the work in making this incorrigible swamp and stream passable, is far from being agreeable.

Since commencing this letter, we have been visited by a heavy thunder shower, and the indications now are, that we shall have more rain and less heat. Thus we live!

Camp near Harrison's Landing
July 15, 1862

The stirring events of the last days of June and first of July, are still fresh in the minds of every one, and perhaps familiar to all by this time, but every one likes to tell his own story, and having just recovered from a temporary illness caused by the excessive fatigue of the march, I propose to tell mine.

The ball opened Thursday, June 26, in the afternoon, and till nine o'clock that evening there was the most rapid firing of artillery I have heard during the war. That night there was a detail of picked men sent to dig a rifle-pit close up to the rebel line. This was rather delicate and dangerous business; the men selected were those that could work rapidly, keep quiet, and fight if necessary. The rest of the regiment—and I don't know but that other regiments were sent out on the same business—went as guard. Very cautiously we crept up to the place we were to occupy, as a hunter would approach a sleeping lion, and all night we lay there giving the officers all the annoyance imaginable to keep us from falling asleep. The muffled sound of the picks, spades and shovels was all that disturbed the silence of the night. At the first appearance of daylight, the guard withdrew and were relieved by the regiments. It was now expected that we should make another step in our journey toward Richmond; we had secured a good position, but alas it was destined to be of no benefit to us. We went back to our tents, but not to sleep, for we were continually being ordered under arms and into line to repel attacks that the rebels persisted in making on our front and just to the left. All day long the battle raged on the opposite side of the Chickahominy, and its progress could be distinctly seen from our camping ground. We could see that our men were apparently driven back. In fact nothing could have been more apparent. It was all a trap of Gen. McClellan to catch the enemy, so the officers said, and this served to allay apprehensions which might otherwise have produced serious evil. The Generals and their aids appeared remarkably tickled with the progress of events, and the course things were taking, and they even proclaimed that twenty-four hours more of such prosperous and successful strategy would open to us the way to Richmond.

Near sundown the rebels commenced to compliment ourselves by throwing shot and shell with remarkable precision directly into our camp. We couldn't stand this and accordingly skedaddled. I suppose we retreated in "good order" though we did it as fast as we comfortably could. Just over a steep bank to the right of our camp, we were comparatively safe. Here we came to a halt and listened to the music of the enemy's shells as they whistled over our heads and plowed up the dirt just beyond us. All at once the artillery stopped firing, and for a moment there was an ominous silence, but it was soon broken by a volley of musketry directly in our front. In an instant every man was on his feet, for we knew that here was a chance for us. Double quick we went out there, and found the Fourth Regiment engaged with the foe, and they appeared abundantly able to give the rebels all they were capable of bargaining for. It seemed they had attempted to storm our position but found a serious impediment in the Fourth, who were already there. Darkness soon closed the struggle and we returned to camp to get a little rest which we very much needed. Thus ended the first day's "strategy."

The next morning we were ordered to pack up and fall in, two orders which the soldier very well knows how to comprehend. We were only going to move our camp to a safer place they told us, which was strictly true, though in a much different sense from what we expected. We marched a short distance to the left when we were set to falling timber. About noon we were compelled to submit to another shelling. We threw ourselves on our faces and every shell that passed a foot above the ground passed harmlessly over our heads. Only one or two were hit, and these were mangled horribly. Our batteries, as soon as they opened made warm work for the rebels so that the enjoyment was not all on one side. The enemy were soon effectually silenced. We laid that night in the woods near by, and in the morning we started on our backward march. We passed through the camp of the 4th New Jersey, which came so near being annihilated in the fight on the right of the Chickahominy, stopping only long enough to destroy a few boxes of hard crackers to prevent them from furnishing the rebels a feast. This was the first time I had seen our own subsistence destroyed, and it was difficult to believe that the necessity for it was wholly premeditated. A little farther along and skirmishers were thrown out of our regiment to the rear, which opened our eyes to the fact that we were not only retreating but we were to act as rear guard. At Savage Station we halted in the woods after crossing the railroad, and rested there a short time. Meanwhile the troops from the entrance, left of the line belonging to Heintzleman, Keyes and Sumner's army corps, came pouring down the road past us. Large piles of subsistence stores and ammunition were burned here. At length when all the rest of the troops had passed we had orders to move on too. We had marched less than two miles when a brisk cannonading was heard back at the Station, and our brigade was immediately ordered to about face—an order that savored unmistakably of a collision. We returned, formed in battle array, the Fifth taking the lead in line of battle, followed by the Second in close column ready to support it on the right or left as the exigencies of the case might require. We charged up hill through the woods bordering on the Williamsburg road where we had stopped to rest. With a yell the Fifth bounded forward for the rebels were retreating. Without stopping to get into a more fighting shape our regiment followed them making the woods fairly ring with their shouts. At the farther verge of the woods the tug of war commenced. The rebels had some pieces of artillery which sifted the grape through our ranks like hail stones making huge openings at every discharge. The Fifth manfully stood their ground, though their loss was terrible. We drove the rebels from the ground and had clear possession of the field when night closed the contest. We took what care of the wounded we could which was but very little for we were soon ordered forward. All night we plodded our weary way, halting just at break of day. After crossing the creek at White Oak Swamp on a small eminence well calculated for defense, we threw down our blankets and assumed a horizontal position without stopping to calculate our proximity to the enemy or our chances of being awakened by a compliment of shells.

Our slumber was short. In the morning we reconnoitered our position to the right and left, to assure ourselves that all was right; then stacked arms and sat down to rest. While quietly sitting here discussing the peculiarity of our position and freely expressing opinions pro and con relative to the wisdom of the strategy which made such mysterious movements necessary, and inwardly doubting whether it was not forced on us instead of being planned at leisure by our Generals,—for the rank and file are by no means indifferent to these important matters—we were suddenly startled by a perfect storm of shells, which the rebels threw simultaneously from perhaps a dozen pieces of artillery which they had shrewdly got into position unperceived. It was as if a nest of earthquakes had suddenly exploded under our feet. Cavalry and artillery horses, some with riders and some without, rushed helter skelter through our ranks,—if ranks there were—frightened almost to death. We repaired to the woods and there formed into line, and each took a position best calculated for defence. Here we endured another shelling similar to that we were compelled to submit to the Saturday previous. A cannon ball passed close by a friend's ear, near me, brushed his knapsack and lodged just to our rear. An inclination of his head—he was lying on his breast—to one side, if not more than two inches, would have secured to him an eternal discharge from all terrestrial warfare.

It was nearly midnight before we were ready to leave. Tired and exhausted as we all still were, we were impatient to get to a place of safety, where we would not be in constant danger of being attacked with a superior force at every disadvantage. As long as I have been in the service I have not yet become educated up to that degree of bravery, that makes the shriek of a shell music in my ears, and I fear I never shall. I ought to have said the rebels' guns were effectually silenced on this occasion, by our artillery without the aid of infantry. They could not cross the creek in the face of such a fire as Captain Ayer dealt them.

Once on our journey again we marched with all possible speed till sunrise when we halted in an open field near the James river. Here within sight of the naked masts of the gunboats we felt that a brief respite of rest could now be enjoyed free from the turmoil of war. Alas, before we had hardly eaten our breakfast we were ordered back into the woods for it was reported that the enemy were advancing. All day we remained in the woods in line, but no enemy appeared. There was, however, fierce fighting on our left during the day, as there had been the day before.

At two o'clock in the morning, we were aroused. The enemy were advancing in three directions. We had got pretty thoroughly rested and began to feel our courage revive in consequence. Doubtless we should have made a tolerably effective show of resistance if they had pressed us to it but they did not. It began to rain early in the morning and till noon it poured as if the windows of the heavens were opened. We were ordered to march, which we had not the slightest reluctance in doing, stormy as it then was. Through the mud and slosh we tramped till we reached Harrison's Landing. We put up our tents on the liquid soil and forthwith repaired to an extensive wheat field where the grain had been cut and bound and probably we cleared that field of every vestige of straw or grain in as short a space of time as it was ever done before. This made us excellent bedding. In the morning we moved our camp back from the river a mile or so to the place we now occupy. It is a pleasant position with plenty of water, and probably much more healthy than the one we occupied on the Chickahominy. The brigade has been terribly thinned, but is now improving in health, if not in numbers. There are many incidents connected with this retreat or "strategical movement," worthy of mention which I leave to those better acquainted with the facts to relate.

Wednesday, July 9th, Co. E lost one of their sergeants under rather melancholy circumstances. He went down to the creek which runs between here and the river with a squad of men to bathe and in swimming across the stream the cramp seized him and he was drowned before assistance could reach him. George E. Allen was a kind-hearted, brave and intelligent soldier, the only son, I understand, of his parents, and his loss will be keenly felt at home as well as in his company. In positions of extreme peril I have often noticed him doing his duty as coolly as though no danger was near, and in the battle or on picket he never showed the slightest timidity or a moment lost his calm self-possession and presence of mind. The country could ill afford to lose such soldiers as he was.

———————

Camp California, near Alexandria
Sept. 6, 1862

Again we are under marching orders, with the prospect of lugging three days' rations, after the ubiquitous Jackson. If a tithe of the reports concerning this bold, dashing General had proven true, he would have been thrice killed, "chawed up" by the Union forces, or annihilated long ago. We had him surrounded in the swamps on the Chickahominy, with his army of five, ten, or twenty thousand as the case might be, times innumerable. Surrender or starvation, has been thrust upon him by our brave boys (of the tongue) at periodical intervals, ever since his name began to attract notice. At the seven days' fight before Richmond, he was positively killed. This was verified by such a host of witnesses, that the fact was established beyond a peradventure. And what made their testimony the more unimpeachable, was the fact that these knowing ones, had nearly all of them, conversed with some one who knew an officer, of high rank, that had seen or heard of an eye witness, which of course made his story remarkably weighty. But, notwithstanding all the straits to which this General had been pushed, and all the deaths to which he had been subjected, there was still enough left of him to give zest and spirit to our march on Bull run, last Saturday. We then had him cornered on the old battle-field, or near that place, with the whole Confederate army of Virginia. Pope was in his rear; McClellan in front and we were hurrying up to witness the grand surrender, which was to entomb the cherished anticipations and plans of our great Rebel antagonist, and upset forever the hopes of our country's traitors. So the boys talked and believed, as we were hurried along that dusty road, without stopping for intervals of many miles to rest our aching shoulders, or moisten our thirsty throats with a drop of water. Of course we believed it, for no less a personage than our Surgeon had said so, and he had seen an aid, who, of course was right from the field where the game was being played. Centreville Heights was reached a little before sundown, and here I for one would gladly have stopped for the night, even if in consequence I should lose a sight of the forthcoming grand denouement. I fancy I was not alone in my desires, for along those ranks could be seen a great many thin faces, whose bodies were weakened by exposure and consequent disease, and who were poorly able to endure so fatiguing a march. Gen. Pope in his official report, speaks of Gen. Franklin's corps straggling enormously, and perhaps with justice. No doubt this state of things in an army is deplorable in the extreme, but it seems to me that something besides discipline is necessary to effect a remedy. When a man is physically unable to walk, all the discipline in the world will fail to keep him in the ranks when the regiment marches. I have seen men follow the moving columns and keep their right place, when they were too weak to ascend a flight of steps without supporting themselves by their hand, and when a "double quick" would have been simply impossible. How can it be expected otherwise, than that straggling should follow, when an army of such men are making forced marches in a burning sun.

Our halt here like all the previous ones that day was just long enough for us to divest ourselves of our encumbrances preparatory to sitting down for a little rest when the order, "fall in" was given, and we were on our way again. Before we arrived at the old battle-field things began to look suspicious. The road was full of wounded, some on foot, some in ambulances, hurrying as it seemed to a place of safety. Instead of shouting Jackson is cornered, the boys now changed their tune and called it Bull run No. 2. And so indeed it proved to be. Jackson had turned both flanks, and our army was actually retreating. We marched on, however, beyond the source from whence the retreating tide seemed to emanate, when, after some preliminary arrangements on the part of the mounted officers who seemed much in earnest with their business whatever it was, riding hither and thither at the swiftest gallop, and speaking in a whisper—we faced about and marched back to Centreville. The roads were completely blocked up with teams, troops and wounded men all anxious to get along as fast as possible and all mutually hindering each other. Regiments were cut in two and sometimes divided in several places. I saw one Colonel riding about in great anxiety and alarm inquiring for his regiment which he had lost. We were in a field of troops and in some careless moment he had probably allowed himself to follow the wrong regiment. Bad as the confusion was, there was probably less disorder than at Bull run No. 1, though it would be hard to conceive how things could have been much worse.

About midnight, we were back again to Centreville, and when the order came to rest, you may be sure we were in a condition to obey it with a hearty good will. It was beginning to rain, and there was a chilly East wind, and we were without any woolen blankets, having come in light marching order, but we made the best we could of our situation. If I felt any disposition to grumble at that time, I was sincerely ashamed of it the next morning, when I heard the boys engaged in the fight, speak of their comrades whom they had been obliged to leave on the field, wounded and dying, without care or help from any source. Monday night, and Tuesday we accomplished our retreat back to this place again.

We are expecting now to march across the Potomac, and up the river to some point not yet made known to us. Jackson is getting into another trap, and I suspect we are to surround and annihilate him once more. I certainly hope that after this campaign, we can write of something beside disaster, slaughter, defeat, and skedaddle. Should victory turn on our side once more, it will give me great pleasure to dilate on the facts in my felicitous style, for the benefit of your inquiring readers.

Meanwhile, Farewell.

Mt. Pleasant Hospital⁹
Camp Convalescence
Jan. 15, 1863

It has been so long since I have written you anything that I fear I shall have to consider myself a stranger to your readers again and commence my acquaintance anew. I believe I promised in my last, which was as long ago as last September, that I would give an account of the pending campaign in Maryland, but that promise I did not fulfill; and perhaps I owe an apology for not keeping my word. Declining health, a misfortune which but few soldiers can prevent, rendered me, physically, incapable of enduring another march and obliged me, with a number of my comrades, to seek a temporary asylum in one of our Army Hospitals. I have noticed a great deal of comment in the newspapers, pro and con, in regard to the management and care of the sick in these hospitals and I presume enough has been said to acquaint every one with their proceedings in these places, but I often receive questions from those having friends here, who are anxious to know in regard to their welfare, so I propose to give a few observations, from my own experience. I shall disclose nothing new or startling, nor do I propose to enter into any profound reasoning whereby you may base the presumption that the sufferings and calamities of this war are soon to close. Any one who has read my former letters knows better than to expect any such thing. I am a common soldier belonging to the rank and file, and whoever reads my letters must expect to find them full of nothing but soldiers' talk. Just bear this in mind, kind reader, and then your disappointment will be less keen if your patience allows you to follow me through to find in my letter so little that can interest you.

My destination, after leaving the regiment, on this occasion, happened to be at the Mt. Pleasant Hospital, which is situated the best part of a mile northward from the heart of the city of Washington, between Seventh and Fourteenth Streets. This hospital is, indeed, situated in a pleasant place, but the altitude of the situation is hardly sufficient to deserve even the abbreviated title of mountain. The building, itself, contains ten wards besides the cook-room, laundry, store-room, dispensary, &c. These wards branch off from the main building or "hall" at right angles like the wings or L part of a dwelling. At first view, from the outside, a spectator would suppose that the wards were two stories high; the height of the buildings and their having two rows of windows would justify such a conclusion. But, on entering them, he finds the space vacant of all partitions or ceilings, from the floor to the roof, making a room at once spacious, airy and well lighted. A large water tank, elevated high above the hospital, supplies every part with pure water. Excellent facilities are afforded each ward for washing and bathing, and the rules of cleanliness are strictly enforced. Those too feeble to help themselves were waited upon by the nurses.

Each ward contained about fifty beds, making not far from five hundred beds in all. The bedsteads were light iron frames admirably adapted for hospital purposes, and each bed was provided with a good mattress or straw-bed, and every one had plenty of bed clothes. Besides these wards there were between fifty and sixty triple tents containing eighteen beds each. So the whole concern made provisions for some fifteen hundred men. The tents are intended for convalescents and those less seriously ailing, while the wards are reserved for those requiring greater care and attention. These are sent to the tents, as fast as they are able, to make room for fresh arrivals. Such was my fate after the first month.

On the 10th of September, Anno Domini Eighteen Hundred and Sixty-two, your humble servant was introduced into one of these wards, to be treated as a patient. As my comrades and I had made our way to the hospital through the exercise of the powers of locomotion which Nature has given us, it need not be supposed that we were entirely helpless, or confined to our beds. Our complaint was that insidious disease, so widespread in our army, the chronic diarrhoea, which we contracted in the swamps of the Chickahominy, and which saps the foundations of one's strength, and makes his existence a lingering duration of misery. I can hardly find language adequate to express the relief I felt when I took possession of the bed which I was to occupy. I had marched many a weary mile when I had not sufficient strength to step on, and raise myself to, an eminence a foot high, without assisting myself by my hands, nor to "double quick" a dozen rods, though it were to save the whole Union; and now the prospect of a few days' rest in a place that would bear, at least, a favorable comparison with the comforts of civil life, was gratifying in the extreme. It seemed too good to be true. I was actually afraid that I should be awakened some morning, as usual, by the inexorable command, "Fall in," and the fond illusion would be dispelled as a dream.

I am aware that there has been complaint made by many of their treatment in these hospitals, but I am unable to see how so many sick men could be cared for better than we were at this place. Other hospitals may be differently managed; I do not presume to judge. Here everything we desired and needed was unhesitatingly granted. There was a very efficient corps of nurses, male and female, and they spared no pains to render their patients as comfortable as lay in their power. I think they entertained heartfelt sympathy for the sufferings of those under their care, and did the best they could to alleviate them. Especially is this true of the women nurses. If any who see this have friends in this hospital, they may take my word for it, they are well treated and have excellent care, and the prospect of their being restored to health is scarcely less than it would be if they were at their own homes in Vermont. The diet prescribed was generally suited to the wants and condition of the patient. Toasted bread with butter or apple-sauce was served every day to the feebler ones. Boiled rice and milk, meal porridge, farina puddings, and almost any article of diet was readily granted by the physician if asked for. I never was refused in a single instance what I expressed a preference for. Those who were able took their meals at the mess barrack together. Theirs was the common army ration, with sometimes a little butter or apple-sauce thrown in for extras. As convalescents we had unbounded freedom, for aught I know, of the country around. I never found any limit placed upon our pedestrian privileges, providing we were in our tents when the doctor came around in the morning, and were in our beds at nine o'clock at night. We could not go to the city unless we had a pass without running the risk of being escorted to the Central Guard House by the patrol guard, which, by the way, was not so very risky, providing one behaved himself properly.

I visited the Harwood Hospital, which is situated about one mile east of Mt. Pleasant, and I regret that I cannot give so good an account of that place, as of the hospital where we stayed. But it had then just received a large influx of patients, larger than there were accommodations to receive, and they were without efficient organization; consequently there was much complaint and considerable suffering. The tents were without floors and many of them had no beds. The very sick were suffering greatly for want of care. I was told that the men were not allowed to dig ditches around their tents to prevent the water from soaking into them in rainy weather, out of respect to the rich proprietor of the land; but I think, if true, it was because floors of boards were soon to be procured, which would render such desecration of the soil unnecessary. There was, it is true, much complaint at one time at this hospital, but I have heard less since. The tent we occupied was always dry, clean and neat. All the tents had good floors, and the tents themselves were of thick, stout material, having a fly, or extra roof, to each one, so that in the hardest rain storm, not even a mist could be felt in the inside. The head surgeon and hospital steward were gentlemen in every sense of the word, and highly respected by all in the hospital. Everything was quiet and the best of order prevailed.

It would be impossible for me to enumerate the many kindnesses we received from benevolent hands during our stay here; but there is one that I will not forbear to mention. Let it not be supposed that the many charitable acts of which we hear so much, are all that is done for the benefit of the soldiers. Multitudes of benevolent ladies who would shrink from having their names made public, constantly employ themselves in ministering to the sick and wounded soldiers, giving freely of their own resources whatever can conduce to the comfort of the sufferers, without expecting a cent in return. They deserve the eternal gratitude of the soldiers who are the recipients of their kindnesses and doubtless they will get it. Scarcely a day passed that some one of these ladies, on their errands of mercy, did not come into the ward with something to give the men. Perhaps it might be nothing more than an apple apiece, or a peach, or perhaps it might be some favorite books that some one had expressed a wish to read. Very often they brought in tracts to distribute among the men, and I never knew a case where one refused to read them. Sometimes they gave stationery to those destitute of funds to enable them to write of their whereabouts and condition to their friends. Let it not be said that the North are ungrateful to their soldiers, and I hope the soldiers will not prove insensible of gratitude in return.

It was my good fortune to receive an invitation from one of these sisters of charity [10]—for such indeed they all were, though they belonged to no order,—to visit her residence in the city, which I gladly accepted. Her husband was a bookseller and newspaper dealer, and he willingly furnished his numerous soldier visitors with all the reading they desired. Books, historical and fictitious, and periodicals of every description, lay upon his counter, which without money or price, were freely proffered us to read. Often has this lady accidentally heard of some particular want of some sick soldier in a hospital, and with as much promptness as if he was her own son, she procures the desired article, whatever it may be, and hastens to the sufferer's relief. On one occasion she took a soldier who was scarcely this side of eternity to her house, nursed and took care of him till he was well and able to return to his regiment. Now he is doing duty in the field, when, but for her kindness, it is more than probable that he would have been forever lost to Uncle Sam and all the rest of the world. A day spent with these folks I considered as second only to a visit at home.

But at last the time came for us to leave the hospital. The order was sent in for every well man to be sent to his regiment, and those still convalescent were to be sent to this camp. I supposed that I was going straight to my regiment, but instead of that I found that I was booked for this camp, so justly famed for misery and uncleanliness. Although I had been expecting for several weeks to leave the hospital, I confess when the time came my patriotism was hardly sufficient to overcome all reluctance to leave. My health was still somewhat delicate, and I must leave my comfortable bed, to exchange it for a rubber blanket and the damp ground. My warm, comfortable tent I must exchange for the contemptible "shelters" of the field. My books and papers, which had been my amusement for many a day must be given up for the musket, and in place of reading by a warm stove, I should have drilling, marching and picketing, with hard tack and salt horse for my daily grub. Soldiers are sometimes accused of trying to "play off" from duty, and I appeal to you if the temptation is not strong at a time like this.

On this occasion a guard was stationed around the camp to prevent any from skulking away, who were so disposed, but, I think, this precaution was unnecessary. The night previous to going away a drizzly north-west storm set in—a kind of weather which is the most disagreeable to soldiers—and, coming as it did at this particular time, it seemed to render our departure superlatively unpleasant. But the boys were bound to be merry in spite of the gloomy prospects before them. They laughed, told stories, sung songs, and did their best, to have a jolly night. At any other time their noisy demonstrations would have been promptly checked as a breach of order, but, on this occasion, no one found fault with them. Morning came and according to the program we bid adieu to the hospital and the pleasant associations connected with it. We fell into line between two rows of bayonets and like a set of criminals were marched to the Soldiers' Retreat, a terrific squall of rain accompanying us all the way. The next day, we were forwarded to our respective destinations.

Next time, if it will do to make promises, after my former delinquency, I will introduce to your readers the Convalescent Camp.

The Convalescent Camp
[February, 1863]

The name of this camp explains its use. It is impossible, I suppose, for the Government to furnish hospitals enough to contain all the sick and wounded men, and keep them there till they are well. As soon as they are considered in a fair way for recovery, they must leave the hospital to make room for more needy sufferers. Often when all the hospitals have their full complement of patients, and all seem to be getting along finely, an order comes to make room for a large number more, and these must be attended to, at all hazards. The only way to arrange this business was to establish a camp, where those the nearest well and best able to take care of themselves could be sent and thus make room for others to whom neglect would be certain death. Hence, the origin of this camp for convalescents.

I shall live to be an aged man, indeed, if I live to forget the day that introduced me to this camp which honest critics have considered of all places the one most miserable. First impressions, they say, are lasting, and if so, this may in part, account for the sombre description I shall give of what I saw here. The day of my initiation was as disagreeable as the elements could make it. Rain and sleet, driven by a northwest gale, was the complexion of the weather, and the most irritating red tapeism the order of the day. In the first place, at precisely ten o'clock A.M., of this eventful day, we were ordered from the retreat to fall into line in front of the office. Here, quite a number were selected from among us, to take some horses down to Fredericksburg. From Fredericksburg, these men could go at once to their regiments. As soon as it became known what this selection was being made for, almost every one of the boys clamored eagerly to be counted with the lucky number. A stranger could have seen at a glance, how anxious the boys were to get to their regiments, and how glad they were to shun the convalescent camp.

After being kept in a line, exposed to a pelting storm, till the impatience of the men was beginning to find copious vent in language not at all refined, we were finally marched down to the wharf, when to our chagrin, we found that the Government boat for Alexandria, had just left for that place. It now became a military necessity for us to wait till its return, and we did so, with perhaps less of patience than patriarch Job would have exhibited under the same circumstances, but still quite resignedly for soldiers unprotected from the storm, and just from comfortable hospitals. In process of time the boat returned and we were taken to Alexandria, and forthwith we commenced to march to our convalescent home. The camp is situated just on the brow of a hill just back of the city from the river, and to the right of the road leading from Alexandria to Fairfax.

In pleasant weather this situation is by no means devoid of beauty. It commands a fine view of Washington and Alexandria and a long stretch of the Potomac, far down below both cities. In a clear day, when the bright sparkling bosom of the river is covered with vessels of all descriptions, from the sprightly little steam-tug to the giant ocean steam-ship moving proudly on in its course, the view from this eminence is truly splendid to behold. The residence at its summit must have occupied no unenviable position in the days of its glory, but all its beauty, except that of position, has been ruthlessly destroyed by the grim demon of war. Here once was the abode of wealth and refinement, and marks of the proprietor's taste in cultivating his grounds are visible all around. But where once stood the nicely pruned cedars, enclosing beautiful gardens, such as Virginians know how to make, now all that can be seen is the stumps of the trees and a bare outline of former beauties. Tents have occupied the ground, which once was sacred to someone by all the endearments that can embellish a HOME, and where once the lily and the rose grew and bloomed, sick men have lain and groaned and died. Alas! this same sad tale of beauty destroyed and homes desecrated is echoed throughout the length and breadth of this guilty secession-accursed State. But I have dropped the thread of my narrative.

From Alexandria we faced the storm till we reached the headquarters of the camp, when we naturally expected to be taken to our quarters, whatever they might be; but we were very naturally disappointed. We found that we had now to submit to a delay more vexatious than all the rest, before anything in the shape of protection from the storm was to be thought of. Our names had all to be taken down, one by one, before any of us could be received into a tent. Probably there was no other way to do the business, but there were enough of us now to make a good sized regiment, and to me it seemed a tedious long while to wait there for one man to take down all of our names. But it was accomplished at last, and by that time it was nearly night. All day we had been exposed to the pitiless storm, without a mouthful to eat, and we were beginning to feel ourselves entitled to good quarters somewhere; and we thought if anybody justly deserved a good supper, it was ourselves. But we were mere novices in the camp, and we bitterly found that we had much to learn.

We were divided up according to the States to which we belonged. New York troops were sent to one part of the camp, Pennsylvanians to another, and the Vermont boys to their particular limits, &c. The prospect before us seemed more dismally discouraging than ever. The rain had converted the clayey soil into mud, or mortar, to the depth of several inches. Inside of the tents, as well as outside, it was nothing but mud. I never saw a more cheerless place in my life for even a well man's habitation, and I have seen those that were gloomy enough in all reason. But this was for convalescent men; men in just the condition to need good keeping, as farmers say, and to need the best of care. Weak and crippled men were consigned to quarters more contemptible than any that a conscientious farmer ever thought fit to offer his swine.

The New England troops, part of them, were taken over to the southern slope of the hill, just back of the city reservoir and facing the Fairfax road. Here was a large field of tents huddled in close together in regular streets, with something like the appearance of order. Vermont, Maine and New Hampshire troops occupied one street. It was with the greatest difficulty that we could find a place here to lay our weary heads the coming night. Every tent appeared to be full. The Sergeant took us the whole length of the street in vain. At every tent he had inquired if there was room for another, and had everywhere received the same gruff reply in the negative. Things were beginning to look exceedingly gloomy. Something must be done. Probably not one of us could survive a night like that without some kind of protection from the storm, accustomed as we had been for some time to hospital living. The little A tents were huddled full of men, and that they were exceedingly averse to receiving in any more was quite evident. One fellow remarked that he would give a month's wages for the simple privilege of lodging that night in one of the city hotels; but a proceeding so unmilitary as that was not to be thought of. By dint of much persuasion and some threatening the Sergeant got us admittance one by one until our number was reduced to three, including myself. Luckily for us we found an old cast-off tent, which we got permission to pitch for ourselves. Even this could not be done without encountering difficulties innumerable. First, we had to dodge all conflicting claims as to locality, then the materials for pitching the tent must be found when there were no such materials to be had; then to get an ax when nobody had one to lend, and strangers were not regarded as men worthy of notice,—all these, and many like perplexities, had to be met to begin with. "But where there is a will there is a way," so our tent was duly pitched, and we crawled into it for the night. I have spent many disagreeable nights in camp, but if any of them were comparable to this the occurrence has escaped my memory.

Just at dark, a young soldier, too young to be here, came to me and begged the privilege of stopping in my tent till morning. He was poor and pale as death, and had evidently suffered greatly from sickness and his sufferings seemed not likely to end soon. He had no blankets nor coats of any description. His thin blouse was soaked with rain, and he shivered and trembled in the cold like a sere leaf in the autumn wind. He was a Vermonter, too, he said, and he seemed to expect sympathy on that account. Most gladly would I have accommodated him, but my two partners, who were New Hampshire men had already given admittance to a fourth person, and they thought there was no more room to spare. I was obliged to turn him away, but the look of disappointment he gave me, made me half wish I was accursed from the tent for his sake. If he has a mother on earth, it was a mercy that God spared her the knowledge of her son's destitution and suffering, that bleak, stormy night. He turned away, and I never knew what became of him, for I never saw him afterwards. The next day I joined the guards. The duty was light, and by doing so, I secured comparatively comfortable quarters.

Everything about the camp indicated the most grievous neglect and mismanagement; in fact there was no management at all. There was no wood to be found within a radius of a mile and a half, and there was no means adapted to provide any. The soldiers received their rations uncooked, and each one had to prepare his own the best he could. In this matter of wood the convalescents suffered immensely. They must go this long distance for it, or they must go without. Nothing could be found nearer. Even the gnarly, crabbed oak stumps were grubbed down to the very roots. I have seen men a mile from camp tugging along with a chunk of wood in one hand, and a cane in the other,—resting at intervals of every few rods, and then pushing forward again; and exhibiting a degree of perseverance worthy of a much wider range of usefulness. And I have seen them obliged to desist from such efforts to get wood from sheer exhaustion, and return to their tents to shiver away the long hours of the day, utterly indifferent whether the results were life or death. How could men be expected to regain their health under such circumstances? Not every invalid can cook and prepare his food, even if the means were furnished him, and do it properly; but when to this is added the discomfort and exposure to the cold, what wonder that men die off so fast at the Convalescent Camp.

If a man wants to see human suffering and human depravity in their grossest phases he need not go to the Kingdom of Dahomey, nor cross the Arabian Desert to find it. Let him go to the Convalescent Camp, and he can see enough to sicken his soul forevermore, unless his heart is harder than adamant. Imagine four or five men in one of these little A tents, strangers to each other, and men who have suffered everything but death itself. These sufferings have soured their dispositions and irritated their feelings, until they are as morose and unsocial as men can well become. They care nothing for one another, and seem to care but little for themselves. Once they were robust and healthy, their nerves flashed fire, and their chief glory was in their physical prowess, and all things were joyous to them and full of hope; but when hardship and exposure in the field, had robbed them of their strength, life lost its charms, and they became hardened to every thing around them. Men have slept unheeding, while their companion by their side has gasped and died. I was told of an occasion when a man was thrust out of a tent to die, because those tenting with him did not wish to be disturbed by his dying groans.

If this account is reflecting upon the authorities here, the fault is not mine. Col. Belknap who commanded the camp seems to be a humane man and anxious to alleviate all the suffering in his power, but what could he do with ten thousand men. There were a half a dozen, or more, doctors in camp, but they seldom visited their patients; their patients had to visit them. At nine in the morning the surgeon's call is beat, and whoever wished to, could fall in with the crowd and go to the dispensary and there wait his turn to go in. This might not be till noon. When at last he gained an audience with his medical adviser his story must be brief, and his prescription is made out without much thought. There was a way for men unable to attend the surgeon's call to get medical attendance, but it involved so much circumlocution that but few ever found it out. A sick acquaintance of mine tried his utmost to get medical relief but he tried in vain. He sent to the head surgeon who referred him to the officer of the day; but that officer was nowhere to be found. The messenger went again to the head surgeon and this time was referred to one of the assistant surgeons. The assistant surgeon had nothing to do with that part of the camp. He went to another assistant surgeon, but with the same result. He was sent to a third, but the third was nowhere to be found. He went to the head surgeon again who promised to send some one of the doctors to his sick comrade's tent but the promise was never fulfilled. Probably it was forgotten the next moment.

Many men have suffered and died in this camp, when with ordinary care in a hospital their lives might have been spared. True, there was a hospital in the camp, but many have died here without ever finding it.

One bitter cold night I was stationed to guard the sutler's shanty. The keen northwest wind only mocked at clothing, and every gust felt its way to the very skin. It was tedious being out anywhere that night, and especially so to the sick. I took my post at nine o'clock. Before I had been there many minutes, a fellow, thinly clad came shivering from one of the tents, and curled down by the wooden shanty to get away from the wind. He was quite unwell as his looks abundantly showed. He had just come into camp that day, he said, and was put into a tent already crowded full. They, according to his story, were opposed to admitting him, and had then just driven him from the tent. At eleven I was relieved, and my two hours was all that I felt able to endure there, although I possessed a considerable share of health, and was well clothed. When I came to my post again at three o'clock, I found the sick man was still there. I tried to persuade him to go to the officers and have them provide him a place more comfortable, for I was actually afraid he would perish there, but I could not. He was much too bashful to be a soldier. Before my next two hours' duty was done he had gone. I never knew where he went. He had threatened to desert the service, and if he did attempt the hazard, I can hardly help wishing him good success.

But I am making my letter much longer than I expected. Incidents crowd upon my mind which seemed important to me, an eyewitness, but probably they would be too tame to relate at this time of stirring events. But I am happy to say the Convalescent Camp has improved since the time of which I have been writing. It has been moved some three miles toward the height opposite Washington, where wood is more plenty and other comforts more abundant. Barracks are being built, and it is to be hoped that before summer the men will have quarters more decently comfortable. It would be a lasting shame to our Government if this eyesore was left unremedied.

I have sketched thus much Mr. Editor, of what I have seen and known of this place, and if you think it worthy of the room, you may give it to your readers with my prayers that they may never be sent, as we have been, to this Convalescent Camp.

Camp near White Oak Church, Va.
March 14, 1863

Once more I am back to camp and once more with the old Second Regiment in the field. You may be sure it was a most pleasant experience to meet my old comrades in arms, those whom battle and disease has spared. Now I propose a short chat with the *Freeman* which has so kindly indulged me many times before. Six months have flown into eternity since I was with the regiment before, and during that six months many changes have been made in the army and in the regiment. Our much loved General has been removed, our Colonel and Lieut.-Colonel have resigned and gone home, and many of the line officers have had their places filled by others. But nearly two years of war has made still sadder havoc among the men in the ranks. Scarcely twenty-five per cent of the men who originally composed this regiment are left. Last winter four of us tented together and of the four two are dead, one killed at Savage Station and the other died in a hospital, and one other is at home in a state of health by no means hopeful. On the Peninsula, at Newport News, four others and myself one stormy day went into the woods, a little one side of the camp, and built us a comfortable log house, covering it with our rubber blankets, and there we mutually pledged to stand by each other in time of danger, and many were the plans we laid in the air of our future prospects when the war was over. Of the four one has been discharged, but the other three are sleeping their last sleep. Such is war. Many and indeed most all that now are left could relate similar experiences. But I was going to speak of events more recent.

Wednesday, March 4th, a squad of convalescents was sent from the military hospital at Brattleboro, Vt., to their regiments, and among them might have been seen your humble correspondent. The boys left the hospital in the best of spirits, as they have always had the name of doing when duty was to be done, for we Vermont soldiers have made it a part of our creed not to grumble or whine at inevitable necessity no matter how disagreeable it may be. I will not presume to say, as most newspaper correspondents do, that the boys were *eager* to join their regiments or over anxious to measure swords with the foe in the field, though doubtless most of them would rejoice to take part in a battle that would bring, for once, a victory glorious and decisive to our arms. But there was no complaining that injustice had been done them in sending them so soon to duty. Most of the boys that left their regiments just after that second disgraceful retreat from Bull Run, retain the spirit of discouragement which that event, in connection with previous disasters, cast over the whole nation. Defeated in every issue, from causes beyond their control, they have lost heart, and when they see the great contest, which every one, at the beginning, supposed could be speedily decided, assuming more and more gigantic proportions, and when, after every sacrifice of life and the utmost display of valor, they find their efforts fruitless as at Fredericksburg, what wonder that the boys do not feel "eager for the fray," and who blames them that they are tired of the war. And to add to these causes of discouragement, their favorite leader, McClellan, has been removed, and removed as they think, because like a true-souled patriot he tried to maintain a consistent policy in the face of disunion, fanaticism and political trucksters. The proclamation of freedom is represented to them by the hellish imps of the Jeff Davis persuasion, as an instrument to convert the war from its avowed purpose of restoring the Union, to one for the freedom of the blacks. The antipathy of the soldiers to the negro race, is well known, and whoever panders to this prejudice for political purposes or for any other purpose, is guilty of blacker treason than the rebel who meets us openly on the battle-field. These peaceable copperheads tell us that McClellan was removed because he manfully resisted the effort to prostitute the war for abolition purposes. They tell us the Government is on the verge of bankruptcy, and they do not scruple to hint that it is more honorable to desert such a service than to be made tools of by abolitionists of the Greeley school. I write only what I have seen and heard, and can assure you this manner of spreading disaffection among the troops, is more extensively practiced and has greater effect than many may have imagined. So if the army of the Potomac is demoralized, who is to blame?—certainly not the soldiers, wholly. Nor is it altogether a want of courage among the troops, that there has been so many desertions of late, from this army. Let the blame be laid where it belongs. Those who assail the Administration as abolition fanatics, and seek to disseminate the virulent poison of this doctrine among the soldiers, are doing more to contribute to our defeat and ruin, than if they enlisted under the banner of treason, and fought us face to face in the open field. It is not the army that is demoralized, it is the citizens at home. If they will stand by the soldiers, the soldiers will stand by the flag till the last. It is a shame that men at home should be discouraged first; and is it not so? But it was not my intention to write a lecture.

At half-past three o'clock on the afternoon of the day alluded to we left Brattleboro, and before midnight we were soundly sleeping in the berths on an elegant steamboat, somewhere in the neighborhood of New Haven, Connecticut. I said the boys were in good spirits and in the main content, but I might have mentioned one cause of dissatisfaction that was keenly felt. The most of the boys were old soldiers, belonging to the first brigade, who had not seen home since they enlisted. When we were taken to Vermont we supposed that this precious privilege would be granted us, but for some unaccountable reason it was denied. No furloughs or leaves of absence were given from this hospital. None went home from there except those that ran away and braved the consequences. We spent the day, Thursday, in the great metropolis. We had but little opportunity of seeing the elephant, as no one seemed to have the power or the inclination to give us passes, and the patrol guard were too vigilant to make it safe to be outside of the barrack grounds without one. One of our number, for merely stepping across the street to speak to an acquaintance, was arrested as a deserter, and it cost him five dollars to get clear.

The bright moonlight evening found us whirling along over the railroad from Jersey City to the seat of war. We made no stop at Philadelphia, much to our regret, for hungry and sleepy as we there were, it would have been a refreshing relief to have partaken of the hospitalities which that city always affords. The soldiers entertain a high regard for Philadelphia. Nowhere else that I have been are soldiers treated with so much consideration and respect as there. If rations are served to us there, it is of a quality good enough for the most fastidious, and that peculiar air, "Good enough for soldiers," seems to be entirely wanting among these benevolent people.

Arriving in Baltimore late in the morning of Friday, we were left to wait till the day was far advanced, before the train left for Washington. The guard cautioned us to be careful what we bought to eat, for two of their number had been severely poisoned in this way by some malignant rebel. The virus of secession still exists concealed in that corrupt city, and only the strong arm of authority keeps it from rising to the surface, as it did on the 19th of April, '61. There is but little that is attractive in Baltimore, and had we ever so much liberty, but few of us would have cared to use it. It was a relief when the shrill whistle of the engine notified us to be ready. So slinging our knapsacks we scrambled aboard the train, and were soon rolling over the rails to Washington. I noticed that the road was guarded by squads of soldiers, stationed at intervals along the line. We reached the Soldiers' Retreat at sunset. Here soldiers from all quarters meet, stopping a few hours, or days, as the case may be, and then are sent to their destination, wherever it is; at the Convalescent Camp, or to their regiments, or in the opposite direction if they are homeward bound. It was a matter of some speculation among the boys whether we should be sent to Camp Convalescence, or to our regiments. Lieut. Chandler, who had us in charge, succeeded in getting transportation for those belonging to the 1st Vermont brigade, the others had to go to that camp. We staid at the Retreat till Sunday morning, and during that time several squads of soldiers, numbering from one to five hundred, came and went. Probably no hotel in the world has more transient lodgers than this Soldiers' Retreat.

There is honor among thieves, as the saying goes, and honor is by no means wanting among soldiers, rude as they sometimes appear; but soldiers often have a curious idea of that quality. No soldier that respects himself in the least would wish to be caught pilfering from his comrades, but in a place like this Retreat, where men from different States are brought together, if one party can "Arab" an article from another, he deems it an act highly honorable and praiseworthy. I left the Retreat a few minutes Friday evening to visit a friend in the city, and when I got back I found my knapsack had exchanged ends of the room, and, by some mysterious means, had found its way under the head of a Pennsylvania volunteer. Another fellow had his slumbers disturbed by some one trying to extract a pair of boots from under his knapsack, which he was using as a pillow. The would-be thief was lying in close proximity to his head, apparently asleep and unconscious of any attempt to do his neighbor injustice. Perhaps he was a somnambulist and in his erratic dream imagined the boots were his own and his right to remove them unquestionable. Soldiers are queer fellows and they have a thousand honest ways for violating the eighth commandment.

Sunday morning, before breakfast, we took passage on the steamer John Brooks, for Aquia Creek, and changing boats at that place, proceeded five or six miles farther on to Bell Plains Landing. The rest of the way, about five miles, we made on foot. We found, as we expected, plenty of mud, but I think it less so than last year at Camp Griffin. This is owing partly to a difference in soil. Wherever it was muddy at all, it was awful muddy.

We found the boys in much better health and spirits than when we left them six months ago. Scarcely a man there could say he was well, and speak the truth, but now, as a general thing, all enjoy a tolerable share of health and seem to be prospering finely. They have fixed themselves up quarters, much more comfortable than I had expected to find them this winter. I had supposed the boys were suffering everything from exposure to all kinds of weather, and indeed they have, in their battles and marches, but in camp, they are comparatively comfortable. They have built them huts of logs and mud, using their shelter-tents for roofs. They are built, generally, with four half-tents together, and occupied by four. Where timber is scarce and the ground is dry the boys dig down and settle the floor below the surface, leaving the walls partly a solid bank of earth, and the rest is made up of logs and mud. A fire-place is easily excavated in this bank of peculiar soil, and there is no need of brick or mortar to make it firm and solid. Here the boys can sit and smoke their pipes and tell their stories, and where is the parlor-spoiled dandy that will say we do not enjoy ourselves? This camp is about three miles from the Rappahannock and eight or ten miles from Fredericksburg.

Thursday and Friday afternoon, we had regular old-fashioned brigade drills. Col. Grant, of the 5th regiment commands. The boys are beginning to think themselves veterans, and I think the "old stand bys" have a right to claim that title. All the maneuvers were executed with great coolness, the weather being particularly favorable for a display of that quality. Away across the river from our camping ground, the white tents of the enemy are pointed out. It is quite a debatable question among the boys, whether we shall be sent across the river at our next move, or whether some other method of attack will be adopted. Bets are freely offered on both sides. The army is under marching orders now; that is, an order has been read on dress parade for us to be ready at a moment's notice, but further than this no move has been made.

Most of the men have confidence in General Hooker. Next to McClellan he is considered the best man to command this army, so far as he is known. His ability is yet to be proved, but we are all willing he should have a fair chance to prove it. Gen. Burnside hardly gets the credit that is due him. Gen. Hooker is doing all he can for the benefit and comfort of his men. His giving furloughs is creating a good feeling in his favor among the troops. Nobody but a soldier, who has seen nearly two years of active service, knows what a boon a furlough is. Our General has provided that the army may be supplied with soft bread, a most agreeable change for those who have subsisted for a long time on hard tack. Then, it is said, he is making arrangements to have express boxes forwarded at once to their owners. For a long time it has been a standing shame, the way this thing has been managed. Boxes sent from friends by express, and containing things that we very much need have been allowed to remain piled up in great pyramids at the landing, until their contents are spoiled. We earnestly hope Gen. Hooker will correct this evil. One thing speaks well for our General Commanding—all that belong to his old division have unbounded confidence in him. The rebel pickets used to tell ours, when both picketed close to the river, that before we could enter Richmond we should have a Stone-wall to scale, two Hills to climb, and a Long-street to march over. Perhaps Gen. Hooker will be the lucky man to lead us over these obstacles to that city. If so we will all shout, "Bully for Fighting Joe Hooker."

Camp near White Oak Church, Va.
April 6, 1863

I can imagine some of your impatient readers, who love to hear of blood and carnage, as many do who are themselves safe are wondering when we are going to commence *our* Spring's work. If any of us knew, we would willingly impart the knowledge, but I doubt if any one, except Him who knows the end of all events from the beginning, could give the information desired. A month ago not a man of us would have hesitated to bet two against one that before this time we should be on the march. We have been expecting every day to hear the order, "Pack up for marching," but that order is still withheld. It is not our fault, good friends, that we are not at work. The Lord knows we are anxious to finish this job as soon as possible, and return to our heart-loved homes. Notwithstanding the discouragements, rough dealing and bad management we have been subjected to, there is scarcely a man that shrinks from the coming contests. Of course there are some that are always finding fault, but in this regiment they are only a piteous minority. The grumblers are pretty well sifted out. Account for it as you may, those who came here from mere love of adventure, with no heart for the work, who were always grumbling at every measure the Government adopted, and found fault when the best was done for them that could be done, these were the first to get broken down and sent home. The staunch patriots, who love their country and are willing to fight for it, are here yet, and will remain here till the regiment is sent home, if not absolutely compelled to do otherwise. The health of the regiment was never better, and when the word comes, we are ready and willing to go forward and do our duty but we may not go till the word does come. Yes, we are *willing* to go forward,—not anxious from mere love of excitement, but like men in earnest, who know they have a great and important work to do, and can comprehend its magnitude. We have seen too much of war to desire its novelty, and we have seen too much of it to shrink from its horrors.

Last Friday our Army Corps was reviewed by Gen. Hooker. I like the appearance of the old hero very much. He is not at all such a looking man as one would associate with the name of "fighting Joe." He has a smooth, pleasing countenance, light hair, a keen eye, though not so *piercing*, perhaps, as McClellan. He looks more like some venerated minister of the Gospel than a General. But I had not the opportunity to get a very distinct impression of him. I only saw him as he rode rapidly by the ranks, viewing each regiment in front and rear. If I was to give my own impression of the man, I should call him of a mild, good-natured disposition, not at all rash or reckless, as some seem to have an idea. His lady accompanied him and his staff wherever they went. She was evidently no stranger to the saddle, judging from the almost reckless ease and freedom with which she dashed from place to place on her mettlesome steed. After the General and his staff had passed around the entire body of troops, they took their position, and we in turn marched past them.

There is something grand and imposing in these reviews, that the lover of the beautiful cannot fail to admire. Ten or fifteen thousand men uniformly dressed, and marching by companies at company distance, all keeping the same step and maintaining the same distance, is what one does not often see, even if he belongs to the army. Such a mass of men moving steadily and regularly forward, keeping time to the most soul-enlivening strains of martial music that ever was discoursed, is certainly a *moving* spectacle. It would eclipse even those magnificent never-to-be-forgotten June trainings that Vermont used to have in the good old times, when the sound of the drum and fife would kindle our boyish patriotism into enthusiasm. I suppose this review was preliminary to an onward movement. At least it used to be so last Summer,—when we had a review the order to march soon followed.

Last Tuesday we were on picket. We picket now, the whole regiment at a time, and generally remain out three days. Tuesday morning brought with it a nasty, disagreeable snow storm. We could barely make ourselves comfortable in our tents by a warm fire, but on picket, nothing need be anticipated but wet clothes, numb fingers, and the prospect of shivering away the long hours over a comfortless fire of green pine, if we are lucky enough to get even that to burn. Gloomy as the duty in prospect might seem to some, it is just such an occasion as the old Second Vermont loves to glory in. Had a stranger been in camp, and seen us emerge from our cavern-like houses into the slop and slosh that was on the ground, and the snow and rain that was still coming, and heard the laughing, joking and shouting, he would have thought the regiment was discharged, and the boys were uproariously jubilant over the prospect of going home, instead of preparing for a three days' picket. Well, we formed into a line, preparatory to guard mounting, and of course had to stand the best part of an hour, that all the ceremonies incident to the duty, might be performed in a manner strictly military, and all the while the keen wind, direct from the North pole, was blowing the snow and rain into our faces. Under these circumstances, it is the most natural thing in the world for men such as compose this Second Regiment to feel "demoralized." So joke and play they would, regardless of the demands of good discipline, and even the officers were glad to escape being made the victims of some sharp witticism. The boys were bound to be merry, let what would happen; it is our philosophy. In course of time we started on our way towards the picket line. Part of the regiment stopped at the big reserve, part went on still further to some smaller reserves, and some went and took their post at once. On the big reserve, where it came my lot to stay the first twenty-four hours, we built us houses of boughs and blankets to protect us from the wind and storm, and made us large fires, so we managed, the most of us, to pass the day quite pleasantly. Night came, clear, windy and cold. Some managed to sleep comfortably, but many couldn't manage to sleep at all. Some had their houses uncovered of their blankets or boughs, and awoke in the morning, as the Irishman said, to find themselves sleeping outdoors.

Next day was April the first. Many had predicted a warm day after our snow storm, but they were nicely April fooled. Last year this day I, with a number of boys, enjoyed a good bath in the James river. This year, unless a man had latent caloric enough in him to melt an iceberg, he would hardly want to venture into the water far enough to wet his feet. We spent this day at the small reserve. Here half of us only were allowed to sleep at one time. The third day we went out to the line, and relieved those who had been standing guard the last twenty-four hours. Supports are distributed along the line where a score, more or less, are stationed. At these supports the men are divided into three reliefs, each relief taking their turn on post two hours, as in home guard. All were required to keep awake on these supports, but sometimes you hear a roguish fellow brag of getting a little sleep there. There are cavalry pickets stationed outside of our lines near the river. Opposite the river some of the rebels' works are visible, and the rebels themselves can be seen, but not plainly without the aid of a glass. Friday morning we were relieved by the 77th New York belonging to the third brigade of this division. Picketing is quite an experience, though any description I could give of it would be tame enough. We got back to camp just in season to get ready for the review. Getting ready for an occasion like that, means to black our shoes, equipments, belts, scour our brasses, brush our clothes, clean our guns, and trim ourselves up generally, as becomes the dignity of a soldier. Some of the boys who were sleepy and tired did not at all relish the idea of going out again so soon, and there was some language used that I should deem highly improper to quote. We forgot our philosophy of Tuesday morning, but when we were told that Col. Walbridge[11] had tried to get us excused, we began to feel a little mollified toward our commanders, and as soon as we were fairly on the ground we were as jolly as ever.

To-morrow we are to be reviewed by his Excellency, President Lincoln. Should anything of note come under my observation I will mention it in my next. But I will draw this letter to a close immediately, for I greatly fear, Mr. Editor, you will scold me by and by for sending my letters so long.

Camp near White Oak Church, Va.
April 13, 1863

Of course you know that we are still idle here, and if I should tell you that all "was quiet along the lines," I don't think it would cause any one a very deep sensation of relief. Yes, we are fairly surfeited with idleness and indolence. To be sure we have our regular routine of duties—guarding, "fatigueing," besides drills occasionally, and roll calls regularly. To go "on fatigue," as probably everybody knows, means to go to *work*. Generally it consists of either shoveling or chopping. But we have no rifle-pits to dig, as last year, nor breastworks to throw up. We have had as yet, no Chickahominy swamps to bridge over and corduroy, nor acres of timber to fell, but it is not too late for all these things to happen yet. So far we have been prosecuting a vigorously inactive campaign, and the prospect is favorable to its lasting for some time to come. Of course we are satisfied so far as idleness can satisfy. Our drills are none too much for healthy exercise, and to remind us that we are still in the military employ of Uncle Samuel. Less of this than is given us would have a tendency to diminish the military spirit of the troops and lead us to forget the reverence due to our paternal Uncle. Occasionally we have a review or something of that sort to relieve the monotony of our duties, and make them seem less mechanical, but even these are losing the charm of novelty. Croakers are getting scarce now; grumblers are always plenty. I suppose that it would be impossible to raise an army or a regiment and leave this element out. If it is fair weather they grumble because there is a drill, if foul they grumble because it rains. Duties of all kinds are especially distasteful, no matter whether it be a tedious drill or a splendid review, the "order" is full of oppressions and to them is very obnoxious. No order of command can please them. They would grumble if they were ordered to march through the suburbs of Paradise. But this class of men are in a very pitiable minority in this regiment—too small to be noticed.

I don't know what may be the opinions entertained in military circles in regard to the time when and place where we shall next move. Here in the ranks we entertain ideas of our own in regard to this, and we always fancy that we are about right. Certain indications will always rise to the surface to tell of coming events, and everybody knows how quick we Yankees are to learn the art of guessing. When officers begin to look good-natured and their wives begin to multiply in camp, we guess at once that an "immediate advance on the enemy's works" is not contemplated. But after all, our calculations for staying here may at any moment be annihilated. We base our calculations for staying upon the following premises:

In the first place, some three weeks ago we received an order allowing us to pack up our overcoats, extra blankets if we had them, and send them to Washington to be kept for us during the summer campaign. Believing that this order foreshadowed an immediate onward movement of the army, the boys gladly availed themselves of this opportunity to save in this way, every article that could possibly be dispensed with on a march, and was worth saving, last year's experience having taught us the folly of trying to carry more than was absolutely necessary. On dress parade, orders respecting rations were read, similar to those we always receive on the eve of a march. Furloughs were revoked, and all absentees called in. Every day for some little time we expected to try once more the road to Richmond,—a road that experience has told us is an exceedingly hard one to travel. But day succeeded day and no move was ordered. It was almost a disappointment. Soon, furloughs were being granted as before, and everything pertaining to the camp, went on as usual. It was even reported that our extra clothing was coming back, but of course this was an exaggeration. Then we were set to work cleaning up our camping grounds. Regular streets were laid out for each company in the different regiments of this brigade. To do this, tents (I suppose it is proper to denominate them tents—we call them "shanties" or "houses" here) which in the hurry of camping here, supposing their stay to be only temporary, had been huddled together in all manner of shapes, had, many of them to be removed and made to square with the company street. We brought pine trees from the woods and planted a row on each side of every one of these, making each street a vista, at once pleasing and beautiful. The officers had their tents encircled by a grove of pine, and many of the men did the same. Our camp now almost has the appearance of a well laid out pleasure ground. At the entrance of each street, an arch is made of poles draped with evergreen, the company letter ingeniously made of the same, suspended from the apex. The whole gives an air of beauty and refinement to the camp, that cannot be without wholesome effect. We think we have a right to consider this at least a minor indication that our stay here is to be prolonged, though last year the order to "police" our camp was so often followed by the order to march, that it became proverbial. This year, things move differently. I suppose the men whose minds are occupied only with the movements of great armies, the raising of men or the developing of gigantic financial schemes and who form their opinions of marches and battles from these, would laugh at our puny ideas, but it may be that we guess the nearest right after all.

If I were to step up into the higher latitudes of reasoning, and proclaim my opinion as worthy of consideration, I should not be at a loss to find evidences from this source, of a prolonged stay in this place. The relative strength of the opposing armies is no doubt proportionately greater in favor of the rebels, now, than ever before. Every avenue to Richmond is closed as secure as skill and science can make them. No position that can be made available for defence is left unfortified. The prestige of victory is with them. Several times when our army was stronger, and theirs was weaker than now, and when the way was comparatively open, we have tried to capture the rebel capital, and so far, we have signally, often almost ignominiously, failed. It seems to me that it must be a rare compliment to the genius of the present Commanding General, to suppose him capable of contending successfully against these great difficulties with his slender means, when others with greater advantages have failed before less imposing obstructions. I have great faith in General Hooker, but I do not believe his skill or genius is inspired with anything superhuman. The soldiers who took part in the battle of Fredericksburg, dislike trying the same thing over again, not because they have lost courage, but because they see in it no prospect of victory. Citizens who live here and know the lay of the land between here and Richmond, say it is a succession of ranges of hills the whole distance, as strong by nature as that we tried to carry at Fredericksburg. So if we succeed in driving them from their present position, they have only to fall back to the next strong position, where we must dislodge them the second time, and so on, fighting them at immense disadvantage each time till finally we may be overpowered ourselves and compelled to act over again the soul-sickening retreats of last summer. Perhaps there is a way of following upon an enemy so closely that he cannot gain advantage by falling back from one position to another, but if there is, our leaders have never yet discovered it.

Parts of this army have been sent off, they say, to operate in other parts. Our corps is to be left to hold this place and cover Washington till new contingencies develop themselves, says the same authority—*they say*. After all it would not be at all strange if we were ordered to "pack up," within twenty-four hours.

The news of the week is meagre enough. We were reviewed by President Lincoln last Wednesday. The honorable gentleman looked thin and careworn. No doubt it would be a great relief to him as well as to the country at large if the nation was free from the dire calamity of civil war. Perhaps my imagination added the unusual paleness to his cheek, and the expression of care that his countenance wore, but, certainly, as he passed by where we were standing, and I had a chance to see his face fully, I, for the moment, doubted the statement, so often made in newspapers, lately, that our President is enjoying the finest health and the best of spirits. Gen. Halleck (I suppose it was him) rode beside the President, and Gen. Hooker behind, followed by half a regiment of staff officers. It was a splendid review, and well worth marching out to Falmouth to see.

For weather, we have all kinds, but mostly cold. March was a very severe month, but the most of us are used to severe Marches. Since April commenced we have had cold nights and windy days—fine sugar weather if it was in a country where maple sugar is made though perhaps not quite freezing enough nights. Our cavalry all started out for rebeldom this morning. Reports are rife that the rebels over the river are evacuating. If this should prove true we shall not long remain idle. Meantime we quietly abide the issue of coming events.

———————

On Picket
St. George's County, Va.
April 19, 1863

Picket day has come around again, and being once more on this duty away out from camp, out of sight of all dwellings and habitations save a few negro huts, or hog pens, one can hardly tell which, such as are visible throughout the whole of slavery's accursed territory,—what could suggest itself, as a means of passing the time more agreeably in a place so lonely as this, than to hold a little written conversation with you, and perhaps, through your kindness, speak to many other good friends who love to hear of our welfare, and on whom our thoughts will sometimes linger in spite of the rough gaiety camp life evokes. I cannot tell you exactly where I am, but it is somewhere on the boundary line, between the United States, what there is left of them, and the Southern Confederacy. I need not tell you, Mr. Editor, that it is quite a romantic place here to sit and talk, or write, and one's thoughts can hardly help being inspired by the beauteous scenery so lavishly spread out by Nature all around. We are between two hostile armies, both of them drilling and exercising their men, and teaching them, as fast as they can, the arts of killing each other, and practicing those that are already learned, that they may not forget them. Brethren once, born under the same flag, reared under the same beneficent Government and prosperous by the same happy Union, now at deadly variance, seeking to imbrue our hands in each other's blood, and striving by all the means we can command to injure and destroy each other. Already has mourning been spread throughout the land, and poverty, suffering and desolation scattered everywhere. What a fearful load of guilt the band of traitors who caused this calamity have to meet at the bar of justice, when the Father of the fatherless, and the Judge of the widow calls them to their final account. If there is a pit in hell deep enough to receive them it must be a very deep one indeed.

Yes, it is a beautiful place here—beautiful to-day. The forests of pine are beautiful, so clear and transparent they look in the bright sunshine of to-day, so soft and furry as they appear when viewed from a greater distance. And the music is beautiful, Nature's own, that comes from a thousand branches, poured forth from a thousand tiny throats; sweet melodies making cheerful the passing Spring, and welcoming approaching Summer. The ground itself is beautiful too, as its carpet of green begins to relieve the deadness of the shrubbery around. The meandering brook, that finds its way along the winding valley close by, shall not be denied its claim to beauty. Everything of Nature's make that man has not spoiled is beautiful; and yet, the place is lonely, gloomy and desolate. Beautiful as most of the farms are in Virginia, there seems to be, or to have been, but few inhabitants who have occupied here to enjoy it. Few and widely separated are the dwellings here, and yet, occupying land that in Vermont would soon be covered with trim cottages, owned by a thriving, happy population. God must have made a great many acres of handsome forest here in Virginia for nothing, or else he made it to look at himself. But there are fields well cultivated and in a high state of improvement. What seems strange to a New Englander is, that it should take so much area for so few inhabitants.

One can hardly suppress a feeling of regret, to see land so fair so ruthlessly destroyed by the demon of war. Miles on miles of as finely timbered country as was ever produced, are stripped, laid waste, bared to the earth wherever the army has been. Fences have been converted into fuel, and houses without number burned to the ground. Universal ruin is marked everywhere. It cannot well be otherwise. Soldiers will not respect forest nor fences when they are benumbed with cold, nor will they be content to take any less than their needs require for the sake of economy or to spare the pockets or the homes of the secesh inhabitants. Virginia is a guilty state, and the day of her retribution seems to be at hand. It will be a long time before she can recover what she is now losing; and the end is not yet. Omnipotent wisdom alone can tell when the end will come, or the extent of ruin that will be accomplished when the end does come. If Virginia and her sister conspirators against our good Government were obliged to bear the whole burden of their guilt, it would be well, but this cannot be. The whole Nation is involved, and deep grief and poignant sorrow must be borne by the North, to expiate the crimes of the South. The issue as yet seems uncertain; and yet it cannot be uncertain so long as God is just. God does not love slavery; there is no slavery in Heaven. God does not love rebellion; rebellion could not live there. He hates oppression and oppressors. He loves liberty and a respectful obedience to just law. No, the issue cannot be uncertain—

> "For right is right since God is God,
> And right the day must win!
> To doubt would be disloyalty,
> To falter would be sin."

There is no other way,—there can be no other, for peace or for prosperity,— but to fight out this rebellion to the bitter end, subjugate and destroy it. After all the toil we have undergone, all the sufferings we have endured and dangers we have outlived, it is certainly an occasion of grief and indignation to us to hear of those at home who are talking of peace, to be purchased by concession *now.* There are soldiers here that would rather their bones should rot in Virginia than to have anything happen to our Government so humiliating. Possibly we may be obliged to surrender and give up to rebels, but it is cowardly to believe so, and it is doubly distilled cowardice to think of any such thing now. Shall we confess to the rebels that we have been wrong and they have been right; that we have been murdering them, and they only killing us in self defence? Shall we confess that we have been all the whiie the aggressors, while they were only resolutely contending for their rights? Shall we confess that twenty millions of the hardy sons of the North, with all our advantages, were unable to cope with less than half that number of proud Southern aristocrats? Shall we put our mouths in the dust and sue for peace to the very men that are despoiling our Nation of its glory? To talk of peace now means just that. It would rob us of our self-respect. All the world would despise us, and none more so than these same Southerners, whom we are so anxious to conciliate.

I hope the reader will excuse me; I can't help remonstrating in a feeble way against this hideous deformity of political faith. We have a big job to do and we need all hands to help, and whoever throws his influence in the way to hinder, should be summarily dealt with. No doubt the burdens of war press heavily, but look at our enemies and profit by the spirit of determination they display. It would seem as if the conscription act had made cowards of many and they were afraid their own precious blood would be spilled. It isn't fair play. We have borne the brunt of the war so far, and by and by, as our terms expire, and others are wanted to take our places, it would be the manly thing in them to go, and not talk of throwing away all we have done, and giving up the country now. Drafting is only drawing cuts to see who shall go to war, and no man of honor will shrink from running his chance. Those who complain of the war the most are generally those who have suffered the least. Those who have spent the most and suffered most are almost invariably the firmest patriots. Ask the widows and orphans throughout the land, whom the war has bereaved, if they want the blessed heritage for which their fathers and husbands fought and died lost forever, and there can be but one answer,—Never!

There are but very few men in this regiment that desire peace on any terms short of entire submission on the part of the enemy. There may be some, there always is in every regiment some who care but little whether the North or South whips so long as they can have a jolly, easy time. A few days' hard marching with short allowances of hard tack and meat, is very apt to convert such soldiers into violent copperheads. But they are not the rule, they are exceptions, and there is hardly enough of them to make a decent exception. I wish these peace politicians could come into the old Second Regiment just for the experiment, and pick out their worshippers, and have on the other hand the unconditional Union men select out those who will stand by them at whatever hazard, and let the moral and intellectual capacities, and all that go to make up a *man,* of each, be put into a balance and see which way the scale would tip. It would be as between a pile of froth and a wedge of gold. If the copperheads would not be ashamed of this party here, then there could hardly be found anything outside of the infernal regions that would shame them. I do not say that it is absolutely impossible for a man strictly conscientious to desire peace through disunion and compromise. Paul consented to the martyrdom of Stephen, and afterwards claimed to have lived "in all good conscience" to that day. So a man may consent to see our Government martyred, and if he don't know any better, charity may reluctantly admit, perhaps, that he is sincere and honest; but if a man is endowed with conscientiousness, bravery and wisdom altogether, he will hardly fail to feel a personal sacrifice or personal risk. Turn this regiment loose, and I know the boys would hardly brook to hear the treasonable talk about peace that is sometimes echoed from home. They would consider that it tarnished their honor and robbed them of the praise and glory that would justly belong to them as benefactors of the country. It is as much as our patience can bear to hear the secesh, that live about here, continually twit us of our inability to conquer the rebels, and the folly of our trying to do so. But we expect this of them. We don't expect friends at home will imitate them, however. It is really remarkable how exactly similar the arguments of the rebels here and the rebels at home are. The points most prominent in both are always "abolition" or "nigger," "Lincoln's tyranny" "State rights" etc., blaming the North and excusing the South. If our friends at home join hands with the citizen rebels here and advocate their cause, they will expect to receive the same regard from the soldiers that we give these; and that is just what we are obliged to give them and no more.

All the way up the Peninsula, these citizen rebels, male and female, told us of our certain defeat and probable destruction. We laughed them to scorn, and marched proudly and confidently on. By lack of management on the part of our leaders, and through no fault of ours, as these leaders are willing to testify, their prophesies proved true, and we were obliged to accept their bitter taunts, and skedaddle for our lives. A vast change then came over the feelings and spirits of the boys. From being bold and confident, proudly conscious of our strength and prowess, we were humbled in a great measure, and seriously distrusted our ability to cope with the enemy. We respected our enemies more and ourselves less. Demoralization was the certain consequence, desertions frequent. But defeats are not the only means to demoralize our army. Preach to them the justice of the rebel course, dwell largely on their grievances, speak of the injustice and corruption of our own Government, and if soldiers will believe you, you have done more to demoralize the army than the enemy could by a thorough victory of their arms. The numerous desertions which has so marred the reputation of this army, were caused as much by copperhead ideas—I don't know what else to call them—as by any reverses they had suffered. They thought it useless to struggle any longer. The South must in the end succeed, and after all, they were not so much to blame for seceding. The North were the oppressors, and their government was very corrupt. In short, the sentiments of almost every one that deserted would almost exactly square with those of Fernando Wood[12] as expressed in some of the recent political meetings in Connecticut. If the honorable gentleman himself was in the army, I don't believe but that he would try every means to get out of it, though I do not doubt but that he is as courageous as a lion.

There has been a great change for the better, in the minds of the men of this regiment during the last few months respecting the war, and no doubt the whole army are improved in the same way. A while ago it was no uncommon thing to hear men answer to their names "Here, but it is the last time," and often they made true their statement. Officers as well as men spoke frequently of their determination to desert, and not help carry on an "abolition war." It is very materially changed now. Good discipline is effectually restored. Confidence in the Government, and respect for it, is re-established. Many a time have I heard boys, with more perverseness than good sense, remark that they would never carry a gun against the enemy again. There is but little of this disposition manifested now, and it is becoming decidedly unpopular. As the soldiers see more fully the depths of principle involved in this controversy, and the wisdom of the policy the Government is adopting to bring it to an issue that God must forever approve, the more determined and anxious are they to carry the war out successfully. Whatever tends to weaken the faith cannot be born of patriotism. But I owe the reader an apology for presuming upon his patience so long. We soldiers have a personal feeling in this matter of fighting or surrendering, and it may sometimes be that we are almost oversensitive in regard to it. Having taken up the subject I hardly knew when to drop it.

Camp near White Oak Church, Va.
April 26, 1863

We have not moved from our old camp yet, although we came so near it once that we considered it a foregone conclusion. Last week every possible preparation was made for such an event; the usual orders were read, some more stringent and particular than ever before. The order in regard to straggling was read by the adjutant to each company separately, besides being read, according to usual custom, on dress parade, twice. Great stress was laid upon the importance of preventing a practice so demoralizing and weakening to the army. Regimental and Company officers were to be held responsible and, besides other punishments threatened, leaves of absence and furloughs would be withheld from those regiments where straggling was permitted.

The order in regard to rations informed us that we must each of us carry eight days' rations of bread, coffee and sugar, three days' rations of meat—the remaining five days' rations of meat were to be taken along on the hoof. This was making far greater provision for ourselves than had ever before been required of us, and seemed to bode heavy, fatiguing loads for our backs, or else extreme destitution in the matter of blankets and extra clothing. We were not exactly ordered, but very strongly advised, to take only our rubber blankets, and leave our woollen ones in the care of the Quartermaster. Everything else, except a change of underclothing, must be left. Once before we had been ordered to send off to Washington everything worth saving that could possibly be dispensed with in a summer campaign. We thought we had been remarkably self-sacrificing and had stinted ourselves to the lowest possible extreme, but this order pressed us down another notch. Some sent off their woollen blankets and even their dress coats,—their overcoats had been sent off before. They saved nothing but their rubber blankets and their blouse coats, or fatigue jackets. Others determined to keep their woollen blankets at all hazards, and if sorely weighed down on the march, they could throw them away. Inasmuch as we didn't move, these saw the wisdom of their decision. Those that sent off all their things consoled themselves with the philosophy that they are as well off in camp without them, as they would be on the march.

But all of our preparations were nothing, as present appearances indicate. It is quite amusing, though, to be in a camp like ours on the eve of a march, and hear the debates, suggestions, and decisions in regard to a thousand little valuables,—whether they should be left behind or carried. Things of no special merit, but which had contributed to our comfort or convenience, were heedlessly thrown aside or destroyed. Many an article that a few days before would have been gladly bought at a high price, were at once valueless and could not be given away. Often a knapsack would have to be unpacked and its contents sorted over and over again, and other articles selected out and doomed to stay behind, to the no small regret of the wistful owner. No bigger article than a can for butter, or a frying-pan, would be made the subject of earnest debate, but the question, "how can we get along without them?" was confronted by one still more inexorable, "How can we carry them?" If we only knew where we were going? but we did not know that, and it was wisdom to prepare for the worst. That night it rained like a deluge, and marching the next day was rendered impracticable. It would be the merest guesswork, to undertake to tell when we shall be called upon to get ready for marching again.

The boys were never in better spirits or in better health than now, and they were never in better condition to endure the fatigues of a march than at the present time. But very few of the men are on the sick list, and those that are are mostly recruits who are not yet fully acclimated. The boys "feel their oats," as the saying is, immensely. I have never seen the time when the boys would engage in all manner of athletic sports with such eager relish as now.

There is none of that thin, gloomy, woebegone expression to be seen in the faces of the men that was visible upon almost every countenance at the end of last summer's campaign. The boys never felt more *boyish* than they do now, and they never enjoyed themselves better. We can get up a sham fight that might look a little rough to some of our milder acquaintances at home, perhaps, but it passes with us as good, earnest boy's play. Rough as the Second boys have the name of being—and rough customers we certainly are, to those who are foolish enough to proclaim themselves our adversaries—a quarrel among ourselves is an unheard of thing and "difficulties" quite unknown. Almost perfect equanimity and good feeling exist throughout the entire regiment. Our guard-house remains empty, or in fact we have no guard-house at all, the apology of a thing we once had having become totally ruined and demoralized for want of use and care. The whole institution is nearly obsolete, and putting men under arrest is well nigh played out.

The 26th New Jersey regiment belongs to this brigade—a regiment of nine months men who came out here with big bounties, and, of course, has seen more hardships, endured more privations, and suffered more generally than any of the old soldiers ever dreamed of. The boys call them "two hundred dollar men," and they take wicked delight in playing their pranks on them whenever they have a chance. Our boys have no particular grudge against the Jerseys, but their mischief loving propensities must find vent somewhere and the Jersey regiment furnishes them abundant victims. It will be a long time before the boys will allow them to forget the dog scrape we got them into when we tempted them to steal a nicely dressed dog, which was duly served up to their officers in fine style. They stole it out of pure mischief and a desire not to be outstripped in that line of business by our boys; and doubtless it tasted remarkably sweet in consequence, as stolen articles proverbially do, but the joke leaked out, and it will be a long time before they will hear the last of it. It must be very provoking to them to hear the *barking* that springs spontaneously, as it would seem, from our regiment, whenever we pass the Jerseys, but nobody can tell who does it, and the Jerseys have to "grin and bear it." Our boys love to make them visits occasionally, after roll-call at night, and, as they generally come back in high glee, with a mouthful of stories to tell, it may be safely considered that the visit was a pleasant one to at least one of the parties. In one of these nocturnal visits some of our boys, for some reason or other, probably a misunderstanding, got caught, and were put into the guard-house. But the guard-house didn't hold them long. They run the guard and outrun the guard's bullets, and, though the Jerseys did their best, they couldn't imprison them again, nor tell who they were. After that our boys generously offered to stand guard for them, but our services were declined. Some time ago some officers of the Fifth advised the Jerseys to let the Second boys alone or they would find more than they could handle, and the Jerseys are beginning to think it best to accept this advice.

The paymaster made us a visit about a fortnight ago, and this has contributed not a little to keep the boys in good spirits, for there is nothing in the world that will make the boys feel so good-natured as it will to get their pockets lined with Uncle Sam's greenbacks. We received four months' pay. It made quite a little sum for us, but it is easily spent here. Some are beginning to borrow already. While every luxury (we call them luxuries, though any one but soldiers would consider the term "necessaries" more appropriate) that we have to buy rules so high, as here in the army, money is of but little account. For instance: butter is 60 cents a pound, cheese 50 cents a pound, apples 5 cents apiece, papers tobacco at the rate of nearly $3.00 a pound, whiskey $1.00 a drink or $3.00 a bottle, and so on to the end of the chapter. For five dollars a fellow could get a pretty good dinner at the sutler's. It is unnecessary, in order to tell a big story, to quote prices in Jeff's dominions; here in the Union army we can beat the rebs all hollow even in that.

The weather to-day and yesterday, has been remarkably fine. The sun shines clear and pleasant with scarcely a cloud to intervene. A stiff northwest wind has been blowing steadily, in regular April style. In Vermont it would be considered excellent weather to make sugar, as well as to dry the land and prepare it for the plow. Here it is still quite cool, and a sunny side is preferable to a shade for comfort. With this weather Virginia mud must soon disappear. Something besides mud will have to be our excuse for remaining here much longer. There has been some curious rumors afloat to account for our not moving. In the first place Gen. Hooker had broken his leg, by being thrown from a horse, and therefore could not be with the army. Then it was said that he ordered a movement to be made, but the President countermanded the order. Upon this, it is said, Hooker resigned and Fremont was now in command. They are all about equally true, probably. But whether we move or stay, as the boys say "it is all inside of the three years."

Quite a disgraceful affair occurred the other day with the 5th regiment which perhaps I ought to mention. Five or six from Co. D, of that regiment went out to a house near the picket line, for purposes too foul to mention. The guard stationed at the house was relieved, who reported his suspicions of something wrong at the nearest picket reserve. A squad of pickets was immediately sent to arrest the guilty party. They succeeded, but were fired upon and two of their number hit. I do not know the extent of the injuries received. The affair will soon undergo an investigation, and some think the death penalty will be inflicted upon one or more of the culprits.

On the Field
May 2, 1863

I might safely call writing under the present circumstances, a labor under extreme difficulties. We are every moment expecting to fall in and move. All our "effects" are with us; our clothing, bedding, and eight days' subsistence, besides our trusty rifles and a complement of ammunition. Our equipments we constantly wear, so that in a sudden emergency we may not be found without them. Our knapsacks are kept packed and we are expected to be ready in a moment, at the word of command. While the cannon is booming occasionally, and the wind blowing exceedingly, I have pulled out my portfolio, and as the Major has just given the command "rest," and gone out on an eminence to look at the rebs with his glass, I take it for granted that we shall have a few moments' respite; so be the time longer or shorter, I am bound to improve what there is of it by scribbling a line or so to you.

We have not done any big fighting yet, but we expect there is some awful strategy going on, and by and by when matters have developed themselves to the proper pitch, we expect to wade into the contest and cover ourselves and all Vermont with glory.

Tuesday we prepared ourselves according to the oft-repeated order with our eight days' rations and everything else we wanted to carry. It rained, of course, but not quite hard enough to prevent our marching or to dampen our spirits. We pulled down our tents, burned up our love-letters, packed up our knapsacks, threw away our novels but kept our Bibles, and at quarter before twelve A.M., we took up the line of march Dixieward once more. The mud grew heavy, and so did our knapsacks, but we trudged along, not minding either. It is not the gloomiest thing that ever was, to march, even if it does rain, and we know we are marching where death and destruction are going on, or going to go on; at any rate, it isn't for the Second Vermont. The boys are full of wit and fun, which comes out in spite of everybody, and all the discipline in the world couldn't keep it in. Sometimes a citizen is pounced upon, and if he undertakes to reply to their sallies, he finds himself far up the salt river in no time; sometimes a pompous black is made the victim of a joke, that even the blackest Republican can hardly help smiling at. Occasionally we get up a song and rest ourselves singing, and occasionally we sit down on our knapsacks and rest ourselves laughing. Besides what we got up ourselves to enliven the journey on this not very eventful day, we passed by, or rather, around, near where an excellent band was playing, and their music was so rarely excellent, that the boys were willing to be quiet as we passed, and listen to them. Further on we come to the ground where the Professor's balloon operations were going on, — for I suppose it is generally known that these operations have to be carried on partly on the ground as well as up in the air. The aeronaut would hardly dare trust his balloon or his own precious skill and learning very high in the air, without some connection with good, loyal, United States soil. We halted just as we were passing there, which gave us a good opportunity of viewing their movements. The balloon car has two ropes from it which are held by men below, and they let it up or pull it down as a boy would a kite. Either for their own amusement or somebody else's, for it was too foggy and rainy to make observations, the balloon was elevated and drawn down every few minutes that we were there. The balloon had the face of Washington on one side and his name on the other. The countenance of the revered patriot must be very large, for it looks quite natural and life-like when the balloon is so high in the air that the man in the car looks scarcely half as big as a mosquito's bill.

We halted for the night on the eminence that overlooks the fertile valley of the Rappahannock and the historic city of Fredericksburg. During the night the pontoon train moved down to the river and laid their bridges. The whole operation was brilliantly conceived and successfully carried out. Gen. Brooks' division moved across at daylight and drove the rebels out of their first rifle-pits and occupied it themselves. They had a short, spirited skirmish, and gained an important position by it.

In the morning we moved down nearer the river and remained during the day. At night we spread down our blankets in the mud, and laid ourselves down to dream of parlors and feather beds. Some put up their tents and some didn't, for every moment we expected to be called upon to move—perhaps a dozen miles or perhaps as many feet. At midnight it commenced raining, and, as I had preferred sleeping in the open air, I had the full benefit of it. The soft clayey ground all around me was fast converted into mud, and everytime one went by my bed, as they often did, making a gulchy noise like driving a yoke of cattle through a barnyard where the muck is belly deep, and spattering the mud into my face, I felt that there was more than one way for a man to suffer for his country, and that this must be one of them. If this wasn't the dam—pest kind of sleep I ever tried to enjoy, I wouldn't say anything about it. It kept drizzling nearly all of Thursday forenoon, but in the afternoon it cleared away, and bid fair for good weather during the impending struggle. All day firing was heard upon our right, and we very naturally felt the keenest interest to know what was going on. An order was read to us from Gen. Hooker to the effect that he had pushed their left flank, and had now got the enemy just where he wanted them — where they must either come out and fight in open field or surrender. I saw a correspondent of the New York *Tribune,* who had just come from the right, and he spoke of the prospect as very encouraging. He said that Gen. Hooker's plan, so far, had been carried out with complete success. This intelligence enkindled our hopes amazingly. We began to think that, after all, here was some prospect of seeing Richmond and giving three cheers in the capital of Secessia.

Yesterday we hadn't much to do only to fall into line occasionally, and then fall out again. We moved out of the mud up the bank that encloses the wide beautiful intervals that border the river and here we had a good chance to watch the rebels and our men on the flat over the river. The fertile valley of this river from Fredericksburg away down almost as far as one can see, comprizes some land as handsome as ever pleased the eye of a farmer. The flat on both sides of the river, I should think, was nearly two miles wide; perhaps it would average more. In Vermont it would be worth from $100 to $150 an acre. I have been told it was valued at that here. It is encircled all around with hills and bluffs, thus forming a kind of basin that Nature evidently intended should be highly appreciated, and would have been if she had peopled it with Yankees. The hills are the strength of the rebels' position here. They are mostly hidden by woods, but enough of them can be seen to show that they are sufficiently formidable to try the pluck of even Vermonters. Their skirmishers and ours are so near together over there, that from here it looks as if they could commence hostilities without their rifles, — that they could throw brickbats at each other. Till to-day both parties had remained perfectly quiet, but to-day the rebels have been annoying our skirmishers considerably, they being protected by a high bank along the road. I couldn't see as our pickets replied. Our old Brig.-Gen. commands over there. Gen. Howe, our Division General, asked him if he didn't want his men relieved. "No, G—d d—n it," (the Gen. always swears) "if you want a position fight and get one."

I saw some boys a few minutes ago belonging to a nine months Rhode Island battery. Their term of service is about to expire, but they have unanimously voted to stay and see the termination of this movement. They are brave and patriotic fellows, and will probably do good service somewhere in the coming contest.

A few hours ago we started out to go on picket up the river where our pickets are this side. Part of our regiment has been deployed out, but we are moved around in so many shapes that it is difficult telling what kind of duty we are doing.

From the bluff, a few rods from us, our battery is playing occasionally, just for the amusement of the rebels. A few minutes ago a shot struck among a loose squad of rebels that were walking leisurely along over a knoll, and scattered them instantly, except a few that couldn't scatter without help.

But here comes Major Tyler,[13] and I know by his looks that he is going to order us to fall in. The pickets on the other side are firing at each other with considerable spirit, and I shouldn't wonder if we were to go over there and have a chance at the enemy ourselves. So I will close this rambling letter, hoping the next time I write I shall be in less of a hurry, and have something more important to tell.

———————

The First Day's Fight at Fredericksburg
Camp near White Oak Church, Va.
May 9, 1863

Undoubtedly every incident connected with the late battle of Fredericksburg is perfectly familiar to your readers, long before this time, so that anything I could say would be but mere repetition, entirely superfluous and uninteresting. Nevertheless, it is my habit to like to speak of brave deeds, and there were so many performed on this day that I shall not omit the opportunity offered now of telling what I saw, although aware that my account will be but the relation of my own experience and will feebly compare with those of more extended observation. The temptation to write would be much stronger if I knew how to convey anything like an accurate idea of the exciting events of this day's fight.

Last Saturday night, as soon as it was dark, we crossed the river and halted on the plain opposite. The whole transaction was executed very quietly, and everything was very still. We spread down our blankets in the bright light of a full moon, and sought repose, expecting on the morrow to march against the foe and measure swords with him once more. Nothing occurred to disturb our rest, only we were aroused once or twice to move a few rods to the right, and then to move a few rods to the left, and finally to come to a halt almost exactly where we were in the first place. At midnight they called us up to have us draw half a dozen more hard tack apiece; we had but eight days' rations of them in our knapsacks, which probably rendered this insignificant addition indispensable to the safety of the Union. After this we slept without interruption till the day was beginning to dawn. As soon as the morning twilight began to appear we were promptly in line, ready to move forward. We took our positions a short distance in advance, sheltering ourselves in the road. The batteries took their positions on the flats and fired over our heads at the rebel works. The enemy's shot, as well as our own, passed over our heads, and their music was quite lively and interesting. Occasionally a shot or a piece of shell would come so low as to hit some one in the road, but for all that the officers found it almost impossible to make the men obey the order, "keep down." About 11 o'clock there was a consultation among the officers in regard, I suppose, to making a charge and taking the rebel works on the hill, — the very works that General Sumner tried so desperately and with such immense loss to take last winter, but utterly failed to do so. Simultaneously with the assault here another attack by assault was to be made from the city, about three-quarters of a mile above, where there was another range of strong works, and if both succeeded we should be in possession of the key to the whole position. The 26th New Jersey was to take the lead, ours to follow and support them, and other regiments were to advance on our right and left. The boys started with confidence and alacrity, cheering as they went. The rebels opened on us from every piece they had, from a 24-pounder to a pocket pistol. Our batteries played over our heads and helped us all they could. The air seemed to be full of hissing shot and bursting shells. The roar was terrific and it required men of nerve to stand it. The Jerseys faltered; they did not run, but their regiment became so completely broken up that but little could be expected of them. There didn't seem to be any ranks anywhere. They were scattered all over the ground, so that a shell could hardly burst amiss. Behind every tree, stump, or whatever would shelter them, they could be seen hiding away from the storm of iron hail and completely paralyzed with terror. Some of them we forced into our ranks, but such were found to be too demoralized in the knees to be capable of effective service. We approached a deep ditch and, as we expected, it was filled with the trembling cowards, who seemed to be dying a thousand deaths. A rebel shell struck in the ditch just as we came up to it, filling our faces with dirt, and burying a number of the Jerseys, where the boys maliciously hoped they would remain till the resurrection. Col. Grant saw at once that to expect anything from that regiment would be hanging his hopes on a rope of sand, so he ordered the Second Vermont to the right of them, and we rushed up the hill ahead. Some from the Jersey regiment, more brave than the rest, joined with us and fought like heroes till the engagement was over.

The hill up which we charged, was covered with brush besides being very steep and every way difficult to climb. At the right there was a deep ravine also filled with brush and felled trees. The right of the regiment had to make their way up through this. The rebs had set fire to the brush on the top of the hill, and the hot, suffocating smoke drifted into our faces, but we moved straight onward, regardless of everything. The air was intensely hot and sultry, the fire of the rebel musketry as we neared the top of the hill, was hot, too, but not a man flinched. While we were crossing the flat and till we got to the foot of the hill, our regiment kept in as good a line as if they were on a drill. Among this brush and smoke and bullets, this, of course, was impossible. We halted a moment in a rebel rifle-pit to take breath, when at the word from Col. Grant, "Up now, my brave boys and give it to them," we pushed forward as fast as possible. There were plenty of opportunities for cowards to hide and skulk from duty, as we were getting up through that brush, but I do not know of a single man who availed himself of them. Our skirmishers drove the gunners away from two excellent pieces of artillery and captured them.

At the top of the hill we were met with a more terrific shower of bullets than before. For a moment our regiment wavered. A little way beyond us through the smoke, the rebels could be seen hesitating the same way. Their officers were trying to rally them. It was a critical moment. If our men would come forward now they would certainly drive them; a moment more and all might be lost. The crisis was imminent, immense consequences hung poised on a few seconds of time. Some of the rebels were panic-stricken and running, some were rallying to renew the fight. A bold attack from them just then, would certainly have driven our men, so would a bold attack from us drive them. Now was the precious moment to strike. Oh! if our boys only would rally, — thank God they did. They rallied in stoutly, and drove the rebs to the eminence beyond. Here they held a line for some time, but by the time our supports came up, they had skedaddled out of sight. This was the sharpest fire our regiment has been under. The men fell fast on right and left. It is difficult to realize in the time of an action, the extreme peril one's life is in. Death there seems of less consequence than anywhere else, one gets so used to it. Let a railroad accident happen, or a factory tumble to the ground, mangling a great many, and terrifying numbers more, and the whole country shudders, but the same number may be killed and maimed in a brisk skirmish, and the affair is very "brilliant." Such is the acknowledged difference, and it is well that it should be so. But when the excitement is over and we go back to camp and see so many comrades whose society was our pleasure, missing, we feel very keenly the loss we have sustained.

During this fight a brave little fellow just to my right was shot through the neck. The ball cut the jugular vein and he died immediately. He was told that he could not live and asked if he had any word that he wanted to send to his friends. "Tell them," says he, "that I was a good soldier," and truly he had been one. He had been with the regiment from the beginning, and was never excused by the surgeon but five days during the whole time, and two of those days was in consequence of a wound received at Fredericksburg before. The country has had his services and his life, and more than this no patriot can give.

Bullets play curious freaks sometimes, and every battle has its hair-breadth escapes. One fellow had his gun shot out of his hands, and another close by had his life spared because his gun intercepted the bullet. Sergt. Davis of Company E, was struck in the breast with a ball, but an account book in his pocket was his life-preserver. Capt. Ballou, Company H, had the skin scratched off his nose by a rebel minnie, and that is shooting a man almost within an inch of his life. I might multiply incidents like these to an almost endless extent.

The smoke of the battle cleared up and gave us an opportunity to rest ourselves and slake our thirst — an opportunity that we very much needed. We took a number of prisoners, Mississippians. They said they never had been driven before. They were old troops. They had plenty of bacon and hard biscuit to eat, and their appearance hardly justified the idea that they were in a starving condition. They had no coffee, and they were destitute of many little luxuries that we enjoy. Some prisoners that came and delivered themselves up as we were charging up the hill said they came in to get something to eat; they were tired of fighting on an empty stomach.

There were other Vermont regiments in the fight of Sunday, but none lost so heavily as the second. The casualties in this regiment that day exceeded a hundred. It is unnecessary for me to give any names, as you will probably receive a list more correct than I could give long before this reaches you. Quite a number of officers were wounded while gallantly doing their duty, but I omit to mention their names as I fear I should not do them justice if I did. The severest was received by Capt. Crossman, of Company F. He has had to have a leg amputated.

———————

Camp near White Oak Church, Va.
May 11, 1863

Just one week ago to-day we had our second day's fight with the enemy, which is almost long enough ago for news to spoil, but as I never aspired to be a news-teller, and only write when I have nothing else to do, just to keep myself out of mischief, I will venture to give an account of that fight as it looked to me, without comment or apology. The task would be much more agreeable if it related to a glorious victory instead of another repulse and another hopeless retreat. We really think we ought to have one general victory after so much hard fighting, and so many times driving the enemy, but we will try and not be unreasonable.

When we had finished the fight of Sunday we returned to the road where we had left our knapsacks, and strapping them to our backs once more, started in pursuit of the "flying foe." We marched up through the city of Fredericksburg, which looked sullen and gloomy as though it brooded revenge for the mutilated buildings pierced by the shells in the former battle. A few grinning darkies were seen at the doorways and at the corners of the streets, gazing in childish curiosity at the men as they passed along by. We asked them where all the white folks were. They said they were in the house out of sight. I could not exactly divine the meaning of their answer.

Passing on through the city we marched westward to where Gen. Brooks with his division was fighting, that we might render him assistance if necessary. Before we reached the battle-field, however, we met large squads of stragglers, some wounded, but the majority well as ever, which told us plainly enough that some regiment had got broken or scared to pieces. As the fighting was all over before we got there, we marched off to the left of the road through the woods and brush, and took up our position for the night. Tired almost to death, and hungry enough to eat our hard tack without coffee and not grumble, for no fire to cook was allowed, we finished our plain repast, and were soon wrapt in blankets quietly sleeping in the dense pine thicket, totally unmindful of the dread excitement we had gone through, or the bloody task which to-morrow's duties might require of us. We were not aroused till we had had plenty of sleep, and ample time was given us to prepare and eat our breakfast. Everything seemed to be as well as heart could wish, and our anticipations rose high of an easy and glorious victory. But our hopes were quickly annihilated when a volley of rebel shells fired from the very hill we had taken Sunday, came hissing over our heads and bursting in our midst. This sounded in our ears as the death knell of all we had been toiling and hoping for, and we knew enough to know that instead of marching triumphantly on to Richmond, the prospect of having to skedaddle for our very lives was much more imminent. We packed up instanter, faced about and marched back to take up a position for defense. We marched from place to place, taking position in one spot, and then moving to another, so that to the enemy it might appear that we had a considerable force. At last we halted in an open field sheltered by a slight swell in the ground while a strong line of battle was posted in front of us. Pickets were thrown out and everything was quiet till about five o'clock in the afternoon when the attack on us commenced.

Our line was in the shape of an ox bow, with both ends resting on the Rappahannock, and covering Banks' Ford, some four or five miles above Fredericksburg. We were on the eastern side of the arc, facing the city where the heaviest attack was made. Gen. Brooks' division was on our right and Gen. Newton's on our left, while another brigade guarded the bridge at Banks' Ford. Our line was far from being strong enough to resist such a bold attack as the rebels brought against us, outnumbering our forces three to one.

The attack was made in regular Jackson style, and for a while we supposed that that intrepid General had brought large reinforcements against us and was leading them in person, but the prisoners said that Gen. Lee was there in command and that he intended to capture the whole of the sixth corps.

In front of the Vermont Brigade was a deep hollow covered with trees, mostly low pine. The hill beyond commanded Fredericksburg on that side. Here our skirmishers were deployed while troops in line of battle were posted close behind them. About five the occasional crack of a musket warned us that the attack had commenced and the enemy's skirmishers were engaged with ours. In a few moments more the continuous roar of musketry announced that the attack had begun in earnest and the enemy were close upon us with a heavy force. At first we could see that our men were falling back, but as they approached us the woods hid them from our view. We waited in suspense for the issue of the contest, but we did not have to wait long before we could see the ground covered with our men emerging from the woods in wild disorder, completely panic-stricken. They had the same old story to tell; their regiment was all cut to pieces and there was no use fighting, the enemy were coming in five lines of battle and would surely overwhelm us. Some of these men were forced into our ranks and compelled to fight, but as a general thing, they were too thoroughly frightened to be of much use. One fellow that was forced to take his place in the rear rank a little to the right of me was so beside himself with fear that he discharged his gun as soon as he could after getting into his place, without waiting to even raise his piece from the ground. We were lying on our faces, and it so happened that he fired directly under his file-leader in the front rank, the ball going his whole length but so close to the ground that it did him no injury. The escape was almost miraculous. The Captain concluded after that, that it would be as safe to let the skedaddlers run. Some of these men belonged to the 21st and some to the 26th New Jersey, and others belonged to the 20th New York.

Meantime the rebels were coming in all their fury. As soon as they were fairly through the woods so that we could see them, we arose at the word, and let them have it without mercy. They were completely taken by surprise, and such a fire was more than they could stand; when finding that they could make no impression on our right line they beat a hasty retreat back out of sight. The left of our regiment suffered severely; the right was partially protected by the rise in front which deceived the enemy so that nearly all their shots passed over. The Sixth on our right charged on the retreating foe and captured a large number of prisoners. Gen. Howe complimented us very highly for our bravery and steadiness. Said he to the Colonel, "You have reason to be proud of your men. They did well yesterday and they have done well now. They have saved the day." We formed the last line and had the enemy broken it he would have had everything his own way. I don't see how a man in the whole corps could have escaped. I do not wish to be understood as trying to convey the idea that this regiment did all the fighting or was braver than every other regiment. I only bear testimony to what I saw. Other regiments fought equally as well, no doubt, perhaps better. There was some as brave fighters among the Jerseys as can be found anywhere in the army. When we charged up the hill Sunday, some of these fellows left their own regiment and joined us and fought bravely to the end. They did the same here, and seemed to feel ashamed and mortified at the conduct of their regiment, which they said was caused in a great measure by the inefficiency of their line officers. Their field officers they said did all that men could do to rally their men, but the company officers were nowhere.

Notwithstanding we repulsed the enemy so handsomely we were obliged to fall back. Between the Second regiment and the Fourth on our left, was an intervening space large enough for two regiments to stand in line, which was left vacant because we had not sufficient force to fill it. There was a sort of ravine between us into which the enemy threw a column of men to get into our rear. They were trying to flank us also at another point further down to the left. Of course we could preserve our lines only by falling back. "It is too bad to leave this position," said Col. Grant's aid as he delivered the order, "for I believe we could hold it, but your regiment is ordered to fall back to the rear of that house," pointing to a house about a hundred rods to our rear. We started double quick, and some of the other regiments seeing us run, gave rise to the story that the Second was driven back by the enemy. It was sorely against our will to fall back at all, but when the order was given we executed it promptly; but we were not under fire and what we did was done deliberately.

We took our position once more and awaited another attack. Daylight had faded, but a full moon shone brightly and an enemy could be seen almost as well as in the day time. A few pieces of artillery was posted just to the left of us and as soon as the enemy advanced from the woods they opened on them with grape and cannister. The effect was grand. I never saw more splendid artillery firing. At every discharge the grape could be heard rattling against the trees like throwing a handful of pebbles against the side of a building. No enemy could stand such a fire, and they were soon driven back.

We took a position once more in a road a little to our rear—the embankment making a good breastwork for our protection. We did not remain here long before we fell into line as quietly as possible and marched for the bridge at Banks' Ford. Large numbers of troops were there impatiently waiting for their turn to cross. After waiting there a short time we were ordered to fall into line which we did most willingly, for we were anxious to reach a place of safety where we could rest. Instead of marching across the river, however, we were ordered back to act as rear guard to protect the army. Some of the boys thought it a poor return for brave fighting that they should be obliged to do extra duty. But it was reported, with how much truth I cannot say, that Gen. Howe dare not trust any other troops but Vermonters to protect his rear at this critical time. Skirmishers were deployed out ahead and we waited as patiently as we could for the rest of the troops to march off. The rebels got a piece of artillery where they could throw shell to the bridge and among the troops about there, but I do not know how much damage they did, though they could hardly fail of doing some. There was a delay and all was quiet for two hours or more; and the rumor came to us that a shell had destroyed the bridge. Another rumor said that a rebel officer had assumed to be a messenger from the commanding General, with an order countermanding the withdrawal across the river.

It was a relief to see the troops in motion once more towards the bridge, for it was getting to be nearly morning. After all the rest had gone we withdrew from our position with the utmost quietness and marched across. It was sunrise before we halted. We did not remain here but a short time, for a rebel shell bursting directly in the midst of the Sixth regiment, and another one close by, told us that if we were marching for a place of safety we had yet further to travel.

Camp near White Oak Church, Va.
May 19, 1863

The smoke of battle has cleared up, giving us a chance to look over the ground and count the cost and consequences of our late bloody campaign. As we are considered fighters by trade, the last attempt in our line of business will have prominence in our thoughts and be the leading topic of conversation till another "rip" comes off. It may be an old story in Vermont by this time but it is not exactly so here. We all have our stories to tell, and where they are deficient in fact we supply the lack from imagination.

It is quite amusing to see the accounts the newspapers give of our proceedings here subsequent to coming this side of the river. Hooker, it was coolly said, was over the river again and pursuing Lee's fleeing forces into the last ditch. The Philadelphia *Inquirer* (I believe) shrewdly observed that the next battle would probably be fought somewhere on the Pamunkey and then the door to Richmond would be thrown open to the victorious Yankees. The backbone of the rebellion, so long on the point of breaking, would be able to sustain the pressure no longer, and the starved-out Confederacy would succumb at once, letting peace and prosperity once more shine into that slavery-darkened region, while the Flag of our Union should float triumphantly over all. This looks very fine in print, and if the papers would only fight the battles for us and give us an open road to the rebel capital we should be abundantly satisfied to walk in and make that noted, as well as notorious, city ours. It is vastly easier to win victories on paper than on land, and experiment has proved that to drive Gen. Lee and his army from the Rappahannock to Richmond is an operation attended with considerable personal danger. We had no idea that we was to start for Richmond again after being drove to this side, till we saw it in some of the leading dailies, and then, it is needless to say, we didn't believe it.

I notice the New Jersey papers claim that the 26th New Jersey regiment with the Vermont brigade captured the rebel stronghold on the heights of Fredericksburg. That is strictly true, but it strikes us that the mention of the 26th is entirely gratuitous and unnecessary. It reminds one of the Dutchman who in the excess of his vanity to make a display for himself, boasted that he and the Squire owned forty cows, when it would have been equally true had the "he" been left out, for the forty cows all belonged to the Squire.

But after all, that regiment contains some as brave boys as the country affords, and it is a pity they should have to serve in such a miserable organization. It is not necessary to have the men all cowards to have the regiment break and run. Fear is one of the most contagious diseases that ever afflicted a soldier, and when one timid fellow loses his heart, others are apt to be affected in the same way. It takes a fellow of more than ordinary courage to come up to the scratch when others desert their post to hide away from the bullets of the enemy. Every man that leaves and runs, encourages the enemy, and prompts them to crowd a little harder, and when one after another has skulked away and the ground is getting covered with wounded and dying men, while all the time the enemy are pressing harder and harder and bringing up heavy supports as they did in the second day's fight, leaving our men no hope of driving them back, but only of holding their ground and gaining time, it takes but a word to start a panic that no power on earth could stop.

No matter how brave a man may be when that event takes place, nor how much he may deplore the event, if the rest run, he must run too, or be overwhelmed.

When the Jerseys broke in the 5th, on Monday afternoon, some of them fell in with us, willingly, and some fell in with the 6th regiment, to show the Vermont boys that they were not a set of cowards, and when that regiment charged, they charged with it, and they kept a long ways ahead, making themselves the most conspicuous mark for the enemy, and plunging first and foremost in every encounter, doing their utmost to retrieve their honor, and the honor of their regiment. Bully for such fellows as that, and all like them, belong to what regiment they will!

The anxious question, When is the Army of the Potomac going to move, has been practically answered. We have moved on to the enemy's works, and moved off again. We slept one night in the rebels' nest, and should have slept longer there, perhaps, had we not been forcibly reminded by them that it was a safer place for us this side of the river. Some sanguine writer said, When Gen. Hooker moves on the enemy, God help them; but the prayer was unnecessary; they were able to help themselves. On the whole, the most of us are willing to admit that we got a very neat little whipping over there, and General Hooker will have to be more successful than he has been, or his boys will think Old Lee, the rebel General, is too much for him. Our reports claim a sort of victory on the whole, and so do the rebels, but the rebel newspapers will lie, and ours won't. If we accept the rebels' own calculations that one Southerner is equal to two Yankees, we may safely infer that battles like the last ones pay pretty well, after all; but the rebels can hardly make out as much for them, unless they change the premises of their argument, for they, by no means, killed twice as many of us as we did of them.

Let no one say that the recent battles have had a tendency to demoralize the army. Far from it. The more we get used to being killed, the better we like it. Positively, the army is in just as good fighting spirits to-day as they were the day we left our old camp. I was talking with some New York boys a few minutes ago, whose time of service has nearly expired. The late battles, I found, had not discouraged them in the least, and a large majority said they contemplated re-enlisting after they had enjoyed the luxuries of home a while but they would not bind themselves to any paper at present, preferring to wait and see what would "turn up," as they expressed it.

Last evening I was talking with some boys belonging to the 5th Wisconsin. They had a share in the late battles, and, of course, were full of stories about it. They thought the different accounts of the battles had hardly given them the credit that is their due. They lost heavily. One Company, they said, that deployed as skirmishers, lost upwards of thirty men. They were sent out to draw the enemy's fire, and they did their duty, and did it without flinching. To detail men for a duty like that, is like selecting men for a sacrifice, but the 5th Wisconsin are not the boys to quail before the deadliest danger. They charged through the death-dealing fire of grape and cannister, and captured the rebel fort — neither sharpshooters nor artillery-men being able to check their advance one moment. The enemy kept their position and refused to surrender, even after our men were within the fortifications, and fairly outnumbered them. One rebel boldly bared his breast and told our men to shoot him, he would never surrender. Perhaps he hardly expected to be taken at his word, but he was; a dozen bullets pierced him at once. Another rebel was seen loading his gun, after our men had charged by him. "You G—d d—d son of a B—h," said a sergeant, who happened to see him just in season to save his own life, "I'll learn you to shoot our men after you are within our lines," and he clubbed his gun which he had no time to reload, and placed him *hors du combat* on the spot, without ceremony. The fellow who told me the story, did not know whether he killed him or not, but he thought he might safely predict that in future he would be more circumspect in selecting opportunities for shooting Yankees.

Since we have been this side of the river, we have enjoyed the utmost luxury of ease and laziness that hot weather can afford. We are about two miles from our old camp, nearly north. We have fixed up our new camping-ground in as good style as we know how. It is situated on elevated ground in the edge of the woods where the cool air and shady pines make our position almost enviable. Water is plenty, and of the purest quality. The rest of the brigade is situated near. Everything goes on as of old, and as yet I see not the slightest sign of a move. A bakery has been fitted up, which is calculated to turn us out a loaf of soft bread apiece every day. This bakery institution stands high in the estimation of the boys. No benevolent enterprise could rival it. I have heard men say they could tell in a minute by the men's appearance whether they were living on hard tack or soft bread. The difference is as wide, almost, as between rye-straw and grain provender for horses. It behooves Uncle Sam, therefore, to feed his soldiers well and keep them in good, healthy order, for bounties rule so high now-a-days, and recruiting is so slow, that a new soldier is getting to be quite a costly article. Uncle Sam understands this; hence his disinterested benevolence in giving us soft bread, in place of his "cast-iron biscuits."

The old man played us rather a mean trick during the late Federal raid, as the boys call it, around Fredericksburg. We were obliged to start with eight days' rations which we did without murmuring, trusting that our appetites would gradually diminish the load. But hard bread was brought to us every day except one, and sometimes it was brought to us in the night, and we were expressly required to keep the sacred eight days' rations untouched. When we recrossed the Rappahannock we supposed we were getting to a land of peace and plenty, so we very naturally forgot the reverence due to these fragments of hard-tack which had been kicked about in our knapsacks so much that they were constitutionally entitled to a discharge — mine had got reduced to flour almost, and had a way of baking that I didn't like — and some of the men threw them away. They thought they had earned a right to rely on the commissary department for a supply of grub; but they were mistaken. It was precisely eight days to a minute before we drew anything, and those fellows who were destitute and could neither beg, buy, nor borrow, had to go without or steal.

I am bound to call that a little mean, because in the first place, we had to use our knapsacks for everything. It furnished us a seat in the daytime when we stopped, and was our pillow at night when we slept. It was our bed, band-box, and storehouse. The hard-tack suffered every indignity, and were positively unsuitable fodder for anything that claims to be human; as soldiers sometimes do, being created, they think, by the government a little lower than the niggers, and being endowed with certain qualities that might be called human as well as a great many that are almost inhuman. A Captain's waiter offered some to his horse and he refused to eat them, and I think it no exaggeration to say that any intelligent pig possessing the least spark of pride would have considered it a pure insult to have them put into his swill.

Speaking of rations reminds us of the warm discussion some of the boys had in regard to what is allowed and what is not. We all know that Government gives us besides our bread, meat, and coffee, sundry articles such as hominy, meal, peas, vegetables, and so forth, but which we seldom ever see. The army regulations allows us these, or something in "lieu thereof." As these articles so conducive to health in hot weather are not provided us, we sometimes feel it no impudence to inquire in what shape the "lieu thereof" is coming. Undoubtedly it is all right — the officers say it is — but we wish they would make it a little plainer for there are some who pretend they "can't see it."

As yet we have not been called out to drill, but we probably shall be before long. The rebels can be seen every day drilling on the plain below Fredericksburg with their usual assiduity. The balloon goes up to reconnoitre the enemy every day, as usual, but up to the moment of going to the post-office, all was quiet along the Rappahannock.

Camp near White Oak Church, Va.
May 24, 1863

Since the battles everything on the surface of events here has looked remarkable smooth. There is no bustle or preparation nor a curious anxiety in regard to some important move, that may be at any moment expected, nobody knowing when it will take place or what it will be. Everything is as quiet and comes along in an every day sort of a way, as much as if we had always stayed here and always expected to. No eight-day ration orders are issued periodically for constant observance, no talk in military circles, or in circles not so military, of an approaching summer campaign, and we are not compelled to be eternally "ready," as we were for a month or so previous to our last adventure in Dixie's Land. There seems to be a tacit understanding that for the present our work is done, and now it only remains for us to rest idly on our oars content with the work already accomplished, and unconcerned for the future.

Camps are fast assuming a slick, summer-like appearance. Policing, alias sweeping, is the rage of the hour. As far as pine boughs, made into brooms, can make a camp look clean, they are so, and nothing offensive shall be allowed to lie loose anywhere about the camps to breed disease and make the air unhealthy. Yankee ingenuity is taxed to its utmost in devising means to counteract the sun's burning rays, and make our tents as cool and as comfortable as possible. Natural shade is taken advantage of when convenient, and when not convenient artificial shade is made in its place. The 4th and 6th regiments are very neatly situated. The ground is a gentle swell covered with low bushy pine trees which have all been trimmed up to a certain height, and where not thick enough others were planted leaving the tops to form a complete canopy of boughs overhead, and making the grounds have the appearance of some cool subterranean abode, well lighted and airy. The streets are cleanly swept and everything looks neat and tidy. The 5th seems to have been less fortunate in the selection of a location, not so much for want of taste as on account of the unhealthiness of the place. It is said nearly half of the men were sick or so enervated as to be unfit for hard duty. The surgeon attributed the cause, I understand, to the water used, and very likely he was right. They are doing better now. The 2d is situated apart from the rest, as usual — in consequence of our singular character, I suppose, — on an elevated piece of ground in the edge of the woods, where the cool breezes, when there are any, can fan away the heat, and where the shade of the tall pines can mitigate in a measure the burning of a Virginia sun.

The art of building up comfortable quarters, like every other art, improves greatly by practice. Certainly we have never fixed up our "shanties" in a way more pleasant and comfortable than we have them now. Our shelter tents we fasten to poles and stakes several feet from the ground on all sides. We build our "bunks" to the same height under them. Here we have a place to sleep clean from the ground, and where the air can circulate freely under and all around us. We have a roof to cover us, and, if we wish, we can close up the ends of the tent and curtain the space from the eaves to the ground. Plenty of old material for doing this can be picked up in the camps of those regiments that are going home, and the boys are not slow in finding it. Thus it can be seen we have all the advantages of a good wall tent, minus a great many of its disadvantages. The brigade is in the neighborhood of four miles from Falmouth and about two from Potomac Creek. Here we live, move, and have our rations every day. So far we have had but little duty to do in this camp, except such irregular duties as could be handily devised to keep us out of mischief. We have had our guard and picket duties, as usual, of course. Drilling has not yet been inaugurated, but it soon is to be. We are not long to be so generously let alone. Last night an order was read on dress parade for morning and evening drills, each an hour, just enough for healthy exercise and good discipline. We shall have them every day except Saturdays and Sundays.

Last Wednesday we were reviewed by General Sedgwick. The day before, Col. Grant had reviewed us to make sure that we were capable of making a respectable appearance before our corps commander, for Col. Grant is as proud of his men as his men are proud of him.[14] He well knows that his Vermonters can out-review any other troops on the ground.

Last Monday we had a large fatigue party detailed to clear off a place for Gen. Hooker's headquarters. There was nothing connected with this day's work that is materially worth writing about, but I mention it as a specimen of the vigorous way we have of prosecuting such kind of business. It almost always brings a scowl to a soldier's face to be called upon for this kind of duty, but wry faces never amount to anything only to relieve the patient of a little surplus ill-nature, when he is as cheerful as ever. The day in question we knew was going to be hot and sultry, and as we were required to take our dinners along with us, it was evident that we were booked for a long day's siege. This was sufficient to warrant a little extra hilarity and joking, to say nothing of a bit of swearing mixed in occasionally just to spice the proceedings; for I suppose it is revealing no secret to say that now and then a soldier will swear, and if he swears at all he will do it just before going on "fatigue." We did a big day's work that day, — at least the General in charge said we did and I suppose he knew best. If any of our hard-working men up in busy Vermont fail to "see the point," it is their fault and not mine.

Well, we fell into line, formed into a battalion, marched over to brigade headquarters, where we were joined by other details, and then started for our destination. We knew as little where we were going as the man in the moon, and we cared as little as we knew. We marched (or walked as you please to have it) as near as we could calculate, about three miles, though, as the crow flies, I doubt if the distance to our work would have been more than one mile. We halted and sat down till ten o'clock, or near that, when General Warren — I believe that was his name — rode up and took us away off in back of the place where the work was to be done. Here we found a large oval elevation of land, covered in part with standing trees and brush wood, and in part with felled timber and brush, but mostly with small pines that were to be trimmed up, and the brush carried off. To clearing this we were set to work, a whole army of us, and we went at it like a hive of ants, only, perhaps, we told more stories, and did less work according to our size than these busy animals would have done. Indeed, we were very busy when the mounted officers came around. We had to work every alternate two hours and be relieved the other two. In this way they kept us at work until it was hard on to five o'clock in the afternoon. But the meanest of it all was for the old General to send us in without even standing treat. I am afraid some of the boys will never forgive him.

In due time we got back to camp, cross and tired, very tired. Of course there was no getting us out to dress parade that night, and as there were not men enough left in the regiment to make it paying business, dress parade was postponed. To have ordered us all out indiscriminately would have involved the necessity of building three or four more guard-houses. At roll call we managed to get out and answer to our names, because we couldn't reasonably dodge it, but we felt that a soldier's life was a dog's life indeed. Had we been charging up some more Fredericksburg Heights instead of "fatigueing" we should have been all right.

Camp near White Oak Church, Va.
May 29, 1863

We had a very pleasant surprise last night. We were out drilling, as usual late in the afternoon, for we generally take that time in order to avoid the hottest part of the day, and besides, we can wind up with dress parade, and come in and call it all one. We had but just got fairly interested in our drill, when the drum beat. It was entirely out of season and we all wondered what it meant. It was not for dress parade, but was an orderly and an officer's call. The inquiry "what's up?" could be read in every countenance. Pack up for marching, seemed to be the inevitable solution. So we went immediately to our companies and remained in line until the officers had answered their call, that we might be told the result. "Boys fall in as soon as possible, every one of you and, — *sign the pay rolls.*" Bully, bully, was the enthusiastic response, and we needed neither sergeant or corporal to prompt us to execute this order. Instead of having to look hard marching, hard fighting, and hard skedaddling in the face, the prospect of looking in the face some more of Uncle Sam's good-natured greenbacks, seemed imminent. Before midnight, instead of being on the famous road to Richmond, the most of us were sleeping very quietly in our tents, for how could we help sleeping under the magic power that a full money purse inspires. Government got ahead of our expectations this time. We had deliberately made up our minds that the paymaster's next visit would be sometime in October. This unusual promptness surprised us completely. If Uncle Sam would always be as prompt to supply his boys with the coveted article, they would be much more eager to help him settle his family difficulty.

Our pay came in just the right time, as we have but little else to do than to spend it. Our duties are light, but none too light for the hot weather we are now having. Besides our military duties we devote an hour or so, occasionally, to the cleaning of our camp. We have literally swept the entire woods, and made it as clean as a park. Our camp now has a very clean, healthy appearance, and it almost makes one feel healthy to look at it. The health of the regiment is remarkably good, and the disposition to meet the enemy is good also. Only give us plenty of soft bread and fresh beef, and let the paydays come along pretty thick, and we shall soon be "spiling for a fight."

My tent-mate has just brought from the fire a savory dish of "hash" which he has prepared from hard tack and fresh beef. He has a very excellent way of making such material eminently palatable. Assuming that no one else knows how it is done, and that every one would like to know, I will explain the process:

He takes a small bag, like the one inside of our haversacks, and puts as many crackers into it as he thinks his appetite will demand. And then with a cudgel, or something else, he pounds these crackers till they are as fine as flour. He cuts up his meat as fine as his patience will allow, using his jack knife and fingers instead of a chopping knife and tray. The next thing is to get a spider and pour into it some broth or "pot-liquor" that he saved when the cooks boiled the fresh meat, and which would otherwise have been thrown away. Into this he puts his meat too, and then pours in with it as much water as he has broth, and as a general thing a little more, for he says it would be too strong and too salt, and taste altogether too "beefy" unless it is a little mite reduced. As soon as this is made to boil, the cracker flour is stirred in. If he has any potatoes, which he frequently doesn't, he boils and smashes them, and mixes them in too. It doesn't need to cook long, and when it is done, he has a dish good enough for anybody, — a super-excellent one for soldiers. I have heard unimpeachable critics pronounce it *bully*, and as that is the most expressive word in the soldier's vernacular, it precludes the necessity of further comment.

The boys have just come in from picket. They are complaining in no very complimentary term about the officer in charge, whose ignorance of the way had made them march two or three miles more than was necessary, both in going out and in coming in. This extra marching in a burning sun was too much for even the good-natured "Green Mountain Boys" to stand. They were not, therefore, very choice in the selection of epithets for their officer of the day. Some, however, who were more charitable than the rest, concluded that so long as it all went to help put down the rebellion, they ought not to complain. The corporal, who is a very close calculator and shrewd mathematician, positively affirms that the rebellion went down two inches during that dusty suffocating march. He further hints, in a modest way, that he could, in time, worry the rebellion down alone. Perhaps so, he is a tip top marcher, and very patriotic, but he will have to march so well that he won't need to march it over again, or he will find himself in the same unpleasant fix that our commanding generals do when they attempt the same thing.

The expedition of the 8th Illinois cavalry returned while they were out. From Mr. Fassett of Co. E, who saw and conversed with the officers and men, and took some pains to ascertain the incidents of the raid, I have the following statement:

This regiment of cavalry, under Col. Clendennin, left the vicinity of Brooks Station the 16th inst., nearly 500 strong, and started for Heathsville, a small place at the lower extremity of this peninsula, near the mouth of the Rappahannock river. After a little more than a day's march, the rebels began to suspect that all was not right and sent over a squad of cavalry to reconnoitre and ascertain what was going on. The cavalry had passed by, so the rebs signalled back to Gen. Lee that if he would send over 2000 men, artillery and infantry, to their support, they could bag the whole Yankee force. But Yankee ingenuity outwitted them. There happened to be among our troops a man that could read the rebel signal, and thus their plans were penetrated and easily foiled. Col. Clendennin sent at once to his Commanding General, and informed him of his position and the intentions of the enemy, and had a small brigade of infantry and artillery despatched to his assistance. They came just in time to frustrate the enemy's movements and drive him back across the river.

The cavalry proceeded on — part of the time pretending to be rebel troops, and part of the time Union, whichever circumstances demonstrated to be the best policy. They visited every Court House the whole distance, eighty miles or more, besides many other places of some note. They said they respected Union property, but the property of rank secessionists they were less particular about. They found many who professed to be strong Union people, and they manifested their loyalty by many acts of kindness which the men will not soon forget. In some instances the women sat up all night to cook for them, and the best they had was always freely given. They had started out with but three days' rations and were gone ten days, but the men said they had never enjoyed themselves better. When among secesh people, if nothing was offered them they compelled the women to cook for them, but always kept strict watch in such cases, that they might not mix with their food anything unwholesome. They estimated that they had captured $100,000 worth of property and destroyed enough more to make the total loss to the rebels exceed a million. They captured 400 horses, some of which were very valuable; one four years old blooded horse valued at $2,000, 200 mules in excellent condition, 8 yoke of oxen, and a large number of buggies, open and covered, doctors' sulkies, team, wagons, carts, &c. They brought a large quantity of dry goods, in the shape of hats, bonnets, ribbons, broadcloth, boots, shoes, gun caps, cutlery — nearly all of which had been smuggled through the lines from Baltimore and other semi-secesh places. They also found, used and destroyed almost any quantity of brandies, wines and liquors of various descriptions, besides an immense quantity of kerosene oil. In one place they knocked in head thirty-two barrels of whiskey. They captured five smugglers and thirty-five prisoners, citizens and soldiers. There was among them a lieutenant colonel, a major, one captain, and other commissioned officers. The prisoners were mostly from the rebel army on a furlough. Mr. Fassett saw these prisoners and says they appeared not at all concerned or chagrined at the change in their social and political position and status.

There was one captain, Robert H. Tyler of the 8th Virginia cavalry, who was captured under circumstances very amusing to his captors, though tantalizing in the extreme to him. He was married last winter and had been in the service ever since. He was in the last Fredericksburg battle, and had just got a furlough for eight days. He had just got within sight of his home when the cavalry overtook him. The wife saw him coming and ran out to meet him, but seeing the Yankees she called, "The Yankees are coming!" So, leaving his lovely partner, he struck off into the nearest woods, to escape the Yankees if possible. But the unfeeling Illinoisans had no respect for the tender feelings of this now unhappy couple, but started off after him in the highest merriment. They fired four shots after him from their carbines, but with no effect only to frighten him to surrender. This captain found it very difficult to appear as cheerful and contented as his fellow prisoners, though he appeared to be a brave and respectable rebel.

The expedition had no fight, and lost no men killed. Two were wounded by citizen bushwhackers — one severely, the other slightly. On one of the bushwhackers the boys swore deadly vengeance. They tried their utmost to find him, but he eluded them. They burned his buildings and did him what damage they could. They chafe exceedingly to make him another visit. Their wounded comrade they say shall be avenged.

Among other articles taken by this cavalry was a large lot of brass buttons, such as are worn by our staff officers. They might have wanted them for a disguise to pass themselves off as our men on a battle-field, or to allure them into a snare, but I can see no other use they would wish to make of them. I omitted to mention that they captured 700 contrabands, men, women and children. A large share of them were said to be as white as other people, though my informant did not see these, as they had been shipped from the landing the day before. The cavalry boys were in the best spirits and looked eagerly forward for another such an opportunity of scouring the enemy's country. When they do "may I be there to see."

_____

Camp near White Oak Church, Va.
June 4, 1863

We have just come in from another three days' picket sweat, ill-natured and covered with dust. Our guard mounting this time had been enlivened by the newly arrived Brigade Band. We have been for a long time eagerly expecting this Band, and it was no small satisfaction to see these musicians with us. It is getting to be quite a rare treat now-a-days, to hear good martial music, but this seemed all the better for being sent from Vermont for our special entertainment and gratification. Fifes and drums lost their charms long ago, if, indeed, they ever had any. This Band made a fine appearance, their music was excellent, and it turned off our guard mounting quite agreeably.

After guard mounting we proceeded to our posts, a distance of some two miles or more. The fine dust in the roads, in places, was like ashes, and before we had gone far, every man was so covered with the gray dust that he looked for all the world as if he had just been immersed in an ash-heap. All the fine effect of the music was spoiled by this dusty march in the hot sun. The first day we stopped at the small reserve. Here we had but to get into the shade, read books, if we had them, and make things as agreeable to ourselves as we pleased. We had nothing to disturb the harmony of our leisure, except that we must fall into line, whenever the officer of the day came around, that the proceedings might in every particular be done up at the highest military standard. Although this might often spoil a precious nap, or interrupt a pleasant story, it was clearly too small a task to occasion any grumbling, and no doubt he of the red sash was in every way satisfied with our promptness. The next day we were on the outposts and stood guard two hours out of every six. We were stationed near the Potomac creek, where the prospect of seeing an enemy was about equal to the prospect of taking Richmond. Standing guard there is dull, listless business. Who, three years ago, in his wildest dreams imagined that he should be divorced from his peaceful pursuits and engaged in an occupation in itself so utterly profitless. It is a strange anomaly for our heaven exalted land.

I recollect that we did not get overmuch sleep that night for which I am willing the mosquitoes should have as much credit as our vigilance in watching the rebels. I didn't see but one good thing on that support, and that was two canteens of milk, that one of the boys borrowed — of somebody's cows. There was some Jerseys with us, and every one was loud in asserting that their time was out the 3d of June, while the Government claims them till the 18th. They were evidently not overanxious to be engaged in another battle. Some of the croaks that came out with our grub spoiled one fellow's appetite by telling that they were under marching orders again with another eight days' rations.

The third day we were back on the large reserve, where we might pitch quoits, play poker, or amuse ourselves any way most convenient to our inclinations. I had reserved my hour for sleep till night, intending to lay in for a little extra of that luxury, and, if possible, make up the lost time. But the Captain spoiled my plans by detailing me to stand guard over the guns. Generally we had done this duty by taking turns which, divided among so many, was not worth minding, but this time the captain had made a different arrangement, on his own hook, and one that I decidedly disapprove. However, I did my first two hours' duty as any patriotic soldier should, and had it not been for the blunder I made in going back to somebody else's quarters instead of my own, when I was relieved, so that, unfortunately, when the next two hours came around the corporal could not find me, I should probably have done my whole duty, for I never shirk. As it was I got a bully night's rest, but I had to apologize to the corporal in the morning, and that is something I always dislike to do; for apologizing, under such circumstances, to a fellow of his resolute calibre isn't always the safest kind of business.

The fourth day we were relieved by the other brigade. The new pickets said the camp was full of rumors. That morning they had had to stand in line under arms, *a la* Chickahominy. The First and Second Army Corps were on the move, some said up the river, some said down, and others said they were not moving at all. All seemed to think that some important work was in contemplation.

They had a splendid ball at Gen. Howe's headquarters Wednesday night. It was a select party, no lower caste than field officers were admitted, unless they were particular favorites, or had a lady, which, for the sake of a full attendance of the fair sex, was an especial recommend. An affair like that, so suggestive of the pleasures of home, and so strikingly in contrast with camp scenes in general, excited the curiosity of a great many of the boys, and forgetting the demands of decorum, they huddled around to get, if possible, an outside view of the enchanting show. Among these impertinent outsiders, they say, was a large number of the Second boys. Our boys were bound to have some fun out of the performance — and they like fun, as they do chickens, geese and pigs, all the better if it is obtained at somebody else's expense. The boys had the greatest respect for this assemblage, but their pride was a little piqued by being gratuitously informed that they could not on any account be admitted. A large hall had been improvised for the occasion. It was built of evergreen boughs and was all the more interesting from its romantic situation and warlike surroundings. It had a well laid floor, and probably no hall in America was ever occupied for a dance with better enthusiasm than was this one. The dance was lively and interesting. Good music, pretty women and a fascinating dance, who can blame the boys for trying to be spectators of such a lovely scene. The temptation was too great to be resisted. They were not content to stand outside the guard, but they made a charge *en masse,* and about that time there might have been seen multitudes of eyes peering through the boughs, from the outside, upon the happy throng within. Unless the sum total of enjoyment was greatly increased by the presence of these uninvited visitors, they must have subtracted heavily from the pleasure of those who occupied the floor, for the boys outside enjoyed their view amazingly. The aids tried to order them away, but what is the use of an order without the means to enforce it. After they had satisfied themselves and punished the privileged ones all they wished, they retired in good order under cover of the night, no one trying to molest their retreat. If any different account is ever given of this ball than what I have written, the reader will please pay it not the slightest attention. Let him read my letter and he will be correctly posted.

Our regular drills have become an established necessity. We have two per day. As they last but an hour or an hour and a half, it is not a very cruel task, even if it is done under a burning sun. But all that time is not occupied in drilling. We have our "rests," when, as at recess in school-time, we can play with and plague each other as much as we please. Co. E and Co. I had one regular pitched battle. For shells they threw at each other empty _____ bottles. (The confiding reader will excuse me for not telling what kind of bottles they were; for as true as I live I do not know.) It was lively sport for a few minutes and one had to look sharp and dodge quick to save his head. The loss was about equal on each side, and was finally settled by compromise.

There has been no rain since the 14th ult. Everything is getting dry, awful dry, almost as dry as this letter. There is always plenty of wind and the dust flies everywhere. There are significant signs of a move soon. Unless we are favored with rain, dust and not mud will be our evil genius.

On Picket
June 10, 1863

Friday, the 5th, we bade adieu to our old camp, packed up, and started once more on the same old road to Richmond. The order came in the morning to pack up everything but our tents; about noon the tents were struck. Where we were going, or what was to be done, was more than the shrewdest of us could answer. There was an inexplicable air of mystery about the whole movement that defied penetration. It could hardly be possible that we were to attack Fredericksburg again, but it might be. It is just like Hooker. We were ordered to take three days' rations, but the order was subsequently increased to four. It was dry, hot, dusty marching, and there seemed to be a dead dullness and silent gloom about everything, contrasting strangely with some of our previous marches, or else my imagination was at fault. But little was said by anyone; we marched on in silence.

The boys were not in good spirits — they hadn't even whiskey. Besides, they had no relish for storming the Heights of Fredericksburg again. Perhaps, for the sake of telling a good story, I ought to say we were in the best of spirits — anxious to meet the foe — confident of success, and with unbounded faith in General Hooker — but I shall say no such thing. Soldiers are not much different from other people, and they have their opinion of Gen. Hooker, pro and con, just as so many citizens would. And as for being anxious to meet the foe, all my experience goes to prove that to be nicely situated in camp with good tents and all the little conveniences which ingenuity can devise, where we can have clean, tidy quarters, with but little to do and plenty to eat, is decidedly preferable to fighting, marching, advancing or retreating. To march several miles and fight several battles, to say nothing of the dangers, is very hard work and soldiers love their ease as well as anybody. I never hear the order to pack up, but that I deplore more sincerely than ever before that the rebellion ever broke out. But we had had a good resting spell and not a word was said to indicate a timid reluctance to move. Perhaps this grim determination on the part of the men, would be considered the "best of spirits" by those who are judges of human nature.

We started from camp about 2 o'clock that afternoon and marched straight to the Rappahannock river. We passed by the celebrated White Oak Church, which has given name to a large camp ever since the first battle of Fredericksburg. It is a miserable, insignificant structure, dilapidated and steepleless, and seems to have belonged to some former age. It looks very much like some ancient horse shed and barn that may be seen in some of our less thriving villages. What kind of people they were that could recognize the sacred name of church applied to that building is more than I can imagine.

We struck out into the same road that the army had tried before — the same road that our regiment had traveled three times to meet the enemy, and apparently we were traveling it again for the same purpose. Of course the prospect for us could not be more than usually hopeful; for in what conceivable particular were we better prepared than we were five weeks before? It seemed almost like a forlorn hope. One bluff, brave fellow said he hoped if they put us on to those heights again, and he got his head blown to pieces, he should have to be helped off by men on crutches, and that was almost the only remark I heard that in any way indicated the *animus* of the troops.

We moved down to the river. There were but very few troops ahead of us, but more were coming. The pontoon train was there, which fact put at rest all doubts as to whether we were to cross the river or not. Batteries were placed on this side of the river and at a given moment opened on the enemy.

It was a smart cannonading; it might almost have been heard in Vermont. The rebel pickets occupied a rifle-pit on the side of the flat, across the river. The shot and shell from our batteries fell thick and fast in among them, tearing up the ground on the flats and raising so much dust and smoke that the rebels could not see what was going on, or render any assistance. Under cover of this fire the 5th and 26th New Jersey crossed over in pontoon boats, and captured the rebels in the rifle-pits — about 150 in all. The rebels made a spirited resistance, and their fire was extremely annoying to our men as they tried to cross. The Jerseys say they took the rifle-pit, and the 5th say they did, but probably it takes them both to tell the whole truth. We followed soon after, crossing the river in the same way, for we had not time to wait for the bridge to be built. Our skirmishers advanced, took road and posted themselves beyond it. We took our position behind an abrupt rise in the flat a hundred rods or more from the river. Here we waited as the troops kept coming in in squads, a boat load at a time, to see what disposal would be made of us. We were about a mile and a half, I should think below Fredericksburg, on the same plain where so many of our troops have bit the dust and died in former battles. Were more to be sacrificed?

Tired of waiting for orders, and tired, too, in a more genuine sense, for we had marched rapidly, the boys one after another, dropped to sleep on their knapsacks. Some pulled out blankets and covered themselves for a night's sleep, choosing to make the most of the present and let the future take care of itself. If called to fall in in haste, they might have to leave their blankets and perhaps get left themselves, but we run the risk. Fortunately we were not disturbed. The next day there was some sharp picket firing, but no advancing. Our pickets suffered severely. A great many were killed and wounded, some say as many as forty, mostly from the 6th regiment. They held their ground, however, against these rebel sharpshooters, and finally the firing died away. Other troops came over the river, but I think in all there was but one brigade besides our division. We had batteries placed in position in front of us. All this time the rebels remained perfectly quiet, except now and then a random shot on picket. No doubt the rebels had batteries that could have annihilated us if they had seen fit to have opened on our men, but for some reason they remained quiet. It was a strange move. If we were going to attack, why wait? if not, what were we going to do? The best solution we could get of "the situation" was that we were only feeling to see if the rebel force was still there, and if not, pitch into them; if we found they were, we meant to keep them there to watch us. The Richmond *Sentinel* of day before yesterday, that we borrowed of a rebel picket, says that the whole affair is probably a *ruse,* but it says if we advance, we shall surely be driven back.

Sunday night we fell into line, and after waiting for a long column to come up from the river who were to relieve us, we crossed back again to this side. We pitched our tents on the high bluffs that overlook the plain on both sides of the river — the Stafford Hills, and remained in easy supporting distance of our troops across the river. The rebels took pains yesterday to demonstrate that even this place is not out of their range, by sending a few shots plunging through the camp in a manner quite the reverse of pleasant. I dislike occupying a camp where our safety depends upon the magnanimous forbearance of our foe. But we have artillery further up toward the city that is capable of teaching them a wholesome lesson any time their actions may call for it.

Monday night we were ordered to go on picket. We were to be posted away down the river, nobody knew where, but long before midnight we found the right place and got duly posted. The rebels occupy one bank and we the other. Yesterday I was on post, and we held a long conversation with them. They were frank and candid in their talk, and expressed feelings in regard to the war very similar to those expressed by our boys on this side. They were tired of it they said and our boys responded an amen. The corporal suggested in an off-hand kind of a way that we privates get together and pare'off, each one going to his own home, and let the war take care of itself. The idea tickled them amazingly. As far as *they* were concerned they would willingly do so, but they supposed there was no other way but to fight it out as things were now. They told us if we would use a certain sign when we met on the battle-field, they would spare us. They asked what regiments we belonged to, and when we told them they said they had heard of us before; they were North Carolinians. Some South Carolinians came down to the river and we asked them what they were fighting for. They said we ought to know, and refused to give a direct answer. It was in vain to repeat the question, the reply was the same — "you ought to know." We told them they were fighting to save their niggers, which they seemed to resent a little. The niggers might go to h____, it wasn't them they were fighting for.

They wanted to know why we didn't advance. We told them they ought to advance on us. They said they did the last time, and now it was our turn. They said when we first crossed over, Friday night, we might have taken the heights, as there was but few men there; the main army under Lee having gone down the river to counteract a movement they supposed we were making in that direction. But as soon as they heard we were moving here they hurried up their men with all possible dispatch and now it would be impossible to take them. They had some papers which they were very anxious to exchange. We asked them the news from Vicksburg, and they replied that it was very favorable for their side. They said Pemberton would hold it till he had eaten his last dog before he would surrender. They said Grant and Banks had lost nearly 40,000 men trying to storm the works at Vicksburg and Port Hudson. They held the newspaper in their hand that had an account of it. I had in my pocket the Sunday Morning *Chronicle* (Washington) and a *Freeman* a week old which I offered to give them if they would come across with their papers and, besides this, other boys offered to give them as much coffee as they could carry back. We would let them go back in good faith. One fellow started, but the whole thing was spoiled by Lieut. Wooster's coming along just then and ordering him back. It was against the orders on both sides to talk across the river, much less to swim across. We told him to wait awhile till the officers got out of sight (I hope Lieut. Wooster won't see this letter) and then he could come across, but no favorable opportunity offered. Further down the river a fellow crossed, exchanged papers with them and had a friendly chat. They shook hands cordially, and one offered to go and get a blanket to cover him while he stayed that he might not take cold. After he had stayed there as long as he thought proper, these affectionate enemies shook hands, bid each other good by and parted. This morning a corporal went over and got a paper which was printed yesterday in Richmond. He carried over a N.Y. *Herald,* the Boston *Post,* and last week's Windsor *Journal.* The rebels have been respectful and courteous, ready to talk sensibly on any subject, and they are ready, too, to blackguard and fight if we choose. I was highly pleased with our social visit. I couldn't help thinking it a great pity that we should have to shoot such good hearted fellows.

Camp near Fairfax Station
June 17, 1863

At this present moment the 1st Vermont brigade has halted to take breath in a woods near Fairfax Station. The Court House is some five miles further on. Being too restless to remain idle I have dropped almost involuntary into my old habit of writing to you without ever reflecting that nothing worthy of record has yet transpired. True, we have done some pretty tall marching as we are apt to do when the rebel army is behind us, though this time we are not so sure whether our crafty foes are in the front or rear.

When I wrote last we were on picket, where we had a jolly time, and was not relieved till last Friday towards midnight. Aside from the disagreeable necessity of being aroused from a comfortable sleep, those of us that were on the reserve, we were not all anxious to go back again to camp. We rather enjoyed this picket, partly because there were so many of us that each one had but little to do, but chiefly because we like the novel society of our neighbors over the river. They furnished us with the Richmond papers every day, and sometimes brought over letters to be sent to their friends in the North. These letters were not sealed and our officers were requested to inspect them, according to the rules of war, that we might be sure of fair play and that nothing contraband was contained in them. We sent letters over there — those that had friends in the South — which they promised to forward them, and without doubt they will do as they have agreed. Of course this intercourse was contrary to orders, but so long as we were not caught in it by any one whom it might concern to enforce a penalty, we considered ourselves all right. One fellow had a letter that a colonel wished him to get across and very likely he had but few, if any, conscientious scruples in the matter of breaking orders when his sins were winked at and upheld by an officer of that rank. One rebel sent a letter to his parents in Connecticut. He said he would most gladly leave the rebel army and go home, but he had a wife and one child inside the rebel lines that he did not wish to leave to the tender mercies of such enemies as would surround them if he deserted the rebel cause. Several fellows did swim across the river and give themselves up. A rebel Lieut. and 40 men gave themselves up on the other side of the Rappahannock last Wednesday. Two other fellows came down to the river to swim across for the same purpose, but our picket this side, through sheer timidity, refused them the privilege. They went up the river and surrendered to the pickets on that side. Friday the rebels maintained a frigid silence. They were forbidden the least intercourse on account of these desertions. No exchanges could be made unless they were made very slyly. They regretted the prohibition as well as we, and probably more. If the rank and file of each army could have their way they would soon manage some way to inaugurate peace. But the war is on our hands and it must be fought out to the bitter end. A few bad men have conspired to destroy our Government and build another on its ruins, thus drawing thousands of others into the vortex of rebellion, and, for the iniquity of these comparatively few, millions who have no personal feelings of animosity, must meet in arms and in cold blood slay each other. A day of fearful retribution must await those ere long, but while they live the mischief goes on. Meantime let Satan look out for his laurels.

Saturday night we received orders to pack up and be ready to march. Just after dark the order to march came. We had just been visited by a plentiful shower which gave us considerably more rain than was absolutely necessary to lay the dust. In fact in less than thirty minutes the roads, which had been filled with fine dust, and lay like a heap of ashes all along the way, were converted into a slippery bed of mortar. Had it not been for the difficulty which men perfectly sober found in keeping their feet under them, the rain would have been considered a decided advantage. As it was, marching of a dark night, through woods, in a snake like path where small stumps intrude everywhere and deep ruts are found on every hand, a sprinkling of dust, I think would have been preferable to this slippery mud. However, we made the best of it we could, and when some unlucky fellow fell headlong into the mud, gun, knapsack and all, we considered it a rich joke, and immensely aggravating as it might be to the victim, it was lively sport for the rest. Quite a number threw down their arms that night, though not so much for the lack of patriotism as for lack of cohesion under their feet. Before morning we reached the railroad near Brooks Station, where we remained till Sunday night. Troops, baggage wagons, ambulances and artillery were constantly passing all day. Near by the corps hospital was cleared out and much of the stuff burnt. It was the same heart-sickening sight that we have seen so often before. Must it always be so? At a commissary establishment the boys got a quantity of potatoes, Indian meal, sugar, dried apple and other stuff out of which we had a good supper, and what we preferred to take along with us, instead of hard tack and pork. The commissary sergeant said he had a number of good overcoats that were to be left, which he said we were welcome to appropriate if we wished. They were behind a certain tent; but I saw nothing there but a pile of coffins, so I concluded the sergeant must be only joking.

It was after dark before we started on our march again. The boys were not at all affected by the peril "the situation" was apparently in. They got up a spirited battle on their own hook, just as the heat of day was passing off, throwing socks, with the toes filled with dirt, for the shells, and one needed the agility of a cat to keep clear of the fast flying missiles. Advantages were rapidly gained and lost on either side. Charges were boldly made and boldly repulsed. Victory alternated from side to side, but capriciously refused to crown either. Men were literally knocked down, but with a cheer they jumped to their feet again and pitched into the melee with more enthusiasm than before. It was exciting sport. The General and his officers enjoyed it immensely. A spectator from a distance, hearing the cheering, and seeing the dust we kicked up, — for the shower hardly reached to here, — might have thought a battle was actually in progress.

We were on the road all that night, but we made but little progress. Teams of troops continually clogged the way , occasioning the most vexatious delays. I don't know as I could explain it, but it is a fact, nevertheless, that it tires a soldier more to have to stand still half of the time than it does to march straight along without interruption. I had rather march fifteen miles in reasonable time, than spend the same time in marching five, unless we can sit down and rest. Morning came, but with it no rest. We halted a few minutes, just long enough for a good many to get soundly to sleep, — and it did not take long to do that, for we had lost two nights' rest, but their sleep was very brief. The unfeeling order was passed down the lines, and every sleeper had to "take up his bed and walk." Those who had preferred sleep to breakfast lost the latter for a very pitiful allowance of the former. All day long we tugged our weary knapsacks in the broiling sun, and many fell out to fall in no more. It was very hot and very dusty. The dry dirt seemed to be particularly adapted to draw the rays of the sun, and the blistering heat that the road reflected, seemed like the breath from a furnace, seven times heated. The road was lined with stragglers, and many fell dead in their tracks. Our corps alone lost forty-six men from sunstroke. Some say that other corps lost upwards of a hundred each. I have no means of knowing how many died from the effect of heat and exhaustion, but I know that dead men lay along beside the road in sufficient numbers to prove that our marching strength was being pretty well tested. About five o'clock we reached Dumfries and halted for the night. In some of the regiments less than one-third of the men were in at the time of stopping. A Bible full of general orders couldn't have prevented straggling that day. At half past two o'clock the next morning we were ordered to pack up again, and as soon as it was fairly light, we were once more on our way. It was a little cooler and we marched and rested more systematically than the day before, so that but few were left behind. At nine P.M. we reached this place, having made, according to the statement of a citizen, twenty-five miles since morning.

The reader probably understands that there is a great difference between marching in the ranks with a column of troops, and walking the same road alone, at will. Anything that obstructs the way, hinders the whole column, and all have to wait for the rest. One cannot slacken his pace over rough ground, and quicken it again when the going is smooth; he must jostle along with the crowd, and, perhaps hurry where hurrying is the least possible, or be continually hindered where the ground is the most favorable to rapid progress. The temptation for a half sick man to straggle along on his own hook outside the ranks is very strong, and not always successfully resisted. In this way many keep up that could not, if obliged to keep their places.

We reached Wolf Run Shoals, where the 2d Brigade has been in camp, about three in the afternoon, having marched nineteen miles. All the Vermont regiments of the other Brigade had gone, except the 14th. Here we rested two hours and a half, which gave us a pleasant opportunity of greeting our friends in the 14th. They had contemplated providing a good dinner and giving us a hearty reception, but found it impracticable, as the time of our arrival could not be definitely known. As the cool of the day approached, the inevitable order, "Fall in," was given. With a regular Vermont cheer, the boys obeyed. The last nineteen miles siege had not tamed their spirits, and the next half dozen could not. The column moved along very rapidly, and some of the boys mischievously inquired of the mounted officers when they were going to stop to change horses. We finally reached our journey's end, and filed off from the road into the woods, where I hope we shall remain at least till I get my letter finished. Where we shall go to-morrow, Gen. Hooker only knows. The rebel Lee, they say, is up in Maryland cutting up mischief at a saucy rate, and probably we shall be put where we can bother him the most. We expect more hard marching, but shall either get toughened to it, or, as the boys say, die toughening. General Hooker knows how to plan hard marching and hard fighting, but whether he knows enough to catch Gen. Lee remains to be seen. After our severe march yesterday and the day before, we were surprised to learn that we had reached this place twenty-four hours behind the time General Hooker had ordered. If we get whipped this time, the kind reader will not blame the boys if they sing long and earnestly,

"Come back to us, McClellan."

Bristoe Station
June 21, 1863

We are making some strange movements now, movements entirely beyond the comprehension of your intelligent correspondent. At this present moment we are some four miles from Manassas Junction, southwest. We have made some very long marches during the week past, the great strategic result of which has not yet been developed. Our course has been something in the shape of the figure 6 with the top at the Rappahannock, the bottom on the line of Fairfax Court House, and the right hand portion curving around by Centreville to this place. Whether this movement is simply a reconnoissance in force or a grand advance does not yet appear, but at present only our division is here, and, certainly, unless we are reinforced we cannot offend against the enemy to any great extent.

We have had plentiful showers of rain since Thursday, which has made the air refreshingly cool. The ground had become very dry and parched. Vegetation suffered extremely, especially grass. Thursday night the rumbling of distant thunder announced the probability that the long and anxiously hoped for rain would soon gladden the thirsty earth. It came. Just at night the large rain drops, with a mixture of hail, fell freely and copiously on the baked ground, which, in this vicinity, I should think had long been deprived of this invaluable blessing. Soon the unyielding soil was softened. The immense reservoirs of dust were closed up and the verdure of the hills around assumed a cleaner and brighter look, as if itself instinct with life and overflowing with thankfulness for the precious gift. Friday, too, was somewhat lowery, and an occasional dash of rain showed how hard it could rain now it had once begun. Another heavy shower Friday night, which left the roads for our yesterday's march entirely free from the annoyance of dust, and made the air cool and bracing. We had marching orders Friday afternoon at four o'clock but they were counter-manded. Saturday morning they came in an hour we thought not of, and liked to have caught some of the boys away from camp, who had gone out on an ex-pedition in search of sutlers, caring more for their appetite's demands than they did for their country's service. When we started, the head of the column took the Centreville road and turned toward that place.

In my letter last Wednesday I left the regiment near Fairfax Station, and, that I may not leave a gap in this most sublime portion of history, I must not omit to mention that our march of about five miles Thursday morning brought us from that place to another about one mile this side of Fairfax Court House. There was the strongest medley of guessing Thursday as to where we were go-ing, what for, and in what direction, that any one but a soldier ever hears. Some said we were going to Chain Bridge, some said to Leesburg, some *knew* we were going to Alexandria, while others doubted if even the War Department knew where they wanted to take us to. But all the while we kept on in the uneven tenor of our way over the rough roads, which had a very uncivilized ap-pearance, and in due time emerged from our barbarous course, in full sight of the familiar Court House at Fairfax, Va. The head of the column steered straight for the village, then turned square to the right on the Centreville road. Our brigade — "the shrewd cusses," as a straggling New Yorker called us, — struck across lots, at a hypothenuse angle with the others, thus saving about a mile of travel and a long uphill road. We halted in the edge of a woods, stacked arms, and then sought the best shelter we could find among the bushes and trees from the fierce heat of the sun.

Here we had ample leisure to reflect upon the peculiar predicament of "the situation." Lee was in Maryland. Our army was singularly scattered. Parts of it were on the way to the Upper Potomac, and parts of it were going in the op-posite direction. What great portion of the programme of ejecting the crafty ring-leader from the loyal States was to be assigned to us, was more than we could divine. The militia of Pennsylvania and other States were flocking with wonderful alacrity to repel the invaders. Would they be able to do it? The old soldiers have a perfect contempt for these raw regiments. Last year, they said, they broke and run before the enemy had fired a half dozen rounds, and a great many think the influence of their example would do greater injury on a battle-field, than their services would do good. This is an error of prejudice, and it is a great mistake. What noble deeds of heroism could be pointed to in our own country's history that have been performed by raw militia! But old regiments that have served a term in the war are returning, and if enough of them volunteer, it is possible that our rebel visitors may find that they have been playing a dangerous game.

Saturday morning a move was ordered. Where — whether east or west, north or south — was a most perplexing mystery. It mattered but little, however, to us, only if we were outgeneralled and were trying to make the best out of a desperately bad case, it would be very gratifying to know it; but such information as this is always studiously withheld. We were in good marching trim. But very few of the boys were on the sick list from our previous hard marching. They were as ready to shoulder arms and move towards the enemy's works as if they had rested a month. Had sutlers been a little more plenty so that we could have filled our haversacks with something more palatable than hard tack and pork, the boys could have given their "inner man" less grounds for complaint. As it was this inexorable gentleman appealed loudly for gratification. There were a few sutlers in the village, and these were thronged continually with a crowd that one might suppose had but just been endowed with the gift of eating, and were intoxicated with the novel desire that appetite awakened. No matter what exorbitant price was asked for the most insignificant article, if it was eatable it was bought, and all the quicker for the swindling extortion. If the sutlers don't fill their pockets at such times, it is not the soldier's fault.

We paid our annual visit this year to Centreville and Bull run a little earlier than usual, owing, perhaps, in a measure, to the forwardness of the season, but much more, I think, to the forwardness of Gen. Lee. The old Heights at Centreville had a familiar look. There was an old camp there occupied by a New York regiment, the 115th, I think. We passed down to Bull run, crossing that stream a little to the left of where so much bully running was done two years ago, proceeding by the way of Manassas Junction to Bristoe. The plains of Manassas were indeed an excellent place for an open battle — altogether too open and fair to make it in any degree probable that we shall ever fight on them. I saw but few works from the route we took. Probably there are more, or I should wonder where the much talked of wooden guns were placed that the world supposes frightened us so long. For a farming country I should consider these plains a long way below par. There was an extremely lean crop of grass, ripe enough to cut to-day. I doubt if it would yield a half ton of hay per acre. I don't know how much allowance should be made for the ruinous tread of armies.

From Manassas we took the railroad— not the cars— to Bristoe Station. It was getting to be near night. We were tired, foot-sore, and anything but good-natured. Besides, the prospect of a drizzling rain all night was much too imminent to be agreeable. "Two miles further, boys, and we shall stop," but a weary traveler knows how much lingering misery may be concentrated in the last two miles.

All along the railroad were wrecks of cars that had been burned and smashed to pieces — some of them quite recently. Perhaps it was when the 15th Vermont was driven away not long ago as we saw letter envelopes addressed to that regiment.

We came to a halt just at dark, having marched about eighteen miles. Bristoe Station consists of a two-story house, which probably answered for a dwelling-house and a depot, and a woodshed. Here we threw down our knapsacks, picked up some boards that were lying about loose, and some that were not so loose, built our fires and made our coffee. Sleep, however, we were destined to be cheated out of. We must go on picket. The two right companies, H and F, were ordered out first. With a good rousing cheer, that showed very plainly what manner of spirit they were of, they started for their posts. Six more companies went out soon after; the rest were a reserve.

Today is the holy Sabbath, though if it were not for my almanac I should hardly have suspected it. Heavy firing is heard in the direction of Thoroughfare Gap, where it is supposed Gen. Hancock had gone with the second corps. How long we shall stay here remains to be demonstrated by Gen. Lee. When we move the report is that we are going somewhere else.

Our communications are cut off, I suppose. At any rate we can't send out any letters, and we don't receive any. So if this letter never reaches you, Mr. Editor, and all its contents are lost to the world, you will know that it is Uncle Sam's fault and not mine. I hope not the slightest uneasiness will be felt on our account. We are all right. We are supposed to have on hand three days' rations, though I doubt if half of the men have enough to last half of that time. The contents of my haversack consist of a few broken crackers, some bits of hard tack, and now and then a piece of army bread. Besides this I have got four cubic inches of solid cheese, for which I paid 75 cents, that I might have something to fall back upon in case of hard times, but I hope we shan't see anything of the sort. Hard times are played out.

There is a rumor, on the sly, that Gen. Grant's army has been completely whipped and used up. Now it only remains for the Western rebel army to pitch on to Gen. Rosecrans and spoil his army, and then the rest can be easily disposed of in detail. Meantime old Lee is running riot in Maryland and

Pennsylvania, and when he gets ready he will just gobble us up, and then he can place Jeff. Davis firmly on his throne, so that no power on earth can disturb him. Hurrah for the Southern Con — found it, I shall get demoralized.

On the Battle-Field near Gettysburg, Pa.
July 3, 1863

Once more we have met the enemy, or overtaken him, whichever you please to have it, and once more the hissing shells and whistling bullets are filling the air with their deadly music. Gen. Lee has transferred, as he said he would, the war from Virginia into Pennsylvania, but whether it will result in such overwhelming disaster to us, and such triumphant success to him as he predicted remains to be seen. Perhaps quite the reverse will happen. Long before this can reach you the event will probably be decided, and all the particulars generally known. While we are waiting here in position, in line of battle, I see no better way to hurry off the time than to tell you of our long and severe march from Bristoe Station to this place.

We had staid there five days. All was quiet along the lines during the time, affording us ample opportunity for leisure and rest, more than we really needed. Herein is the great objection to camp life; when we rest we have more rest than we require, and when we are called upon to act, we have more action than any necessity of our physical being demands, decidedly more than our inclinations ask for. Regular drills had begun to be inaugurated at Bristoe, and things looked a little as if they were going to fall back into the old channel of camp duties. Still, there seemed to be an air of mystery about our movements and position that seemed a little strange and hard to account for. Teams came up there with supplies very shyly, and quickly retreated back to a place of safety. Something evidently was wrong. It really looked as if our Commanding General had become bewildered at the bold strategy of his adversary, and hardly knew what to do with us. We saw no enemy, guarded no railroad, and why were we here? Drilling seemed in very bad grace, and the boys would not interest themselves in it. Gen. Howe drilled us by the whole division three hours Wednesday, the day before we left, but we failed to give him satisfaction, and another division drill was ordered Thursday, in place of our drills by battalion;

but a greater than Gen. Howe saw fit to order something else of more serious practical moment.

That day orders were received to march at 7 o'clock P.M., and at 7 o'clock we started. All the week it had been dry and hot; now it commenced to rain as we commenced our journey, giving us all the luxury of another night's march in the slippery mud. We made pretty good time, however, and reached Centreville about 1 o'clock in the morning. We spread down our blankets on the saturated ground and soon forgot rain, marches and everything else in sound, refreshing slumber. Our time for sleep was short, but we made the most of it. As soon as the earliest daylight appeared we were ordered to pack up, and, without breakfast or coffee, started on in the direction of Leesburg. The Second Vermont Brigade had camped that night but a short distance from Centreville, and as good luck would have it we passed directly by them. I never could account for it exactly, but it actually so happened that when we were opposite their camp the column halted, giving us an excellent chance to see our acquaintances in that brigade. It was the first time the two brigades had been together, and for a time there was a confused, noisy clatter of tongues that might have rivaled Babel itself. But the order, "Forward march," put an end to our friendly greetings, and we left them with mutual blessings and wishes of good luck in the crisis that seemed impending. They were to follow us, they said, and join us in the next fight. Even now, as I write, the story is being told of their bravery and success in yesterday's battle, and today they are engaged again. No doubt they will give a good account of themselves.

I have not the time to write of all I saw, or the long forced march, and perhaps if I had no one would take the trouble to read it. In order to see and appreciate everything in a beautiful country, like Maryland, one needs to march through it with from sixty to eighty pounds of luggage strapped to his back, and then everything that looks like comfort or enjoyment stands out in bolder relief, from very contrast. At any rate, in such a case, he will have a realizing sense of distance, inasmuch as his transportation is so dearly paid for.

We reached Drainsville that night, having marched, according to the best testimony of the citizens and guide boards, about thirty miles, through the mud and rain. We camped that night in the woods, and as soon as it was light we were on our way again. Many fell out in that march, and had to be brought along in ambulance, who had always been equal to any emergency before. I saw some feet there that night that if they had been on me, I should consider had done their duty faithfully, and if it lay between me and them which should carry the other, I should hardly have had the heart to ask them to carry me any further. Blistered and raw, every nerve was a magazine of pain, and every step exploded them. But without a written permission, no one was allowed to fall out, and it would never do to give a whole command almost, the right to straggle. We marched only about ten miles that day, crossed the Potomac on a pontoon bridge, and bivouacked this side till Sunday morning. At early dawn we started again towards Canada. We marched up to the east of the Sugar Loaf Mountain, over ground familiar to the regiment, as this same road had been passed over before on a similar expedition last fall. We passed through Poolesville and Drainsville, and that night camped at Hyattsville, making a march of twenty miles or more. The next day we marched thirty miles and stopped at Sam's Creek. Tired as the boys were they had strength enough left to ransack the village and purchase everything eatable, from a mince pie to a loaf of brown bread, including chickens, hams, eggs, etc. The stores were drained of all groceries as fast as the goods could be handed out and the money received for them. Farm houses were besieged and everything that extravagant prices could buy was bought, and even then there was hardly half a mouthful apiece. When all other resources became exhausted we resorted to the grist mill, where flour and corn meal could be had, out of which we made cakes and puddings in the most approved primitive style. Probably the most of us manufactured a supper out of material not expressly mentioned in the army regulations. But the time consumed in this, was so much extracted from what we needed for sleep, and much needed too, for the time allotted to us for that since we started had been an extremely stingy allowance. At last we lay down in the bright light of a full moon, and soon were unconscious of pain or weariness in our refreshing slumber. How bright and beautiful the moon shone that night. As I looked upon that pure, silvery orb, I could half imagine how her light would become dimmed with sorrow were she conscious of the cruel desolation being enacted under her light. Perhaps it was so, and for very grief she had hid her face behind a cloud, for before morning it rained quite hard, and when some of the boys awoke they found to their surprise that their blankets were soaking wet.

We were generally allowed till six o'clock to dry our blankets and get our breakfast that morning, when we were ordered forward again. Weak and weary, stiff and sore, we plodded along, taking the Baltimore pike, which there runs parallel with the Baltimore and Ohio railroad to Ridgeville, when we turned to the left a little and took a road directly north through Winchester, to within about a mile of Manchester. We called it that we had traveled twenty-eight miles. At night we were put on picket. To this we had no objection because we fancied we could "forage" a little, and the thing wasn't impossible but that some good Union lady might be induced by the tempting display of greenbacks to bake us a loaf of bread. Our hard tack and pork were at a discount there, good, legitimate bread and butter having the preference. Besides there was a lavish abundance of cherries, large, ripe and luscious, although they grew without cultivation, and of these we partook as much as we pleased. That night and the next day we picketed there, and it seemed the most like living and enjoyment of anything we had seen for a long time, though I must confess, the vacant stare of my purse, was sometimes a little annoying. Not all the citizens there could be accounted good Union men; there were many rank secessionists. One fellow told me that fifteen men from Manchester joined Lee as he passed through. This place was in Carroll County in the north of Maryland, within seven miles of the Pennsylvania line.

Winchester was a very pretty place. We marched through in an orderly manner, carrying our guns in a uniform position, and keeping our step and places in the ranks as if we were trying to play Fourth of July. The General requested us to do so, that we might show the people how well good Union soldiers behave. The streets and buildings had a more thrifty appearance than most of the large Maryland towns that I have seen. It was almost equal to our northern villages. Although it rained quite hard, the men, women and children thronged the doorways and windows to see "the soldiers" as we passed by. The boys remarked that it had the most cheery, home-like appearance of anything we had come across for a long time.

That night orders came just at dark, to pack and march. We had heard the firing during the day and we well knew what was wanted of us. We started back towards Winchester and went within two miles of that place west, then took the main road towards Gettysburg. It took all night to march about seven miles, the roads so clogged with teams and other things to hinder. Marching by rods is like dying by inches, and it gets an impatient man into a hell of a misery. Scolding and swearing is dispensed at an awful rate when a regiment is compelled to halt and wait every few rods, if the road is good and the journey long. We marched that day thirty-five miles. We were in sight of the battle-field when the battle commenced yesterday, although some distance from it. We moved forward as rapidly as possible, which at this time was not over and above rapid, and reached the ground between five and six o'clock; but it was long after dark before they discovered where they wanted to put us. Finally they placed us here on this left flank, so that if we are attacked here we can prevent the army from being flanked. Yesterday they came very nigh turning this flank and winning the day. If they fail at every other point they will undoubtedly try this. We have constructed us a sort of breastwork on our own hook, of rails and dirt, that we fancy will help us some, though I dare say it is not very formidable. I noticed the General smiled as he rode by and saw it a minute ago. At any rate it will stop the minnies; but if the rebels place a battery in the woods yonder and throw solid shot they will poke the rails on to us and make the splinters fly so that our engineering will be worse than nothing. Perhaps they won't attack us here at all. I hope not, though by this, I by no means admit but that I am very brave. All day long I have been summoning up my patriotism, honor, and sense of duty, to get my courage to the sticking point, and I guess now I can make it stick. But I promised to make this letter short, and it is growing longer and longer. I see plainly if I stop at all I must stop at once.

On the March
July 13, 1863

Another spare moment having chanced along on an angel's visit, I will improve it in trying to bring up the rear, for my account of our proceeding here, is getting sadly behind the time. A laggish correspondent is the last man to expect forgiveness. Nevertheless I desire to go back, if the reader will go with me, and commence where I left off before.

It was July third, the day of the severest fighting at Gettysburg. Although we acted a part there, our regiment was not engaged. Part of our brigade was on the skirmish line where there was some firing, but of comparatively trifling importance. Our position was on the extreme left, and as we acted on the defensive, we had nothing to do unless attacked. It was a hard day's fight. The cannon's roar was beyond all precedence of anything I have heard during the war. It fairly made the ground tremble, lasting with unabated fury for several hours. Of course our eagerness to know how things were going on was intense. Every straggler had his own story, and each formed his own opinion from some trifling circumstance that happened to come under his own observation, making it extremely difficult to form any conclusion as to the general result. The officers continually represented things as favorable. They always do. Night closed the struggle, and we lay down tolerable sure that the battle had not gone against us. Saturday, everything was quiet, scarcely a shot being fired on either side. Sunday morning the order came to pack up for marching; the rebels were falling back. We fell into line and marched through a short piece of woods on the battle-field. This part of the field was covered with jagged rocks and huge broken stones of every conceivable shape, — the ugliest looking place for a battle, or for anything else that one could easily select. Over this forbidding looking ground, the rebels had made several fruitless charges, and many of their men, and ours too, fell here to rise no more. The most of these had been buried. Further on through another belt of woods the dead were still unburied. Here the troops halted for a short time, and those that wished to had an opportunity of looking over the field. I saw but a small portion of it, but I saw all I wished to. The rebel dead and ours lay thickly together, their thirst for blood forever quenched. Their bodies were swollen, black, and hideously unnatural. Their eyes glared from their sockets, their tongues protruded from their mouths, and in almost every case, clots of blood and mangled flesh showed how they had died, and rendered a sight ghastly beyond description. My God, could it be possible that such were lively and active like other people so shortly previous, with friends, parents, brothers and sisters to lament their loss. It certainly was so, but it was hard to realize it. I turned away from the heart-sickening sight, willing to forego gratifying my curiosity rather than dwell upon the horrors of that battle-field. I thought I had become hardened to almost anything, but I cannot say I ever wish to see another sight like that I saw on the battle-field of Gettysburg.

There was a rumor that the enemy were intrenching themselves a little further ahead. We moved on, formed in line, and speedily prepared us another breastwork of rails and dirt, but it was not needed. In a short time we were ordered forward. We undertook to move forward in line of battle, but the thing was beyond the range of possibilities, for softer mud I never saw. The way lay through a corn field, and to march across it was like walking in a bed of mortar a hundred feet deep. The mud would adhere to our feet until we were unable to walk. It would have been a sorry undertaking for the rebels to have charged our position across that field, and it would have been poor policy for us to have advanced upon them had they been there. Nature never contrived a better slaughter pen.

A little further on, we passed by what looked to be a rebel camp, but proved to be their hospital, filled with rebel wounded and those left to take care of them. They reported the rebels just left. We had been marching west, but turning to our left we took a southerly course towards Fairfax. Just before reaching that place, however, we met a couple of rebel shells that informed us that our further progress was disputed very decidedly. Our batteries sent back shells enough to pay them and leave a heavy balance in our favor. Our brigade formed into line in the wrong place of course, or else how shall I account for changes we kept making every five minutes, moving first to the right and then to the left, forward, then backward, making endless maneuvers till our patience was entirely exhausted. I do not pretend to know the reasons for all our vexatious movements, I had rather find fault. I know on this occasion we made an endless number, and if I ever have an opportunity I want to "speak my mind" and that never takes me but a little while, so here goes:

You see it was nearly night, and we were hungry, and imagined that we were pretty tired, and that is generally worse for us to bear than if really tired. We formed in line on a steep hillside that sloped towards the rebels, where it would have suited us to have remained during the night, and if the rebels pitched on to us, why — pitched them off again. The artillery firing had ceased and everything was profoundly quiet along the lines. After considerable painstaking the line was straightened to a hair, for we are very precise about these things when danger is not very imminent, and were ready to throw off our knapsacks and make our coffee etc. But the line was not in the right place, we must move forward to yonder field. We moved, formed another line with systematic precision at the same time watching with uneasy interest, the rapidly falling twilight, for when night came on, rainy and dark, how was we going to see to find good water to fill our canteens or to steal good rails to make us a fire?

Again we had to move forward and form anew. Daylight had gone entirely, so there was no need of further anxiety on that point. But we were wrong again. Once more we must move and form our line, — yes, twice, and all for nothing. I tried my best to be patient, and I succeeded remarkably well, for I didn't swear at all, but I was in a desperately supperless condition, and somehow had got the idea that I must have a good hot cup of coffee before I could eat or sleep. The next order was to move back to almost the very place where we formed our line in the first instance. Some laughed and some swore, but we obeyed the order the best we could, feeling our way, over stumps and stones, in the dark, until finally we got organized, and as soon as we were assured officially that we had at last found a stopping place for the night we threw off our knapsacks, built us fires, and prepared our evening meal. This eat, we were the best natured fellows you could find on the globe. By midnight we were ready to lie down and sleep. Now, in cases like this, it is clear we ought to have moved directly on to the right spot the first time, thus giving the men more time to rest and less cause to complain. Why we don't do so the General has never told me.

Pretty soon after sunrise we were packed up ready to march. We didn't march far, however, we only moved to the right a short distance, where we remained till nearly night, when we resumed our march. The rebel skirmishers were but a short distance in our front. They fell back and the 3d brigade of our division followed them, skirmishing as they went. The way from Fairfield to Emmittsburg lies through a mountain gap, though both places are on the same side of the main range. We marched over this road that night, a distance of about seven miles. The soft, liquid mud was all the way from three inches to three feet deep in the road, and there was no use on that dark night, to try to dodge it, or to be dainty about the matter; so we plunged right along as if all was dry and solid. At the dwellings along the road the women came out with lights to see "the soldiers" as they passed by. They must have admired our interesting appearance on that occasion; if so, the sentiment was certainly reciprocal. We reached Emmittsburg about midnight, turned to the right on the Frederick road and camped in a field till morning. I will not attempt to speak of the direction we took, for to me it seemed that our march had been west over the mountain, when we had turned exactly north, but as the sun arose in the morning exactly in the west, I had to reverse all my calculations. We marched down beside the mountain towards the old Potomac, passing through several unimportant villages, sometimes carrying our guns at "right shoulder straight" and keeping step to music in regular order, just to please the ladies, and sometimes observing no order at all, just as it pleased ourselves. But on we went through mud, mire and water, on and on, and on, till, as night approached, we began to anxiously expect a halt. Never before had a march seemed to drag so wearily as this. We left the road and struck out, across meadows and through woods, to a field at the foot of a mountain, where we supposed we should bivouac for the night. But no such good luck awaited us. The mountain must be crossed before we stopped. The distance was seven miles. It was four miles to the top of the mountain. The road was narrow, crooked, and rocky, closely hugged on either side by the thicket of trees and bushes. The night was dark as inky blackness, and the rain poured as I have seldom seen it pour before. The road was steep, awful steep, so steep that one fellow, who was perhaps a little inclined to exaggerate, declared it was worse than perpendicular, that the hill rather canted under. Nevertheless, we should have accomplished this march, as we have accomplished a great many other impossibilities, if we could only have marched right along without hindrance. But the road was continually blocked up by some obstructions ahead, so that we had to halt three minutes where we could travel one. It was vexing beyond all control to stand there and hold our aching knapsacks, with that gigantic, never-ending hill looming up in front of us, and the long, hard journey in prospect. We rarely halted long enought to sit down, but if we did the column would invariably start just as we were fairly seated. Men fell out, whole companies at a time. Some companies took a vote to stop, and all fell out, officers and men. One Colonel said he rode on till his men all left him, and he found himself without a command, when he concluded he would stop too. As for your humble servant he trudged on till he got to the top of the mountain, when, with a comrade, he concluded to follow the multitude and camp on his own hook. Heretofore he had kept with the regiment, but he pleads conscientious scruples to justify his course on this occasion. He had seen men whom the Government could ill afford to lose march till they died, and he was exceedingly loth to deprive Uncle Sam of another of his valuable soldiers, if by stopping he could prevent it. Perhaps he wanted to live to give somebody an awful "blowing up" for marching us so outrageously that day. If so, no one should complain.

The first step I took from the road I stumbled over a sleeping soldier, who swore and threatened terrible vengeance on "the blundering d—d fool" as he called me. I felt very sorry for him, but I couldn't help it. Jumping from him I landed square in the stomach of another. He roared with pain, but without stopping to apologize I sneaked off into the bushes as far as I conveniently could, and without inflicting any further misery on the miscellaneous sleepers so thickly scattered about, we spread our blankets and laid down for the night. It was already past midnight and still continued to rain with unabated fury. There was not a dry thread in our clothes, but for all that we slept, and soundly too. In the morning there was nearly a pailfull of water on the rubber blanket under us.

We started down the mountain on the opposite side and soon came to where there were more of our regiment who had fallen out, and they had a large, comfortable fire blazing from a pile of rails, where we could straighten our benumbed fingers and cook our breakfast. Stragglers kept streaming in and huddling around the fire, their rubber blankets, dripping wet, thrown over their heads, and looking for all the world like a flock of sick turkeys in a stormy day. One fellow had made up his mind that that kind of soldiering didn't pay. He had spoiled his rations by allowing them to get wet, and it had cost him three dollars for one day's expenses, and then he got but two pies, a slice of wheat bread and a drink of whiskey. This, of course, exceeded his day's pay by quite a heavy fraction, hence his conclusion that his country's service was a losing business. He took such an obviously selfish view of the matter that I had to forbear discussing the subject. Of course I couldn't sympathize with him.

I had an excellent breakfast that morning; if you doubt it, allow me to tell you what I had. I had a slice of fat pork, good enough for anybody to eat, plenty of hard tack and coffee. I had a tin plate and tin cup; on my plate I fried my pork, and in my cup I made my coffee. My hard tack I converted into fried cakes, superior to ordinary doughnuts, from the fact that they had the benefit of an extra cooking. I had forgotten my supper in the rainstorm, and my appetite had been accumulating all night. I don't recollect of ever eating a breakfast that relished better than my fried pork and hard tack and coffee did that morning. I doubt if ever the Prince of Wales enjoyed a meal better. My breakfast operated to a charm. I felt like a new man, good for twenty-five miles marching, the toughest they could bring on.

But there is always bitter with the sweet. When I got ready to join the regiment, which was but little further down the mountain where the whole brigade fell out, I noticed my gun had changed its appearance most remarkably. The decently clean and polished musket that I left there had become transformed into a carelessly kept and miserably rusty affair that any other soldier would have been ashamed to carry. Evidently somebody had swapped with me. I had always supposed that it took two to make a bargain, but this one had been made by one I have never seen, and one I fear I never shall see.

In course of the forenoon we came to a full stop near Middletown, and our adventures over the big mountain were at an end. Napoleon crossing the Alps will no longer be mentioned as the climax of heroic achievements. Sedgwick marching over the Catoctin Mountains has entirely eclipsed that. That was undoubtedly bad enough, but it bears a feeble comparison to what we did.

Camp near Warrenton, Va.
July 28, 1863

For a strange rarity the army of the Potomac is not on the move to-day. Since Saturday night we have rested here in camp on a conspicuous elevation in the vicinity of Warrenton. Our brigade is in a splendid place for a camp, affording a most extensive and beautiful view of a large portion of Virginia. Away to the east as far as the eye can reach, hill succeeds hill, until the view is lost where sky and earth meet in the dim distance. On the west the jagged and imposing range of mountains composing the Blue Ridge, are seen in all their grandeur and sublime beauty, their loftiest peaks piercing the clouds, and their green sides, so smooth and unbroken as they look in the distance, seem to speak a nobler purpose in their creation than that they should be a mere barrier between two hostile enemies. It is just such a place here as nature's lover would wish to occupy that he might see and admire the vast panorama she has spread out before him. It is a cool and airy location, too, where we have plenty of the purest water and where we are free from the pestilence-breeding filth of low and unhealthy camps. I should have no objection to serving out the remainder of my term in camp here; but it is not our habit to stay long in so nice a place, and now we are almost momentarily expecting to receive the order to pack up and march at a double quick pace, and I must crave your indulgence accordingly.

We have been on the move every day for the past week, except one. We have marched in all directions, north, east, south and west, with how much result may never be accurately estimated. We have seen no enemy, fought no battle, but we have accomplished toil enough to win a dozen victories, and it ought to have some saving effect on the Union. Often we have been on the march from four o'clock in the morning till ten at night, then, after a brief rest, start on again at daylight. Last Tuesday we remained in camp near Philomont, a little village about twenty miles from where we crossed the Potomac. Here the boys had an opportunity to wash and mend their clothes, clean their guns, pick berries, write letters, and steal chickens. It was a busy day with the most of us, if the army was still, and one day was all too short for the many things we needed to do for ourselves. It was not till in the afternoon of Wednesday that we resumed our march, and as time lingered and we delayed moving, we began to think another day was to be given us to rest. Some of the boys ventured to put clothes in the wash, some went berrying. I even went so far to pull out my portfolio to write you another letter, but long before I had completed it, the order was given to march. I had to lay aside pen and ink, and shoulder my musket and knapsack and trudge on again, leaving my ideas to get scattered beyond the hope of recovery. I had a long story that I wanted to tell the boys at home who read the *Freeman,* of our campaign in Maryland, but it is so long ago now that an account of it from me would be a dull affair to read; though I can assure you our Maryland trip was quite an interesting event to experience. It was hard marching every day, sometimes hard fighting, and all the time hard living. It is more pleasant, to be sure, to march through even so friendly a country as Maryland, than to march where all are enemies; but all the friendliness in that State, and all the kindness of a thousand such principalities and powers, couldn't have separated us from our hard tack and pork, unless a regular system had been arranged to provide us something better.

Perhaps all do not know how eager the boys all are when on a long march to get that to eat that will bear some resemblance to a favorite dish they were fond of at home, or how difficult it is to gratify any such eagerness. In some cases it is a mere whim of the soldier, a sort of natural desire to get something different from what is provided, but in many cases it is essential to health, and often to life itself. But those that needed this kind of nursing the most were not always the ones to get it. Once in a while a lucky fellow would get a woman to bake him a haversack full of biscuits, but their number was comparatively few. They were costly luxuries when obtained. One might have to roam all over the country to find them, and then perhaps have to wait half of a day or more for his turn in getting them cooked, and finally pay from 25 to 50 cents a dozen for very cheaply made biscuits, scarcely large enough to be visible to the naked eye. But the good people were not to blame for these grievances. Let a woman undertake to bake for the soldier and forthwith her kitchen is crowded with "brave defenders of our country's flag," respectful, perhaps, but awfully impudent and all eager for the first loaf of bread, or the first batch of biscuits, as the case might be. The first man to visit such a place will, if he is shrewd, offer about ten cents a dozen for biscuits of a very fashionable size, and perhaps strike up a bargain for quite a number. But other customers begin to come and soon there is a crowd. The position of the cook is now more laborious than pleasant. The demand for soft bread or biscuits so exceeds the supply that the price bounds up to a marvelous figure. One will offer 25 cents for a loaf of bread or a plate of biscuits; another to overreach him will offer 50 cents, and take out the money and urge her to take it to clinch his claim. A third will produce a dollar greenback, and beg the woman to give the bread to him, as he has had nothing to eat for three days, — and if that doesn't touch her sympathies, he will make it three weeks; while perhaps a fourth individual, unheard of before, will step forward and claim that the bread has been promised to him. If the woman doubts his statement he can furnish positive proof that it was so. The woman gets confused dealing with such strange characters, and she hardly knows what to do. Her room is getting crowded full of men; her cooking is interrupted; her fire goes out, or her bread gets burnt; her cakes mysteriously disappear, until in despair she gives up the lucrative business, shuts her stove, and with as much politeness as she can assume, invites the men to clear out. No other alternative is now left us, but to go to some other place and try again, or else return and be reconciled to our slighted and abused crackers. For me, in such a case, it was a very easy question to decide, especially after marching from twenty to twenty-five miles and carrying a soldier's pack and under a dog-day's sun.

Our brigade had one day of hard skirmishing near Funkstown, as you are well aware, in which the Vermonters did all the fighting with characteristic success and pluck. I saw in the Baltimore *Clipper*, the next day, a flattering notice of how the "Vermonters" drove the rebels, and were with difficulty restrained from rushing on after the retreating foe. The *Clipper* might have told how our bare skirmish line received and repulsed a determined charge from the enemy made in regular order in three lines of battle. "Mr. Johnny Rebs" thought he was going to crush our thin picket line, but the whistling Minnies from our accurate rifles came most too thick and close for their courage to stand. They hesitated. Their officers tried to urge them on; they shamed and threatened them; they told them that there were but few of us, and we could easily be captured. Some turned on their heels and run, some rallied again to the charge. They came on a few rods further, when their ranks broke, and the whole battalion, officers and all, skedaddled for their very lives. They had discovered that they were blundering on to a nest of Vermonters. No wonder it was difficult to restrain the boys from rushing after them. Wtih a few more Vermonters we could have annihilated the whole crew. No other part of the corps did any fighting that day, except our artillery.

Since we have crossed the Potomac we have had no fighting to do, but plenty of marching. Till Wednesday noon our marching was in a style quite reasonable and human. At that time we had got as far as Rectortown Station, on the Manassas Gap railroad, almost the last station this side of the gap. We rested at that place till two o'clock, and we expected to rest longer, but some unforeseen contingency made it necessary, I suppose, for another long forced march. As we waited we had a glorious opportunity to gather a quantity of ripe, luscious blackberries, for if nature had intended us a banquet of this delicious fruit, she could not have offered them at a better time, or in more lavish quantities. The bugle note to fall in sounded when some of the boys were a mile or more from camp, and these fellows had to make remarkable good use of their legs, for the corps moved forward as if it had important business ahead. We marched on down beside the mountains as fast as we conveniently could, and somewhat faster, passing near White Plains, through Salem, to Rix's Cross Roads, where night overtook us; but, without supper or rest, we turned to the right and took a jagged, miserable road that led us, in a westerly direction, over what appeared to be a sort of gap in the mountains, or rather the suburbs of the Blue Ridge. We finally found a halting place in a field, where the vine blackberries were so thick we could almost pick them by handfuls, even in the night, had we felt in any way inclined to do so. But the boys were too tired by far to pick berries, and many were too tired to even cook their suppers, but sought repose as soon as they could, comforted only by the expectation of being drummed up at daylight in the morning and ordered forward like a flock of cattle, not knowing where they, or for what purpose, were going.

In the morning we took a north-westerly course, going, as it seemed to me, almost directly back to where we started from the day before, only we were on the opposite side of a huge mountain, and fortunately for us we happened to discover the error of our way in season to halt before we were quite back to Rectortown Station. The boys were all getting "short" for rations, but by dint of pretty energetic foraging they managed to secure enough to hold starvation at a respectful distance. Some found chickens and geese; some calves, all the way from six months to six years old; and some run across a garden of early blue potatoes just large and ripe enough to be eatable. After an hour or so of delay, we had orders again to march. We divided our plunder and took along with us what we could of it, and left the rest. Do not harshly condemn us, honest reader, for this seeming lawlessness, nor consider us a mere roving gang of thieves and plunderers. How could we have done differently? Besides, the men whose property we took were secessionists of the rankest kind, many of whom are now in the rebel army, murderers, perhaps, of your dearest friend — your father, brother, husband, or son, — and doing their utmost to bring into contempt the Government we have always delighted to honor, and to dim the lustre of that starry flag, our nation's pride and glory. When the alternative is presented of taking property of these men or suffering from hunger, it takes a different nature from mine to hesitate long, on grounds of moral principle, which of the two to choose.

We fell into line and marched back the way we had come since morning, and continued on in a southerly course towards Warrenton till dark, when we halted again for supper and sleep. A threatening demonstration on the part of the enemy at Manassas Gap was the reason of our marching so far out of the way. We heard the firing, and knew right well what it meant, but the trouble was disposed of long before we got there. Infantry and artillery came back along the same road together, which always makes marching very vexatious and inconvenient. Many of the men fell out, but not so many men as horses. The battery boys said if this kind of marching was kept up much longer they would be left without sufficient horses to drag along their pieces. We have already marched, since leaving our old camp, about 320 miles, averaging over 20 miles per day, counting the days that we marched.

Sweet as the voice of a friend is the order to halt, after so long a march, and brief though our night's rest may be it is wonderfully recuperating. On this occasion, we turned off from the road, through a piece of woods, to an open field near the bank of a brook, where water and rails were plenty, and in short time our camp fires were burning brightly and the boys were engaged in cooking their evening meal; and the most of us had that that no one need be ashamed to cook or eat. I should have been loth to have swapped my supper that night for the best farm in New England. We had orders to start next morning at five o'clock, but as our supply train had arrived and the boys were all out of rations, the General very kindly condescended to allow two hours more, to draw and issue enough hard tack and pork to last us another day. We were behind one day, or rather, our rations were, as we had subsisted one day on nothing (?) and we all considered it a first-rate plan of Gen. Sedgwick's to stop us long enough to draw some more.

We came here into camp that day, and although it took us almost a whole afternoon to find a camp-place to suit, I have no fault to find, for they finally led us to a very good one. We hope to stay here long enough to get thoroughly rested, for the men are thoroughly exhausted. A sutler's visit, too, would be gladly welcomed, for such articles as writing paper and the like are more scarce here than gold in Dixie.

Camp near Waterloo, Va.
Aug. 3, 1863

How very hot the sun shines this morning; how hot it shone yesterday. Long shut out behind clouds and mist and rain, for it rained almost every day in July, and now, just released, the great king of day seems to glory in his liberty and power, and as if to make amends for time lost, pours down his flood of heat with more than redoubled intensity. It almost reminds one of that bourne from which no sinner returns. It would be cruelty refined to order a march today. No man or horse or mule could long endure marching or any kind of labor in this intolerable heat. At least it seems so, as we sit in our tents undergoing a vigorous perspiration, and feeling too languid and too indolent to undergo the least exertion, or think of it with composure.

As I predicted in my last, we have moved camp. Military men know why; I don't. The charms of our former camp are not re-produced here, nor its equivalent furnished. I should be strongly tempted to grumble at a change so little desired and so seemingly purposeless, had I not learned that it is expedient in whatever situation we are placed, therewith to be content. Many of the movements that to us in the ranks look so aimless, and often absurd, have proved, afterwards, to be of the most vital importance. The most simple are apt to be the most complaining. Hence so much vituperation in my own letters. But we only moved about a mile — merely exchanged a lofty, airy and healthy location, for one that is not lofty, and which the wind seems to disdain. It is situated on a small hill side sloping westward, in a field covered with rocks and small bushes and hemmed in on all sides by hills that have no peculiar charms to recommend them. The situation, however, is good enough in all respects, only having been removed from a better one it is hard to like this.

The boys entertain the idea that we are to stay here for some length of time. There seems to be considerable excuse for thinking so. Lee's army has escaped from us. They have taken up their line of defence where it best suited them. Our army has been weakened in many ways, as every one knows. The nine months men have gone home, the two years men have gone too, and the remainder has been most lamentably reduced by hard fighting, hard marching, by sickness and by exhaustion, until there is but a remnant of the Army of the Potomac left. To advance with this at this time of year and attack Lee in his chosen position, would seem to us like an adventure too foolhardy for a madman to attempt. Success would be impossible. If the army hesitated to attack when we had the enemy cornered against the Potomac at Williamsport, it surely does not look as though, with the same army to oppose us and all the advantages reversed, we should now be anxious to bring on a collision. It frets the North more than anything else except the draft, to have this army lie still, but in the very selfishness of their desire to see the Army of the Potomac move, they must desire success also, but success cannot be had without proper means, and it requires time to secure these. The men are worn out and exhausted and loudly call for rest. These long forced marches have told fearfully upon the best constitutions. A rest is imperatively needed or the army will be too much weakened by disease to be capable of effective service. No particular malady affects the men, but a sort of general debility, a relaxation of the whole system that has long held out against severe and protracted hardships. The surgeon's call is lately well attended. The long train of sick, lame and halt that find their way to the surgeon's tent every morning, shows conclusively that something is needed to repair the physical vigor of a great many who have been heretofore proof against the severest privations and hardships. Give us good food, something less concentrated than hard tack and pork, and let us rest and recuperate our strength awhile, and we shall soon be able to astonish the world again by our long marches and hard fighting. Do not think, dear friends at home, because we have no sympathy just now with the impatient spirit that asks so often, "why don't the Army of the Potomac move?" that we are indifferent to the cause, becoming demoralized, willing to sacrifice our country's interests to our love of ease, or are in any way losing the spirit of patriotism or the spirit of war which we trust has characterized our efforts from the outset. On the contrary, our very desire for success demands inactivity just now. You have called us brave, heroic and self-sacrificing, and whether we have deserved it or not we have accepted the compliment, but after all it is no more than the truth to say that the bravest and best of us would be almost as willing to see the Constitution of the United States destroyed as to see his own.

But before anything great can be done we not only need health, but we need reinforcements. Men at home are being drafted to fill our thinned ranks, and some of these — such as have no convenient $300 to spare — we shortly expect to see out here. These men will need some experience in drilling and camp life before they can take the field. What better time for that than now? The paymaster, too, is expected, and all of us are quite willing that he should come as soon as he sees fit and discharge any obligations he may have to us. Taken all in all, we think we have quite forcible reasons for thinking that we are to go into permanent camp here. After all, before this letter is read in Vermont we may be on the move again, and more fiercely engaged with the enemy than ever before.

The army is a world almost exclusively by itself now. Without money and without sutlers, dependent on our own resources, and independent of every one else, we can live on without care or trouble, knowing that our commissary can always be relied upon, and that hard tack will ever be abundant. Lovers of tobacco appear to be the principal sufferers. Those who love tobacco, and have borrowed till they can borrow no longer, have indeed a trouble that makes them of all soldiers the ones most miserable. It must certainly be a most excruciating annoyance for those who affirm that the use of the peculiar weed is the soldier's principal comfort, to be deprived of his idolized luxury, but as I do not use the article myself, I presume I shall never be thanked for pitying those who do, for I am not a fit person to sympathize with them. No doubt there will be pedlars here soon who will remedy the evil.

A week ago yesterday, we had the rare entertainment of Church service, the first we have enjoyed since in camp near White Oak Church. It seemed all the better because held in a *bona fide* meeting house. This house was built in a very secluded spot, on a by-road, screened from view by a grove of bushes and trees. It was where one would scarcely think of looking for a building at all, much less for one of that sacred character. The reasons for placing it so out of sight were obvious as we came to view the house more closely. It is very ancient, old fashioned, and rudely constructed. The walls are built of logs and mud and neither inside nor out is there the least attempt at ornament, or any indications of refinement and taste in the whole construction. It is about as large as an ordinary barn in Vermont, and not a whit more substantially or classically built. The ceiling covers about two-thirds of the area with a large opening over the pulpit and this second floor I suppose was the gallery. It was supported by roughly hewn posts, not painted or even white washed, but in the same condition that the workman's broad axe left them. The pulpit was a small miniature concern scarcely big enough to hold a man, and looked from the opposite side of the room more like a cupboard or a library closet than like a preacher's desk. Whether it was abject poverty or a woeful lack of appreciation for the good and the beautiful in these people, that made them build such an uncouth sanctuary for divine worship, is more than I can tell.

The meeting was conducted by chaplain Stone of the sixth regiment, and chaplain Mack of the third regiment. Notwithstanding the quaintness of the surroundings the services were impressive and full of instruction. After singing some familiar hymn, as we always do in these meetings, chaplain Stone spoke at some length from the words of Solomon: "He that governeth his own spirit is better than he that taketh a city." After fully illustrating the meaning of the text, he proceeded to show how every one of us could be more heroic, wield a more difficult authority than our best and ablest officers and generals. His application was quite practical and forcible. To rule even our own spirit we needed fixed principles laid down, and a constitution, as it were, to guide us. Was it best to swear? Could any one say it was? Whether it was or not he left it for us to decide, but in either case he advised us to make a law in regard to it, and fully live up to the law. Was it best to play cards and gamble? If it was, then on every opportunity, make it a business, and take the consequences. If it was not, then make a law to leave off at once and see if we had moral heroism enough to keep the law. Other vices incident to camp life were enumerated, and dealt with in the same practical manner. He was followed by chaplain Mack, who spoke of some pleasing reminiscences in his connection with the soldiers, made some very practical and instructive remarks in his usual clear and entertaining manner, when, after singing the doxology, the meeting dispersed. The boys went back to their tents to digest thoughts of no inferior consequence, though too often forgotten in the hurly burly of a soldier's life. We wish we could have more such meetings to record.

P.S. In letter 31, I noticed in my haste I had made one or two unimportant mistakes. Darnestown in Maryland was written Drainsville. Westminster, Winchester, and in letter 32 in one place Fairfield in Pennsylvania was written Fairfax.

Camp near Warrenton, Va.
Aug. 10, 1863

This camp is, I believe, without an official name at present. We are within about five miles of Warrenton, and about two from what was once the village of Waterloo. Warrenton is on your left, and Waterloo on your right as we face the enemy. You will perceive since writing my last we have moved our camp once more. This remarkable event occurred last Wednesday. I cannot say whether it was a military necessity, or a military convenience, or some other motive that prompted the change, but so far as my humble opinion can judge, I think the move a wise and judicious one. We went almost directly back to where we were encamped at first, only swinging in a half a mile or so nearer the Rappahannock. This may not be quite so good a camping place as that, but it is better than the last one, and makes a very acceptable compromise between the two. So, having become somewhat domesticated in our new position, I see no better way of employing one of the fairest mornings that Virginia ever saw than by writing a line or so to my always welcome visitor, the *Freeman*. To be sure, nothing has transpired worth noticing, and there is nothing to write about; but incessant talkers and scribblers can generally manage to make themselves sufficiently troublesome without the aid of these superfluous auxiliaries.

Living in camp is a peculiar kind of life, but like every other situation one may become so accustomed to it that the evil and the good bear a relation to each other very nearly approaching to what may be found in almost any other pursuit. It may often seem dull and irksome, imposing burdensome restraints and duties not at all agreeable, but only the croaker will say the days are all dark and cheerless. We certainly have had hardships and privations to endure, and sometimes pretty severe ones, too; but we have also, now and then, a time for sport, joyous, health-inspiring, and full of fun. We have our games of chess, backgammon, draughts, cards, and others, to make merry many a dull, listless hour. We get occasionally a book to read, sometimes a paper, or what is often better than either, a letter from home. These last are the chinks that fill up many a useless, if not burdensome, hour, presenting to the soldier's mind something tangible that his thoughts will love to dwell upon. Many hours are pleasantly spent in answering these letters, many in visiting our friends in other portions of the camp, many more in fishing and foraging; and thus the day often closes before we are aware or wish to have it.

Since we formed our new camp we have been employed principally in making our tents comfortable and convenient. I would like to introduce the reader in to our camp this morning that he might see what pleasant houses we can improvise at short notice and very little expense. If you can imagine a pole or rail, whichever happens to be the handiest, elevated a little higher than one's head and held horizontally by two crotches, or by being strapped to two other rails that are perpendicular, which are inserted in the ground, one at each end, you have an idea of the first starting point in putting up a tent. The principal difficulty in all this is to get an ax or hatchet to cut a pole or sharpen the stake that is to be driven into the ground; but sometimes a big jack-knife will answer the purpose. The next thing is to throw our tent, which is nothing more nor less than two pieces of cotton or linen cloth, about five feet square buttoned together, over this ridge-pole and fasten the lower edge, or eaves, to small stakes as near the ground as we have calculated to have the tent come. The boys generally prefer from two to three feet. Here then is a tent for two men. Others can join on to the ends indefinitely, thus making a continual line of tents and have it all one. Along the centre of this we can build our bunks, running lengthwise, if we have tents sufficient, at a convenient height from the ground, making us a good seat or lounge in the day-time, and a bed for the night, or we can build them crosswise, if we prefer, and thus economize the room. Being open all around, the tent has the freest circulation of air, and we escape the unhealthy damp of living on the ground. Some of the boys fix themselves up stands for writing-desks, and cupboards for their cups, plates, and fragments of rations. Many other conveniences are constructed as necessity demands, or ingenuity invents. Generally we provide ourselves with all the proudest aristocrat needs to ask for, while the whole establishment would be costly at five dollars.

But in order to tell the whole story, which seeing I have begun I might as well continue, it will be necessary to speak of the manner in which the boys often procure the boards to build and ornament their singular habitations. The rapid disappearance however of barns and sometimes houses in the vicinity of where a new camp is being formed disclosed the secret. In our last camp the boys had begun to render their location quite pleasant and tasteful, supposing that the promise to stay there was made in good faith, and were quite loth to leave in consequence. Boards were plenty there as the Village had been vacated but not entirely destroyed. Every building there, of whatever description that was not occupied was speedily sacrificed to the boys' greediness for comfortable tents. They had been polluted with the heresy of secession, and the boys could not be made to feel any compunction for their downfall. As soon as a building was struck it was doomed. The first blow became a signal for a general attack, and soon all that was left would be a few scattering timbers and fragments of boards, while the road to camp would be lined with soldiers sweating under their loads of plunder.

There was one old miller left in the village of Waterloo, and I believe he is the last of his race in that spot. The village was burnt last summer or destroyed when we came, except one negro shanty. It used to contain two stores, a woollen factory besides the grist mill and blacksmith shop. Waterloo is on the Hedgeman river or Rappahannock proper, which stream is the southern boundary of Fauquier County of which Warrenton is the capitol. It is about sixty miles from Washington in a direction a little south of west. It is represented as having been a very thrifty place but like many of her sister towns it has become totally crushed out by this desolating war.

The camp of the 2nd regiment since moving from Waterloo, is on a small ridge crowned with a grove of bushes which unfortunately was not so extensive but that both ends of the regiment extended out into open sunlight. The 3rd, 4th and 6th are camped near by; the 5th are guarding Thompson's Ford. We have found lumber much more difficult to obtain here than at Waterloo. "But where there is a will there is a way" and where there is plenty of boards only two miles distant, who would be willing to lie in the dirt and go without them? Certainly not Vermonters, if we may judge from the throng that has been continually streaming back to that place over the hills and brooks and coming again with a load such as no lazy man would ever put on his shoulders. The officers had teams to bring their boards, but the men being more independent brought theirs on their backs. By dint of much perseverance and industry we have again established ourselves in camp pretty much to our satisfaction. Next week I may be able to chronicle another move.

Perhaps some one will question the constitutionality of our confiscating secesh boards and buildings in the manner I have described. I can only say it is a way we have of managing affairs here, and our officers had much rather help than hinder us. This morbid tenderness towards secesh property has been stifled by the rebels themselves, in their uncivilized conduct toward Union people when the power has been with them. Still I must confess it looks a little barbarous to go into a man's door yard, almost, as we did the miller's at Waterloo and tear down his barn and shed under his very eyes. This "erring brother" could only look demurely on and witness the progress of the destruction; he was powerless to prevent it. But they not only tore down his buildings they carried away his garden fence and ransacked and spoiled his garden. Excuse me reader, but I too went into that garden to help harvest the immature crop, and should have carried out my intentions, perhaps, but when I saw the woman and one of her children looking in sorrowful submission from the window at the wasteful destruction going on in their own garden — and it was a pretty one — my courage failed me, and I withdrew without taking so much as a pod of peas or a handful of potatoes. I never was caught stealing sheep or any thing of that sort, but I fancied I then had a very realizing sense of such a culprit's self-importance. It is impossible I suppose in war time but that such offences will come, and doubtless, in most cases they are well enough deserved, but when they are to happen to women and children that appear innocent in this case, I thought it would be as safe for me in the end to shirk the responsibility, and let them come through some one else; and certainly it was as consistent with my inclination on this particular occasion. Generally I am not behind when secession sinners are being punished after this fashion.

Camp near Warrenton, Va.
August 13, 1863

The "hot season" for this year is evidently over — and all around us. Last Sunday a citizen said his thermometer went up to 104 degrees in the shade, and to-day it cannot be much below that. It is absolutely impossible to keep cool or to keep good-natured. No matter how thick the shade one keeps himself in, he cannot prevent perspiring freely — so freely sometimes that every garment is wringing wet with the perspiration. August so far has made ample amends for the cool, lowery weather of July, and we are beginning to hope anxiously for this intense heat to relax its severity. It has been almost uninterrupted since the closing week of July. Flies, too, are becoming miraculously abundant, and as annoying as they are abundant. We have the most prolific species of this insect here that I ever saw. I believe they increase fourfold every day, and have done so in regular geometrical progression ever since dog days commenced. They swarm everywhere and torment a fellow from daylight till dark. They hover in his face, fly into his mouth and nose, and with their little tickling feet irritate the flesh wherever the saucy imps can find it. There seems to be a peculiar species of the fly kind that infests our camp. They bite almost as quick as a bee can sting, and their bite is almost as painful. The rebels could never boast of being more troublesome than these same little flies. It would be untrue to say that we are idle; we cannot be in such a nest of flies.

Last Sunday we had an inspection on a scale ranking a little higher than usual. It was a division inspection, superintended by Gen. Howe himself. He wished to have every man provided with a suitable outfit of clothing, and have it kept clean and neat. Every man was required to have at all events a change of under clothing, shirts, drawers and socks, but other articles, such as blankets, coats or pants, it was left optional with us to take or not, as fancy or necessity might suggest. It may be supposed that no one would need to be urged to carry two shirts, one to wear and the other to exchange, but a great many of the boys prefer to change the same one. That is, when the garment needs washing they pull it off and wash it, and then put it on again often without pretending to dry it at all. This style of doing business is not exactly satisfactory to the authorities, though quite convenient on a march, and very economizing of knapsack room. Very many had no knapsack at all, and some had allowed their affections to become so alienated from these troublesome articles in the late campaigning, that it was difficult to persuade them to adopt another. Haversacks and canteens were also missing. These had to be accounted for and others provided. I imagine some twenty-fifth or thirtieth mile of some of our long marches could account for some of these delinquent articles, and show where they had gone, for when men were too tired to carry them further they bid them an everlasting good bye, and dumped them beside the road and went along without them. Hard as it was to be driven to such an alternative, it was better than to fall behind and run the risk of being "provost marshalled."

During the preliminary arrangements of getting the men into military shape, which took the best part of two hours and all of our patience, several men from the other brigade fell, under the effect of the heat, and had to be helped off from the ground. Besides this the inspection passed off very pleasantly to all, unless we except a few officers that stumbled into a hornets' nest and had to retreat in disorder, leaving the enemy in possession of the field, and themselves in possession of a sore head. When we were arranged by company in line, in open ranks, the inspecting officer passed up and down between the rear and front ranks, which were facing each other with their knapsacks spread out before them, and if any article was seen in them denoting a lack of care on the part of its possessor, he was sure to have some disagreeable questions to answer. I observed that some of these inspecting officers could be very personal in their remarks to a soldier that should exhibit an unusually slovenish or negligent appearance.

We had a thanksgiving last week I suppose in common with the whole nation, although it passed without any demonstration here, and probably a great many never knew when it happened. We had not so much as an extra ration of hard tack to celebrate the day, and how should we know or remember it? But as for the victories we have been thankful for them ever since they happened, and I doubt if in this we have been exceeded by the most favored in their peaceful holidays at home.

My friend and I came very near having a canteen of milk apiece to help make us thankful; in fact we did get the milk, but it turned sour before we could use it, and thus cheated us out of our feast. It is of no use to mourn over milk that is spilt, and it is worse than useless to cry when milk sours; but to lose one's thanksgiving in that kind of a way is harrowing in the extreme. We had been obliged to go nearly three miles to get this one luxury, to cross two streams, one on loose flood wood and the other on the trunk of a huge sycamore tree, where the torrent dashed and foamed as if it would delight to engulf us for ever milk and all, and this in a dark night after roll call when good dutiful soldiers who love their country dreadfully, as we do, should have been abed and asleep. But we got across the Rappahannock and its tributary, and got back again safely, got into camp in season to dream of milk and honey, thanksgiving and flap-jacks, and to wake in the morning and find our milk curdled, our thanksgiving spoiled, and all our epicurean dreams of feasts and felicity but miserable false prophets to cheat and betray us. When Vallandigham and Fernando Wood have inaugurated their peace policy we hope these things will have an end.

Where is there a friend of mine that will not pray for peace?

We made our purchase of a respectable colored man, who, with his able partner, occupy a very substantial two story house of the better sort, but which has felt the effects of war in its most practical form, it having been pierced in several places with solid cannon shot and an almost endless number of bullets. Everything within this house had the appearance of scrupulous neatness. The walls, chairs, ceilings, and whatever furniture I noticed was cleanly kept and tidily arranged, evincing considerable taste, and refinement even, on the part of the occupants, "niggers" though they were; that was apparent to the most casual observer. Yet this dwelling was occupied by two Africans, well advanced in years, belonging to a race whose title to respectability we are loth to recognize, and who are excluded from the pale of the proud Caucasian's socie-ty. I couldn't help wondering, as I talked with this man — had I ought to say nigger? — so respectful and gentlemanly in his demeanor, and thought how universally he was avoided and despised, whether He who made his skin black and mine white, would endorse my title to exclusiveness in that other world where we conclude there are no such visible distinctions made, and where he was evidently much more fitted to enter than my humble self. I found him well informed in regard to the war, as well as the citizens generally. He was conscientious in his religious beliefs, as almost all of his race are, and, as is their nature, would rather suffer wrong, than wrong another.

This man had never been a slave, and has consequently possessed many advantages that are denied to slaves; but if his superiority to the common negro is attributable mainly to freedom, it only furnishes an argument against this institution of bondage that all the sophistry of the infernal regions cannot overthrow. If the soul of the African has sufficient elasticity to rise to such a height, when released from the pressure of slavery, it must be a fearful responsibility for a nation to keep them down. This nation has run the risk, and is reaping the consequences. It is of no use to speak of the prejudice against that race; but when this prejudice leads to the revolting scenes that were enacted in New York during the late bloody riots, it throws off its mask and shows its hideous deformity. A hatred that leads men to murder women and children, burn orphan asylums, and makes it dangerous for a colored person, however innocent, to be seen abroad anywhere — and all this from no provocation whatever, except the crime of color — must be wholly wrong, unnatural and unjustifiable. What if Jehovah should espouse the cause of this despised race, and shift the inequality to the other side, where then, my negro-hating friend, would your arguments and your boasting be? Should Omnipotence punish our insolent pride in that way, we must not lay it all to "radical" teachings, nor make the Republican party responsible for our damages.

Transport Steamship Ericsson
Chesapeake Bay
Aug. 20, 1863

This letter is not dated from our new camp, nor from the field of battle, but on the smooth, placid waters of the Chesapeake. The boat is the one that the famous builder of the Monitor designed to have propelled by caloric or heated air, but, failing in that, it was converted into a steamer bearing his name — Ericsson.

Last Thursday night, when everything was quiet — the flies all still, the air cool, and everything favorable for the most invigorating repose, and every boy vigorously improving it, the order came — that same everlasting order — to pack up and be ready to march immediately. We did so, and almost as soon as light we were on the road, marching in the direction of Warrenton. Our visions of a long rest in camp, of exemption for a time from the arduous toils incident to a perilous campaign in the field, and our hopes of ease and comparative comfort, such as camp life sometimes affords a soldier, were ruthlessly dissolved, and the sternest realities of war seemed again to frown down upon us from the mysterious future. It was the most sudden and unexpected order we have ever received. Our eyes had to be rubbed several times extra that morning before they could perceive the true state of affairs, and even when fairly awake we half believed it was a dream or some big mistake. All the week we had been making improvements in our camp, we had built us a brigade bakery, cleaned up our camping ground, and had received the strictest orders to attend to our personal appearance, a matter that is entirely left to our own discretion when the enemy are hovering near. But it was useless to waste words or indulge in vain regrets, the order had come to march, and march we must.

Night brought us to Warrenton Junction, a distance from camp of about sixteen miles. The day had been very hot, and as a very natural consequence there were some that fell out. I passed one of those unlucky fellows, lying prostrate under the shade of a tree, overcome with heat and fatigue. His comrades were trying to relieve his sufferings which appeared to be very severe, and to restore his strength, though it was but little that they could do. We had been marching through the dryest place for water that we have seldom seen, and all were destitute of the first drop. They brought him some from a pool in the road that had lain there since the shower, thirty-six hours before, and that half of the brigade had marched through, and this was the very best they could do. I had no time to stop and see the result, but I think, bad as our commissary whiskey is, it would have been better for this man to drink than such miserable water.

It was nearly sundown when we stacked arms at the Junction to wait for the train that was to take us to Alexandria. During the interval a load of troops from the latter place arrived at Warrenton. They claimed to be conscripts and substitutes, and were mostly from New York and Boston. Some of them had their pockets well lined with money, as the price for which they sold themselves to Uncle Sam. They were jolly, hearty fellows, full of fun, fight and frolic, and looked capable of becoming the best of soldiers as soon as they were fairly trained to the yoke. One or two campaigns after old General Robert E. will make them as "handy" as old veterans.

Noticing some soldiers coming continually from a certain place, with sutlers' goods in their hands and throats, a number of us started to find the source of this stream of pies, cakes, and other etceteras, and perhaps do a little in the way of purchasing for ourselves, as we always imagine we are going to want everything when we start out from camp, and we imagine that each chance is going to be the last. We found a quantity of sutler's goods piled beside the railroad, evidently just unloaded, which a simple, honest man was dealing out as fast as he conveniently could, yet not half fast enough to supply his customers. This sutler was an open-hearted, unpretending man — quite a stranger with his class, and evidently quite unsophisticated in the ways of the world, — certainly so in the ways of the soldiers. He regarded his property with a nervous apprehension, for he saw in the face of the crowd a power that might sweep everything from before him, leaving him destitute, and without redress. In the first place he had been loth to bait the crowd with any of his good things, preferring to wait till he was safely in his destined camp, but the troops there clamored so eagerly for the privilege of purchasing, that he was obliged to yield. They huddled around him so that it was impossible for him to supply half of their demands. They soon got to waiting upon themselves, which so agitated the mind of the sutler that he hardly knew what to do or how to act. He tried to persuade the boys not to rob him, and appealed to their feelings in a most Christian like manner, but it was of no avail. The boys would listen to neither arguments or persuasion. He could not convince them that they were ungrateful and ungentlemanly, though he made almost superhuman efforts to do so. They had neither pity nor compassion for his helplessness. While he was selling a pie to one, another would help himself to a handful of lemons, and when he would turn to drive them away from his lemons some one would steal a pie. He implored, entreated, and sometimes threatened them. "O don't boys, please don't. I am a poor man and this is all of my property. I brought this here by special permission, that I might accommodate you with things that you need. I am willing to sell you my goods reasonably, only don't rob me. I have invested my all in these goods, and it will ruin me if you take them. I am trying to earn an honest living and to support my family, and it is very cruel and very wrong in you to treat me so." Thus he kept pleading with them, but the unfeeling crowd not only stole his goods, but they mocked his agony. He was very earnest and vehement, and evidently sincere and truthful. He told them he was a man that had seen a great deal of trouble in the world. He was unable to labor, and through the especial kindness of some officers, he had been allowed to bring that load of goods to the army that he might earn a trifle that way. He had two sick daughters at home; they had fits and might not live long. The boys heard his story with apparently the gravest respect, but they loved his pies better than they did his sick daughters, and as there was nothing in particular to hinder them, they took what they wanted. A general rush was made in the end, and each soldier grabbed what they could from the ruins, until all was consumed. This is what the boys call "rallying on a sutler." It was cruel sport to this man, but the boys enjoyed it immensely, and it was more from love of sport than from any other motive, that made them bother the sutler so, and steal his goods as they did. Had it been some sutlers I should have had no pity, but I could not help feeling heartily sorry for this man. His goods if properly sold might have brought him several hundred dollars.

About ten o'clock that night we got aboard a rickety train and came to Alexandria. We camped near the railroad till Wednesday morning, when we came aboard this boat. During the interval of our stay at Alexandria, the paymaster made us another visit and paid off part of the brigade. His visit was quite in time, as there was a glorious chance there to spend money, which many could not have improved had it not been for the opportune arrival of a supply of the welcome visitor. Pedlars of every description swarmed through our camps, and all were more or less patronized. Having been long in the field away from trade of all sorts, we had many wants to supply. Doubtless, of the money paid us, Alexandria retains the largest share. The Third Regiment came very near getting no pay at all, being paid, I am told, at the eleventh hour, while the Fourth got not a cent. The cause of this was some defect in the making out of the pay rolls. The Fourth boys are highly displeased with such bad management. They think it hardly fair that they should have to suffer that way for the blunders of others. But there are other injustices that speak even louder than this, and certainly call for redress. I allude to the way men sick and off to a general hospital are sometimes accounted for on the company muster roll, or rather how they are not accounted for, when their right to be so is as unquestioned as if they had carried arms and had done their duty with their regiment every minute of the time.

At my elbow at this moment sits a fellow who was sent away to a general hospital from Harrison's Landing, and who was absent till we left our camp near White Oak Church the last time. He was sent away by the regimental surgeon, and has been kept in a hospital or at a convalescent camp every day since. His officers knew where he had gone and knew that he no more intended to desert the service of his country than he did to commit suicide, yet they marked him a deserter and struck his name from the pay roll. He has not, during all this time, received a single cent of pay, and cannot get any now. At the present time his health is none too good, but he has filled his place in the ranks and borne the brunt and fatigue of the late tedious campaign, yet his status as a soldier is not recognized by the Government he has been fighting for, and he has no claims above that of a common deserter. Uncle Sam treats his negroes better than that. Had he died in the hospital or been killed in battle, the matter might never have been straightened out, and his back pay been lost. He brought certificates from the hospital surgeons, but from some defect the paymaster could not give him his money. Had he been apprised, when away, of the disposition that was being made of him in his company he could have done no different from what he did, but he was not acquainted with the facts till he had been absent a long time. Had he heard that he was a convicted murderer he could not have been more surprised than he was to hear of his desertion. But there was no remedy. A soldier in a hospital cannot return to his regiment when he chooses, he is completely at the disposal of the surgeon in charge. Had this soldier run away from his surgeon to his regiment he would have been considered a deserter from the hospital and perhaps got himself into a double dilemma without extricating himself from any. Let an officer be affronted and he can generally get satisfaction, or if he cannot do that he can generally resign and leave the hardships of war in other hands; but for us there is no alternative, in cases like these, but servile, slave-like submission. We were willing to leave our homes and our business to fight for the government, and, if duty requires, we are willing to do more; but we indignantly protest against being robbed of our good name and declared a criminal, or being deprived of our pay, unless there is some shadow of a cause for it.

Washington Square, New York
Sept. 1, 1863

The situation we occupy as I write to-day, differs in some respects very widely from what I have usually attempted to describe. To be sure we have a camp as usual, live in our little shelter tents as we always have, and sleep on our blankets now as has been our custom; but the rattling of carriages, the constant passing and repassing of well dressed ladies and gentlemen, and the busy hum of peaceful life, are things that we have long been strangers to. The interior of our humble tents may not differ sensibly from their former appearance, and the beautiful shade trees in the park give our camp and its immediate vicinity a resemblance to some of those selected in war-worn Virginia, but we are not accustomed to occupy ground laid out with so much taste and skill, or preserved by so much care and pains. The trees in this park have been kept almost too sacred to touch. The greensward has been constantly guarded by large notices to "Keep off from this grasss," and not the slightest thing that would defile a lady's parlor floor, has been allowed to remain here. The park has walks in all directions, paved with slabs of stone as smooth as marble. There is a large fountain and reservoir in the centre, which is not only a beautiful ornament to the place, but furnishes us a liberal supply of Croton water, the purest and best nature affords. Then we are surrounded on all sides by the lofty, elegant mansions owned by men of large wealth, in which we suppose people of culture and refinement dwell, and which I notice differ most essentially from our simple tents in point of comfort and convenience, if we can be allowed to judge of the magnificence of some of the apartments when brilliantly lighted, as we view them from the side of the street opposite. There are so many splendid luxuries in these mansions, that it seems to me any one would have to live a great while to enjoy them all. Some times I find it all I can do and more too, to enjoy the little that our unpretending tents afford.

The 2d and 4th Vermont, and nearly two regiments of regulars occupy this park for a camp. What we are here for, how long we are going to stay, and where we shall go when our stay here is ended, are questions that almost any one can ask easier than he can answer. We do but very little except to keep one another in camp. That is, guarding is our principal duty, and we have a great abundance of this. If there had been any attempts at rioting while the draft was proceeding,[15] we infer that it would have devolved upon us to show these rioters how public enemies are treated. A few of our lessons I fancy would have effectually satisfied their curiosity. Among all the old regiments brought here, I have seen no New Yorkers.[16] When we came here it was said that our President was afraid to trust Gov. Seymour with his own State troops, in case of riot. I am not sure whether it was the Governor or the troops that was the most distrusted. It was said that Gen. Howe was ordered to send here a brigade composed of other men than New York or New Jersey troops, and some of the best men that he had, and he concluded to send a brigade of pure Vermonters.[17] Evidently that General well understood his business.

We had quite a pleasant voyage from Alexandria, as pleasant as could be expected with a disabled engine, a strong head wind, and a sufficient admixture of sea-sickness with our sensations of pleasure, to maintain a natural equilibrium. We were four days coming from Alexandria to New York. We were packed into the boat from the hold to the upper deck, in a manner very similar, I take it, to that adopted by slave pirates in disposing of their cargo. Every available spot on the floor was a soldier's bed, and at night we were obliged to lie in rows, with our heads apart, and our feet and legs locked together dove-tail fashion, to make room. If our feet got to quarreling, it was a matter of their own, we seldom troubled ourselves to interfere. Sometimes, when a poor fellow, tired and sea-sick, came along, trying to pick his way over this corduroy of legs, the temptation to demand toll by intercepting his steps with our feet, was more than we could resist. If he fell headlong upon somebody else, we were willing to call it even, but we furnished him no safeguard that the next man should not, through anger or mirth, demand an additional penalty. The motion of the boat was everything in our favor, it took but little tripping to bring a man down. Only the sailors and other boatmen had free passage. We reckoned without our host when we tried to stop them.

Some of these boatmen had been engaged for considerable length of time in the transport service. I heard one of them, that appeared to occupy a superior position, descanting at great length upon his experience in this line of business, and what he had seen. It seemed that he had become a strong anti-administration man, owing to its peculiar negro policy. Having felt out the sentiment of the soldiers, he tried to convince them of the fact patent to everybody, as he thought, that the Government cared less for them than for the blacks. He told them he had been with transports loaded with soldiers, as we were then, only much worse, and he dwelt largely upon their sufferings in those miserable leaky vessels. They were always huddled in together, three times beyond the boat's capacity, in damp, dark rooms, and although they had repeatedly tried to have Government remedy some of the evils, they had always tried in vain. He had had them come to him continually for brooms to sweep away the mud, that they might have some show of a chance to spread their blankets. They had come to him, wet and shivering, and begged the privilege of warming themselves by his fire; and, as far as was in his power, he had always accommodated them. Well, he said this same steamboat of which he was speaking, fell into the hands of the Sanitary Commission,[18] who tore the inside all out of it and rigged it over as good as new, and now it was used exclusively to transport black troops and contrabands on the Mississippi and Gulf coast. This partiality for negroes was more than the steward's patriotism could stand, and so from that time he has been decidedly "down" on this "nigger war." If some of the boats were as bad as he described, then the Government or the Sanitary Commission were perfectly justifiable in repairing them, even if they were to be used only to transport wild beasts, but they were guilty in not repairing them before, as then they would have saved a great deal of suffering among the soldiers, and prevented this man from becoming an abuser of the Administration.

I suppose our appearance when we arrived at New York would hardly compare, in point of neatness, to the fancy soldiers the people had been accustomed to see. Our clothes were begrimed with dirt, for we had worn them through the summer campaign, and they had acquired a dirty look that all the soap and water in the world would not relieve them from. Our faces, too, from long exposure to the open air had been relieved of that delicate paleness which the dandy admires, but which the fighter for his country never wears. There was nothing of the ornamental sort about us, nothing superfluous or fanciful; we only had what stern necessity required. It was not our fault if we looked seedy; to look otherwise they must keep us out of the field. We had done the best we could. We had submitted to an inspection every day on the boat except one, and then we were too sea-sick to be inspected, we had scoured our brasses, blacked our boots, brushed our clothes, and did all that our means allowed, that we might present a passable appearance to the fashionable city of New York. We did not wish to come back from the field to be laughed at for our looks, certainly not in the copperhead city of New York.

But as we passed along the streets in Washington Square I noticed we did not entirely escape the critic's eye, and I heard some remarks that did not at all flatter my vanity. We were among the first of the troops that arrived from the army. I heard one man remark as we passed him that we were just from the field he knew by our bronzed faces and unpolished appearance. Another replied that we were just the men he had been anxious to see. We were men that could be relied upon, for we had been thoroughly proved. He had rather see one regiment of such troops as we were, than a dozen regiments of fancy militia. That man possessed a remarkable capacity for judging of human nature. None but the rioters can disagree with him.

A requisition for clothing was forwarded as soon as we got here, but it was not filled till last night. It was a large requisition, as nearly all the boys put their names down for almost an entire suit. If we get this clothing and have to throw our old ones away just as we are ready to go back again, we shall have no reason perhaps to be disappointed, after having so much experience in the circumlocution of war business, but we shall feel that we have not been treated like gentlemen, nor hardly as good soldiers ought to be. After wearing our old clothes during our stay here, it will be a waste that we can poorly afford, in these times of high prices, to throw them aside and take new ones into the field.

We were mustered yesterday for another two months' pay. We expect to be paid this time with less delay than usual. An order was read on dress parade the other evening for the muster and pay-rolls to be made out and forwarded as soon as possible, as there was a man in the city authorized to pay us, and we might be paid immediately. The New York people are shrewd, and doubtless they mean to figure the matter to have the soldiers spend their money here. It will suit us as well, for one dollar here is worth five on the Rappahannock.

Washington Square, New York City
September 4, 1863

We bid farewell to our little shelter tents to-day, and have just got us new A tents, and just got them furnished according to our rank and station, the best our means afforded. Indeed, the most of us have fixed ourselves up quite comfortable homes, in this beautiful park, so well that I am afraid the order to move will be shortly forthcoming, and I hasten to improve these spare moments that I may not lose the privilege of writing from them, at least one letter to the *Freeman*.

I have no great warlike achievements to record, nor particular exploits of bravery to mention. Firing on picket, even, is not heard here, and I know of no reason why I may not report all quiet along the lines. I certainly might were it not for some noisy venders of produce, who are continually challenging the boys to purchase of their goods, which we do, trading across the "lines" entirely regardless of the articles of war, and all other articles except the ones we wish to buy. This contraband traffic is carried on in the utmost good humor on both sides, and flags of truce are entirely dispensed with. We have had to skirmish through the camp occasionally, to drive out the juvenile population, but in these operations we are not always so brilliantly successful, for the ubiquitous rascals will either flank us, or spring up spontaneous in our rear. Getting rid of them is out of the question. After all, it is quite convenient to have these youngsters around, for some of them are the most accommodating fellows you ever saw. They are always on hand to run on errands, such as filling canteens, purchasing knicknacks, whatever we may want, always, of course, expecting a respectable commission. If we happen to have money of large denominations, they know right where to get the exact change wanted, and they generally manage to get it so effectually changed that it is never a trouble to the owner afterwards. If anyone has surplus rations, or anything else laid by, they are perfectly willing to relieve him from all care concerning their safe keeping. Once in a while there is a boy among them that would steal the meat from between one's teeth, almost, and they have a skill in their dishonest tactics, that would shame many an older accomplice.

We have had to preserve a line of sentinels around the camp here to keep the men from straggling away without passes. Besides the sentinels, there is, to prevent this, an iron fence of good, lawful height, which it is considered a breach of good conduct to jump, but a great many of the boys are just breachy enough to do it. At least I am told there are, especially after the roll call at night, when everything is quiet, and there are no indications of any enemy. I do not state this as a fact, but I have strong suspicions that it is so, for when I was on guard the other night, and walking my beat with all the dignity of a young veteran, I noticed a number of soldiers leaning against the fence near one end of the beat, and when I had walked to the opposite end and returned, I noticed these same fellows wasn't there. I had no means of finding out where they had gone to, for when I inquired, the boys only laughed, and said they were taking a walk. Perhaps they were. I noticed a number of fellows about that time walking rapidly down Fourth Street to Broadway, clothed in Uncle Sam's uniform, and they bore a strong resemblance to these. I felt very much grieved to have the rules of camp violated in such a manner, but I couldn't possibly prevent it.

But the best fun of all was to stand guard to keep the little children out of the park. They seemed to have the faculty of dodging a guard every way at once. If we told one to stay out of the park, and threatened him if he didn't, the next minute we might look to see him scampering like a wild cat away to the middle of the camp. They would seem to fly over the fence, invisibly, at least no one could see them till the thing was done, or else they would vanish from the street and scamper in the park. When other expedients failed, they would offer to bring a canteen of ice water for some of the boys, which of course we could hardly find a heart to forbid, and this would pass them in. Children when their parents were with them, were allowed to come in. I noticed many children followed parents that the latter did not own.

One day I was on guard before the camp was fairly organized, and the rules were, as they always are at such times, without head or tail, or all head and no tail. Children were not allowed to come in at all. The regulars had then a separate guard. There are three skeleton regiments of regulars in this park, the 3d, 4th, and 6th, but all three are not larger than one Vermont regiment. They occupy the southwest portion of the park. They guarded their own gates that day, and we guarded ours. At that time it so happened that these sentinels had received no instructions to keep the children away from the park, and the children soon found out that there was ingress there, and it was sought all the more because forbidden on our side. My post was on the west side. There was a large gate there for teams, which was kept closed, only when used, and on each side was a small gate for travelers on foot. I guarded one of these small gates and a regular guarded the other. My orders were strict to let none of the little brats into the park, but the regular might let in as many as he pleased. Troops of frolicking children were continually pressing to enter, but my bayonet afforded an inseparable barrier at that gate. It was amusing to notice how quickly their look of eager glee changed to one of grim despondency when I told them it was against the orders to let them in, and they saw I evinced a determination to keep them away. If they happened to think of it they would try the next gate, and when they saw there was nothing to hinder, they would march in in the greatest triumph. Of course it was a matter of perfect indifference to me, but when they turned and gave me a salute with their thumbs to their noses and their four fingers dangling in the air towards me, I began to appreciate the importance of my position, and to see great advantages arising from winning the respect of the rising generation thus early in the day. These young ones would certainly admire my firmness in preserving order, and they had here a lesson on the consistent management of the war, which they could understand, and which was a fair specimen on a small scale of the way the whole concern is carried on. Since that time, the guards have been united, and each regiment took their turn. The regulars are considered as one regiment. Matters are better arranged by this time. But the children carried their point; we have given up trying to keep them out.

But these youngsters were not the only ones to be affected by the annoyance of superfluous sentinels. Citizens at one time were proscribed from walking certain paths. A sergeant of police wished to know of me what our rules were. He said that as he was coming down through the park he was stopped by a sentinel and ordered to take another path. Very deferentially he complied, though for the life of him he could not tell what for. On the other path to which he had been directed, he was met by another sentinel and ordered back to the path he was traveling at first. Here was an awkward dilemma. He concluded to mark out a path for himself by taking a shorter cut down between the two sentinels and thus flank them both. He always made it a matter of conscience to obey all orders; but he said he could hardly see the use or the utility of our rules.

This police sergeant was what the soldiers would call a "bully fellow," and just the man to be highly popular among the boys. He could be trusted, so we asked him how it would fare with us if we were arrested for playing truant, and brought to his station house. In reply he said a number of our boys were discharged that morning after answering a few brief questions. The old Judge would ask them what their punishment would be when they returned to their company, and if he thought it was severe enough, he gave them some good advice and let them go. Twenty-four hours "log drill" would be sufficient for getting drunk and getting into a small row; twice twenty-four would pay for a big one. The sergeant told us very confidentially that if we wanted to go out to go, he should know us, and if we were arrested and brought to his station house, he would — a sly wink told the rest. Now we wish to have this kept a profound secret, because one of these nights we are going out on a regular "bum," and if we get back safe to camp through that sergeant's instrumentality, it would be the height of dishonor to get him into a scrape. That sergeant is a brave man, though he contends he could not stand the whistling minnies. He has charged pell mell upon gangs of rioters, and had received some hard knocks in his day, and still he persisted in saying that cold lead would be more than he could stand, and that he could never make a soldier. There was a roguish twinkle in his eye that made me discredit his statement, almost as much as he discredited it himself. I believe the old fellow would stand almost anything except copperhead ideas.

There has been a large influx of visitors from Vermont to see their friends here. Soldiers' wives have come to see their husbands and parents to see their sons. Visiting is done, however, to a disadvantage, as the general order grants no passes for a length of time exceeding two hours, and unless we can go out, one almost feels that it is like being visited in his prison. But where men can be trusted, our officers grant them all the privilege in their power, and sometimes more. The Vermonters have the name here of being the most orderly and civil troops that have been called to the city. Copperheads and rioters scowl because we occupy their beautiful parade-grounds, but other citizens are pleased to have us here.

———————

Poughkeepsie, N.Y.
Sept. 12, 1863

The past few weeks have found our brigade more scattered than perhaps at any time before since it was created. The 4th regiment remains at New York, the 3d is at Newark, N.J., and the 5th and 6th are at Kingston, some seventeen or eighteen miles from this place. There were vague reports of a little disturbance there yesterday, but they need confirmation. I believe it is generally allowed that we have kept pretty good order here in New York since we have been made the instrument of executive authority here. Hitherto our regiment has seen nothing but peace and good will, and it seems not unlikely that we shall go back to the war without having a chance to show the New York copperheads our remarkable prowess. It will be just as they see fit to have it; it is a matter of perfect indifference to us.

We came here a week ago to-night a little after midnight. There was no opposition shown as we quietly took possession of the town, and no attempt has yet been made to dislodge us. I don't know whether it was especially intended that we should land at that unseasonable hour, a day sooner than we were expected, but it was very convenient for our friends, and enemies too; it saved them the trouble of a reception. There was no demonstration of any kind. Not a drum was beat nor a brickbat thrown. We marched quietly by the barracks built for the 150th N.Y.S.V., just east of the city, and appropriated them for our comfort. The daily *Eagle* said next morning that we marched through the city in a very soldierly manner, our closed ranks and quiet behavior giving evidence of the discipline we had acquired during two years' active service. We had no idea that we were behaving so remarkably well till we saw it in the newspapers, and we imagine it must have taken an "eagle's" eye to have discovered it. The same paper went on to give a very flattering account of the "roll of honor" that the "war scarred veterans" of this regiment had by their bravery won. It gave a short history of our career during the war so far; of the thirteen battles we had fought, and complimented us upon our personal appearance. (We had blacked our shoes that morning according to orders, and have drawn our new clothes as I told you before, so I expect we *do* look first rate. The ladies say we do, and their opinion is worth everything in such matters.) The daily *Poughkeepsian* tried to puff for us a little but it came far short of the *Eagle*. This excited their envy and they turned upon the *Eagle's* enthusiastic reporter and showered upon his unsuspecting head a scorching tirade of criticism. His grammar and rhetoric was wickedly ridiculous, and to close, the *Poughkeepsian* thought if the brave Green Mountain Boys could stand such a fire of ungrammatical stuff as that, we certainly deserved great credit. Well, Mr. *Poughkeepsian,* we think we can stand it. We have no objection to being spoken of in that style, and even if the reporter should fib a little when facts run short, we believe we could stand it all very well. We sincerely wish the *Poughkeepsian* to be relieved of any further distress in this matter on our accounts.

We have had the finest of weather since we have been here, and we have finely enjoyed it. A number of the soldiers telegraphed for their wives as soon as they got here, and as the papers said next day, "many had already arrived, and happiness beamed upon the countenances of all." A great many had their parents and friends from Vermont come here to see them, so that coming here was almost as gratifying as a furlough. Our Colonel, one of the finest of men, gave these men privileges to be absent from camp all that they could reasonably ask for. As our new A tents that we had received at New York just in season to occupy for a day and night, were brought along here, some of the married soldiers pitched them just outside of the camp and gave their wives a practical instruction to a soldier's life in real camp style. We never have been in a camp that has seemed so cheerful and pleasant as this one. So many neatly dressed ladies and gentlemen, so courteous and civil, mingling constantly with us, it makes the soldier forget his roughness, and the wholesome restraints of civil society are strongly felt.

We drill here two hours each day; a company drill in the forenoon and battalion drill in the afternoon. The order specifying the hour for these drills and the hour for dress parade is published every day in the daily papers, and large numbers of the citizens are always present to see us perform our military manoeuvers. Every afternoon as the hour for drilling arrives, a stream of carriages of all descriptions begin to pour in until at four o'clock there is quite a concourse of people collected in camp and on the hillside that overlooks the parade ground below. The boys take pride in drilling before so respectable an audience of spectators, and I know Col. Walbridge was not dissatisfied with our drilling on the last occasion; his smiles of approval told us plainly that he was not. It has been some time since we have drilled any before, but we believe we have not quite forgotten how. We gave our audience some practical illustrations of a few of the manoeuvers on a battle-field. The Colonel deployed one Company as skirmishers in front of the regiment and ordered them to lie down and load and fire. They went through with all the motions as we have been instructed in such things except actually firing — loading on their backs, then turning on their faces, fire, and immediately reload. The skirmishers being sorely

pressed, he ordered them to fire in retreat, while the regiment behind supporting them pitched in a few volleys and then charged. With a shout, not quite so
full of energy perhaps as one we gave on a certain occasion near the city of
Fredericksburg, but something like it, we rushed forward double quick, when
at the command "down," we were prostrate in an instant. As soon as the
enemy's volley of shot and shell sent to annihilate our charge was supposed to
be fairly over, we got up and resumed operations once more. The ladies
laughed and the children shouted with delight. It was fun for them, and for us
too on this occasion, but we have seen these same manoeuvers performed when
the attending circumstances made the operation a little less pleasing. Were it
not for that part we take it our drafted men would be more acquiescent.

The draft here now is the all prevailing topic. But little seems to be said or
thought of anything else. It is now just completed. The city draft was made last
Monday. The conscripts here submitted to their fate with philosophical
coolness. They had a grand evening parade that night and seemed to feel highly
elated at the distinguished honor Uncle Sam had conferred upon them by taking them into his protection or sending them to protect him. The draft here as
everywhere falls very hard on some. One young man with a wife and three little
children who had just built him a new house and was commencing a prosperous
business was elected to go. It seemed worse than death to him to be torn from
his interesting family and have his business prospects ruined. He was too much
in debt to pay $300, and if he went to war there was no chance for him to pay
for his house. Surely this is a "cruel war." I saw women returning from the
Provost Marshal's office, when the names for the city of Hudson were drawn,
their eyes red with weeping, having I suppose heard the name of some of their
dearest kin announced at the fatal wheel. I saw other young men who said their
names were drawn, and I felt heartily glad of it. They could go to war as well as
not. But these were the very ones that were going to make the disturbance.
Three young fellows whose names were drawn told me in conversation of their
plans for escape. One had lost his front teeth and he expected to be exempt
because he could not bite off a cartridge; another had had a very lame hip years
before and since the draft it was worse than ever, he expected to be exempt on
that; the third had a rich father-in-law that he expected would pay his $300. It is
needless to say that every one of these fellows if they were now in the service
would have to stay there. Some declare that old Abe shall never get Uncle
Sam's clothing on them at any hazard. They calculate probably to fight the law
or flee from its enforcement, but they are making a very sorry calculation. They
are fighting against their country and against their God — fighting in the service of Satan and Jeff Davis and they are fools if they think they shall win in

the end. Occasionally a man of principle evinces a determination to go and do his duty the best he can. God bless such men.

Unless a man has patriotism of the most exalted kind, a high sense of duty and an undoubting faith in the righteousness of our cause to lean back upon in his hour of trial, he has a poor support. It is only the man that truly loves his country, and believes that we are fighting for God and humanity, that can cheerfully submit to his fate when drafted. It is utterly impossible for any others to do so. Standing target for the rebel minnies, is one of the most uncomfortable positions a man was ever placed in, as I can tell you from experience, and we do not wonder that some men pray to be excused when the country calls for such work. But the man who has resolutely made up his mind to do his duty like a worthy American citizen, who scorns to pay his $300 or plead disability, all honor to him. We ask your hand. With you we will willingly, gladly fight side by side, and when this dark cloud of war has passed away, and the clear sunlight of peace shines out once more to gladden our beloved country, we will walk this blessed land of freedom with a prouder step and a nobler heart, from the consciousness that our own efforts contributed to rescue the country from ruin and disgrace when traitors in arms plotted against it. But the poor copperhead, whose soul is in his pocket, we need not wonder that he resists when called upon to risk his precious life for the nation's welfare. It is the most natural thing in the world that he should do so, and we will have all charity possible for him.

Camp near Culpeper Court House, Va.
Sept. 25, 1863

We are once more back again with the Army of the Potomac in our accustomed place, and doing our accustomed duties. Our recall from New York was rather sudden and unexpected. The draft to be sure had been accomplished, but the men had not been taken away, and then was when the trouble might be expected if the draft was to be resisted at all. Our services would then be needed if ever. But the order came for us to return. Meade was contemplating an advance, and no doubt felt keenly the weakness of his army while we were away. The rebels were sending away troops to swallow Rosecrans, and now was the golden moment to strike for Richmond. But what could the Army of the Potomac do without its Vermont brigade? We saved it from destruction in one campaign, and Gen. Meade is not so fool-hardy as to risk another while his main dependence was absent. So in all haste we were re-called to the army, leaving our dear friends, the copperheads, to work out their own destruction. Well, we are here, but I fear the golden moment is lost. The celebrated "eight days' ration" order is in full force and we are liable to move at any time. We may be ordered on towards Richmond and then — Heaven save the mark — may have to skedaddle back again. Our wide awake foes will have whipped the Tennessee army and be back here ready to whip us before we are half prepared for our punishment. It would be no more than we deserve for our proverbial remissness. Should it turn out so, the North ought to sit in sackcloth and ashes and count it an honor to kiss the dust from Jeff Davis' feet. They ought to be excluded forever from the family of nations as unworthy the sacred trust. The poorest scholar can't help seeing that if the North would only rise now like a lion conscious of his strength we might smash the Con-federacy all to atoms in a very short time. But instead of that the North hangs back, only doling out a few miserable conscripts, or substitutes rather, now and then when they can't help it, who are more trouble to us than they are worth, and whose courage consists chiefly in daring to desert. The rebels themselves shame us, and compel our very respect by their dogged perseverance. They can call every man into the army, and it does not seem to require a large portion of their army to enforce their conscription. They work to win; we work because we are obliged to. It is more respectable to be a live worker on the wrong side, than a drone on the right side. But we have not ad-vanced yet, so of course we are safe at present, and while we are awaiting orders I will give a brief account, in my homely way, of our journey here from New York.

We left Poughkeepsie Sunday, the 13th inst., at noon, in the Knickerbocker, and stopped that night in New York harbor. We were transferred from the Knickerbocker to another steamboat whose name I have forgotten, which took us the next day to South Amboy, on the Jersey coast, some thirty miles from New York city. At this latter place we got aboard the cars and came by railroad to Washington. The latest style for soldiers are simply freight cars with boards propped up for seats. For windows, we had the benefit of two side doors to begin with, but long before our journey was concluded we had plenty of ven-tilation, owing principally to the energetic use of the butt end of somebody's gun-stock on the boards at different places on the sides of the car. Each car was filled as full it would hold of men, knapsacks and rations, huddled in together promiscuously. It took a shrewd genius to identify himself in that place.

It was near midnight when we got to Philadelphia. At the Cooper Shop Volunteer Refreshment Saloon we found a glorious supper ready prepared expressly for us. Bread of an excellent quality, butter and cheese, pickles, hot coffee, and all that a hungry soldier need ask. It was not soldiers' living at all; it was good enough for a first class hotel. This is the first place of the kind that has been opened since the war broke out, and I doubt if any more modern, can surpass it. It came just in time, for we were both tired and hungry, and we could not possibly compose ourselves to hard tack and pork so soon after leaving Poughkeepsie, and this was all that was provided us. We had fasted with wonderful patience till then. I imagine the proprietors of that Shop have no insignificant ideas of our capacity to dispose of good food when we can get it. Supper over, we formed into line again outside, where we had stacked our guns, and giving three hearty cheers for our reception, we started on our way through the city to take another train. Here we were packed into the cars again as before. There was every shade of difference between that and a regular sleeping car, but notwithstanding that, I slept most soundly there till morning. I might have slept there till this time, for ought I know, if my next neighbor had not accidentally put his boot into my face, which made sleeping so uncomfortable that I concluded to wake up. Almost all the boys in that car slept as soundly as I did. I have read of travelers who were prone to regard sleeping cars as a failure, saying that it was impossible for one to compose himself to slumber while he was being rattled over the road at locomotive speed. I wish such a man could have looked into that car about three o'clock that morning; he would have seen his argument floored most effectually. There the boys lay in all shapes imaginable, and a great many shapes that no one would think of imagining; some on the seats and some under them, some lying down and some sitting up, and some in all manner of positions from a horizontal to a perpendicular, with their knapsacks, equipments, guns or boots for a bed or pillow. The train vibrated along over the rough road, and occasionally shake one out of his position, but still the boys snored on in blissful unconsciousness. The rocking of the car was only a lullaby that wooed them to a sounder sleep. As we were an extra train, we had to wait for every other train and go the swifter when the time was ours. The consequence was that our progress was slow, and daylight overtook us before we reached Havre de Grace. At this place the whole train, engine and all, was ferried across the bay. There is a bridge to be constructed here, and its foundation is being laid, but it is as yet in its infancy. At this place we stopped long enough to buy us a breakfast all around at the groceries near by. It is curious how quickly the prices of eatables advance in a small place at the advent of a regiment of soldiers. The moment we stopped I stepped into a bakery and bought a loaf of bread for five cents. Handing this to a friend, I returned to the same place and found bread selling rapidly at two loaves for fifteen cents. A few minutes later and the price was ten cents a loaf, and still going up. The price of cheese went up to 25 cents a pound, and that of butter was more than doubled. I hope the people had their shopping done for that day before we got there. All at once the whistle sounded and the train started. More than half of the boys were off the train, and for a few minutes there was a nimble scampering from all points converging upon the moving train, and making all possible haste to get aboard. Freight cars are not the prettiest of vehicles to get on to when in motion, and had one fallen and broken his neck on that occasion, no trial short of a court martial could have made him out a criminal. At half past eleven we entered the city of Baltimore. We made a stop of about an hour, which gave us a chance to eat dinner and all the watermelon we wanted, when we were put aboard another train and started towards Washington. This train was crowded to overflowing inside and on the top. Before, all had been kept inside. The officer of the day peremptorily ordered one of us who had climbed to the top to enjoy the cool breeze and fine prospect, to get down from the cars and ride inside. Now the top of the cars were covered, and the same officer of the day never noticed us. Military necessity they said made the difference. Some of the boys persisted in seeing it in another light. They said it was for their convenience then to ride on the outside, but the officer for the day forbade it; now it was for his convenience to have us outside, and he made us ride there. Circumstances are quite apt to alter cases.

It was after nine o'clock when we got to Washington, and an hour later before we got straightened around so as to know where we belonged. We went into the Soldiers' Retreat and took our supper, and then were marched to the barracks. Our fare at the Retreat, was far below the Poughkeepsie or Philadelphia standard, and some of the boys who had eat their fill of dainties along the way, considered themselves abased because their appetite failed them on this occasion. I remember a time, when a meal there was a rare luxury. There was no disturbance, however, owing partly to Colonel Walbridge's presence, and that of other officers. The Colonel told the boys, that the bread was good and the meat was good, but if we did not want it we could let it alone — a common sense deduction truly. His firmness prevented any disgrace.

The next day we went over to Alexandria, and Friday we started for the army. We had to march the whole distance, and escort a long train for the army's use from Alexandria. The day we started the rain poured in torrents. I have seldom seen it rain harder. It seemed as if the windows of heaven were opened, and doors too. It was rather of a rough introduction to the war again. Some of the boys had scarcely a dry thread in their clothes, but they were all full of fun and frolic, and never seemed to enjoy themselves better. "How are you New York, and how are you Poughkeepsie;" the contrast was so great that it was considered a joke and laughed at accordingly. It takes more than one equinoctial storm to sober such a brigade as the First Vermont. We didn't make a very long march that day; it was impossible. We halted before we got to Fairfax, put up our tents, built us fires, and made ourselves as comfortable as possible. Some of the boys took off their clothes, gave them a thorough wringing, then put them on again to dry. In this process they were assisted by a keen northwest wind, for it had stopped raining, and the wind had shifted to that cold quarter. The next day we made the distance to Centreville, and Sunday we proceeded on to Catlett's Station. At all these places along the Railroad, a large guard is left to protect the road from guerrilla depredations. The Eleventh Corps has this comparatively easy duty, by virtue of their being such excellent skedaddlers in time of battle. Our boys were cruel in their jokes on these fellows, and take every occasion to let them know that their peculiarities are appreciated. One of them happened to be walking very rapidly in a direction contrary to ours. "Is there a battle going on in front?" asked one of our boys of him with great apparent sincerity and earnestness. Not that he knew of, he replied. "What in h—l is your hurry" was the rejoinder. On another occasion, which I shall poorly describe, a group of their men and ours were talking together and laughing quite loud, when one of the boys mildly recommended, that we should be cautious and calm in our conversation for in case of too loud talk or excitement, we might "get the Eleventh Corps to running." The occasion and the peculiar drollery of the expression are indescribable, and the victims themselves were obliged to laugh. They bore our joking with remarkably good humor.

Monday night we pitched our tents on the rebel soil of the Rappahannock. Tuesday we finished our journey, and from the length of my letter, I think it high time that that was finished too.

Second Vermont Regiment
Warrenton, Va.
Nov. 5, 1863

We are off picket to-day, an event not so very remarkable in itself, aside
from the fact that it gives us a short respite from ordinary camp duties, and
leaves us free to employ the time as our inclinations may choose. So military
duties being for the present disposed of, I shall turn to the next duty in order,
which it is plain can be no other than to write to my old friend the *Freeman*. I
notice that my letter No. 42, written from Centreville, did not appear, but its
place was too well occupied to make either the public or the writer feel very
deeply its loss.

The news here in camp is not of very charming importance. We have remained here long enough to become thoroughly accustomed to the place, and
to begin to regard it with the respect due to an old camp. We drill every day and
sometimes twice a day. We have our company drills and our brigade drills, our
battalion drills and our division drills, to say nothing of our skirmish drills and
reviews without number. We have our reviews as often as the commanding officers see fit to order them, which has been remarkably often for the last week
or two. They had a division review last Wednesday, while we were on picket,
and therefore we cannot speak of its faults or its excellencies, for being away we
were obliged to lose the whole benefit of it, and if I should give you any account of it, which I shall not do, you would have to take it second-handed. The
boys that did act a part in that review, represent it as a very fatiguing affair,
and I have not seen a single soldier that considered it any way amusing or interesting. We soldiers are not always disposed to appreciate the beauty of these
drills and reviews, especially when they are tediously prolonged, and when the
orders to execute the different manoeuvers are pretty thickly interspersed with
the order to double quick. Gen. Sedgwick was the reviewing officer on this occasion, and in order that he might entertain as exalted an opinion as possible of
this superb division, every man was ordered out that could go, and a great
many were ordered out that pretended they were sick and couldn't go. Even a
part of the brigade guard — the relief off duty — was ordered to help swell the
ranks on this occasion, and one fellow who was tired and cross when he came
in, positively asserts that several who were dead and buried barely escaped being ordered out, their escape being due not so much to the fact that they were
dead simply, but because they were buried out of convenient reach, besides

being on that account constitutionally discharged from further service in the Army of the Potomac. I shall ask no one to endorse an opinion quite so extravagant.

Last Sunday we were reviewed by Gen. Howe. Monday a detail was made for picket, taking from a dozen to fifteen or twenty from each company. We were ordered to take with us two days' rations, an order that we could not for the life of us obey, from the fact that there were no two days' rations to be had. I know of one fellow that couldn't rake or scrape together a dozen hard tack, either by begging, borrowing or buying, and I know of another — the corporal himself — who had but seven crackers, and four of these he borrowed unbeknown to the former owner. We were obliged to trust to Providence and go ahead. The first reserve was down to the foot of this frigid pinnacle, near a citizen's house; the second reserve was still further out from camp, and at this reserve we were ordered to halt. We were to stay here all day. We stacked arms, and at the word halt, we concluded the most comfortable place to dump our knapsacks was on the sunny side of a stone wall, and here we stationed ourselves, and picketed for the next twenty-four hours with all our might. The succeeding twenty-four we spent on post. All day long we remained faithfully near this reserve, according to strict orders, employing our time principally in falling into line and presenting arms to certain officers every time they came around. Every soldier is aware of the peculiar faculty these officers have of coming around just as we are busily engaged perhaps in reading a story, perhaps in trying to indite a letter to a friend, or perhaps endeavoring to make a cup of tea, or drink one that is made, in which case they will always make it a point to stay till our tea is cold and our appetites spoiled. After they have remained long enough to impress us with the importance of their errand or a sense of their own personal dignity, they kindly condescend to allow us to break ranks again and resume our own unimportant avocations. Of course we accept such a kindness with the meekest gratitude, and straightway forget that that officer and ourselves bear the remotest relation to each other. Reckless soldiers often swear about very small things, and we have known them to indulge their profane propensities quite freely on occasions like these. One fellow, at the time of which I am speaking, had been assiduously preparing him a cup of coffee for his dinner, and which he seemed to regard as of more than ordinary value because it was the last that he had the material for making. He had, by dint of considerable perseverance, started a fire, and had just got his coffee heated to the boiling point, when the officer of the day came along and he was ordered with the rest of us to fall in. Everybody knows that when coffee first boils it takes a mischiverous fancy to running over, and at that critical moment it has to be attended to or it will waste. This fellow in his anxiety to see his coffee in a safe condition to leave waited a little too long. His coffee made out to boil, however, but in his hurry to remove it from the fire he spilled the whole of it, and burned himself in the bargain. This was not a very important event of itself, but it was more than this soldier could master, and the consequence was that he invoked terrible imprecations of wrath upon the heads of all officers in general and this one in particular. If the supreme control of events had been left to his discretion, we should have trembled for the fate of that officer, engaged as he was, in the innocent discharge of his duties. We do not wish to be misunderstood as trying to speak lightly of these military transactions, for as a means of discipline, no doubt they are very useful, but a common soldier is apt to overlook that point and consider only what important bearing they can have in putting down rebellion.

Night came, and we built us great rousing fires of rails, that we appropriated from a fence close up to this citizen's house. In Vermont we should have thought such sacrilege unpardonable, but here it was a very comfortable necessity. The next morning, when we went to buy a canteen of milk of the lady there, we could not help noticing the wearing effect that a daily contemplation of the desecrations going on here was having upon her health and spirits. She was worrying herself to death. The provost guard, who had been stationed there to protect her and her property, and who probably was allowed liberties that a stranger might not assume, advised her in our hearing not to "care" so much. He warned her that she was killing herself, and she did not attempt to deny the truth of what he said. I never saw a more complete specimen of a broken hearted woman in my life. Nothing but the presumption that she might be notoriously rebel in her inclinations could have prevented me from giving her my fullest sympathies. As it was I had no heart to burn any more of her rails, or commit any other depredations whereby she might be the sufferer. I know nothing of her history or her circumstances, I only judge from what I saw.

The next day we went out on to the line. We were strung along in small supports of about six men and one officer, commissioned or non-commissioned, at each. The line itself was a little further out, and each support kept two men out on the line all the time, relieving one another at regular hours. In this way the day passed off and night too, and morning came, when we were to be relieved. The relief did not come however at the appointed time; they were to stay and attend the review before relieving us. It was now a question of a pretty serious importance what we should do for rations. Every one of us was out, and some had fasted since the noon before. Our distress was only aggravated by the cook's coming out with barely hard tack enough for dinner, but with none to atone for the last supper and breakfast. Matters began to look quite serious. What was to be done? One fellow proposed on his own responsibility to go into camp and see what he could get. Rations had been drawn the night before, and we must have them. The corporal, who deserves a high promotion for his faithful performance of duty under all circumstances, dare not allow one to go to camp without the captain's consent. Possibly that consent could be obtained. There was no harm in asking him. Back we went to the last reserve and stated our case to Captain Wales. We had the captain's sympathy, but he candidly told us that he had no authority to let us go in from picket. We were to be released he said at four o'clock. The captain knew as well as we did that the relief would not get to us till after dark, if it did then. He thought we could stand it till four o'clock, and so we could without anything, but we felt that the North, with all her immense resources, ought to furnish us with a few more hard tack. We told the boys the result of our mission to the captain, and they began to think the case was hopeless. But we could not give it up. We looked at our haversack, it was entirely empty, and our stomach felt equally void. We thought of our scanty breakfast, and the thought made us hungry and indignant. We thought of our supper the night before, and the thought made us so hungry that we couldn't stand it any longer, and so indignant that we wouldn't. We determined at once to go into camp and risk the consequences. The corporal was asleep and the captain was out of sight, so shouldering a haversack, in utter defiance of all reprimands, guard houses or court martials, we posted into camp and returned with it full of hard tack. We could feast now to our heart's content, and in our condition it was hardly necessary to ignore the fact that they were wormy and full of bugs. But to make short a tedious story, we will simply say that we were duly relieved at nine o'clock that night and allowed to come back to camp.

We learned on reaching camp that a sad accident had occurred to one Goodell of Co. E. A fellow in Co. K discharged his musket, and the ball, after destroying one of his own toes, lodged in the leg of the man, and inflicted so serious a wound as to render amputation necessary.

Second Vermont Regiment
November 13, 1863

Doubtless your readers have long before this time read every particular of the fight near Rappahannock Station, where the 6th army corps surprised and captured upwards of a thousand prisoners, and where the 5th Wisconsin and 6th Maine covered themselves with glory, and the battle-field with their dead. I shall not attempt to give you any particulars of that interesting, though bloody affair, beyond what has already been given. I only wish to be allowed to tell my story of the events as they appeared to me, and tell it in my own homely way.

We left our camp at Warrenton Saturday morning, a little after sunrise, with knapsacks packed, and with six days' rations. The movement took us by surprise, although we knew that such an event was liable to occur at any time. As usual we were preparing our tents for comfort, not exactly as we used to in summer, but exactly as we are obliged to in winter or freeze, of which I hope I may have occasion to speak more particularly in some future letter. The boys, of course, dislike to labor patiently on their "house" for several days, and then leave the house and lose their labor; but on this occasion the officers were as much the losers as we in that matter, for nearly every one of them had made fire-places to their tents, and chimneys to their fire-places, and apparently were as ignorant of any intention to move as the least of us. Friday, the day previous, an old-fashioned brigade drill had been ordered, which was to take place at two o'clock, the usual hour, but just before that time arrived, we were notified of the impending march, and told that the drill was to be postponed, and we could devote our time to our own benefit as each man chose. The principal military business that we had to attend to was to draw six days' rations, and the principal private business was perhaps to write a letter or so, when we were ready for any event that might be called for. Long before morning the orderly came to each and every tent to be sure we were all of us awake, and by the time appointed, early daylight, we had shouldered our knapsacks and our six days' rations, and a little later we were on the road once more to Dixie's capital in as high spirits as if we had never travelled that way before. We made remarkably good time on our march, the weather was cool and we kept our ranks closed in a manner as gratifying to the officers as to ourselves. We accomplished twelve miles or more before noon. By that time we began to feel that to halt and rest for a short time would be an agreeable exchange for so much marching, and that a few moments' attention to the contents of our haversacks would be by no means unpleasant. We noticed in an open field in front of us that the troops were huddling in together in various shapes, and we hardly knew whether they were forming *en masse* to give us our customary hour's "nooning," or what disposal they were going to make of us. We had a line of skirmishers marching on our right flank, who were deployed a few rods in front of the troops, and these were halting and moving as if in doubt of what they really ought to do. Still further ahead as we faced to the right, away to the top of the hill, could be seen another line of men, and there was quite a discussion in the ranks whether they were friends, or foes. Before we halted to rest, our regiment was swung round into line on the right, where we stacked arms and rested till the middle of the afternoon. Whether the line of men alluded to were rebels or not, it was now pretty evident that we were in the near vicinity of the enemy, for the positions that the different commands were assuming were almost exactly like those we always assumed when we approach the enemy, or are actually on the battle-field.

During our halt the important preliminary operations are going on elsewhere, and when the time came for us to act our part we were ordered forward. Skirmish firing had commenced with vigor, and the object of our mission was no longer a matter of conjectures. We marched in close column by division through a piece of woods where we halted at the foot of the hill, on the top of which we had seen the rebel line of skirmishers. A strong line of battle now occupied the crest of the hill, of an identity ummistakable, with their faces leeward, while the rebel shells were bursting over their heads in a manner that might have unnerved any but the bravest of troops. Sharp musketry firing was heard just over the other side of the hill. This "hill," I might say in passing, is not at all like Vermont hills, abrupt and steep, but a long continued swell, rising barely high enough to hide those on one side from being seen by those on the opposite. A cannon-ball fired on one side would describe an arc that would almost exactly correspond to the lay of the land, and many of the rebel shot and shell fired at the line on the top of the hill came screaming over and lodging unpleasantly near us, so much so that we were obliged to change our position once to get more out of danger. I don't know that any one in our regiment was hit or hurt, but I know that just on my right there was a soldier, a knapsack, and six days' rations tumbled into a promiscuous heap on account of a cannon-ball plunging dangerously near them. As no one was hurt, and only one fellow very much frightened, we concluded that we had a right to laugh at this fellow's mishap, although it was a miracle that he was not killed dead on the spot. These cannon-balls as they came tearing along through the air almost exactly in our range, could often be distinctly seen although the batteries from which they were fired were over the hill out of sight. Some of them appeared to be oblong chunks of iron, and looked like a bird flying swiftly through the air, though they moved so very rapid as to appear to the eye a mere speck, utterly incompetent to make the shrieking noise that always followed them.

We expected to be ordered forward every minute, but the regiments engaged needed none of our help, and we remained where we were until the firing had ceased, and night had come on. It was quite cold, and we soon had great rousing fires built, and our coffee made, when the order came for us to go on picket to their support. We remained in line all night and till noon Sunday, when the order came to advance. All had been quiet that forenoon, and no firing heard except now and then a gun fired by some timid picket, aimed probably at some imaginary rebel, or else fired by some mischievous soldier, aimed at a rabbit or a pig (by mistake of course), but which is of too frequent an occurrence to occasion any remark. The story was told of our brilliant success the night before, which was cheering enough. Our men had captured 1200 prisoners, took their battery, and drove the enemy out of sight and hearing. The rebels fought well, but were caught in a trap and had to surrender. One rebel lieutenant showing fight after he had surrendered his men, had his brains knocked out by the butt of a gun for his cowardly audacity.

On our way back we passed over the ground of the fight, covered, as such places usually are, with pieces of cartridge boxes, muskets and other broken implements of war. There were graves being dug, and a little further along were several rebels sleeping their last sleep, and only waiting their turn to be laid away in their last resting place. Alas for them! Even the soldiers hardened by war, whose duty it was to consign them to their rough tombs, felt a touch of sympathy for their sad fate, and for the moment forgot that a few hours before they were engaged in deadly strife with the senseless handful of clay that lay stiff and dead before them.

We crossed the Rappahannock just above the earthworks that are on each side of the river at this place, on the rebels' pontoon bridge. The railroad bridge that we burned a month ago, was just below these same earthworks. We moved forward in a shape to give or receive battle any time that our enemies were willing to accept a fight. Marching in line of battle is the hardest way in the world to march, but we advanced to Brandy Station in that way, a distance of about five miles. This same distance and same ground we had marched over once before in the same way. It was a month lacking four days before; and on that time we were reconnoitering to see if Lee was trying to chase us; now we were sure that we were chasing him, and to all appearances quite successfully. We slept in line of battle, at least such was our position, for we were on a good place, and expected a fight, but so far as sleeping was concerned, we had very indifferent success, for the night was intensely cold, and the raw north-west wind utterly disregarded all the blankets we could pile on to us. We built us fires of material that we had to glean from far and wide, for troops have passed and repassed over the ground so much that every rail and every bit of fuel has been picked up and burned long ago. Each fire had a circle of men around it, who would warm themselves, and then lay down and sleep till the cold drove them back to the fire again. We remained here till Monday night, when we marched further upon the right to our present position. We are now about six miles from Rappahannock Station, and about half that distance from the river.

––––––––––––

Second Vermont Regiment
Nov. 20, 1863

We have just returned from a corps review by Gen. Sedgwick, and as these reviews almost always precede an onward movement, I will venture to improve the present opportunity, and write you a line or so, before I find that I have no opportunity to improve.

Our review came off just out in front of our camping ground. There was not much connected with this review different from all other reviews, and these have occurred so often, and have been so frequently described, that they no longer excite the interest that they used to, and we regard them as a matter of course. After all, a review is quite an imposing affair. The Sixth Corps when it is all together, artillery and all, makes quite a little army by itself. On these occasions, we brighten up our guns and our brasses, and brighten up ourselves, so far as soap and water and clothes brushes will do it, and try to make the best appearance possible. I fancy we had pretty good success in that, at this review, and I believe old Sedgwick thought so too. Our regiment happened to be placed clear to the left of the whole corps, and when the General and staff passed around from front to rear, he had a better flank view of our regiment than he did of any of the rest, except the regiment clear to the right. We stood in close column by divisions, that is, each division (two companies) stood in line, ranged one behind another, and the distance of one company's length from each other. We were in open order, the rear rank of each division four paces behind the front rank, and in this position it is supposed that the General and other officers can have the best possible view of us. The other regiments, brigades and divisions, were formed along on our right, in the same way. We stood in line, as straight as chalk work, and looked as brave, as tidy, and as intelligent, as Vermonters always do, and I know Gen. Sedgwick thought our regiment was a capital good one, or else his countenance told an enormous fib. He looked satisfied beyond measure.

After he had passed around and viewed us as we stood, he took his position on a convenient eminence, with a whole battalion of mounted officers ranged on either side of him, among whom were some foreigners with their square-top caps and elegant uniform, and before these officers we "passed in review," in the same position relatively that we occupied as we stood, only we were in "closed order" and spread out twice the distance between each division. By the time the whole corps had stretched itself out far enough to double this distance between each regimental division, those that started first had got back to about where we were, when it came our turn to start. At one point we passed over a prominent knoll where we could see the whole circle, and it was quite an interesting spectacle to witness. The whole body was moving along in regular order, keeping time to good music, which gave a peculiar, undulating motion to the moving column, and an effect to the view that never can be transferred to the most natural and life-like pictures.

We moved to this place a week ago last Monday. About that time we were having some weather that we called most uncomfortably cold. We moved from Brandy Station that night, a short distance of between two and three miles in nearly a northwest direction. The rebels have had their camps all around here. These worthies had built them some very nice quarters here, as if they intended to remain here all winter. They had their log houses "mudded up," and their fire-places of a peculiarly serviceable pattern, that even we shrewd Yankees have, in some instances, copied after to advantage. From appearances, I should judge that we had driven them out from here in rather unconvenient haste, as they had left more camp equipage, old clothes and the like, than we generally find in camps that they have left.

But very few of us put up any tents, and I imagine but very few of us slept any that first night, unless they had a great deal better success than I did. The keen northwest wind direct from the frigid zone was our tormenter, and we couldn't get away from it. Cover ourselves over ever so nicely with blankets, head, ears, toes and all, and a current of air like a current of ice cold water would feel us out, and spoil our comfort. Night passed away but the cold weather did not. For several days and nights it remained the same. We gathered wood with all our might, and built us fires large and high, and in this way managed very well to keep warm. The exercise of gathering the wood, however, deserved the principal share of the credit, for the fire would burn but not warm us. The camp is in what was a short time ago a magnificent oak forest, but many of the tall trees had been culled out by the rebels, and now we have nearly destroyed the remainder. A continual pecking is heard all through the camp every day, and especially during this cold weather. Every axe and every hatchet that we could borrow, by fair means or foul, were put to their busiest use. The crashing of falling oaks was constant. The Army of the Potomac was obliged to be busy; the cold weather drove them to it. But we have had some very mild, pleasant weather since. For the last few days it has been the finest of Indian Summers.

We had left Warrenton with what they told us must answer for six days' rations, but mine, for some reason or other, entirely disappeared about the fourth day, and many of the other boys were in the same *unrational* predicament. Cold weather, and the duties and exposures we had undergone, had sharpened our appetites, and when one day's rations were not enough, we always borrow from the next so long as we have the next day's rations with us and when the next day comes if we can't buy anything of the commissaries, as we almost always can't, nor at the sutlers, and these are never around at such times, there is no other alternative but to go without till rations are issued again. From an inventory of the contents of my haversack when we started from Warrenton, I noticed that I had just forty-eight hard tack, and about one pound and a half of salt pork, besides sugar and coffee of which I had plenty. Now I am willing to leave it to the most abstemious man in the United States, if that is sufficient sustenance for such fellows as we, engaged as we were during those six days. I suppose that many very sensible people would hardly consider it a genteel or interesting topic to treat upon, or care to know what we have to eat and what we don't have, but I must beg the reader's especial forbearance in our behalf, for we soldiers often have but little else to think of, except what we shall eat and what we shall drink and wherewithal we shall get our rations; and sometimes this subject becomes to us one of painful importance. I have lived in this world upwards of a score of years, but up till now I could find enough to satisfy the most unreasonable demands of the "inner man," but at this particular time I could not, and though Uncle Sam generally feeds his boys well, I am prone to call him at this time, outrageously stingy. I wouldn't have exposed the old fellow nor mentioned his delinquency to the *Freeman* if I hadn't promised to do so in consideration of a half a dozen of hard tack and a "drawing" of sugar. I should have promised my hat, boots or undershirt at that time, rather than not to have had these.

I recollect being in just this same predicament once before, and at the risk of being considered tedious or given to finding fault, I will just mention the circumstance. It was about the 12th of October, when we were retreating from the Rapidan. We had marched back from Rappahannock to Brandy Station, and halted there to get our suppers and await further orders. There was at that particular time a great inquiry among the boys, some asking of others if they had any "grub to spare," and some that still had a quantity, inquiring for those that had none, and offering a share to such as were destitute — for the most of the boys are willing at such times to divide the last mouthful, and then, when that is gone, all trust in Providence together. When we left Culpeper for the Rapidan, we took with us eight days' rations, and they had issued them to us several times since, sometimes one day, sometimes two or three days' rations, just as it happened, and we had lost our reckoning so that we could not tell at this time just how many days' rations we were supposed to have on hand, nor when we should get any more. That night we were ordered to fall in about midnight, and march back again to Rappahannock Station.

In the morning when we started on our march towards Centreville, the boys commenced crying "hard tack," "hard tack," and they set up such a yell that the Colonel, to quiet the clamor, ordered them to stop, and threatened to fine every man two dollars that shouted hard tack again. Some of the boys said if the Colonel would only furnish the hard tack they would continue to shout for it, even at the ruinous rate of two dollars per shout. But these seasons of destitution do not always last, and my opinion is that they need not have occurred at all on the occasions alluded to, if those whose business it was to see to these things had done their duty.

A man belonging to the 2nd Rhode Island regiment died in our regimental hospital last week. His case was a sad one. He had been sick with the typhoid fever, and was still convalescent when we marched from Warrenton. The surgeon of his regiment refused to excuse him from duty the day of the march, and he was compelled to take his place in the ranks. The cold, fatigue and exposure of that march was too much for his enfeebled health, and he was obliged to fall out. Our regiment picked him up and brought him along to the hospital here, where he survived but a short time. His name was James Bucha.

Second Vermont Regiment
November 29, 1863

This quiet Sabbath morning while the good people of Vermont are attending their accustomed places of worship, we, here in the army, are engaged in a manner widely different. Our regiment is on picket today, close up to the enemy, and picket firing is going on nearly all the time. I have seated myself by our little fire on the support, and as it will be several hours before my turn will come to go on post, perhaps I shall have no better time to acquaint you with our proceedings for the last week or so, than the present.

We are in what I am told is called here, the Owl's Wilderness, and certainly it would be hard to conceive of a name more appropriate. It appears to be one uninterrupted wilderness, extending fifteen or twenty miles either way, without any other inhabitants than owls, buzzards, and such like animals. There may be, once in a while, a small clearing with a log house in the center, and a high fence all around it, and with some signs of the land having been cultivated in modern times, but these places have strayed away so far from all civilization that it will be hardly worth while to take them into account. The land where we are now, is covered with small second-growth pine, and looks as if it had been under cultivation once, but probably worn out and abandoned for more fertile regions. Part of the woods that we have been through is grown up to oak and other solid timber of all sizes, and has probably been forest from time immemorial. The land is level, and has the appearance of being good soil, and if I am any judge I should call it just such land as would tempt the eyes of almost any practical farmer, if it was up in our Northern States, instead of being here in decayed Virginia.

As to the latitude and longitude of our present whereabouts, the man in the moon could tell as well as we. We have marched principally in the night, and in all directions, so it has destroyed all our calculations as to distance and directions, and all we can say about the matter is that we have crossed the Rapidan and are still on the rebels' side of the river. It is cheering to be able, under such circumstances, to put confidence in others, for we should be in a woeful plight if we were obliged to act upon our geographical knowledge at the present time. The sun rises in the southwest, and I noticed that the needle of the compass points almost exactly the wrong way. If anybody was going to desert just now, I should be a poor guide to direct their flight.

One week ago today we had divine services in our regiment, held by Mr. Chandler, from Brattleboro. As we have no Chaplain of our own, and consequently very meagre religious privileges of any kind, it was quite a rarity to hear any one preach. He is connected with the Christian Commission, and in anticipation of a battle, had come out here to act the part of the Good Samaritan to the suffering, — as a great many belonging to that Commission have done, to the everlasting gratitude of those who have been wounded in action, — and to preach the gospel and distribute religious reading where such services are needed. He had a large bundle of papers with him that were eagerly received.

On the morning of the 24th, we had orders to be ready to march at an early hour. Accordingly, at precisely three o'clock in the morning, our quiet dreams were broken up by the rattling of drums all through camp, and forthwith we commenced to break up housekeeping — for the most of us had built us tip top houses — and to prepare for another campaign or for whatever was to be accomplished. The weather was grim and forbidding, and the rain drops as they came pattering on our tent that morning, driven by a regular nor'easter, had a very dismal sound in view of the prospect before us. A rainstorm is a very uninviting auxiliary with which to commence a long campaign at any season of the year, but more especially now when cold weather has come and when wet clothes can hardly be made to suggest anything but discomforts of the least desirable kind. Our tents had become wet and heavy, and to carry these in our knapsacks with all the rest of the clothing that we are obliged to carry at this time of the year, was going to make a pretty heavy draft upon the strength of a fellow's back bone. It is the last straw that breaks the camel's back, and the addition of a few extra pounds of water might have the same effect on us, for our packs have hitherto been as heavy as seemed possible for us to carry. You may judge of our satisfaction then, when we heard that the order to march had been postponed for two days. Some think that other reasons besides unpropitious weather, was the cause of the delay; if not it was rather of an anomaly in our war experience but none the less acceptable for all that. We shall certainly think we have one good reason for respecting Gen. Meade.

Although we had been expecting to move somewhere for a long time, we had but little idea where we were going. There have been all sorts of rumors in camp, and there always are at such times, and almost every man had a rumor of his own. No honest man could believe two of them at the same time. Sometimes it was reported that we were going to New York. Gen. Stannard had command there and wanted us to do service under him. I heard that some officers had offered to bet very extravagantly that such would be the case. It is curious how such rumors will thrive and strengthen themselves in a thousand different ways. It was coolly told in the third brigade, and believed there, that orders had been read to us on dress parade to draw clothing suitable for garrison duty, when no such orders had been read to us at all, and more than all that, our regiment had no dress parade while we stayed in our last camp. Another story was that the army was going to move down to the vicinity of Aquia Creek, and go into winter quarters there again. Going across the Rapidan to attack the enemy once more, seemed to be hardly feasible at this late season. Morever attacking Lee in his old chosen position, we have tried so many times and failed, that a great many think it is high time that that method of maneuvering was played out.

The day, before we did move, I was up in one of the New York regiments, and they were trying to enlist the men over again for another three years. They were managing this matter with a great deal of shrewdness. Every man that put his name down was to have a furlough and go home immediately. As it had become pretty certain that we were to have a long, tedious campaign, cold and stormy it might be in pursuit of the enemy, it was quite a tempting bait for a fellow to write down his name and get rid of it all, and go home and have a jolly time instead. In some of the New York regiments, the enlisting officers have been pretty successful; in others, the boys say they want to breathe free air once more before they enlist again.

Thursday morning, the 26th, we were drummed up again, bright and early, to prepare to march. The air was clear, and there were no signs of rain nor any probability that the movement would be postponed again. Our knapsacks were packed, tents struck, huge bonfires were burning all through the camp, consuming material that had cost us a great deal of pains to collect. The sun was just beginning to melt away the frost, when we fell into line and filed off towards Brandy Station. Camps without number were being deserted, some of which had been fixed up as comfortable as would be needed for winter quarters. The whole army was in motion. Infantry, artillery, and baggage wagons *ad infinitum,* had suddenly waked to life and were crowding along, or halting in a field for it to come their turn to start. It was nearly noon before we got hardly so far as Brandy Station. The marching all day was very slow. Sometimes we would hardly get a half mile from one halting place before we would halt again. As it grew towards night, and we believed that we had got to cross the river before we halted for the night, we began to grow impatient of these vexatious delays, and anxious to get to our journey's end. Before we reached the river we had got a couple of miles of woods to go through, and there was only one little road hardly wide enough for a file of four men to walk in abreast, while on each side was a dense thicket of all sorts of timber that nature ever invented. If we could have marched right straight along in this road it would have been all well enough, but, instead of that, we could only march a few steps at a time, then wait for those ahead of us to clear the way. We would march about a rod, then wait five minutes, when we could march a rod more, and then wait another five minutes, and all this while the weight of our knapsacks was increasing, and our patience steadily diminishing, until the boys began to curse patriots and traitors without much discrimination. Finally, we halted and sat down. An hour passed, and still we didn't move. Some of the boys ventured to make coffee, running the risk of being ordered to fall in just as they were divested of their load, and enjoying their warm drink. By and by orders came that we might make us coffee, and eat our supper, and we all pitched into the business with a will. We had ample time allowed us to finish our meal, and when we were at last ordered to fall in, the road was clear and we could march along as fast as we liked.

We crossed the Rapidan between Germanna and Raccoon Ford, at Jacob's Ferry on a pontoon bridge. The opposite bluff was almost perpendicular and as soon as we had climbed to the top we halted and camped for the night, or for what there was left of it, for it was past midnight when we stopped. Before sunrise we were ordered up, and soon on the march again. There was skirmishing ahead of us and our advance was slow. We gained but three or four miles from the river all day. Towards night firing began to be more rapid and we were ordered forward into line. The third corps were ahead of us. Our line extended into the woods to the extreme right. About quarter before four the firing commenced with terrible earnestness. To us it looked as though there would be a chance for us to have a hand in it. We could not see the fight, for the wood was so dense that we could see but a few rods ahead of us, but from the sound of the firing, and from the number of frightened skedaddlers that were making swift tracks to the rear, we had reason to fear that the battle was going against us. The firing continued till long into the night. Evidently the rebels couldn't break our lines or they would have been on to us. It was difficult to get any exact information of the result of the battle, but the "sum and substance" of what we could get was, that we had been flanked and forced to fall back; that the rebels had charged upon our line and been repulsed; that we in turn charged them, drove them back and gained some ground at the close of the struggle. The Tenth Vermont was in the fight, and there was a report that night that they broke and ran; other reports contradicted it. I have heard that they bore the test and held their ground like men, although a line ahead of them broke and skedaddled back right through their ranks; and for a Vermont regiment, this is decidedly the most rational story to believe.

After a while the firing ceased and everything was quiet as the grave. We commenced to build fires to warm ourselves and to make coffee by, but an order came to allow no fires on the line. Afterward they concluded to let us have a few small fires, and we eat our suppers and laid down. About midnight we were ordered to pack up and fall in. Our line of march was towards the left. By the number of troops that were in motion, I should judge that all hands left that place during the night. It would be impossible to guess how far we marched before daylight, when we maneuvered around and got into a position here. We didn't march very rapidly, nor very straight, but if I was to make a rough guess at the matter, I should say that we came about a half a dozen miles from where the fight was Friday night, and that now we must be pretty well down towards Chancellorsville. Next time I write, I hope I shall be better informed and be able to write a more intelligent letter.

Second Vermont Regiment
Near Brandy Station
Dec. 8, 1863

Being detailed for fatigue, and out a couple of miles from camp, with but little prospect of returning for at least ten days from the commencement of the detail, I have pulled up my knapsack close to the fire, fully determined to write you another letter by firelight, this evening, unless I am driven from my purpose by the smoke, which persists in drifting directly into my face, let me get on to which side of the fire I will. To be bent down over an outdoor's fire on a cold December night, might have a very inspiring effect for a poetical nature, but for me it is a most uncomfortable position, and sometimes places my patience in great jeopardy. But if I wish to narrate the events of the past few days, I shall probably have no better opportunity to do so than now, and to deprive the public of this important delinquency that I never should have the face to ask forgiveness for.

The last time I wrote, I believe we were on picket away out in the wilderness among the rebels, where we expected every hour to be let against the enemy. We were not let against them while we were there, for reasons known only to the higher authorities, though without doubt it was because we found the enemy much stronger in his position than we expected. Gen. Meade did not wish to inaugurate another Lee's Mill's affair.[19] There was a deep creek between us and the enemy, and the rebels had been busy digging rifle-pits and strengthening their position ever since we came up to them. Both banks were abrupt and steep and difficult to get over, while on the rebel side they had added to these disadvantages by placing every conceivable obstacle in the way of our advance. Trees were felled, abattis made, breastworks were thrown up until they occupied a position that if *we* had occupied we should have considered impregnable against all the rebels in the universe.

Army correspondents, I notice, all have it that "the men" were in the best of spirits, and eager for a dash at the enemy. Now all such statements, though meant, I suppose, to be complimentary, need a slight qualification, and admit of some exceptions. We are in "the best of spirits" almost any time when we can get the best of spirits to put into us, and as for being eager for a dash at the enemy, perhaps it is all true; I can speak for but one, but there was certainly a fellow there about my size that felt no such eagerness at all. I couldn't look over to those gray-coated devils and see their position and the means they were providing for our reception, with any desire to be ordered over there amongst them. If the order had been given to charge, of course I should have charged with the rest, and if I could hurt a rebel so that he would have had to go home and stay with his mother until the war was over, I should have done it; but after all, to tell the plain truth about the matter, and there is no use in lying, in the event of a charge, I know I should have had a strong preference for running the other way and placing as much distance as possible between those rebel minnies and my own precious self. Vermonters are the very best fighters in the world, so everybody says that knows anything about it; but you never see a Vermonter manifest any eagerness to get into a fight, nor any desire to back out after he does get in.

It was expected by some, that a charge would be ordered that Sunday afternoon when we were there on picket, but it was postponed until morning. Early in the morning we were relieved from post, and went back to the reserve. At precisely eight o'clock our artillery opened on the enemy. They commenced with energy, and from two points, pouring in a cross fire and throwing in shot and shell among the rebels with terrible rapidity. The rebels hardly knew what to make of it. From the picket outposts they could be seen hurrying in all directions, some scattering in confusion, and some being collected together for resistance. There seemed to be an endless number of them. We had stirred up their hive, and found a pretty lively swarm, and as large a one as we need wish to contend with. The cannonading was to continue for an hour, and then, hurrah boys for a charge. As we are on picket, we should take the lead, and act as skirmishers. In about half an hour the firing ceased. Pretty soon the order came to pack up and fall in. We did so, and were ordered about to the right of the line, a mile or so further. All the way we kept back from the edge of the woods far enough to prevent the rebels from discovering our movement. We picked our way through a dense and almost impenetrable thicket of small trees and underbrush. We passed by where a storming party of the 5th corps had piled up their knapsacks and haversacks, and were stripped for the charge. After a while we got into our position where we should remain until further orders. It was very cold, but no fires were allowed to be built there. The Johnnies were having their nice comfortable fires, and they appeared to be but a short distance from us. They didn't appear to be at all bashful about showing their position by building fires or coming out in sight. But we must keep back in the woods out of sight and keep warm the best way we could. By scuffling, knocking off hats, and running around a ring that we made a path for in the woods, we managed to keep from freezing. We expected to be ordered into action every minute. The companies to be deployed were selected, but the order to advance did not come. The boys were tired of waiting. If they had got to charge on the enemy, they wanted to do it at once, and have it done with, and not stand there and dread it all day in the cold.

But the sun went down and our line had not moved. Soon the order came to "left face place." It was clear and cold. We got into line after about our usual delay in marching and halting, and as soon as we could collect the material, we had a bright, rousing fire to collect around, and to eat supper by. We made our beds around this fire and slept till morning. Some idea of the weather may be understood from the fact that several of the canteens that I helped fill late in the evening, were frozen solid in the morning, and some had burst open and were spoiled. The next day we had nothing to do but to keep ourselves warm and speculate on the prospects before us. We were on a portion of the plank road that leads from Culpeper to Fredericksburg, and could at any time we chose, move down and take possession of the heights of that place. The enemy were only covering Gordonsville. They were south and west of us, and we were the nearest Fredericksburg. All this looked as if it might be so, but there was an air of mystery and doubt about it that made some of the knowing ones feel incredulous. Our hesitating to attack the day before looked a little as if everything was not so well for us as some pretended to believe. They had a strong position and doubtless were so disposed that they could move down and occupy their old position by Fredericksburg, or they could fight us there; in either case they held us to a disadvantage. It really looked as if Gen. Meade had failed in some brilliant maneuvre by which he had intended to bring Lee out on an open fight, and in this failure, inasmuch as we had declined to fight and give the rebels their advantage, it seemed pretty likely that we should fall back across the river once more. This was rendered certain when night came and we were ordered to pack up and fall in. After marching two or three miles, or such a matter, we halted and formed into line. Skirmishers were thrown out, and we were told that we should remain at least two hours.

It was a certain thing then that we were retreating, and that a part of our brigade was acting as rear-guard. We spread down our blankets, determined to steal a little sleep if we could. The next thing we have any recollection of was of being aroused from a good sweet dream, and ordered to form. We had been there three hours instead of two. We were completely chilled through, and it was quite fortunate that we were awakened when we were, for we were shivering with the cold, and trembling like a man of ninety. We fell into line, and before we had marched far we were warm enough.

It was about daylight when we reached and crossed Germanna Ford the next morning. We noticed as we passed down to the river some well constructed rifle-pits and breastworks, from which the enemy had no doubt intended to dispute our passage across the river, and which we were enabled to dodge through the foresight and generalship of Gen. Meade. We marched about a mile this side of the river before we halted for breakfast. The 5th corps had preceded us, and their men were lying in the bushes on each side of the road, as thickly as they could possibly get together. After breakfast we marched on a little further, and finally in a woods for all day, and the next night. Thursday morning we were ordered to pack up and fall in, which we did, and marched towards our old camp. We marched up to Stevensburg and crossed the Mountain Creek at that place, some distance above the place where we crossed the same stream on our way down a week before. As we came along by the camps of the 5th and 3rd corps we noticed that they were occupying the same houses, and, the same places exactly, that they occupied before we moved. At Brandy Station everything was alive with business. One sutler's wagon was actually unloading from a platform car, just as we passed by. This was an important event, for sutler's goods have heretofore been too scarce to be obtained even by officers, and those who feel that they have a special right to these things. We marched straight back into our old camp. Those that had not burned up their houses before they left had only to put their tent overhead for a roof, and they were as comfortably situated as ever; but some had completely destroyed their houses, and material, and consequently if they built again, had to commence anew. We were told that we had better not make any extensive preparations for comfortable quarters, as our regiment intended to move to a more pleasant locality, which has since been done. Friday night the order came into camp to pack up everything, and be ready to move at a moment's notice. The rebel cavalry had crossed to this side of the Rapidan, and possibly we might be attacked. The officers and men had been given a ration of whiskey that night, and all hands were pretty noisy, though nobody supposed that that had anything to do with the rebel scare. Matters quieted down after a while, and so did the boys, and no enemy disturbed us that night. The next morning we were detailed for this "fatigue," and here we have been ever since. We are building a corduroy road along by the side of the railroad from Rappahannock Station to camp. Our supplies they say have got to be carried over this road. The railroad only carries forage to Brandy Station.

But it is getting to be well on towards midnight, and my fire is nearly gone out. No one would disagree with me, if I should say, it is time this tedious letter was brought to a close, for I am beginning to feel almost as dull as what I have written.

———————

Second Vermont Regiment
Near Brandy Station, Va.
Dec. 17, 1863

The "Old Brigade" is still occupying about the same position that we have occupied since the battle at Rappahannock Station, with the exception of the week that we spent on our reconnoissance, as the boys call it, down in "the wilderness." The 6th regiment and ours have changed camps for winter quarters, if we are allowed to have them here, but the other regiments remained just as they stationed themselves a month ago. We have all been as busy as bees to make us comfortable houses, and we shall very much regret to move away and leave our labor to begin anew.

Our regiment moved nearly a mile eastward from where we were, and we have secured ourselves a very pleasant situation and one that we are perfectly willing to occupy until spring if our commanding General sees fit to allow us the privilege. The ground here is nearly level, sloping just enough to permit the water to run off during the muddy season, and of a nature less adapted to that universal sloughy condition so peculiar to Virginia. The land here was covered with an oak forest, similar to the camp we have just left, but which has been removed by one or the other of the contending armies. Now and then there is a line representative of the forest's former glory, but in a week from now, if we stay here, these will have perished with the rest. A little further east the woods remain undisturbed, so that at present wood is within convenient reach, but every day its border recedes further and further from camp, and by the time that we have spent our winter here, if we should happen to do that, we shall begin to see a value in the fire wood that we are careless to appreciate when wood is plenty.

Yesterday and the day before there was a rumor that we were going to fall back across the Rappahannock before we should be allowed to consider ourselves in winter quarters. How much foundation this rumor may have, I cannot say, but it rather lacks confirmation, although such an event is highly probable. The line of the Rappahannock would be much easier to hold during the winter, while there can be but little advantage in maintaining an advanced position on this side of the river. We may be better able to keep a strict watch of the rebels, perhaps, but we certainly do not occupy so good a position for defensive operations as if a river lay between us and the enemy. Now this moving camp at this time of year, is a matter of serious moment to us, and all the probabilities in regard to it, pro or con, are discussed around our tent fires with eager interest. But a few moments ago I was listening to a couple of debaters who were arguing this question of moving back across the Rappahannock, and from them I got a pretty clear view of the subject, though hardly enough to warrant me in making a decision in the matter. One point that we brought forward to prove our going back, was the fact that so many "veterans" were going home on furloughs, by virtue of their re-enlisting, some as individuals, some as companies, and some as whole regiments, according to General Order No. 376, from the war department. These furloughs, if the veterans enlist very extensively, as we hope they will, cannot fail to weaken the army very perceptibly, and hence oblige us to seek a stronger position. There are some at the north that will grumble as they always do when they hear that this army is moving towards Washington, but they ought not to grumble because old soldiers re-enlist.

One argument advanced to prove that we were not going to move, was because all the men and some of the officers, who are men sometimes, were so busily engaged in putting up their "houses" so nicely, which it was urged, indicated that all expected to stay here all winter. This argument, however, was quickly disposed of, for it is everywhere known that the men in the army of the Potomac will work as busy as beavers to build their houses, although not assured of remaining in camp a single week. A fellow will work all day for the sake of a good sleep at night, and this taking good care of one's self here in the army, is a business that pays handsomely in the long run, otherwise the chances are that his run will be very short, and that he will fall a prey to some malady, or at best, cripple his constitution and seriously endanger his life. The exposures at this time of year, are very severe, and the boys have learned that it is the best way to build as well as they can, whether we are going to stay or not, and the extra comfort we derive in a majority of cases, well pays us for all of our trouble, although we have been sadly vexed because we were ordered out of comfortable houses scarcely completed. More than all this the boys take pride in fitting up for themselves the very best houses they can whether we are going to stay or not, so that the simple fact that we are putting up houses on a scale not warranted by the prospect of remaining quiet, is a poor argument that we are not going to move, and it would be impossible to prove that we are not going to move from the opposite conditions, for we do not allow any such conditions to exist. As another argument that we are not going to move, was mentioned the building of the corduroy road along side the railroad, which was noticed in a former letter. It certainly would be ruinous policy to rob the forests in this vicinity of all their small trees, to say nothing of the labor of building these roads, and our Generals would hardly think of undertaking so heavy a job if they contemplated retreating to the other side of the river. So the important question whether we be allowed to remain in our quiet camp or compelled to forsake this place for the woodless region near Warrenton, must remain unknown to us until the lapse of time shall prove the events.

Speaking of building corduroy roads, reminds me of a little incident, which, though of no great importance in itself, will do to mention for want of something better, and which shows how we sometimes treat non-combatants, or rather how we treat their property. Near by where we were at work, lived an inoffensive citizen, who happened to be the lucky possessor of a grindstone, which, for aught I know, is the only one outside of the army in Culpeper County. Sunday afternoon we laid by our axes and quit work, either because it was the Lord's day, or for some other reason that might have been considered more valid. Our axes had become dull from some cause that no one could divine, and it was proposed by some to confiscate this grindstone, and impress it into the service of Uncle Sam by the most practicable method, whether strictly constitutional, or not. The captain sent a corporal with a squad of men, and a team, to capture the article and bring it to our camp. Arriving at the house we walked boldly into the man's door-yard, took his grindstone and loaded it on to the wagon. We wasn't quite sly enough to get off without attracting the attention of the provost guard, and of course it was his business to object to our proceedings, and demand by what authority we presumed to appropriate a citizen's property. We explained our case to him very minutely, but we had nothing to show, and our predicament in a more august presence would have been extremely ridiculous. With an air of injured impatience, to settle the parley and satisfy the guard, the corporal told him that he would get him a written order from the captain, which, if the guard had known it, he had no more business to recognize than if it had been made out by the writer of this letter. Of course Mr. Shaw, who regarded his grindstone as we do diamonds, more on account of the scarcity of the article, than its intrinsic worth, was loth to part with his property without some guaranty that he should get some compensation for it, or be assured of its return. He had allowed it to be used by everybody, and charged no one a cent, and now he was willing to let the boys come there and grind as much as they pleased, and be welcome to the privilege, but he thought it very ungracious in us to force him to part with his property in a manner so obviously unjust. The man appeared so consciously upright, and so gentlemanly in his manner, that I really wished, as I talked with him, that Uncle Sam had a grindstone of his own, and thus precluded the necessity of our robbing this citizen. The corporal returned with the order duly written, which the guard handed to Mr. Shaw as if he had done his duty in the true spirit of military law, and he ought to be satisfied. Mr. Shaw took the order, for he didn't know what else to do, though he had no more idea of how it could avail him anything than an Australian would have of a ten cent Confederate shinplaster. "Well," he said, for he must say something "don't destroy my grindstone, boys; bring it back when you are done with it." It was very easy to lie, under the circumstances, so we told him we would, and drove off with our prize, feeling as if we had captured — not Richmond — but a grindstone.

———————

Second Vermont Regiment
Near Brandy Station, Va.
Dec. 20, 1863

The great topic of interest in camp just now is that of re-enlisting. The Vermont boys are as anxious as any troops in the field, to turn "veterans" and they are enlisting to an extent quite unexpected. Probably, before this letter is printed and read, there will be in Vermont quite a respectable representation of "veterans," from the Old Brigade, enjoying their furloughs which were given them for re-enlisting.

About a week ago, at our dress parade, our Colonel talked the matter over with us, and he told us of a plan that General Howe was confident he could get approved at the War Department, which would allow all, except conscripts, to enlist. His plan was to have those who joined the regiment at Yorktown, on the Peninsula, and those who joined us at Hagerstown, Maryland, in the fall of '62, re-enlist now, and when two years of their term of service has expired, they should commence to receive bounties in regular installments from that time, the same as the others that enlist now. This plan General Howe had great confidence would succeed. He took measures to ascertain how many would re-enlist, providing they could have this matter arranged as he proposed, and the whole Division get a chance to go home to recruit and have a good time generally. This was fully explained to us to the minutest particular. We had several dress parades, in which the exercises were limited to hearing a full explanation of all the advantages that might be expected from re-enlisting, and at one time we had a brigade dress parade, when Col. Grant took the stump, or the saddle, rather, to explain a great many mistakes that he supposed we might be possibly laboring under. He was very anxious, he said, to have the whole brigade go home as a brigade, and claim all the dignity of veteran soldiers. He told us of the probabilities of a speedy close of the war, and though he was not of those, who, when he first came into the field supposed the war would be over before the first three years had expired, he now most certainly could not think the war would last three years longer. Col. Walbridge ventured the expression at another time, that if we went home as a regiment or brigade, we might never be called back.

War is an uncertain game, and by this time we ought to have learned better than to be unduly elated at our successes. I remember about the time we left Camp Griffin, nearly two years since, the New York *Tribune* said, in view of our successes, that within a few months, in all probability, the war would close. When we were at Lee's Mill, a little later, the New York *Herald* even more enthusiastic, after summing up a careful review of "the situation," declared there was a prospect of peace within *two weeks!* Just now it looks as if it was impossible for the rebellion to survive much longer. We have cut huge slices from their miserable confederacy, and have captured all their best strongholds. We have got the Mississippi river, and thus severed their country in twain. We have nearly cut them in two again at Chattanooga, and if they persist in surviving after receiving many more deadly blows like these, it will truly indicate a vitality wonderfully tenacious. But after all, these things may be changed within a short time. A great battle may be fought, the rebels may get to a very important position first, or a brigade may break on our side or a charge be annihilated, and the rebels may gain a more important advantage than they have possessed for a long time. We had better not expect too much, and then it is less likely that we shall be disappointed.

There is a strong probability that the 5th regiment will enlist in sufficient numbers to entitle them to the privilege of going to Vermont as a regiment, officers and all, and some think the other regiments in this brigade will, excepting, perhaps, our own. Three quarters of a regiment or company must enlist to secure that privilege. The 2d, 3d and 4th have had conscripts assigned them that are not included in this veteran arrangement at all. This gives these regiments less of a chance to go home all together than those without conscripts, for it can hardly be expected that the old boys will be unanimous enough to get a majority sufficient to overbalance the other, conscripts and all. Besides in our regiment the original members, of whom there are about 240, are to be mustered out the 20th of next June. These had rather wait six months longer and be free indeed, free to enlist or free to stay at home, than to bind themselves for another three years now, and receive their bounty and furlough. Those that have got to serve through the summer on their present term of enlistment, and who think another summer's work here will crush what is left of the rebellion, very naturally think it for their benefit to re-enlist, pocket their $402, and get leave to visit their heart-loved homes for a short time now.

Last Friday we were taken out to witness the execution of two deserters that belonged to our brigade. Their names were John Tague and George Blowers. The first was from Co. A, 5th regiment, and the other was from Co. A, in our regiment. They were sentenced to be shot to death by musketry on the 18th of December, in the presence of the division. There were seven soldiers that suffered the same penalty in this army on that day. I never was obliged to witness a sight like that before, and I sincerely hope a long time may intervene before I am thus called upon again.

Just outside the camp, in a little hollow, are the graves of these unfortunate soldiers. To this place the whole Division was taken last Friday to witness the execution. These men were made examples, and executed in the presence of the Division, to deter others from the same crime. Alas, that it should be necessary! Such terrible scenes can only blunt men's finer sensibilities and burden them the more; and Heaven knows that the influences of a soldier's life are hardening enough already.

The troops formed a sort of hollow square around the fatal spot, except behind the prisoners there was no troops. Two graves had just been dug there, and after we had got into the place assigned us, ordered arms, and all was still as death; two ambulances drove on to the ground with two live men, and two coffins to contain them, and these were to fill the newly made graves. It seemed as if some horrible tragedy in a theater was about to be enacted, rather than a real preparation for execution. I have seen men shot down by scores and hundreds in the field of battle, and have stood within an arm's reach of comrades that were shot dead; but I believe I never have witnessed that from which any soul shrunk with such horror, as to see those two soldiers shot dead in cold blood at the iron decree of military law.

If the men, generally, were unmoved at the sight, they were not more so than the prisoners, especially John Tague. He threw his hat on to the ground in bold defiance, and stood erect, facing the officers as the sentence of death was read without betraying the slightest agitation. After the sentence was read, the chaplains stepped forward by their side, and after reading some select passages of scripture, they offered prayer, the prisoners kneeling as they prayed.

The band discoursed a dirge-like piece of music, when the prisoners were conducted to their coffins, on which they kneeled, and the guard filed around and took position in front of them, scarcely half a dozen yards distant. A sergeant put a circle around the neck of each, from which was suspended a white object over the breast, as a target for the executioners. The prisoners were not blindfolded, but looked straight into the muzzles of the guns that shot them to death. The guard were divided into two platoons, one firing at one prisoner, and the other platoon firing at the other prisoner, but there was no reserve to be ordered up in case of failure. Blowers had been sick, his head slightly drooped as if oppressed with a terrible sense of the fate he was about to meet. He had requested that he might see his brother in Co. A, but his brother was not there. He had no heart to see the execution, and had been excused from coming. Tague was firm and erect till the last moment, and when the order was given to fire, he fell like a dead weight, his face resting on the ground, and his feet still remaining on the coffin. Blowers fell at the same time. He exclaimed, "Oh dear me!" struggled a moment, and was dead. Immediately our attention was called away by the loud orders of commanding officers, and we marched in columns around the spot where the bodies of the two men were lying just as they fell. God grant that another such punishment may never be needed in the Potomac Army.

Second Vermont Regiment
Near Brandy Station, Va.
Dec. 31, 1863

Camp life is about as dull as a soldier need wish it to be. A cold, drizzling rainstorm is just now upon us, and the pattering rain drops are making merry music on the canvass overhead, while not a few of them manage to find their way inside of our little shanty. At every crack, under the eaves, and all around, the water persists in obtruding its unwelcome presence in our midst. Some of these impertinent raindrops, with a presumption quite unpardonable, pay no attention to the roof of our house, but rush through and drop inside as if aware of the superior comfort to be found near our fire, which they have nearly put out. The consequence of all this is that our floor of mother earth is becoming very muddy and slippery; our blankets, our beds and our knapsacks are becoming soaking wet, and everything in the tent is beginning to present a horribly untidy appearance. Notwithstanding all these unfavorable circumstances, I have secured myself a position on my bunk, with two knapsacks for a seat, and in the dryest corner of the tent I could find, and here, regardless of surrounding events, I have determined to pen you a few lines, at all hazards.

The muddy season has fairly commenced. We have had rain upon rain, and, as a natural consequence, the mud has been growing deeper and deeper. Persons who have always lived in the dry climate of Vermont, can hardly conceive of the extreme disagreeableness incident to a muddy region like this. Here one must confine himself in his house, or if he ventures out he finds himself in mud ankle deep if not deeper, and woe to the fellow that is poorly shod in this sloshy, slippery, sticky, everywhere present mud. A man's shoes must be well tied on or he will leave them buried in this red clay mortar. Go where you will, there is no relief; everywhere it is the same universal mud. However, we soldiers have one good consolation from this evil, for as long as it continues to rain and be muddy, there is no danger that an advance movement will be made, and we are pretty sure of being allowed the privilege of remaining quietly in camp. We have not been called out to drill for a long time, but we have had a very liberal share of guard and ordinary camp duties to do. Rations are abundant, sutlers are plenty, and for the present, we mean to have a good comfortable time.

By some, in speaking of going into winter quarters to remain inactive for a time, it is mentioned as something repulsive to the inclinations of the soldiers, they preferring the excitement of marching and fighting, to the dull monotony of camp life. My experience, so far as it goes, proves quite the contrary.

I should have but little fear of making a mis-statement, if I should say that scarcely anything is more acceptable to troops that have "roughed it" all summer, than to be allowed to put up their quarters for winter, and prepare for a good long rest. Perhaps soldiers think of home more when idle, but I doubt if they suffer any more from homesickness. If they do it is because that during a tedious campaign, homesickness is drowned by trials more stern and severe.

Re-enlisting here goes bravely on. The Fifth regiment left for home last Monday. They go as a body. I hear that they met with a serious accident on the cars between here and Alexandria, whereby three were killed and several injured, but perhaps it may not prove true. The re-enlisted men from the sixth regiment, except one company that goes as a whole, started this morning. The other regiments are waiting for the paymaster that they may settle with the Government for their old term, to commence again anew, and then they will be ready to start too. This regiment will turn out about a hundred "veterans," the noblest and best the country affords. Cos. E and I will produce fifteen each, C produces thirteen, and the other companies a still less number, but all are represented. The furloughs were made out for the "veterans" in this regiment day before yesterday, and those that preferred going home then, to waiting for their pay, had that privilege, and quite a number accepted it. The majority however, are now waiting for the dilatory paymaster, who is at work at the present time in the other brigade paying off the veterans there. The furloughs are for thirty-five days, and this must cover all the time that the soldier is away from camp. They are not dated till the soldier that receives them starts for home.

The question about moving back across the Rappahannock, so generally talked about a few days ago, seems to have been decided in favor of our staying here. It was decided in council so to do, as I am told. All were in favor of moving back to Warrenton, except Gen. Sedgwick. It was his opinion that we had better remain here for the present, perhaps all winter. His reasons were, that if we wished to make a move it could be more easily done from this side of the river. And then if we moved back to Warrenton the enemy would come in here and fortify again along the Rappahannock, and perhaps for a vigorous defence between here and the Rapidan. Besides this the men had built themselves firstrate quarters and preferred to remain; and he believed that the line could be as easily defended here as anywhere. We had plenty of teams, and where camps were considerable distance from any wood they could be employed to haul it for them. General Sedgwick's opinions prevailed. So an order has been issued that every regiment may have as many teams as they want to draw their wood. The third division had hardly any chance at all to get wood, previous to this order.

It is reported that seventeen rebel deserters came into our lines this morning. The cavalry that picket on the outer line, say that the rebels are continually coming into our lines, sometimes in squads and often with their officers with them. One cavalry man said it "beat the devil" how the Johnnies were deserting. He says the rebel commissioned officers have to stand picket on their outposts, to prevent their men from running away. They like their status better under President Lincoln's proclamation than in the rebel army.

Day before yesterday, a member of our regiment, was carried to his last resting-place. Funeral scenes are always sad, but the saddest of all, it seems to me, is the soldier's funeral. There are seldom any mourners here to follow him to his grave, and no tears of sympathy and grief fall on his coffin, as it is lowered into the silent tomb. Stranger hands bear him to his long home, and stranger hands bury him from mortal view. In this instance the Rev. Mr. Mack, of the 3rd regiment officiated as chaplain. He read some select passages of scripture, offered a prayer for the living, for the friends of the deceased, and for us all. He admonished us not to forget the lesson here taught us by the Almighty, and as we fired the salute over his grave, we felt that life is held by a very frail tenure indeed. Somewhere among the wild hills of Vermont there are dear friends of this man, whose hearts will be pierced with sorrow when they see that name mentioned among the dead. And to know that he died among strangers, with no friendly hand to minister to his last wants, will be the keenest pang of all. But such events occur every day till we begin to scarcely notice them.

This man's case was a peculiar though by no means a solitary one. He came out here as a substitute for a drafted man, and since he joined the regiment he has been unable to do any duty. He had previously been a soldier, and was once discharged and before he had recovered his disability, for a sum of money he consented to enlist again. Perhaps he thought he had sufficiently recovered to make it safe for him to join the army once more; or perhaps he thought there would be no difficulty in getting discharged again. If so he made a fatal mistake. The bounty he received was the price of his life. The boys who knew the circumstances of his enlistment had but little sympathy for him, and whatever he suffered, they thought it a punishment well deserved. Boys that have served so far through the war without any bounty or extra compensation whatever, are apt to be envious of those more favored, and to refuse that cordial sympathy to them in time of need, that they would cheerfully render to one of their own comrades; especially if, as in this case, they have cheated the government, and after getting out here are unable to do their share of the duty; and this feeling is shared not only by the men, but by the officers and surgeons and all concerned. Perhaps this is wrong, but it is a fact nevertheless, and those who have once been discharged from the service, or any others who are not physically sound, would do well to take heed before they accept the bounties so temptingly offered them for enlisting. I never could'see why this man was not discharged as soon as it became apparent that he could never be fit for service here, and perhaps it is not my business to inquire, but it seems to me to have been almost too cruel a punishment to allow a man to die of a lingering camp disease for a crime such as this soldier had committed. I believe a discharge was about being made out for him when he died. Any one that enlists now thinking to get discharged again, plays a risky game in which life itself is at stake.

[Tunbridge, Vt.]
[January, 1864]

Home again; How full of meaning the word *home*. I half doubt my senses sometimes, and am afraid it is not a reality but that I am dreaming some pleasant dream, liable to be disturbed at any time by the sound of the drum or the inevitable order "Fall in." I doubt if there is any other occupation that a man may be engaged in to call him away from home, that will enkindle such a longing to return, or such pleasant realities when we do return as to be "off to the war" soldiering for our country. The contrast between the camp-life and the comforts of home are so great, that a soldier feels their loss most keenly, and learns very soon how to appreciate and value that sacred place, by his tedious and bitter experiences away from it. Furloughs are the most precious privileges that the government allows their soldiers, and the prospect of going home has tempted a great many good soldiers to re-enlist when nothing else would.

It was a glad day for us when we turned our backs upon the old camp with our furloughs in our hands and our bounties in our pockets, at liberty once more to start for home or wherever else we choose to go; and we did not suffer our spirits to be dampened by the thought that our liberty was limited to one month of time. Into that thirty-five days we calculated to concentrate all the enjoyment that we had lost for the last two years and a half, and to make up if possible for all the pleasures that might have fallen to our lot for the next three years to come. This of course will require fast work and people must not be surprised nor blame us if the re-enlisted veterans sometimes appear a little too "fast." We shall all be sober enough no doubt by and by, when we get back to the old camp to commence our new term, our furloughs out and our money spent; but it is a soldier's style to improve the present and never worry about the future.

We left our camp near Brandy Station, on the morning of the 4th of January, several days later than we had intended. The anxiously expected paymaster, who was to settle up with the veterans for Uncle Sam, pay us our bounty, and give us our furlough, did not make his appearance in the Second Regiment till the 3d inst. Of course we had begun to grow very impatient. For over two weeks we had been expecting him almost hourly. The boys began to denounce him as the slowest official in the whole financial department, and that is saying a great deal, although paymasters have generally done their business with us with snail-like alacrity. We had at first expected our furloughs by Christmas, but finding ourselves cheated out of that, we still hoped and expected to get home by New Year's day. But the old year faded away, and the new one commenced, and still the paymaster delayed coming. When we inquired as to his whereabouts, we were always told that he was in the third or the fourth regiment, or the third brigade; but he was always coming to our regiment *immediately*. Sometimes we heard that he had actually come, and we hurried out of our tents to see the important personage, but only to return again, our hope hopelessly deferred, and to think how pleasant it is to be one of the lower grade of government employees, with the privilege of being waited upon by official dignities much higher up. Disgusted with so much delay, Lieut. Bailey, our recruiting officer, went in search of another paymaster, but whether he succeeded in his mission, or not, I never inquired. I only know that the next morning it was announced that the paymaster had really come, and before night we had a discharge paper and a very respectable pile of greenbacks in our hands. The prospect now of going home for thirty-five days seemed to have approached a certainty, as had also the prospect of serving in the army for three years more; but this last prospect we resolutely refused to think of.

Some of the boys started off at once that night, but the majority concluded to wait until morning. Too feverishly impatient to allow the time to pass in its natural way, the boys tried every expedient to hurry the hour along that was to see them on their way home. Some of them were up three or four hours before daylight with their breakfast eat and everything ready to start, notwithstanding, they had been told again and again, by the best authority, that the cars would not leave the station for Washington sooner than nine o'clock in the forenoon. Before five o'clock in the morning some of the boys were at Brandy Station, waiting for their transportation. Every minute seemed an aggravating length, but we had to curb our impatience, for we could go no further till the right hour had come. The provost marshal was still in his bed, and the locomotives that were first to leave the station were to all human appearances sound asleep. But as it grew light the men began to stir. The engines were fired up, and by nine o'clock we had seen the provost marshal, got our transportation to Washington, and soon we were on the way. Was it indeed possible that we had started for home? Parents, brothers, sisters and friends, were we soon going to see them face to face? And then after spending a few short days with them, we were going to return to fight three long years more, or find a soldier's grave in old Virginia. It might be, but there was no retreat now. We had concluded that we wanted to stay and see the war brought to a close now that we had fought so long, and we had put our hands to the plow so that we could not look back now if we would, and we would not if we could.

Having been engaged in our country's service so long, and proved our ability to endure its toils and privations, it never occurred to us that our services brought a lower price in the market than those of new recruits. But such seems to have been the case with the most of us. Some get the bounty offered at home, while others do not. If the quota of any town happened to be full before the Selectmen were officially notified of our re-enlistment, the soldiers from that town get no bounty. A great many expected it, but were disappointed. They did what they could to secure it, and felt that it justly belonged to them, if to anybody; but it depended entirely upon circumstances whether they received it or not. They had only to stand and look on and see the cards played by others, and if they were a winner they could pocket their bounty, but if they lost nobody was to blame. Thus two fellows might enlist from the same company, one would get a bounty that in all would amount to $702 at least, and perhaps more, while another who enlists to do the same duty in the same place, and whose name counts just the same to the credit of Vermont, gets only his $402. It is a strange chance game and very unjust. The New Jersey boys that re-enlist get very nearly one thousand dollars bounty. All who enlisted belonging to New York city, get the County bounty paid there, and so they do in almost every other State. Are not Vermont troops as good as any?

The members of the old brigade will hardly feel reconciled to that kind of usage. Of course it is none of our business if another soldier gets a thousand dollars, or a million even, if we get what is due us; at least such is the style of reasoning that some adopt, but those who adopt it, I ween would be hardly willing to submit to their own arguments if the test was put to them. A farmer may sell his grain to an individual for a dollar per bushel, and be satisfied with his bargain because he could get no more, but if that same individual should buy grain of an inferior quality for two dollars a bushel, would he be satisfied then? So a man might work for fifty cents a day in the hay season from sheer necessity if he could get no more, but he would not do it if other hands less able than himself were receiving their dollar a day. If soldiers are to be bought with money, give all an even chance, and if they are all to be drafted give all an equal chance there.

But we were told when we re-enlisted that there was no doubt but that we should receive the $300 extra bounty and many enlisted with that under-standing. Many more would re-enlist if the thing was sure. Vermont would do well to offer that sum to all of her old soldiers, and let all enlist who will, whether her present quota is full or not. They would be credited to the State, and in the event of another call Vermont would be ready beforehand. And even if another call was never made, Vermont would be loth to have the credit to her honor and patriotism thus gained wiped out for all the money that it would cost her. This would be a simple act of justice to the soldiers, and they would feel as if their services were valued at home. But I was not intending to make this complaint when I commenced my letter. I only intended to mention the incidents of our journey home, which however were not very important, and as my letter has swelled to the length intended already, I will postpone any further infliction till next time.

Second Vermont Regiment
Near Brandy Station
Feb. 10, 1864

To-day I find myself back again to the old camp, the same camp I left with all its familiar associations as of old. The regiment had not been sent to Tennessee as had been reported in Vermont, but remains in its accustomed place with the rest of the Corps. No change has taken place except that the regiment has been filled up with recruits, so that now we have very nearly our maximum number. Our beds have grown no softer in our absence, nor our hard tack any more palatable. My friendly old musket has lost none of its charms, and between you and I, Mr. Editor, it would have taken a greater than Christopher Columbus, to have discovered what there ever was, that was very charming about it. I am in a low spirited mood just now, and nothing will inspire me with sublime emotions. Even my favorite knapsack suggests nothing but long marches and an aching back, and the more I contemplate the interesting subject, the more I wonder where in the enchanted region of rebeldom, I shall be obliged next summer to bid it an affectionate farewell, and to leave it forever "along with its glory." Going home seems like a fairy dream, from which I have just awakened, and if it didn't make the reality seem so repulsive from contrast, I should like to repeat the dream as often as may be, so long as I remain under the guardianship of our dear old Uncle Samuel. But, after all, we veterans are not dissatisfied with the service, nor so very anxious to get out of it, and we do not mean it shall appear that we ever considered our first enlistment a mistake, the consequences of which must be borne with the best grace we can assume. We are not ignorant now of what the service requires, nor do we fully accept the idea of some, that the war will close within a few months, though from present indications, such an event is not impossible. We have embarked on a second three years, with our eyes wide open, prepared for the worst that may happen, but always hoping for the best.

We had a very pleasant journey going and coming. Our transportation papers were procured at Washington, which took us home and back again, at Government expense. So many veterans were going home then, that it was difficult to get the papers made out for us all. Some of the boys paid their own fare, rather than to bother themselves trying to get their transportation, and went on their way rejoicing without any vexatious delay. Others wasted a day of their valuable liberty, and some wasted more, and many after waiting awhile had to give it up, and go home on their own expense after all. The transportation office was crowded all the time during office hours, and at night when it was announced that no more papers were to be given out, the crowd had to disperse disappointed, and impatient at being hindered, and chafing like caged lions to be on the road for home. Our furloughs were handed into the office through a little slide in the door, to a man inside, who marked on them the town and state where he wished to go, and when a certain number had been received in there, the slide was shut until they saw fit to open it for a fresh supply. A prominent notice told us that an excellent room, with a warm fire, might be found in a back apartment adjoining the office, where we could wait comfortably till the aforesaid transportation papers were made out. This was a sort of a reception room, dirty and disagreeable as can be imagined, and this was crowded full of soldiers, some of whom had been waiting there all day, and the most of them appeared as resigned to their fate as if they had made up their minds to wait there forever. There was a little side door a few inches square that opened from the office into this room, and as fast as a dozen or so of papers were made out, the slide was opened and the names called over of those who are to receive them. Two papers were given us, one of which was an order for a ticket from Washington to New York and return, and the other was an order to present to the New York depot for a ticket from there to the place where we wished to go, and return to New York. So we had our railroad tickets to go home and back again, and these tickets were good anywhere on the route designated, at any time we chose to use them. We left camp for home on the 4th of January, and left home for camp just one month and one day later.

The Second Regiment was pretty well represented on the train that took us back from home. Some were lively and jolly, and full of fun, and others were lively and jolly, and "full of the devil," attracting considerable notice, while there were others that quietly minded their own business and attracted no notice at all. The boys told the conductor on the Philadelphia road coming home, as we were rattling along at an uncommonly swift rate, that they wanted he should spare no pains to take them safely home, but when they came back he might run them to "h—l" if he wanted to, they wouldn't complain nor find any fault, and returning they appeared to be as good as their word, for in their recklessness they appeared to be utterly indifferent whether they were landed in that unmentionable place, or carried safely back to the Army of the Potomac.

We arrived at New York about midnight, on the day we started from home, and not knowing exactly where we wanted to go, we yielded to the importunities of a hack driver, who carried us several yards into the city, and charged us a fee for his trouble, that on some conveyances would have been sufficient to have carried us well on towards a hundred miles. I will not mention the amount for fear some spirits more resolute than ours, will wonder how men claiming the title of veterans, can be made to submit to such extortion. The hack left us in front of a stylish looking hotel, where a soldier with a big bounty in his pocket, would doubtless be a welcome customer, but being of an economical turn of mind just at that particular time, we concluded to look for lodgings elsewhere. Somewhere in that city, was a New England special Relief Association, and this we determined to find. A policeman directed us to No. 172 Broadway, and here we found an abundance of beds for sleepy soldiers, and there were an abundance of sleepy soldiers to occupy the beds. But room was found for us, and my friend and I got a very good sleep that night, and a very good breakfast in the morning, and we were allowed to go away without being charged a cent for our entertainment.

The next night found us whirling along the road to Philadelphia. Arriving there, we found our way (we lost it at first) to the Baltimore depot just as the train for that city had left. There was another train, however, loaded with conscripts that was to follow soon after. The train was loaded and more too, so that the chances of our getting aboard was by no means promising. Moreover, we had tried to get aboard this same train, or at least with these same troops, earlier in the day, but on our refusing to give up our tickets for the whole route at once, we were told that they had no right to carry us. But we were determined to try, and we succeeded in getting passage. We asked a good natured guard at one of the doors if there was room in his car for two more, and without thinking or asking whether we belonged to their company or not, he replied in the affirmative, and we at last got us a seat. This train, like all other trains for soldiers, was a long string of freight cars with rude seats in them, and it appeared to move about as fast as a man could walk, except when it stopped, which seemed to be about all the time. Sometime the next day we arrived at Baltimore. It was quite fortunate for us, getting this ride, for neither my friend nor myself happened to have our transportation for that portion of the road, so what we got there was clear gain. We didn't know whether we had cheated the Government or the railroad company, but we knew we had not cheated ourselves, which is a sin that even soldiers do not rashly commit. We reached Washington at last, but found we could not get to the regiment till the next morning at ten o'clock. A regular passenger train for soldiers and citizens, officers and their wives, runs from Washington to Brandy Station and back, once every day, and it is almost impossible to get passage on any other.

But we got back to camp "on time," back to the old tent and the same associates, and now we have only to look forward to three long years more of soldier's life. But we had made up our minds to stay here and see the war to a close, and we must not let our courage shrink from its duties now. Farewell, then, to old Vermont, with its endearing associations, farewell home and friends, if it must be, for three years to come. 'Tis hard to part so long, but somebody must, and why should I pray to be excused?

I frankly confess that it was with a heavy heart that I bid adieu to home, friends and neighbors, to start for war the second time. It was more severe at the second parting than it was at the first. The furlough had been very brief. Time had flown with tenfold its usual fleetness. The morning soon came that I must take the parting hand with wife and parents, brothers and sisters, for a length of time that only infinite wisdom can predict. Breakfast was prepared, but to attempt to eat was a mockery. We tried to maintain a brave spirit and appear calm, but when we attempted to read a chapter in the Bible together, and invoke God's blessing, as has been our custom from time immemorial,

there were faltering voices and moistened eyes which told of a sorrow that
could not be concealed.

> When forced to part from those we love,
>   Though sure to meet to-morrow,
> We yet a kind of anguish prove,
>   And feel a touch of sorrow.
>
> But Oh! what words can paint the fears
>   When from those friends we sever,
> Perhaps to part for months and years,
>   Perhaps to part forever.

The last moment came when it was perilous to tarry longer. I repaired to my
room to arrange a few things in my valise, feeling a burden almost insupportable, when I heard a light, tripping footstep follow me, heard the door softly
open, and my wife approached, and laid her hand on my shoulder, and pressed
her warm cheek against mine, mingling her tears with mine in mutual sorrow.
Such moments cannot be forgotten. My wife's patriotism and sense of duty exceeded my own. Painful as the separation was, she was willing that I should go,
glad that I was willing to go, and in that extremity I was obliged to borrow
courage from her. I shall not forget the many friendly greetings I received that
morning on my way to the depot, and the many heart-felt blessings, "God go
with you," as we parted. That a watchful Providence may preserve my own
home unbroken till I return, and preserve that little circle of friends complete
till I can join it again, is the fervent prayer of Anti-Rebel.

––––––––––

Second Vermont Regiment
Near Brandy Station, Va.
Feb. 20, 1864

We have had some severe cold weather here during the present week. I
believe it has been the coldest that I have known in Virginia. I cannot tell you
exactly how cold it was, for we had no thermometer, and we needed none to

admonish us that it was necessary for our comfort to remain as closely around the fires as possible. The air produced that sharp, tingling sensation that I supposed was a peculiar attribute of our Vermont climate. The boys, if they had to venture into the open air, invariably clapped their hands to their noses, and whatever it was necessary for them to do they did as quickly as possible. Dilatory traveling was unknown, almost every one by mutual consent adopting the double quick. If an armful of wood was to be brought, or a canteen to be filled, the transaction took place in the shortest possible space of time. There was, however, as little getting about as possible. Nothing unnecessary was thought of or attempted. The men kept in their tents remarkably well. There have been no cases of straggling reported during the present week that I know of. Military law is pretty strict, but I doubt if it ever kept men so strictly in their places as has the cold weather since the commencement of the week, especially Tuesday and Wednesday. Even now the weather is by no means warm or comfortable. My ink-bottle will freeze up in an hour anywhere in the tent, except in the fire-place. Canteens of water are sure to become solid every night, and even in the day time they will freeze if left more than a yard and a half from the fire. It was extremely severe being on picket or doing guard duty of any kind.

According to the fortunes of war, I was detailed for three days picketing, last Sunday morning. Three days picketing, and with such weather as we had then, is about as much as a soldier cares to endure at one time, and it was enough to make him think of the comfortable home he has left behind him.

Sunday was a very pleasant day. I had begun to congratulate myself that morning, as I was doing up my blankets and filling my haversack, that the prospect bid so fair to be pleasant and warm during our picket campaign. But I was doomed to see a serious turn in my luck before I got back, so far as weather was concerned.

Arriving at the line, we were divided up according as we were to be stationed, one half being sent to the reserve, and the other half was distributed to the different posts along the line. A year ago there used to be a big and a small reserve, besides the posts or supports near the picket line itself. Now there is but one reserve, and we spent half of the time there, and the other half on post, making thirty hours on each. The picket line is about two miles and a half from camp. We got there about nine o'clock, and I found myself with those who were counted off to go on post the first twelve hours. There were three men on each post, one of whom was stationed several rods further out towards the enemy, all the time relieving each other every two hours. These videttes are the real pickets, and their "beats" joined together make "the line." I was stationed on my beat the first thing, and received my instructions from my predecessor.

He told me I must walk my beat all the time, must keep a sharp look out, and if I saw anything unusual outside of the lines, anything to excite suspicion that all was not right, I was to report it immediately to the corporal of my post, who was to communicate with the officer commanding the whole detail. For instance, a smoke rising up in the woods just outside of the lines, or a squad of horsemen riding about, would have been considered an evidence that all might not be right. I was to let no man pass through the lines either way. If a man approached from the outside with a pass, I was to call up the commanding officer to examine the pass, who would do as he saw fit about letting him in. If a man approached from the inside, I was to send him to the commanding officer. If any officer were passing along the lines, I was to salute him by standing at shoulder arms, facing the enemy, till they had passed by.

Well I entered upon my duties that morning fully determined to carry out these instructions, without any mental reservation whatever. I walked my beat with all the dignity of a two and a half year old soldier, and never left it at all, except once, and that was when my hat blew off and I took after it, before I thought what I was about. I didn't see any rebs outside of the line, nor anything out of which I could find a reason for supposing that everything was not right. I saw a few ladies once walking across a field, nearly a mile distant from where I stood, but I saw nothing in their appearance that would lead any to suppose that they were going to damage the Union cause a great deal, and so I took no notice of them. Col. Grant rode along the lines once, and I saluted him according to orders. I afterwards heard, that the Colonel expressed much dissatisfaction at many things he saw in the management of pickets and officers, averring among other things, that but one picket on the whole line saluted him properly. That lucky one, of course, was me. It must have been. I could take my solemn oath that I stood at shoulder arms, with my back towards the Union, and I would have been perfectly willing to have manifested my regards for him in a more conspicuous manner if I had not been afraid I should overstep the rules of military etiquette; for such things are regulated by law here. If I was certain I was that one, and had unconsciously distinguished myself on that occasion, I should apply for a promotion immediately.

At nine o'clock that evening, a relief came up from the reserve to take our places, and we went down to the reserve to take their places. Next morning at nine o'clock we came to our posts again, and after staying there twenty-four hours more we went back to the reserve, and remained there till we were finally relieved. The second day on post it snowed, but otherwise was quite comfortable. It grew colder towards morning, and at nine o'clock when we were relieved again, it was very uncomfortable being on post, or in fact being anywhere.

The wind blew all day from the northwest a perfect gale, and it grew colder every minute. We had fires, but they didn't seem to do us any good. The wind would blow the fire all about, and all over us, or it would blow it completely away from us, so that in reality, a fire was more of an annoyance than a benefit. It was even worse come night. We anxiously hoped the wind would go down at sunset, but it did not. It was tough for us, but tenfold more so for the videttes. My friend and I laid down and covered ourselves up with all the blankets we possessed, and tried to sleep. We lay there till we were chilled through, but, finally was obliged to give it up. The boys put up their blankets to keep the wind off from the fire. The most comfortable place I could find was against these blankets, and this position we found was many degrees from comfort. We built us an awful hot fire, so hot that as I sat against those blankets I had to cover my knees with newspapers, and my face with a handkerchief to keep them from burning. If I uncovered my face I couldn't endure the heat a moment. Before me there was intense heat, behind me it was exactly the reverse. The wind made itself felt as much in the rear, as the fire did in front. If some malicious fiend had been sponging my back with ice cold water the sensations could not have been less desirable. Occasionally the torture was varied. A gust of wind would rush around from the other quarter, and blow a perfect avalanche of fire, smoke and ashes all over us. Our clothes plainly showed the effects of this in the morning. That was the meanest experience I have ever had on picket, but it came to an end after a while, as such things always do, and at nine o'clock next morning we were relieved by a fresh detail. Never did a set of shivering pickets look more anxiously for the next relief to arrive than we did then. It came in good season, and we gladly shouldered our muskets and hurried back to our camp well pleased that this misery was at an end; and I think the reader will be pleased that my letter is at an end also.

Second Vermont Regiment
Near Brandy Station, Va.
March 3, 1864

We came in yesterday from a reconnoissance out to Madison Court House, and although we made a very harmless advance, I am tempted to devote a few minutes in writing you an account of our experience out there. We accomplished nothing wonderful, and did no deeds of mighty valor, but after all, in a brief campaign like this there is always enough seen, heard and felt that I am sure would not be uninteresting to others, who take an interest in what we soldiers do, and how we live; and this common every day experience is all that I have to relate. We have marched out to Madison Court House and we have marched back again. We had rather a tedious time of it, but it is over with now and I am glad of it.

Marching orders came last Friday, late in the evening, and we didn't know but that a general movement was intended. We were taken by surprise. We were eating and drinking, and making merry, as usual, when, like a thief in the night, the sergeant came around and told us we must have everything in readiness to march at an early hour in the morning. Now an order like that happened to be of considerable interest to fellows like us, comfortably ensconced in our winter quarters. Of course we are in high spirits, and anxious to take the field against the enemy again — anybody that reads the newspapers knows that — but after all some of us dread the first start. When it is February we are apt to think the weather a little too rough, and want to wait till March, and when March comes we are full as apt to think that it will be a little pleasanter in April, and if it was absolutely necessary, in order to save the Union, that we should remain in camp till May, I presume there are a great many soldiers that would be induced to repress their anxiety to get into the field till then. But here were peremptory orders to march, and evidently the order meant what it specified. They told us in the morning that we might take our tents, or not, as we chose, for we were only going on a reconnoissance, and should probably come back to the same camp again. The most of us concluded to let our tents remain untouched, and run the risk of needing them while we were gone. We packed into our knapsacks all the blankets we could command, for the weather might be cold and stormy, and at best we should have none too many. With our blankets and overcoats we managed to get each of us a pretty respectable load to carry all day, and long before night we became aware that the man with the most blankets was not in any respects the best off. We didn't start till about nine o'clock. We were supposed to have rations in our haversacks besides what was taken along with the teams.

The weather, when we started, was as fine as could be desired. It was not at all muddy, but on the contrary the roads were dry and dusty. Hardly any time last summer were the roads any more dusty than then. We marched through Culpeper, then bore to the right from the railroad towards Robertson Creek. Things did not look at all warlike in and around Culpeper. Ladies on horseback were riding gaily about with officers, and seemed to be having a merry time generally. No other corps but ours appeared to be on the move. We marched through the town in military style, carrying our guns in uniform position, and keeping step to martial music. This is all very fine, though some of the boys can hardly see the point of putting on too many airs in such a rabid secession place as Culpeper is. We recollect going through there once before in grand order, making every citizen that saw us believe that we were surely invincible, that we were in a glorious state of discipline, and bound to march straight into Richmond, and we recollect that we were hustled back through that same city in the night time pell mell, in no order at all, and we had no desire to act the same thing over again.

We made good time on our march that day. Our resting places were few, and very far between. For some reason or other our usual hour at noon for making coffee, was not given us. When we are on a march coffee is almost indispensable. It is food, drink and rest, all in one. It was said that our division commander was severely censured for marching us at such an unconstitutional rate. I do not know whether the story was true or not, but I know it ought to be. The boys began to "play out" pretty fast towards the middle of the afternoon, though the distance marched was less than twenty miles. But our knapsacks were unusually heavy, besides we hadn't yet got accustomed to such marching this season. It made us sore and lame. I saw one fellow marching along with one boot in one hand, and the other stuck on his gun, while his stockings were nearly worn off his feet by the dirt and hard travellng. His feet were swelled and he had several large blisters on them. He was a new recruit, and one of the veterans asked him how much of his town bounty he had paid for that day. Well, he said, they might knock off about a ten spot for that, but he didn't care a damn; he should soon get toughened to it. He is a courageous fellow, — a Vermonter clear to the bone, — and his friends needn't worry but that he will be able to endure a soldier's life. Such men are not frightened to death by trifles.

It was somewhat past the middle of the afternoon when we had the satisfaction of seeing the head of the column doubling up and stacking arms to camp for the night. We filed off into a piece of woods where there was a plenty of hard timber, and in a very short space of time our little axes were busy at work, and soon we had large cheerful fires blazing up all through the woods, and we proceeded at once to make ourselves as comfortable as possible for the night.

I cannot speak for the rest, but I know that I slept very soundly that night, and in the morning felt abundantly able to accomplish any reasonable amount of marching. We were not ordered to fall in till eight o'clock, and then we didn't march but a little way before we halted again. The fires that we had left in the woods seemed inclined to take advantage of the dry weather and our absence, to indulge in extraordinary liberties, for a huge volume of smoke was rolling up out of the woods as if the whole forest was on fire. Out in the field the fires were equally lawless, and we were set to work to put them out. One man would have made a sorry show before so much fire, but the whole army of us soon got the better of it, though not until it had blackened several acres of ground, and burned quite a number of rods of good secesh fence. Further on we came to the same evil. Everywhere a fire had been built it had spread almost indefinitely. The dead grass in the fields and the dead timber in the woods had become so dry that they burned like tinder. In one place we had to turn out of the road to get along, for the fences each side were burning furiously, aided by a vigorous south wind, and from a little pine woods, on one side of the road, the smoke was issuing fast and hot. Companies H and G had been sent to Lookout Mountain where there was a signal station, but all communication with it was cut off on account of the smoke. The fires crawled clear to the mountain, and from where we halted we could see it ascend its sides. The smoke was visible by day, and the fire itself by night.

We halted near Robertson Creek, stacked arms, but were told not to build any fires. There were fences all around us, and the rails looked very tempting, but so long as we were not allowed to build any fires, we had no need for them. By and by an officer came along and announced that leave had been given to build fires, and in less than ten seconds almost every rail had found an individual owner, and in a very few minutes more every rail in that near vicinity had been appropriated. Secesh pigs and chickens fared no better. All squeamishness on this subject is at an end. If we find anything we want we consider it ours.

A couple of sheep got frightened into the crowd and captured, for somebody a fine supper of mutton. The poor sheep made a sad error when they dodged in between our regiment and the Fourth. They appeared conscious of their mistake, and if nimble feet could have saved them, they would have got away. They run first in one direction, and then in another, but were everywhere headed off by an inexhaustible multitude of soldiers. The boys cheered and shouted as the sheep escaped like lightning from one crowd into another, or dodged a dozen boys at once. But they were conquered at last by force of numbers. The Vermont brigade is more than a match for two sheep. They had to surrender to their cruel captors, though they had earned a better fate. But the boys that got them were too mutton-loving to admit of any hopes of mercy.

We remained in that place till Wednesday morning when we come in. It commenced storming Monday night, and the rest of the time it was wet, nasty, and disagreeable enough everywhere. Sometimes it rained, and sometimes it snowed, and sometimes it did both at once. As we had no tents, and had used up our rations, and as rails had begun to be a cash article, we begun to be anxious to go back to camp. The cavalry had gone out and come in again, and from what the cavalry boys said it was evident that they considered their expedition anything but a successful one.

Wednesday morning we had orders to return. The sun rose clear and bright. The trees were loaded with ice. Every bough and twig was an icicle, which sparkled like pearly crystals in the glittering sunlight. The roads were the opposite extreme from dusty. We made the whole distance back to camp that day. The distance will not vary much from twenty-five miles. Many fell out completely exhausted and helpless as infants — some after we had got within sight of camp. It seemed much better to get back to my old tent that night, than it did that night I got back from my furlough home. But I am getting tedious and will close.

Second Vermont Regiment
Near Brandy Station, Va.
Mar. 14, 1864

The army of the Potomac has not moved yet, but if the present weather holds much longer there is a strong probability that we shall be ordered out of our pleasant quarters here into the field of strife once more, and that very soon. It is much less muddy now than two years ago when we left Camp Griffin, and all the facilities for moving are much better now than they were then. But, at this time of year, the weather cannot be trusted. A long rainstorm would spoil the traveling completely at anytime. There is one indication of a move in the army, the women are all ordered away, though this may only be precautionary, as a forward movement is liable to take place at any time. What direction is to be taken when we do move, and what we are expected to accomplish, is only conjecture. We hope some kind of move will be inaugurated that will promise better success than any we have started heretofore. Going to Richmond, and by this route, has been proved a task beyond our ability times enough to satisfy any reasonable mind that our strength and energy had better be expended in some other direction than in assailing the rebel works directly in front. If I was only the President of the United States, I would have all the armies clear around Secessia hammering away at them at once, so that the rebel armies in each quarter would have business of their own to attend to, and this would stop their reinforcing from one point to another. Longstreet should find permanent employment, either here or at Knoxville, and should not be allowed to frighten both this army and that one at the same time. While the army of the Cumberland and Tennessee was thundering away at the rebels opposed to them, I should have the Potomac army flank Richmond by the way of Charlottesville and Lynchburg, thus destroying the communications with the rebel capital on the Virginia Central, and the Virginia and Tennessee railroads. Lee's army would then find itself in a dangerous predicament, and perhaps be obliged to come out and fight us on grounds of our own choosing. Their formidable works along the Rapidan and the Rappahannock would not protect their precious heads, nor should we be obliged to cross any Mine Runs, or any place of that sort, in order to get a chance to fight these national villains. We should have a fair open field fight, and that is all that we want. If we can't whip them then, we may as well acknowledge their Confederacy at once and go home, call ourselves whipped, and make the best of it we can. But such a disaster could not happen. We should succeed if the business was only managed right. There could be no doubt about it. We should scatter the rebel armies to the four winds, conquer a peace, and be at home in season to hoe our potatoes, and celebrate the Fourth of July. But I am not the President, my friends, and I am afraid this war will linger along in the same blundering way hereafter as heretofore; and that your patience is doomed to be tortured for a long time to come, as it has been for a long time past.

We had a brigade review last Monday, and one again Thursday. Notwithstanding it rained the last time, there were some distinguished Vermont citizens, and a few ladies, present to witness it. We have a first rate ground in front of our camp for parades and reviews, and we have had some first rate parades and reviews on this ground. The Vermont Brigade took their places in line here, — and it makes a pretty long line now — and when the order was given "Prepare for review," and we had opened ranks so that the reviewing officer could see both the rear and the front rank at once, Col. Grant rode around the line to the rear and front, followed by his staff officers, citizens and visitors, who appeared to be well pleased with our appearance. Gen. Sedgwick couldn't

resist the temptation to come and see us too. I noticed the old fellow was looking remarkably good-natured, as he passed by in front of where I stood, and he
seemed to be talking with considerable animation to the officers that rode by
the side of him; pointing occasionally to us, as if he was afraid they would
overlook some of the excellencies which he saw. I couldn't tell what he said exactly, but I knew well enough, he was telling them how quick he could take
Richmond if he only had Vermonters enough to do it. When they had passed
around us, they took their position, and we marched around in front of them.
After this, we went through a few of the maneuvres of brigade drill. We made
one gallant bayonet charge on the double-quick, which would give a spectator
some idea of how this was done in actual battle. The whole brigade was in a line
perfectly straight. The field was broad and open before us. At the command
"Forward march," all started at once. "Charge bayonets," was the next order,
and every man grasped his musket with both hands, the cold steel extending to
the front, ready for immediate use. At the word "Double quick" we set up a
yell and started on the run. The line was so long, of course, it couldn't be kept
exactly straight. Some point might swell out a little ahead of the rest, and then
recede, and another portion press a little too hard, but every such irregularity,
though like a wave it might run the whole length of the line, would immediately
correct itself, and only make the whole so much the more interesting to witness.
Our mounted officers and spectators were ahead of us, and they took good
care to keep out of our way. They appeared to be intensely delighted. No doubt
they rejoiced in not being rebels just then.

I am glad to be able to tell you, that we are having good religious meetings in
our regiment now. The Christian Commission has two delegates here, the Rev.
Messrs. C.C. Parker and J.W.H. Baker, both from Vermont. They have put
up a large Chapel tent, capable of seating about two hundred men. They hold
meetings here every evening, and almost every time the tent is filled to overflowing, and sometimes many have to go away without finding admission. This
large attendance is owing to two or three causes. One is because it is something
new, for it has been a long time since we have enjoyed any religious privileges to
speak of. Another is, because it is a very agreeable way to spend an hour — a
pleasant change from the dull monotony of camp life, whether one cares particularly for the meeting or not. Cheerful sacred singing and speaking is pleasant always; but I believe a soldier enjoys them the best of anybody. It is very
natural from his circumstances that he should. These reasons and the desire on
the part of a great many to do good, has so far kept up a full attendance. The
meetings commence at half past six and are held till the drum calls us to roll call
at eight. One of the delegates preaches a short sermon, or rather makes a few

practical remarks founded upon some text of Scripture, and then the time is occupied by any one who wishes to speak, sing or pray. Generally the time is fully occupied, and often two or more rise to speak at once. Many have risen at the invitation to manifest a desire for the others in their behalf, and some have spoken there that never spoke in meeting before. Besides these, a sort of Bible class is held every day in the Chapel, and where the boys that desire it may meet for studying the Scriptures, and for mutual improvement. Tracts and papers are distributed freely. A good work is begun here, one which every Christian will rejoice to see prosper.

———————

Camp near Brandy Station, Va.
March 17, 1864

The equinoctial storm seems to be upon us in all of its violence. More snow has fallen here within the last six hours than we have had before this winter and still it comes. The prospect this evening is that it will snow all night — and, for all of any signs that are apparent now, it may keep on snowing forever. The Storm King seems to have awakened from his inactivity with a determination to make up for the time lost during the mild winter almost past. It is a regular northeaster, and beats right through the tent on to my sheet of paper here as if it was used to the business and liked it, and in a manner as disagreeable as it is familiar. The tent makes a poorer defence against the snow than it used to against the rain, and I believe I never had occasion to commend it too highly for doing its duty in that respect.

"Old Dixie," the army poet and balladist, has been around to visit us again. There is nothing particularly remarkable in this fact were it not that he has been hung as a spy several times, besides having been killed once or twice last summer while trying to act in the capacity of a rebel guerrilla. There are quite a number of our boys that are personally acquainted with some one or more who saw this same man suspended by the neck and dangling from the limbs of a tree near Frederick, Maryland, when we passed through there last summer. He came here last Thursday. I was on guard at the Colonel's tent, and by virtue of my position, I suppose, I had the honor of shaking hands with the old fellow, and I judged him to be possessed of remarkable health for a man that has accomplished such unheard of adventures as he has. I was pleased to see him introduce himself to Colonel Stone.[20] The Colonel was just outside of the tent and about to enter, but not having the same uniform exactly that the officers generally wear, "Dixie" didn't know him. "Is the Colonel in?" he asks. Colonel Stone gravely informs him that he is not. "Will he be in soon, think?" "I think he will." "How soon should you think?" Well, the Colonel was sure that he would be in his tent within a very short time. The Colonel looked a little roguish (he always carries a pleasant face) and when he asked him into his tent, "Dixie" began to mistrust, and inquired if he was the man. Receiving an answer in the affirmative, he gave his name as E.W. Locke, the man that used to sing to the boys on the Peninsula and at Camp Griffin. I believe the Colonel didn't hardly recognize him as an old acquaintance, though Locke seemed to regard the fact that he was so popular with the boys a sufficient passport to the presence of any officer in the army. This man has indeed written and sung us some very excellent songs, and, as far as I am concerned, I am perfectly willing he should live to sing us a great many more. His reputation, I noticed, has reached as far as Vermont. "Brother, when will you come back?" and "we're marching on to Richmond," with some others, are very pretty pieces. I was entertained with the music of some of his songs when I was at home on my furlough, and if I had another furlough to-morrow morning to start for home and hear some more of them, I would be awful glad of it.

I was over to the 5th Maine regiment a few days ago to visit a friend, and I found the Maine boys wide awake, and full of fun. The Maine boys are a good deal like the Vermonters, but they beat us in one thing. They had fixed up a great hall in the woods where they held "concerts" almost every evening unless the weather or their duties prevent. These concerts were got up with considerable ingenuity, and were quite entertaining. Several officers with their ladies were there. The hall where these performances were held, was built of logs, and covered with boughs, made especially for this purpose. Seats were provided for about two hundred men. A stage was erected for the performers in regular theatrical style. For curtains they had half tents but the scenery was perfectly natural. A fee of ten cents was required at the door, and the boys always had a full house. The night I was there it was crowded. Every available spot for sitting or standing was occupied, and many went away that could not get in. Some that were too late to secure a seat, offered ten cents for the privilege of looking through the boughs on the roof at the performance, but the sentinels had too high a regard for the honor of their institution to permit any such undignified proceedings as that. The boys certainly showed considerable enterprise and ingenuity in getting up their "show," and considerable wit in their exhibition of it.

This regiment belongs to the first division of our corps, and is situated across the Hazel Run, on our right. I almost envied them their pleasantly situated camp, and their handy access to wood. They have an advantage over us in this respect of no mean importance. They are on dry ground, and protected from the wind by hills and trees, and they have built themselves log houses that I fancy would be considered quite stylish in some Western settlements, even in time of peace. Our own regiment occupies a camp on a wide plain, which seems to be a peculiar point of attraction for the winds from all quarters, and anybody that had ever lived in shanties like ours, knows how disagreeable a windy day may be, especially if the weather is cold and we are obliged to keep a fire. Fire wood is beginning to be an article of great importance with us. We have to contrive all manner of ways and means to supply our fire-places. Our wood lot was harvested long ago. Nothing but the stumps and brush remain, and these are every day becoming more and more scarce. We are driven to the strictest economy. By dint of considerable perseverance, a man can get an armful of wood from what is left of a much abused stump, or he can go well on towards a mile and get an armful of small limbs from the brush of some tree top. The other regiments in this brigade have not even this poor privilege. Their fuel was all exhausted in the early part of the winter. Their brush was cleaned up and their stumps pared to the ground long ago. The teams bring them a small ration of wood once in a while from beyond the picket line; not half enough, it seems to me, to keep them any where near comfortable, nor one tenth part of what they would use if they could get all they wanted. Our wood lot lasted about one month. The brush and stumps have kept us supplied twice as long. That part of the wood that farmers generally throw away has really served us longer than the part which they save.

Last Saturday a large detail was sent out to clean off the ground near Brandy Station for a big review. We expect Gen. Grant will be here this week to review us. We cleared off the rubbish from a large area, and the ground is eminently favorable for a grand parade. For some reason or other, the whole "fatigue" force for this business was solicited from the Vermont brigade. This was owing, no doubt, to some whimsical notions of our Commanding-General. Our day's work was not very hard. We had a few briars and bushes to cut down and carry off, and that was about all. There were plenty of us there to do it. At a rough guess I should think there was about two handsful of bushes for each man on the ground, and I believe there were some there mean enough to shirk from even this duty. I carried off, myself, as many as a half a dozen armsful of brush as big as I could lift, and I know if the rest had done their duty I shouldn't have had to carry more than two. But I was at work for my country so I didn't care.

And now I must bring my important letter to a close. It is near midnight, and my last ration of candles is nearly burned out. Taps beat long ago, and I have been violating the rules of camp ever since, in not retiring as a good and dutiful soldier should. But the storm has kept raging, and I have kept writing. I have sinned with impunity, because I suppose the officer of the day does not like to enforce the army regulations in such a snow storm. If my readers will forgive me I think the officer of the day will. My tent mates are all asleep, and some of them are snoring dismal strains of sepulchral music, as I write. I have deliberately made up my mind to join them and —— here I am fast asleep.

Snowballing in the Army
Camp near Brandy Station, Va.
March 23, 1864

We had some glorious sport this forenoon snowballing. The weather was fine and the snow just right. The 2nd and 6th regiment had a regular pitched battle, which resulted in the discomfiture of the latter. A squad of our boys, principally from Co. C, went up to the Sixth, and stumped the crowd for a snowball fight. The Sixth came out and drove them back. It was now evident that the squad from the Second must have reinforcements or call themselves whipped. Some of our officers, eager for fun, collected quite a force, and headed by our Major, we rallied to the assistance of the defeated party. Snowballs flew thick and fast, some of the foremost on each side getting completely plastered over with them, head, ears, neck, and all. A reserve of reinforcements coming up in the nick of time, virtually decided the contest. They all charged on the Sixth, shouting and snowballing to their utmost. The Sixth was obliged to fall back, fighting valorously as they retreated. We saw our advantage and followed it up till we drove them clear back to their camp. We started to return, and they attempted to follow us, but we faced about again, and they saw it wouldn't do, and acknowledged that it was enough. Both regiments left off snowballing, and went to shaking hands with each other. All were good-natured, and no one lost his temper. We claim that we captured their colors, and three or four of their officers. Each regiment had a flag improvised for the occasion. They admit a defeat, but think our force was the strongest. It was lively sport "charging" and snowballing, capturing and recapturing officers, though it was ruinous for army coats, and the wear and tear of clothing in some of our encounters was immense. I haven't had time to get a complete list of the killed and wounded, but as our surgeon was on the ground, I am confident that all the wounded were well cared for.

Camp near Brandy Station, Va.
April 7, 1864

We have just had what is here known as a general inspection. The inspection occupied but very few minutes, and as it takes the place of our regular drill this afternoon we shall have nothing further to do till night. The pleasantest way that I can think of to spend these idle moments is to pen a few lines to the *Freeman,* though I am afraid it is almost imposing upon good nature to attempt to offer anything for entertainment when the times are as dull as now. I have been tolerated so long that my self-confident assurance has grown immensely, and if I keep on writing I don't know but that my habit of writing for the *Freeman* will by and by become seated and incurable. But I cannot help it. When I know that the readers of the *Freeman* include but very few sneering copperheads if any at all, and that all are interested in the soldier's welfare, and interested in the cause for which we are here, it is very easy and pleasant to write, and I cannot resist the temptation, and I will not try.

The signs of an advance movement begin to thicken. Sutlers have been ordered away, and there is now, I understand, an order at headquarters for the men to pack up, to be sent off, every article that we do not need, such as extra clothing, overcoats, blankets, and the like, as has been our custom every spring. These are only preliminary movements and really indicate nothing immediate, but so far as we know, the army may be ordered to move within a week. We have had considerable wet rainy weather of late, which will doubtless retard operations some. A few that are prone to prophesy say that it is doubtful if we move from here before May. But we soldiers trust this matter is in wiser hands than ours, and when they consider that the proper time has arrived for action, and order us forward, we shall go cheerfully and confidently, whether the time be sooner or later. It seems to be the prevailing opinion here in the army, that we are at last to have a campaign that will for once be really "short, sharp, and decisive," and I will add, victorious. Great confidence is felt in the plans that General Grant will adopt, and the means that he will have to use in crushing the last vestige of this Heaven accursed rebellion. Having authority that extends from the Atlantic to the Mississippi, from Mobile to Washington, we may reasonably expect a concert of action in the coming campaigns that will ensure us success and victory. God grant that we may not be disappointed.

Success and victory! whose heart does not beat quicker at the thought? What consequences will have been achieved when this great rebellion shall have been forever humbled. It is not merely that this terrible war may be ended, and we safely at liberty again, that we hope to conquer our enemies and be once more at peace, but that the great principles of a free government, whose worth no mind short of Infinite Wisdom can estimate, and which even after the world has stood so long is still considered an experiment, may not be overthrown, and the progress of civilization and freedom may not be rolled back for ages, or receive a blow from which they may never recover. We are anxious of course to get out of this war, for we long most earnestly to return to the almost sacred hills and valleys of old Vermont, but we are not so anxious for this, as we are that the faith of the world in the intelligence and virtue of the common people, and their ability to govern themselves and maintain national unity without being rent asunder by internal strife and discord — a faith that despots the world over profess to sneer at, and hold to be a delusion, and which stimulates the noblest energies of the masses of mankind — that this may be maintained, increased and perpetuated. If these principles succeed, Slavery must fall, and fall forever. The two are so antagonistical that, even if both are right, or neither of them, men embracing each could not possibly live together in peace, unless we are to suppose that God has given them a larger spirit of forbearance than is vouchsafed to humanity in general. There never was a real unity between them, and there never can be. Slavery is a relic of the darkest ages, and the poorest government on earth is better in principle than that. If we are going to have a free government at all, let us have it all free, or else we had better give up the name. Slavery has fostered an aristocracy of the rankest kind, and this aristocracy is the bitterest foe that a really free government can have. Slavery and despotism have challenged war with us, and by it she must abide. Slavery was jealous of the comelier strength that Freedom possessed; and maliciously envied her irresistible march onward to a higher destiny. Slavery drew the sword, and would have stabbed Freedom to the heart, had not God denied her the strength. She could not bear that her more righteous neighbor should be prospered, while she herself was accursed, and in her foolish madness she has tried to rend the Union in twain. With that institution it is success or death. Compromise with Slavery, and restore the Union with Slavery in it still! As well might Jehovah compromise with Satan and give him back part of Heaven.

There never before was a rebellion like this one. Generally a rebellion has been the outbreak of the people against the tyranny of a few. Their cause has usually been the cause of liberty, and more or less just. Knit together by the idea of freeing themselves from an odious despotism, and armed with justice, and backed by numbers, they have often succeeded, and history has applauded their bravery. In this war it has been different. The people have not rebelled against the few, but the few have rebelled against the people. Our government is the people's, and against this government the proud slaveholder has rebelled. With Slavery for a corner stone they hope to rob our government of her honor, and erect within our borders a rival government, which every attribute of the Almighty must detest. Can they succeed? Is the glory of our nation to be destroyed forever? Is the great experiment which our forefathers have made, and which has been our pride and boast so long, to be a failure after all? If the North will do her duty, we answer, Never! And the North *will* do her duty. She knows what it is, and she does not fear it. Never in a war before did the rank and file feel a more resolute earnestness for a just cause, and a more invincible determination to succeed, than in this war; and what the rank and file are determined to do everybody knows will surely be done. We mean to be thorough about it too. We are not going to destroy the military power of the dragon Confederacy and not destroy its fangs also. We have as a nation yielded to their rapacious demands times enough. We have cringed before Slavery as long as we will.

> "Far better die in such a strife,
>   Than still to Slavery's claims concede,
> Than crouch beneath her frown for life,
>   Far better in the field to bleed:
> To live thus wage a life-long shame,
>   To die is victory and fame."

I almost lose my temper sometimes (what little I have got) when I hear men that really ought to know better, call this war a mere crusade to free the negroes, "a nigger war" and nothing more. But even if I was fighting to free the negroes simply, I don't know why I should be acting from a motive that I need be ashamed of. I verily believe that He who when He was on the earth healed foul leprosy, gave sight to the blind beggars, and preached the gospel to the poor, would not be ashamed to act from such a motive. And if he would not, why should I? Fighting to free the "niggers!" Why yes, my dear fellow, we are doing just that and a great deal more. But, sir, I am going to tell you, you would not speak of that so contemptuously, if you had not all your life long fed your soul upon motives so small, so mean, and so selfish, that the sublimer motives of sacrificing blood and treasure to elevate a degraded and down-trodden race, is entirely beyond your comprehension. Should such an event, however, rather help than hinder the success of this war, we trust that you will acquiesce in the result, and when the future of this country shall have become by this means more glorious than the past has ever been, we shall hope that you will find that your own liberty and happiness has not been at all infringed upon by giving the same liberty and happiness to a few ignorant and despised sons of Africa.

But I have prolonged this discussion till my space is full, and I have no room for general news, if any had been needed. The weather has been pleasant since the snow and rainstorms of Saturday and Monday, but just now another storm is threatened. We are to have three drills each day till further orders, two in the forenoon, and one in the afternoon, and this with our other duties, getting wood, and the like, will leave us rather a short allowance of time for idleness.

Camp near Brandy Station
April 15, 1864

The news here in camp is not very startling just now. Cold weather and rainstorms seem to preponderate in the statistics of the weather, with an occasional sunny, spring-like day, just to show how pretty a smile Dame Nature can wear when she chooses to do so.

About one week ago, one dark and very stormy night, several men deserted from the regiment, but were overtaken and brought back again the next morning by the cavalry sent after them as they were missed. There were seven of them, and six were retaken and one escaped. The Rappahannock was swollen by the rain, and these adventurers found it more difficult to cross than they had expected.

That same night two railroad bridges between here and Alexandria were swept away or rendered useless for the time, and our supplies were cut off till they were repaired. The worst inconvenience that we boys felt was in being obliged to fall back upon hard tack, and the loss of our daily mail. This interruption was soon remedied, and now we are enjoying our daily bread and daily mail as usual.

The great topic of discussion and interest just now among some of the "old" boys, who have not re-enlisted, is as to when their time of service will expire. Even those who came out with the regiment at first are not entirely satisfied on this point. Their opinions are divided, some thinking that they will be freemen the first of June, and others not expecting that glad day before the twentieth. There is claimed to be most excellent authority for believing that the old soldiers in the whole brigade will be discharged the first of June. Positive evidence to that effect, it is said, has been received by some from the State authorities of Vermont, and there can be no doubt about it. On the other hand those less sanguine, but more reasonable, believe that they will have to wait till the twentieth of June, which is the third anniversary of their muster into the United States service. Then there are the recruits that have joined the regiment at various times. These have more reason to debate the question than the "old" men.

We have five distinct classes of recruits. The first joined the regiment in the Fall of 1861, at Camp Griffin, the second in the Spring of 1862, at Lee's Mill, the third in the Fall of '62 at Hagerstown, Md.; the fourth class was the drafted men and substitutes that came out here last Fall. The last class are those that have come here under the last call of the President. The two last named do not of course expect to be affected by the expiration of the regiment's term of service. The others do, and enlisted with the express understanding to that effect. The first recruits and the Lee's Mill's recruits supposed they were sure beyond a peradventure that their time would be out in June, 1864, and the Hagerstown recruits were expressly promised by those who ought to have known what they were promising that they should be discharged with the regiment. But Government makes a dodge they were not thinking of. The regiment is not going to be discharged but is to remain here right along as usual, and the men are to be discharged as fast as their term of service expires, but no faster. Men anxious to get home to their families and business, as almost all are who have families and business to get home to, are seriously inconvenienced by this, and quite naturally feel most keenly that there has been bad faith practiced in regard to them somewhere. This is felt more especially by the Hagerstown recruits. It lengthens out their term of service nearly a year and a half.

Re-enlisting was checkmated really when government bounties stopped. There has been some enlistments since, however. Just now there is considerable stir among our Lee's Mill's recruits on this matter of re-enlisting. In the other regiments of the brigade, I understand this class of recruits have re-enlisted in season to get their government bounty of $400. The reason they did not here was because of some uncertainty as to the time they had originally been mustered in. It seems they had enlisted in February and March of '62, but were not formally mustered into the United States service till some time in April, and some affirm that they have no recollection of ever being mustered in at all. It is certain that upon our regular company pay and muster rolls, the date of enlistment and the date of muster are identical, but upon some ancient roll somewhere, the Lee's Mill's recruits date their first muster the 12th of April '62, and the recruiting officer of this regiment did not dare to enlist them till they had served two years from that time. They have served two years now, and they say they are bound to "go in."

Being cheated out of their government bounty, with a very feeble prospect of a local bounty at home, these recruits — I mean veterans — determined to make it up by assigning themselves to New York City, and get the bounty offered there. Should more men be called for by and by, and Vermont need more to fill her quota, and should the towns that claim to have a sort of natural right to these men offer again the usual local bounty to all whose names should count upon their quota, not omitting the re-enlisted veterans, as undoubtedly they would not, these veterans would not have made so much by forsaking old Vermont after all. But the faults of human nature extend even to soldiers, and they are apt to become selfish and look out for their own interests very much as other people do. As for any scruples in the matter, they say their towns don't care for them so long as their quota is full. Towns, they argue, pay big bounties not because they think the soldiers deserve or earn it, but to prevent being drafted into the service themselves. They have served so long without any bounty, and now they deem it their right to secure one if possible. In New York they have $375 paid down, while in Vermont they would only get their State pay, amounting, cash in hand, to but $225. As long as it is likely to make $150 difference whether they go for New York or Vermont, it is expecting a large share of State pride and devotedness to one's own locality to expect that men, some of whom have families depending upon them for support, will make that sacrifice. New York city wants men, Vermont towns do not. New York city gives a bounty, while the towns in Vermont do not. The cause they are fighting for is all the same, the result is the same, and I find the men do not hesitate at all in assigning themselves to the quota of New York instead of going to the credit of Vermont. I am not writing of how they *ought* to act in this matter, I am writing of how they *do* act, and how the question is discussed here.

Undoubtedly, Vermont will make this all right in time, but just now it looks a little unfair. From where I am writing this letter, I can look through the folds of my tent, and see a good-for-nothing recruit, three score years old, and gray headed, deaf and decrepit, who has not done a day's duty and cannot; whom (the boys say) the grave has spoken for, and who will never feel at home till he gets there, and this man was paid $300 by the town he came from, besides the $300 government bounty he is to receive here; was passed by the examining surgeons I suppose at home, and is now installed in all the dignities of a soldier in the U.S. Army. Money in the world's eye when it is given to pay for services, makes rank, and this man ranks several hundred dollars higher than any able-bodied, service hardened veteran, that may choose to re-enlist. Of course men that love to grumble will pick this up, and if they look for an excuse for giving Vermont the mitten, they find in instances like these, and they are quite numerous, such as are suited to their liking. But the reader will excuse my mentioning this. I hadn't anything else to do, and when a soldier gets idle, he almost gets to grumbling, and if he hasn't anything to grumble about himself, he is willing to help those that have.

The Christian Commission
Camp near Brandy Station, Va.
April 26, 1864

The station of the Christian Commission here has been taken away. It was removed a week ago to-day. This was done I suppose because it was thought the army here was about to break up camp. The station was called the Vermont Station of the U.S. Christian Commission, and during its stay here there were four different delegates, though not more than two at one time. Revs. C.C. Parker, and J.W. Baker, were succeeded by Revs. Wm. M. Taylor, from Pennsylvania, and George Moore Smith, from Connecticut. There were all faithful, earnest men — men who appeared anxious only for the soldier's good, both spiritual and temporal. The last few days Mr. Smith had the whole care, Mr. Taylor having left for other fields of usefulness. Mr. Smith preached a regular sermon every evening, attended the Bible class at noon each day beside the multitude of other duties that a clergyman has to perform in a place like this. Portions of the day he assigned for those who might wish to call on him for private religous instruction, besides which he visited the sick in the hospital, the sick in their tents, and ministered to the wants of the needy everywhere. I have seen him a mile from the station, among the other camps with a haversack slung on his shoulder, filled, I suppose, with testaments and tracts that he had been giving away to the boys. He evidently understood his work, his heart was in it, and he did it well. He told me he thought the soldiers much more susceptible of religious instruction than the same number of people at home. It was easier to preach to them. Their susceptibility did not come of ignorance, or stupidity, but, on the contrary, the soldiers were intelligent and earnest in the matter. They required just as good preaching as the average of people anywhere. Their cordial, appreciative earnestness made preaching easy. There appeared to be, he said, entire unanimity among them. No sectarianism or bigotry marred the harmony of the meetings. Nobody inquired of another if he was a Methodist, a Baptist, or an Episcopalian, and no one seemed to care for religious preferences. If a man was a Christian, it was enough. The first Sabbath of this month the sacrament of the Lord's Supper was partaken of by about thirty communicants. Eleven made a profession of faith, and three were baptized.

This Christian Commission has become to be respected by all the boys. Even those who care but little about its benefits personally speak well of it, and think it a very good thing. The idea of an enterprise of such infinitude being carried on and supported by voluntary contributions from those who are interested in our welfare mainly because we belong to the common brotherhood of mankind, and have souls to save, as well as bodies to preserve, carried with it such a weight of argument for the sincerity and power of that christian principle which begets this spirit of benevolence, that no man attempts to gainsay or resist it.

The worst of soldiers know and appreciate what is good in human nature, as well as the best, though they may not imitate it themselves. The world may call us "rough" and "rough" many of us certainly are, rougher than there is any need or excuse for; but, beneath this rough exterior you will generally find a heart that can be as easily touched by kind and benevolent attentions, as the hearts of those who have acquired a more icy polish, and who aspire to belong to a more refined class of people. A Hottentot will appreciate and respect a really disinterested and unselfish act, and I should be loth to admit that any of us soldiers, were less manly than they. I believe the soldiers like these Christian Commission delegates better than they do the regular army chaplains. I mean as a general thing. The chaplains they say, all they care for is to come out here and see the country, hold office, get a good swad of greenbacks every pay day, perhaps preach a tolerable good sermon on Sunday, if the weather is perfectly right, distribute the mail when it comes, and then when they get tired of this, contrive some way to be out of health, resign, and go home. I am half inclined to believe, myself, that some of them "play it" in just that way. If an army chaplain pays no heed to the divine requirements, he can very easily do all the army regulations require of him. Occasionally we have what Beecher would say was God's ideal of an army chaplain, but alas! they are scarce. But these delegates are just the men that the army wants. It is hard work for the most malignant to cavil at what they do. They give their time and their services, and generally work hard, and work willingly. Their term is short, and they endeavor to make the most of it. If they were selfish enough to think of it, they would not want to be outdone by their successor, or by those whom they had succeeded. Not many, however, would leave their charge at home, and come out there to labor for us without any compensation from the Government, or any connection with it whatever unless they were animated with the desire to do good, rather than to make themselves conspicuous. We who receive their ministrations are not asked or expected to give them anything for their work, but on the contrary, they distribute their gifts to us most liberally. Testaments in English, German, and French, are given freely to any and all who wish to receive them, and so are religious books, newspapers, tracts in enormous quantities, and these gifts are received, read and appreciated. For a missionary field, there is none half so promising as the army, none half so white for the harvest as this. No missionary in any field can receive a heartier welcome than the soldier is willing to accord to the delegates of the Christian Commission; and, if my opinion is of any account, no more can be accomplished anywhere else than can be accomplished here. Some who have been with us and seen how easily great results are obtained, have called it a revival, when really it is not a revival, it is only what can be done anywhere in the army, at anytime by the same means.

We shall remember with gratitude what has been done for us here, and some will have all eternity to be grateful in. Probably no other army was ever cared for as ours has been. European armies knew no Christian Commission. Napoleon thought the worse the man the better the soldier. Many of us would be sorry indeed if that principle had sway in this army. Of course, camp life must always present peculiar and powerful temptations. An army collects a great many very bad men, and their example here is all the more pernicious, because it has a wider range of liberty to develop itself, and there is no public sentiment to crush it. Away from the restraints of society, and of home, it is the easiest thing in the world to drop in with the current, call it the "soldier's style," "live while you do live," and let the end take care of itself. The Christian Commission may not be able to wholly remedy this, no man can expect so much as that, but just so far as they are able to bring the influences of home and religion among us, just so far they will counteract the opposing influences of vice and immorality. They may not be able to make the camp what home is, but they can make it a great deal better than it is now. Now, though I say it myself, and surely I ought to know, there is nothing that so stimulates the soldier to endure what he has to endure as that moral strength which comes of the thought, that friends at home are not unmindful of us, but anxious to do us good whenever it lies in their power. The Christian Commission is well got up, ably conducted and thoroughly efficient. All who contribute of their means to this noble organization may rest assured that what they give is not given for nothing, nor is it received into thankless hands.

We were sorry to see our chapel torn down, and the delegates take their leave. We shall miss very much the books and newspapers they gave us, and miss the good preaching we had the privilege of hearing. But, because we broke up our camp, the Commission does not forsake us. It will follow us on to the field, and be ready to assist us just when we shall need assistance most. Hand in hand with the Sanitary Commission they will attend to the wounded men, when but for them, these victims of war might be beyond the need of attendance. God bless them both.

On the Battle-Field
May 9, 1864

I presume you have heard, before this, all the incidents worth relating of the present bloody campaign, so that any further account will be only a repetition of the same or similar scenes, such as we all have witnessed. Being one of that fortunate number that lives to "tell the tale," I am inclined, however, to run the risk and do so, though so completely worn out and exhausted as I find

myself to-day, I should give a very tame account of what I have seen and experienced, for I have hardly life enough left to tell where I have been or what I
have seen. Of course, no one of us can give much of an account of anything
that has happened beyond his own range of vision, for it is difficult to get much
of an idea beyond that ourselves.

On the morning of the 4th of May we left our old camp at early dawn, and
took the war path once more. The morning was bright and clear, the air cool
and refreshing, as we bid adieu to our winter's home, and started on what we
knew to be the most perilous campaign of the war. We took the same line of
march that we did last fall, marching direct to Germanna Ford, and halting for
the night two or three miles beyond.

At daylight next morning we took the plank road, and marched out to its
junction with the plank road that runs from Fredericksburg to Gordonsville.
We saw nothing of the enemy, and heard nothing of them until just before we
reached the latter point, when our column unexpectedly came up on a column
of rebel troops coming this way. After a little skirmishing, the rebels fell back.
Here was a high point of land where the roads cross at right angles, and it is in
the midst of an endless wilderness — "a wilderness of woe," as the boys call it.
The troops massed in here in considerable numbers, and after some moments
got into working order. Our regiment crossed the Fredericksburg road, and
filed into the woods with other troops in line in our rear and front. Pretty soon
the order came to advance. We marched in line of battle on the left side of the
Fredericksburg road, in the same direction that the road runs, and we soon
came upon the enemy. There was one line ahead of us. We followed close to
them, and were equally exposed. The rebels gave us a warm reception. They
poured their bullets into us so fast that we had to lie down to load and fire. The
front line gave way, and we were obliged to take their places. We were under
their fire over three hours, before we were relieved. We were close on to them,
and their fire was terribly effective. Our regiment lost 264 men in killed and
wounded. Just a little to the rear of where our line was formed, where the
bullets swept close to the ground, every bush and twig was cut and splintered by
the leaden balls. The woods was a dense thicket of small trees about the size of
hop poles, and they stood three times as numerous as they are usually set in a
hop yard; but along the whole length of the line I doubt if a single tree could
have been found that had not been pierced several times with bullets, and all
were hit about breast high. Had the rebels fired a little lower, they would have
annihilated the whole line; they nearly did it as it was. Our Colonel was killed,
our Lieut. Colonel and acting Major wounded, and only three captains were
with us after the fight. We all had our hairbreadth escapes to tell of. My

propensity for boasting has already been discovered. I could say that I had a bullet pass through my clothes on each side, one of them giving me a pretty smart rap, and one ball split the crown of my cap into two, knocking it off my head as neatly as it could have been done by the most scientific boxer.

Another line marched up to take our places, and we fell back to the road and that night we threw up breastworks the best we could, considering that we had to dig among roots and stumps with but few tools and poor ones at that. The firing stopped at dark without our having gained an inch on the enemy. We were called up in the morning before light. Our hours of sleep were few and brief. At half past four o'clock we were ordered to advance into the same place again. There were pale and anxious faces in our regiment when that order was given. We had had very insufficient rest for the two nights previous, and the terrible nervous exhaustion of fighting had left us in hardly a fit condition to endure another such an ordeal so soon. There was so many men missing from our number that it hardly seemed like the same regiment. But the order was forward, and I do not know that a single man failed to take his place. We advanced directly down to the same place where we fought the day before. Our dead comrades lay on the ground, just as they had fallen, many of whom we recognized. We would gladly have fallen out to give them a decent burial, but we had no time to think of that. We drove the enemy this time and captured some prisoners. The prisoners were mostly North Carolinians, and some of them came into our lines swinging their hats and saying "the tar heels wouldn't stand that morning!" We advanced about a mile and a half, I should think, when our left flank was furiously attacked and a division of the Second Corps miserably gave way, leaving us in a most perilous and exposed position. We were in the point of the letter V, and the rebels were fast closing up the sides. On they came, double quick, elated with the prospect of capturing a fine lot of Yankees. I do not know how well they succeeded. My legs saved me abundantly. We had to leave our dead and wounded, and without much ceremony, or order retreat out of that place, leaving all that we had gained in the hands of the enemy. The front lines became considerably disorganized, but the rear lines held the enemy in check. Oh how discouraging it is to lose ground before the enemy. So much hard fighting, and so many killed and wounded for nothing. We had lost over fifty men in this fight. One of my comrades was shot dead there. I was lying at the time as close to the ground as I could to load and fire, while he, less timid than myself, had raised himself up, and was loading and firing as fast as possible. The ball struck near his heart. He exclaimed, I am killed and attempted to step to the rear, but fell on to me and immediately died. Just then we were obliged to retreat, and leave him where he fell. He was a new recruit but he had shown himself to be a brave soldier. He gave his life for his country, and those of us that have served the longest can do no more.

There was considerable disorder and confusion in our hasty retreat, and the regiment was more or less broken up. There was no chance for us when the left gave away but to run or be taken prisoner. We were between two fires, and the enemy had every advantage. The road was to be the rallying point in case of disaster. The disaster came, and every man that had good legs was in duty bound to use them. I found myself with a squad belonging to the division that broke and caused the defeat — decidedly bad company to be in. Some of their officers drew their swords and revolvers and tried their utmost to rally them again. They might as well have appealed to the winds. When I got back to the road there was considerable excitement. Generals and their aides were giving and carrying orders in all directions. They thought the enemy were coming in overwhelming force. I had got among a lot of stragglers, and I began to consider myself a straggler, too. At any rate I was shamelessly demoralized. I didn't know where my regiment had gone to, and to be candid about it, I didn't care. I was tired almost to death, and as hungry as a wolf. I had been fighting to the best of my ability for Uncle Sam's Constitution, and now I thought it of about as much importance to me individually, to pay a little attention to my own. They tried to halt us at the first line of breastworks, but I saw fresh troops coming that hadn't been in the fight at all, and I thought they might as well hold the line as me. My object was to find a safe place in the rear, and in spite of revolvers, or swords, entreaties, or persuasions, I found it. A Colonel's horse stepped on my foot and crushed off my shoe, and being barefooted, and lame, of course, I had but little difficulty in accomplishing my purpose. I should have been ashamed of such conduct at any other time, but just then all I thought of was a cup of coffee, and a dinner of hard tack. The regiment might have been ordered into another battle, and every man of them been killed, and I shouldn't have been ashamed that I wasn't with them. My patriotism was well nigh used up, and so was I, till I had had some refreshments. I made a deep impression on my haversack, which nourished my fighting qualities so that I could return to my regiment. I found the regiment had moved to the right, a little on the line, and were stationed behind a rude breastwork preparing to defend it against an attack from the enemy, which was momentarily expected. No serious attack, however, was made directly in our front, but to the left, where we advanced in the first place, they tried to break our lines and they tried it hard. They charged clear up to the breastwork, and fairly planted the colors on the top of it, but they did not live to hold them there long. The ground in front of the works was literally covered with the rebel dead after they left. One

Colonel lay dead clear up to the breastwork. Two were shot on the top of the breastwork, and fell over on our side. I believe I have never heard such a murderous roar of musketry as was made to repel that charge. The rebels fell back and did not renew the attack.

The next day there was no fighting of any consequence. I was on picket. The picket line was advanced farther out than we had been before. We discovered nothing but a few sharp-shooters who retreated as we advanced, until we came upon their line of breastworks. They opened on us with artillery, and having no support we had to fall back. We had been assigned to the second Corps, under General Hancock, during this fighting, and that afternoon we went back to our own Corps.

Such is an off-hand description of what we did during the first few days of this campaign. How much we have accomplished, I cannot tell. You never need to ask a private soldier for general information. He is the last man to get that. His circle of observation is very limited. He sees but little of what is going on, and takes a part in still less. I have told what I saw, which you will please take for what it is worth. If Providence spares my life, and the rebels don't pick me off, I hope before many days to be able to chronicle a decided and glorious victory here.

On the Battle-Field
May 9 [?], 1864

We are for the present moment lying quiet here facing the enemy without any signs of hostile demonstrations on our side, or that of the enemy either, just now. What we are preparing to do, or what are the intentions of the enemy just now does not appear. So little do we know of what is going on from what we can see ourselves, that we hardly know whether to rejoice over a victory won, or nerve ourselves to retrieve a battle lost. Evidently, however, we occupy a more favorable geographical position than we have ever done heretofore after fighting this side of the Rapidan. Unless Lee is gathering on our flank he must be retreating. God be praised if we have whipped him at last.

We are just now, I believe, on what is called the river Po, somewhere between Spotsylvania Court House and Guiney Station, on the Fredericksburg and Potomac railroads. The celebrated Heights of Fredericksburg are in our rear. The enemy are in our front. How far they may be from us I can hardly find two that think alike in guessing. Undoubtedly they will find some strong position to hide behind somewhere between here and Richmond, but we sincerely hope their days for weal are numbered.

Our regiment has been terribly thinned during the late bloody conflicts. Over two thirds of our number are absent. We have lost 410 men, all but thirty of whom we know to have been killed or wounded. The whole brigade has suffered in about the same proportion. All of our former battles put together have not reduced our ranks like this one, and the end is not yet. They have had to consolidate our regiment into four companies for temporary convenience, and even then we have hardly officers enough to keep us in working order. The 11th regiment has joined us. It contains more men than all the rest of the brigade. They have seen no fighting yet but they evince a determination to acquit themselves before long. In the meanwhile we are recruiting our exhausted strength and getting ready to give the finishing blow to what remains of this obstinate rebellion. While all is quiet along our lines allow me to give you a slight sketch of our proceedings since those of which I wrote you a week ago.

After fighting three days for Hancock we were glad to be sent back to the old Sixth Corps once more. "Johnny Sedgwick," as the boys call him, was a favorite General with the boys of his corps, and they had unbounded confidence in his prudence and judgement. But he died with his armor on, and we cherish his memory, emulate his bravery so that, though dead, he still lives with us. Our corps we found back towards the river by the way we had come. We stacked our arms and prepared our suppers, hoping for a good night's rest at last, for we were so much exhausted by our labors that a good night's sleep seemed indispensable. Our hopes of rest, however, were quickly dispelled by the order for us to make haste and eat our suppers for we were going to march again that night. There were rumors of disaster in our rear: the rebels had turned our right flank and got behind us cutting off our communications with Brandy Station. They had captured our pontoon bridge and part of our train and still held part of the road on which our supplies were to come. Were we again going to retreat? As tired as I felt then I was ready to turn peace Democrat if they did. We took the road that night towards Chancellorsville, but it was so blocked up with troops and teams that we made but little progress. We marched, or pretended to march, all night. From Chancellorsville we bore to the right of Fredericksburg toward Spotsylvania Court House. It was burning hot when we stacked arms at noon in an open field where a large portion of the train was parked. It was told us that we were going to be train guard, and we began to hope for an easier time for a few days. We certainly felt as if we deserved it. During the afternoon, however, heavy firing was heard away ahead of us on our left, and pretty soon orders in great haste for us to pack up and fall in. We knew well enough what it meant. Some troops were getting badly handled by the enemy, and they needed the Vermont brigade to help them out of their trouble. We marched as fast as we could but we did not get on to the field till dark. We maneuvered about from place to place until some of the boys who were tired and cross from loss of sleep began to exhibit a state of mind the farthest removed from patience or obedient resignation. Eventually we filed into a dense thicket in a sort of a ravine close up to the enemy's lines. This place is utterly indescribable, and I will not attempt to describe it. A description might confuse the reader as much as the reality did me. It was as Egypt. Picket firing was kept up all around us as it seemed. Our movements were made very quietly, but there was a perfect confusion of orders. It seemed impossible to get into a place that would suit all of our commanders. There was another regiment in line of battle ahead of us, and the Major commanding it was much distressed for fear we should fire into them in case of an attack. No amount of assurances from our officers seemed to pacify him. At length one of our boys ventured to beseech him not to be alarmed for fear of us for we belonged to the Vermont brigade. Vermonters generally understand their duty after being told of it upwards of a dozen times. I am told there was an actual collision between one of our regiments and one of the rebel regiments that blundered on to us in the darkness before they knew what they were about. The rebel sergeant saw our colors and thought they were his and told his men to form on to them. The color guard saw who he was and knocked him down. A few shots were exchanged, and we captured about forty prisoners, and the rest of the regiment skedaddled to safer quarters.

After we had lain down, and were fairly asleep, our officers seemed to have discovered that we were in the wrong place, and moved us on to a ground that looked decidedly more rational for military operations. Here, in the morning, we threw up breastworks and prepared to act on the offensive, or defensive, as the case might be. Sharp skirmishing was kept up all along the line, and not without effect. The skirmishers were continually coming in wounded, and others had to be sent out to take their place. Finding that the rebels declined attacking our works, we determined to attack theirs. We piled our knapsacks and prepared for the bloody work. A brigade of the first division was to lead the charge, and we support them. A hundred rods or so in front of us, we came to an open space in the woods, of perhaps a hundred rods more, and on the opposite side of this space was the rebel rifle-pits. We formed in a ravine, screened from the rebels' view, where we prepared to charge across this open space, and drive the rebels out of their rifle-pits if possible. Our batteries kept up a continual shelling as we were getting into shape, firing over the woods with a degree of accuracy truly remarkable. We formed in four lines of battle, three ahead of us. At the signal the three first lines sprang to their feet, and rushed across the field, determined to drive the enemy or die. We followed immediately after. The rebels mowed down the men with awful effect, but the advancing line was not checked. We drove the enemy out of his first line of works, and captured over 2000 prisoners. Another brigade that was to follow on our left broke and run before they reached the works. Of course this made our position untenable, and spoiled our victory which we had so nearly won. We held our position until we were nearly flanked, hoping that re-enforcements would come, but none came, and we were reluctantly obliged to fall back. We lost heavily in killed and wounded, and so did the enemy, besides many prisoners.

But the most singular and obstinate fighting that I have seen during the war, or ever heard or dreamed of in my life, was the fight of last Thursday. Hancock had charged and driven the enemy from their breastworks, and from their camps, but the enemy rallied and regained all but the first line of works, and in one place they got a portion of that. The rebels were on one side of the breastwork, and we on the other. We could touch their guns with ours. They would load, jump up and fire into us, and we did the same to them. Almost every shot that was made took effect. Some of our boys would jump clear up on to the breastwork and fire, then down, reload and fire again, until they were themselves picked off. If ancient or modern history contains instances of more determined bravery than was shown there, I can hardly conceive in what way it could have been exhibited. This firing was kept up all day, and till five o'clock next morning, when the enemy retreated. Gen. Russell remarked that it was a regular bull-dog fight; he never saw anything like it before. I visited the place the next morning, and though I have seen horrid scenes since this war commenced, I never saw anything half so bad as that. Our men lay piled one top of another, nearly all shot through the head. There were many among them that I knew well, five from my own company. On the rebel side it was worse than on ours. In some places the men were piled four or five deep, some of whom were still alive. I turned away from that place, glad to escape from such a terrible, sickening sight. I have sometimes hoped, that if I must die while I am a soldier, I should prefer to die on the battle-field, but after looking at such a scene, one cannot help turning away and saying, Any death but that.

———————————

Near Noell's Station
May 25, 1864

We are still pressing our way "on to Richmond." We have crossed the North Anna river, and got beyond the Central railroad just above its junction with the Fredericksburg railroad. As I write this we are formed in line of battle, our arms are near at hand, and our equipments are on ready to jump to our feet and fight any moment that we may be called upon. The troops are massing in this field as if something belligerent was intended, but we do not know whether we are preparing to attack the enemy, or preparing to resist an attack from them. We have just halted here in the hot sun, and under the shade of my woolen blanket, which we have propped up on two guns and two ramrods, I have pulled out my portfolio, to give you a little idea of what we are doing now, if they will let us remain here long enough to give me a chance. We are continually shifting from one position to another, and we never know when we are to have five minutes' rest. Our officers know but little better than we. They cannot tell what orders their superiors may give them, and their superiors cannot tell what orders the exigencies of the situation may require. It is only by seizing these fragments of time that I can hope to succeed in writing a letter, and with as much confusion as there is at present I guess my letter will be a miserable success at best. I fear the reader will think I had better not made the attempt.

We are in a large open field — a rich and beautiful farm — flat and level, with good buildings and beautiful fruit trees, kept in good condition by a man of taste. His name, a negro told me, was Anderson. On the same authority I was told that this field was covered with rebel troops last night. They have now fell back across Little river. Their skirmishers are close to ours, and picket firing is kept up continually. We are all eager to know what is going to be done, but there is no way to gratify our curiosity only to wait and see. We boys who think we have considerable sagacity in guessing at these matters, have discussed this subject and come to the conclusion that we are only following up the enemy, that we are ready to give them a terrible punishment if they are so indiscreet as to pitch on to us, but that at present it is not the intention of our generals to meddle with them if they let us alone and continue to fall back fast enough without. Wagon loads of entrenching tools are coming, which give promise of employment to-night.

Yesterday we had a little rest, for a rarity, and we needed it. We had been marching for the last two days, and nights too, almost, and the men were completely tired out. The last part of the march night before last, was made very rapidly. Heavy firing was going on in our front, and we hurried along as fast as possible. We seldom march in the road, as that has to be given to the artillery, but across fields, brooks, ditches and fences, through woods that are almost impenetrable, and through mud holes that are very penetrable indeed, making a mile's marching with a heavy knapsack on one's back, and a pair of tired legs under his body, not the easiest thing in the world to accomplish. We did not get to the river until about ten o'clock in the evening. The regiment had dwindled down pretty small from straggling. So much excessive duty since this campaign commenced, has told upon the strength of most of us. With some it was impossible to keep up. My right hand man and I had threatened to fall out before the firing commenced, but when cannonading and musketry grew pretty sharp, my comrade said he should keep up with the regiment at all hazards, and though I didn't feel half so brave as he did, I felt ashamed to be outdone, and concluded to keep along if possible. It grew dark. The artillery were in the road, and the infantry were in the woods on both sides. Other troops mixed with ours, and it soon began to be hard work for a fellow to tell where he belonged. Stragglers were abundant. I fell in with the current, but alas, I soon found it was only a current of stragglers. I couldn't find a man that belonged to the 2d Vermont, and when I did find some of them they were just as ignorant of where the regiment had gone as I was. Further along I noticed a squad of mounted officers inquiring for their regiments, and appearing to be in the same forlorn condition that we were, and we took courage from their example. They were officers, and on horseback, and appeared to feel somewhat chagrined at the idea of straggling, but we were privates and on foot and what did we care? If the Provost Marshal had been there then to arrest all stragglers, we might have enjoyed their illustrious company, or rather they ours.

In view of such bright probabilities I determined to remain a straggler all night. I persuaded one of my comrades who has seldom ever fallen out on a march to remain with me. We stepped aside into the woods and built us a fire, and soon had some good hot coffee to drink. Our haversacks contained nothing but hard tack. Raw pork that we have abused so much heretofore, has been a rare luxury on this campaign. Occasionally an officer's cook passed us that had some, but we could not beg nor buy a mouthful. But our appetites were keen, and the hard tack happened to be most excellent ones. We found no difficulty in disposing of two days' rations of them on the spot. The brigade stopped but a little ahead of where we were. We joined them in the morning and crossed the river where the fighting had been. It seemed the 5th Corps had partly crossed when the rebels came up in force on their flank, with the intention of driving them back into the river. But they failed of accomplishing their object, and were driven back themselves. Our artillery did fearful execution among them. They claim that they saved us from a disaster there.

We have had a pretty severe campaign thus far. Scarcely a moment has been our own. Sometimes we are building breastworks, sometimes marching, and sometimes fighting. Our marches are not so remarkably long as they are irregular, many of them being done in the night. In the day-time we are continually shifting from one place into another, building breastworks here, supporting a battery there, on picket or on the march, so that there is but little chance for rest, and none for amusement.

It seems to me it must require an extraordinary military genius to comprehend the reason for all the movements that we make, and their result. We take up a position one day and fortify it, and the next day we abandon it altogether. Some times we think we are about to make a regular attack on the enemy, and sometimes we think they are about to make an assault upon us. We make all preparations for a fight, but no fighting is done. If we think we are going to have a day's rest, we are pretty sure to fall in immediately and commence to march, and when a day's rest does come, it comes quite unexpectedly. I will give a short account in detail of the past few days.

Saturday, the 14th, we slung our knapsacks at about half past two in the morning, and started in pursuit of the "fleeing foe." We made a long day's march, though we gained but a few miles, swinging around to our left, and resting on the river Ny. Here we had our tour of picketing and some rest. We built us a breastwork, and Tuesday, just at eight, we moved all our tents upon a line, with company streets, as if we were going to make a stop of several days, when the order came to pack up and fall in. Some were at work on their tents when the order came. We marched all night, and accomplished scarcely half a dozen miles. I have marched twenty easier. In the morning we found ourselves advancing under a pretty sharp artillery fire over the same breastworks that we had captured in our desperate fight of Thursday. About a dozen of our regiment were killed and wounded. We advanced and covered ourselves under one of their inside lines of breastworks. There were other troops ahead of us, but most of the firing was done by artillery. What we accomplished I do not know. We fell back from there about ten o'clock, and massed in a large open field, where we made coffee, and eat our breakfast, or dinner, or both, when we took up our line of march back again. We crossed the Ny that night, and after we had found the place assigned for us, drew our rations, cooked what we wanted for supper, we prepared to bivouac for the night. Some were too tired and sleepy to eat at all. At half past two we were called up again, and the line was advanced close upon the rebels, where we worked all day throwing up breastworks. We held these two days, and then fell back, leaving nothing but a skirmish line which the rebels boldly attacked with three lines of battle. We had fallen back and formed a new line. We had worked like beavers and fortified our new line, and had the rebels attacked us they would have found us prepared to receive them. But they only drove in our pickets and retired. It looked a little as if we were retreating, but the rebels appeared as anxious to get away from there as we. We marched all night with our usual snail-like rapidity, and at two o'clock Sunday morning, the 22d, we halted near Guiney Station on the Fredericksburg railroad. Monday we marched to the North Anna river. Just now there appears to be an obstacle in the way of our marching any further, but how long "Old Useless," as the boys mischievously call the Lieutenant- General, will allow it to hinder his onward progress, remains to be seen.

Near Gaines' Mill
June 11, 1864

At this present writing we are close up to the enemy's guns besieging his works. The breastwork against which I am leaning is not more than 200 yards from the enemy's lines, and in front of us are skirmishers and sharpshooters still nearer. Our line is just outside the edge of a woods, and theirs is partly in an open field, and partly covered by timber in our immediate front. The field is open between us, but it is a strip of land across which no man dare to pass. An attacking party from either side would be mown down like grass. We have abattis in front of our works, and so have they. This is made of small trees, trimmed of their boughs but with every prong and branch left, which packed together with these snarly prongs extending outward are no very pleasant things to get over in the face of a murderous fire at close range. I believe if the enemy should attack us, we could kill every man of them before any could get into our works. They know better than to try any such undertaking, and as far as I am concerned, I hope our officers will know better than to send us over there.

Our skirmishers and the rebels keep up a continual firing. Bullets are whistling over our heads all the time. A man's head isn't safe a moment above the protection of the breastwork. Our work here is built zigzag like a common rail fence, which gives us a chance to protect ourselves from a cross fire. We can only get from place to place, or from one part of the works to another, by walking in trenches that we have dug for that purpose. There is a breastwork just in our rear and a winding sap connects them so that we can pass from one to the other in safety. This front work that we occupy now is an advanced line that we built in the night, and some of the time when the bullets were flying pretty freely. We are building a rude fort here to protect some pieces of artillery which will render valuable aid in offensive or defensive operations. Yesterday they fired a few shots from there, to try the range, and to admonish the enemy that we had implements of war here that it would be well for them to heed. We found, however, that the rebels were not without the means of replying to such a challenge, and they answered us nearly shot for shot. Their aim was too high, and our works were found defective for accurate firing. We have large fatigue parties at work every night, and we are gradually working our way up to the enemy's lines. In one place on our left, it is reported that we are within thirty yards of the enemy.

This is what I call a charming place to sit and write letters. The music of these bullets puts a fellow in a pleasing vein for writing. Since I commenced this one, a bullet has struck the breastwork behind me, spattering the dirt all over my sheet, and another has pierced Col. Pingree's tent just in front of where I am sitting, the base of which has been dug out and settled several feet below the surface of the ground. It came up the line, from away to the right. Its path was exactly where we are passing to and fro nearly all the time, and it was not breast high from the bottom of our paths, but fortunately its path was clear. A sharpshooter has gone out to discover the offender and take care of him.

These bullets have a peculiar sound. Some of them come with a sharp "clit," like striking a cabbage leaf with a whip lash, others come with a sort of screech, very much such as you would get by treading on a cat's tail. Then there are others, the sharpshooters' bullets we suppose, that whistle on a much higher key, and snap against a tree with as much force as if the tree had been struck by a heavy sledge hammer. Some strike in the dirt with a peculiar "thud," others fly high in the air and make a noise similar to a huge bumble bee. They do not tarry long by the way. What they do is done quickly, and woe to the man that stands in their way. To add to the beauties of our situation here we are in an ash heap, as it were. The earth is like a pile of dust, and it dances before every breeze like Vermont snow in midwinter. A man may spread down his rubber blanket for a seat, and one puff of wind will cover it so completely with dust that it will be difficult to distinguish it from the ground around it. Our clothes are filled with dust, and our coffee and everything else we cook is sure to get a clever sprinkling of this fine sand. This dirt goes everywhere. It gets into our haversacks and knapsacks, it fills our hair and mingles with the sweat on our faces. It is universal, and there is no getting rid of it. I saw one fellow get almost swearing mad because he couldn't write and seal up a dainty little letter, (I guess it was a love letter,) without disfiguring its appearance with slovenly looking finger-marks of dirt.

One regiment is not supposed to stay here all the time. They are to be relieved regularly. We came out here Wednesday night, the 8th, after two days' rest, having been here for the two days previous to that, and last night (Friday), we anxiously expected to be relieved, but no relief came. We had to be resigned to our fate. Well, the boys say, we belong to the Old Second Vermont, and we are considered especially fit for any rough, disagreeable duty the army needs to have done. Relieving is accomplished in the night, and as slyly as possible. A volley from the rebels, even in the night, if they knew where a regiment was moving, could be given us with deadly effect. The last time we left here a rallying point was decided upon just to the rear of the woods, and then, from one company at a time, each man left and found his way there on his own hook, the best we could, where we formed again. Wonder if the rebels are bothered in the same way when relieving their men?

Our works are so nearly completed now that not so many are wounded as there were a week ago. Every regiment then lost several every day, exclusive of skirmishers. We lost one man Thursday night, almost the first thing after getting here. He was killed instantly by a piece of shell. He had just returned from a veteran's furlough, and this was his first duty to the front after getting back. His name was Joseph Felton. He belonged to Co. H, and was from Fairfax, Vt. It is a pleasure to bear testimony to his sterling integrity and Christian character. I believe he would have rather died than to have done a wrong act or neglected a single duty. I first became acquainted with him at the Convalescent Camp, where we were both detailed a short time for guard, and I remember his anxiety to get back to his regiment as soon as he thought he was well enough to do duty there. Some of the boys told him to stay where he was as long as he could; it was easier than doing duty in the field. But Mr. Felton was no shirk. He thought it his duty to go to his regiment as soon as he was able, and no argument would avail anything against his convictions of duty.

We are on the famous peninsula once more. The place we now occupy is near Cold Harbor, and about ten miles from Richmond. Gaines' Mill, where the memorable battle of June 27th, 1862, was fought, is about two miles from here, and within the rebel lines. It is to be hoped that the old programme of '62 is not to be enacted over again, with the same result. Both armies have become inured to war since then, and bloodier consequences would follow any such result now. It will be hard work for either army to destroy the other by fighting. It would suit me much better to have Grant capture Richmond by some prodigious display of strategy. Another of his flank movements may bring us a little nearer the rebel city, perhaps as near as McClellan reached in his celebrated campaign two years ago. It is beyond me to tell how the remainder of the distance will be accomplished. That another such flank movement may soon be made begins to be evident. It is rumored that orders have been received to evacuate at the White House, and bring the supplies to City Point on the James River. We know that a part of the troops to our rear have moved away somewhere, rumors do not agree where; and we all know, without any ifs or buts, that we were not relieved last night as we ought to have been, which must surely mean something or nothing. All these facts, with many others, we weigh as evidence that we are going to evacuate here and go somewhere else — probably to the left again.

But I will close this useless scribbling. I find after all, that it is impossible to write anything sensible in a place like this. I have not told you of our severe marching to get here, nor of the charge we made when we arrived, June 1st. When I have a more convenient season I will endeavor to do so. Just now our attention is directed chiefly to the "Johnnies." Some of the operations here are quite amusing. A few minutes ago there was a lull in the firing, and the boys hallooed, "Wake up there, Johnnies! It is getting dull here." A half dozen shots was the only reply. The other night after it was safely dark, the rebels were as "bold as sheep." They jumped upon their breastworks, and invited the "Yankee sons of b_____" to come on. They said it would take a long time for us to *dig* into Richmond. Our boys replied that we should dig them into hell and *walk* into Richmond.

But I told you I was going to close my letter, and I will do so before I forget it.

Near Petersburg, Va.
June 19, 1864

Another flank movement has been made by the army, and to-day we find ourselves within a mile of Petersburg with our old enemy in front. For three days there has been pretty severe fighting here, but this time our corps escaped the worst of it. Our division reached the front night before last. The Second Regiment was sent at once on to the skirmish line, from which we were relieved last night after twenty-four hours hard duty.

We left Cold Harbor the night of the 12th. It was a bright moonlight night, just right for marching, except that the air everywhere was filled with choking dust, which the dampness of evening could not lay. We fell into line at the order, and the most of us guessed where we were going, but our calculations were a little puzzled, when instead of marching off to the left, we started out "right in front" and marched back on to the right flank. It soon became evident that we were sent there only as a rear guard, and after remaining behind good breastworks till midnight, we changed our course towards the Chickahominy. The interval we improved the best we could in catching a little sleep. It was short, and less satisfactory than sweet, scarcely better than none, for it makes a fellow feel more stupid than ever to call him up suddenly from a refreshing sleep just begun. At daylight we halted an hour for breakfast, then pushed on again through the dust and heat till night. We crossed the Chickahominy at Jones' bridge just before sundown, but continued our march a number of miles further before we came to a halt. I don't know exactly how far we marched, it is variously estimated at from twenty to twenty-five miles, but the choking dust and heat and the many crooked turns we made, made the march doubly difficult. We were completely exhausted before we bivouacked for the night. Those last miles were doled out in suffering by inches. If a man wants to know what it is to have every bone in his body ache with fatigue, every muscle sore and exhausted, and his whole body ready to sink to the ground, let him diet on a common soldier's fare till he has only the strength that imparts, and then let him shoulder his knapsack, haversack, gun and equipments, and make one of our forced marches, and I will warrant him to be satisfied that the duties of war are stern and severe, whether we march or face the enemy on the field of battle. A fellow feels very much like grumbling at such times as that, and when we march on and on, expecting every minute to halt but still hurrying forward, when every spark of energy seems about to be extinguished, and the last remnant of strength gone, tired, hungry, sick and sore, who blames a soldier if he finds it hard work to suppress thoughts of a quiet home he has left behind him, with its comforts and endearments, and if he sometime turns his thoughts to himself and wonders if he, as an individual, will ever be compensated for the sacrifice he is making. What if the rebels are whipped, and what if they are not? How does it matter to him? One blunder of General Grant's may make final victory forever impossible and all our lost toil go for nothing. I tell you some of our hard marches put one's patriotism severely to the test. It finds out a fellow's weak points if he has got any, and we don't claim to be without them.

About ten o'clock that night we were ready to lie down for our night's rest, and at four in the morning we were called onto our feet again. We advanced towards the James River, just before Harrison's Landing, where we had a camp two years ago. It would have been quite a treat to have visited that old camp again, but we did not have the opportunity. We crossed the James River the night of the 16th on a pontoon bridge and came directly to this place. The first and third division of this corps, more fortunate than ourselves, were carried to City Point on transports while we made the distance on foot. The whole movement was well planned to save time.

As we were coming on to the ground, we had positive assurance that Petersburg was taken, and of course felt highly elated at the cheering news, but we found when we got here that the news was not quite so good as reported, although we had captured their outer line of fortifications and were almost within musket range of the city. Burnside's negroes claim a large share of credit in taking these works. They made a splendid charge, capturing the whole line of works, thirteen guns, and some prisoners. The negroes were remarkably well pleased with their prowess on this occasion. It was a glorious day for them. They won great favor in the eyes of white soldiers by their courage and bravery. I am sure I never looked upon negroes with more respect than I did upon those soldiers, and I did not hear a work of disrespect towards them from any of the boys. Yesterday they made another charge here, and it was done in excellent style. The best military critic could hardly find fault with it. In a steady straight line they advanced right over the crest of the hill and right up to the enemy's works, under a terrible fire, but without wavering or faltering, compelling the enemy to leave his works in the hands of the blacks. The stream of wounded that came pouring back, some leaning on a comrade and some carried on stretchers, told of the bloody work they had done. Our picket reserve was in the road where they passed by. They captured some prisoners and brought them off. The proud Southerner might have felt a little humbled to be taken prisoner in open fight by a class of people that they refuse to recognize as men, and be conducted off the field in charge of a negro guard. But this they had to submit the best they could. One of the guard, a small, comical looking darkey, rolling up his large white eyes and looking at a tall rebel with a peculiar expression of triumph inquired, "Who rides a horseback now?" The rebel did not deign a reply. He bore the shout that followed with philosophical coolness. Sometimes the negroes treat their prisoners rather roughly in remembrance of Fort Pillow, and similar outrages. I have no doubt, if the truth were known, that many a rebel lost his life at their hands at the taking of the first line fortifications after they had fallen into our hands. Their wrath was especially directed against the officers. The rebels would plead with them, tell them they had no desire to harm them, but the negroes would say, How was it at Fort Pillow?[21] and pay no attention to their entreaties. One of our officers who was a free mason, told of rescuing a rebel brother mason whom the negroes decided to kill. He drew his revolver and peremptorily ordered the negroes who had gathered around him to disperse and had the wounded rebel cared for, otherwise he would have counted as one to pay the terrible bill of retaliation that we have against the enemy. Such a kind of warfare is too horrible to contemplate, though we cannot blame the negroes under the present circumstances.

Notwithstanding the negroes fight so well and show so much bravery, they have hitherto been allowed but the bare pittance of seven dollars a month.[22] Chaplain Hunter, of the 4th U.S. colored troops, a colored man of remarkable ability, denounces with just indignation this rank injustice. He says there are men in his regiment who have left families at home, and seven dollars a month in times like these, is not enough to keep them from actual suffering. In a conversation with a Major General a short time since, he said he asked him in a case of a battle where all the commissioned officers were killed or wounded in a company or regiment, who would take the command. (Commissioned officers are white but the non-commissioned officers may be black, but a negro is never commissioned — miserable compromise to an unreasonable prejudice.) The General replied that it would devolve upon the ranking non-commissioned officer of course. Then said the chaplain, when the regiment comes to re-organize and new officers be chosen, what will you do with these men that, according to military custom, are entitled to the position they have filled, and who have proved that they are worthy of it. Well, said the General a little puzzled at the annoying question, Congress will have to settle that.

And Congress has wrangled over that question all winter trying to settle it. It seems strange that a question where justice and injustice, right and wrong, are so plainly apparent, should require any wrangling or debate at all. They seem to think that it is degrading to the white soldiers to pay the blacks equally as well.

Do they think we are afraid of fair competition with blacks? If negroes can fight as well as we, can we not have magnanimity enough to acknowledge it. Certainly to propose especial legislation to keep our *status* ahead of the blacks is acknowledging them our superiors and in a most humiliating way. Whether it suits our tastes or not, it is doubtless true that the golden rule applies to colored as well as to white people, and Congress as well as everybody else will do well to bear this in mind and act accordingly.

Near Petersburg, Va.
July 2, 1864

Strange as it may seem, the Vermont brigade is enjoying comparative quiet just now. For the last twenty-four hours, we have had nothing to do but bring water, fix up shades and endeavor to keep ourselves as cool as possible. The twenty-four hours previous to that, we only marched about five miles, but in that five miles there were several cases of sunstroke, it being so extremely warm that marching was almost impossible. The report now is that we are going to stay here several days to recruit our wasted energies, and prepare ourselves for future emergencies.

Last Wednesday, we went out to the Petersburg and Weldon railroad, at the point about ten miles from here, and tore up the track for several miles. This railroad is the highway for supplies from the various points in North Carolina with the rebel capital through Petersburg, and by spoiling their communications here, we effectually cut them off from all that portion of the Confederacy. There are three important railroad lines that center in Petersburg; the Suffolk, Weldon, and Lynchburg roads, only one of which we have had entire control. We now command the Weldon road also. We have now only to destroy the Lynchburg road, when Petersburg and Richmond will be completely invested, and must fall of their own accord unless they can raise the siege. In order to do that they must come out and fight us in our own position, which is exactly what we want to have them do. There are all sorts of rumors in regard to our operations on the Lynchburg road, and not knowing what is reliable, and what is not I will not venture to speak of them. When we started out Wednesday, it was reported that our cavalry had gone out to Perkersville, where the western railroads from Richmond and Petersburg unite, and that in coming back they had encountered a rebel force in their rear, which made it necessary to call for the assistance of infantry forces. Our corps was the nearest, and we were ordered out to Reams' or Lonesville Station for that purpose. We got there just at night. There was no fighting except a little with the skirmishers. I am told that the Third Regiment which advanced, lost three killed and one wounded. We were put in the skirmish line as soon as we got to the station, and remained there till after dark Thursday without getting sight at a single rebel. Our position was in a thick wood, and all we could see or hear of what was going on, was a thick cloud of smoke coming from the railroad in our rear or the clanking of railroad iron that was being destroyed.

We had begun to fix us up a very pretty summer's camp before we were ordered out to go there. We had been there but two days, but in that time we had made such a transformation in the looks of the ground, that I doubt if the squirrels or rabbits themselves that abound here would have known the spot. The line was extended to the left, and when we moved on to it Monday a more unpromising looking place for a camp I seldom ever saw. There was now and then a scattering pine tree for shade, but the ground was covered principally with low bushes and tangling briars through which the fire had run, destroying every vestige of green vegetation, and leaving the ground covered with ashes and black nasty soot. There seemed to be a peculiar property in this black dust to draw the sun's heat, and while we waited for all to get into their right position, it seemed like being tortured in a red hot oven. But there was no dodging our destiny. The line had been laid out, and the portion of it assigned to us was right *there,* and *there* we must make our camp though an Eden's Garden might have been found a little to one side. We went to work with a will, cleaned off the ground and put up our tents. From the ruins of a house, or rather from a house that we ruined, we got a supply of boards, and made us beds elevated from the ground in regular summer style, and if we could have stayed there long enough to have got thoroughly cleaned up, our bodies and our clothes, I am not sure but we might have thought we were human beings after all. But there was no grumbling when we were ordered to leave this place. Compared to what we have been ordered to do heretofore, and what might still be in store for us now, leaving a good camp is too insignificant a matter to grumble about. We had enjoyed two whole days' respite from military duty, when we had not been promised five minutes, and the order to advance came as a matter of course.

This position was at the extreme left of the line and as the line bends round like an ox-bow to protect the flank, our position was nearly in the rear of the main army. Our brigade has been throwing up breastworks and occupying different portions of this line the most of the time since Thursday the 23d, when the rebels attacked our pickets, and captured nearly all the Fourth and First battalions of the Eleventh regiment. At the present time we do not appear to be on any line. There is cavalry and infantry east of us, and there are siege guns and rebels to siege west. Our own front is about south. We are about six miles southwest of Petersburg, not so far but that we can hear heavy firing in front of the city every night.

The weather has been for the last few weeks of the hottest kind, and the temperature is daily increasing. It seems already to have reached about as high a point as human nature can stand. There has been one or two attempts at rain, but since the first of June, I have not seen enough to lay the dust. The sun only mocks at our little shelter tents. With the hot sand underneath, and the burning sun overhead, our little tents are so many little ovens, and a fellow is well nigh roasted alive in one of them. Curled up in one of these tents, Turkish fashion, is your humble correspondent at the present time, with his portfolio on his knee, occasionally writing a line, but devoting his attention chiefly to wiping the sweat from his face, neck and head. It would be absurd to think of writing anything sensible in a place like this, and I claim to have committed no such folly. But it is going to be four long hours before the mail comes in to bring me a letter from home, and how else could the intervening time and hot weather be disposed of so easily?

After all, we could get along tolerable well here if cold water was not so difficult to get. Water is getting to be an article of high commercial value with us. There are a few small springs near by, but where there is one cup of water there are ten men to drink it, and there are always careless ones enough to spoil any spring in a very few minutes. Yesterday I started out with the full determination of finding some water if there was any in Virginia to be found. I discovered about one mile and a half from here an excellent spring of pure water, almost as cool as ice water, and I was just beginning to congratulate myself upon my discovery, when I was coolly informed that no one was allowed to get water there but such and such regiments, among which the 2d Vermont was not included. So my important discovery was barren of results after all. But our regiment is going to dig wells near by with good prospects of finding a supply of water. If we fail it will be a serious matter with us.

The boys are beginning to want to see their old friend the paymaster. Four months' pay was due us the first of July. The story is being circulated that we are not to be paid for two months to come. It is said that General and Staff officers are to be paid now, but the rest of us must wait till September. The boys will feel unjustly dealt with if this report is true. A soldier's wants are limited, but they are imperative, and it is very trying to be destitute of money. Sutlers are just beginning to bring in a small quantity of goods and all want money to patronize them. Almost all use tobacco, and it requires a pretty liberal amount of pocket money to keep a fellow supplied with that.

The "old" men that did not re-enlist left the regiment the 19th day of June, one day before their time was out. The regiment numbers now one hundred and sixty-five guns all told. There are two hundred and thirteen men and three officers now present with the regiment. Upon the company rolls, counting those that are wounded and in hospitals, there are five hundred and forty names still belonging to the regiment. This is exclusive of those unaccounted for and marked missing, of whom there are not more than twenty. There are one hundred and ninety-nine men whose names were borne upon the rolls to be mustered out the 20th, their term of enlistment having expired, but only about fifty of these were carrying guns in the ranks at the time. There has been an order issued to consolidate the regiment into fewer companies, and it has been contemplated making six companies of the ten, but this method is very obnoxious to the boys generally especially to those whose company organizations will be broken up, and the men distributed to fill the other companies. It will be seen that we still have a sufficient number of enlisted men to entitle us to a regimental organization, and if possible we hope to avoid a consolidation. The regiment is now divided into four divisions. Companies D, B, and H, form the first division, F, and E, the second, C, I, and G, the third, H, and A, the fourth. We have no line officers with us. Each of these divisions is commanded by a sergeant acting as Lieutenant, Sergeant Stone, of Co. A, (brother of our late Colonel) commands the first division company, Sergeant Morey, of Co. E, commands the second, Sergeant Taylor of Co. I, the third, and Sergeant Harrington of Co. G, the fourth. Sergeant Harrington, the tallest man in the brigade, came up with the regiment as color bearer, and has carried our colors up to the time the present campaign commenced. Captain Johnson of Co. D, commands the regiment. Tall, good looking, good-natured, strict and impartial, he is just the man for us. The boys call him a "bully officer" and all like him. If he leads us into another engagement we will show him that there is some Green Mountain *pluck* left in the regiment yet.

———————————

Steam Transport Webster
Off Fortress Monroe
July 11, 1864

While we are being carried smoothly over the placid waters of the Chesapeake, this beautiful morning, I will sketch you a hazy account of this sudden change in the programme of our operations. It is a pleasant relief from our rough campaign to take a boat ride up the Chesapeake Bay, though being crowded together as soldiers generally are on these transports, it is difficult to realize the full effect. But perched upon the upper deck with a cool western breeze to fan away the heat, watching the barges and transports of all description, as we meet and pass them, or the distant shore covered with its forests of pine, with now and then a neat white cottage peering out from its beautiful retreat, as one gazes upon the calm, quiet waters, spread out in panorama before him, he would think the loveliness of nature itself was sufficient to reprove men of their wickedness, and make them ashamed of treason and war. But at the present moment we are only leaving one scene of strife and hurrying forward to another.

We received orders, at ten Saturday night, to break camp and be ready to march. We were not entirely ignorant of where we were going. Two days before we had had orders to hold ourselves in readiness to move. The Third Division of our corps was reported to have gone to City Point to be transported from there to Washington and rumors were strong that we should follow. Maryland was again invaded and the old soldiers were needed to drive the invaders back. But as nothing more was said about the matter, we boys began to consider that the occasion for it had passed, and that we shouldn't have to leave our camp after all.

That very afternoon we commenced improvements in our camp, arranging our streets and raising our beds from the ground and we had just laid down and were comfortably at sleep, when the order came to pack up and march. Not a word of murmuring was heard as we prepared as quickly as possible for an all night's march. It would have suited us of course, to have remained there on the reserve and rested awhile, though we know that it was expecting too much in times like these, and when it was known that the enemy was making an invasion to the north, despoiling the country and robbing our citizens, we were not unwilling to march to the rescue, though we regretted that it should be necessary. It was but natural, however. With the railroads from Petersburg and Richmond under our control, Lee was put in desperate straits to feed his army and the famishing inhabitants of Richmond, and if he could send a portion of his army into the fertile fields of Maryland, to gather the fat of the land he would be quite likely to make a desperate effort to do so. And now was his time, while Petersburg remains impregnable. The prospect of its falling into our hands eventually is as sure as anything of the kind can be, but not so immediate as we would wish to have it. We have tried to carry their works and have failed. The bare facts are the rebels are too strong in their position to be beaten in a direct assault, and every day they are adding to its strength. By our failure to capture them at first they have gained time and have improved it. So long as they act on the defensive they have the advantage. One man behind a good breastwork is worth three outside, and unless we can oblige them to fight us in open field, or, what would be better, make them attack us in our breastwork, they have us to a serious disadvantage. If Lee could supply his army he could hold out against us indefinitely. If a part of his forces could hold the works against us and leave another part to operate elsewhere it isn't beyond the capacity of a child to see exactly what "old Bob Lee" would be likely to do. There is no very great display of rebel shrewdness in it after all. Petersburg is a city that we cannot very well siege. The rebel heights that command the city are separated from our army by the Appomattox river which renders their stronghold doubly secure. Heavy artillery can sometimes batter down forts but they can have no effect in "reducing" a river. Place *us* in a position as strong as the rebels have got, with a river between us and them and we would defy the whole Confederacy to drive us out. And it is the same with them. The rebels know how to fight. We showed them how it was done when we fought them in the Wilderness, and they know their advantage if we attack them.

The only thing we can hope to do at Petersburg is to cut their railroads and give them no chance to procure supplies for their army and city. It was at first thought by many to be impossible for us to do this, but we have occupied every road except the Danville road, and that is so much at the mercy of our raiding parties that it is the same as useless. If the rebels could get no supplies over these roads, they would be forced to do one of three things: to come out and fight us, with a glorious chance of getting licked, to starve in Richmond, or else make a raid into Maryland with the forlorn hope of collecting supplies there. It seems they have chosen the last alternative. Necessity drove them to it. Lee sends his best corps into Maryland for plunder, and Grant sends his best corps to intercept them.

It was a dusty march we had Saturday night. I doubt if there is another place in the world, where so much of this annoyance is to be found in a dry time as along the James River. Dry, light dust, as light as ashes, was piled along in the road several inches deep, and it yielded to the feet like light snow. It was literally "over shoe" in the road, and often the dense clouds of it that we had to pass through, was almost suffocating. Cleanliness was not to be thought of. Sweat and dirt was supreme.

We reached City Point about sunrise, having marched sixteen miles. This city, at the junction of the Appomattox and James rivers, occupies a site level and beautiful, though already scarred by the visitation of war. There was much activity at the landing. New wharves were being made to accommodate the rapid transportation of supplies by boat and rail. But little delay will be necessary, when the whole work commenced there is completed. Cars run from the wharf to near Petersburg. The boys will be pleased if they perfect their arrangements so that soft bread can come through from Alexandria before it becomes moldy. It would appear as if this place was intended to be permanently occupied, but those long acquainted with army operations know how short a time it takes to evacuate a place like this, and destroy all that has been done.

The Sanitary Commission in its work of benevolence was represented here. A large boat load of everything that a soldier can imagine himself in need of was waiting at the wharf to be unloaded. Many of their articles of food were distributed to the boys as they were getting aboard the transports. Pickles, soda crackers, hot coffee and other luxuries were given to many that had not tasted for a long time of such necessaries as these are to an army in a hot climate like this. At one place they had a table fixed up where they gave any hungry soldier a dinner that needed one. The fare was simple — hard tack and pickles, with hot coffee — but it came at a time when we could not have got anything elsewhere half as good. The Commission has a wonderful tact of supplying the right things at the right time. If they have tobacco to give away it is when the boys are entirely destitute with no money to get any more. If it is in the shape of food it comes when there is no other way to get it. Here, we had plenty of hard tack and pork in our haversacks, but doubtless the most of us would have gone on in a dinnerless condition but for the Sanitary Commission's pickles and hot coffee which some of us eat as we were waiting there at the landing.

We left the landing about the middle of the afternoon, and steamed nearly down to the mouth of the James river, where we anchored for the night. Harrison's Landing was pointed out to us, where two eventful years ago we had a camp, after being driven from in front of Richmond, and we could but hope that its counterpart in history was not begun in the present movement. God grant that it may not require another two years to subdue the rebellion. But to insure us victory, there must be more fighting and bloodshed. The rebels will fight as long as they can, and fight with all the energy of despair. Their determination is unyielding. It is hard work to conquer a people so united and determined as the rebels appear to be. At Petersburg we fight the whole rebel population. Up to the right of where we were encamped, near the Weldon railroad, was a rifle-pit made to defend the road, and thrown up, so some negroes and citizens told us by old men, women and children, black and white. They meant to protect that road at any cost. All this toil and sacrifice is made that the stars and stripes may not wave over their soil. Love is a strong principle, and so is hate. We fight because we love our government, and they fight because they hate it. A war like this, once begun, will not close without achieving important results. What that result will be, unless our national sins are past forgiveness, no one that believes in a God of justice, can for a moment doubt.

Near Leesburg, Va.
July 18, 1864

The old Sixth Corps after marching once more across the Potomac into Virginia in pursuit of the enemy, has today a Sabbath of rest. It might not, perhaps, compare with the sanctity of the Lord's day in quiet New England, but though shorn of all other privileges, the privilege of rest with us just now is so rare, and therefore so well appreciated, that we will not murmur for the others. We are spending the day on the top of the Kittoctin or Catoctin Mountain, about three miles west of Leesburg. The enemy passed by here yesterday. We arrived here last night after marching from Poolesville, Maryland, following close up to the enemy all the way. We shall probably pursue them further to-morrow. But our waiting here gives me a chance to write you a little description of our movements since my last, though we have done but little except march, and that is beginning to be an old story with us. We have no communications with the rest of the world. No mail has been brought to us since we left Washington, and we have had no chance to send any out. This letter may become spoiled of old age before there is a chance for it to reach you, but I cannot resist the temptation to write, and I believe it would be actual sin to spend all this day in idleness. It is a pretty place here on this mountain for a camp — plenty of green apples and ripe blackberries for sauce are near at hand, and plenty of clear, good spring water, the coolest and the best, is to be had here.

We have a fine view of the country from this point. Nearly all of Pleasant Valley, the name given the beautiful country between this mountain and the Blue Ridge, can be seen from our camp here. Off to the east lies a vast plain, as it looks from here, covered with fields and forests as far as the eye can reach. It is almost a libel upon human nature that a country so rich, and fair, and beautiful as this valley, should be the scene of so much bloodshed and suffering. Yet it is so. Hostile armies have marched back and forth across this land and fought many bloody battles here, and the tale of misery is not all told yet. We hope it may be soon.

We left City Point the 10th inst., and reached Washington the following night. As soon as we disembarked we started at once for Fort Stevens about four miles north of the city. We were not a moment too soon. The enemy were approaching the city at this point with the intention of entering it, and probably would have succeeded but for the timely arrival of our division. The third brigade was engaged at once. There was some pretty sharp skirmish fighting Monday night and during the day Tuesday, but the enemy finding old troops in the Fort, concluded that it was best to keep out of the range of its guns, and accordingly left Tuesday night. The rebels supposed that they could march at once into the city. They supposed that only citizens and militia were defending it, and were much surprised to find the old Sixth Corps there. Judging from the determination and spirit shown by citizens and militia they might have been as much surprised at the resistance that would have been offered them by such troops, as they were at seeing the inevitable Sixth Corps. The most of the inhabitants were cool, and ready for any emergency. Of course we except secession sympathizers and the constitutionally timid.

Wednesday the 13th, all was quiet around the fort. Our dead were brought in and buried. I saw twelve Union soldiers buried in one grave near the fort, but did not learn how many there was of them all. The rebels were buried where they fell. Several squads of prisoners came in during the day. Their clothing was badly worn, and some of them had no shoes on. They had seen hard marching, having been on the road nearly all the time, and making forced marches every day since they commenced their raid. One of the prisoners said they had met the Sixth Corps in the Wilderness, at Spotsylvania, behind the works of Cold Harbor, and now, here in Maryland, they met us again. They thought the Sixth Corps must be everywhere. They hardly believed us when we told them that the Sixth Corps was the smallest in the army of the Potomac when we left camp, and that its proportion is still smaller now. One of the prisoners was in the skirmish line that first advanced into our works after we left them at Cold Harbor. He said his corps did not follow us at all, but started immediately to head off Hunter to Lynchburg. After driving him back they pushed for Maryland. They made long marches every day, calculating to accomplish all that was possible before we could intercept them. They gathered forage and took all the cattle and horses they could lay their hands on in Maryland, whether it was from friend or foe. They had strict orders, they said, not to burn any building or wantonly destroy any kind of property whatever.

We started Wednesday afternoon in the direction of Poolesville, and reached that place Thursday night. Marching through the fertile fields of Maryland, is a much more pleasant affair than marching through the desolate regions of Virginia. Everything has a look of thrift and prosperity in Maryland, while in Virginia on every hand one sees nothing but evidences of decay and desolate abandonment. The inhabitants treat us cordially, as if grateful for the toil and sacrifice we were making for our country. Anything it was in their power to do for us, they were willing to do, and seemed to account it a pleasure, although it can be no desirable thing for a man to have his fields the highway for an army, whether that army is friend or foe. The citizens here have suffered greatly from this raid. One man that had a large farm and much team work to do had all his oxen and herds taken from him, leaving him without the means to gather his crops or to do any other necessary work. His neighbors were in the same plight, and there was no remedy.

Friday we remained quietly in camp near Poolesville. The cavalry were out scouring the country and harassing the enemy all they could while we were waiting to give them battle whenever we could get a fair opportunity. We witnessed the execution of a rebel spy there that day. He formerly belonged to the 67th New York regiment, and had deserted and joined the enemy. He had added the double disgrace of deserting to the enemy and then turning spy against us. The miserable man was caught in one of his attempts against us, and here paid the penalty of his crimes on the gallows.

The next day we marched out and crossed the Potomac at White's Ford between Edwards and Conrad's Ferry. There were some of the enemy visible on the opposite bank, but after a short and vigorous shelling from our batteries, they were much less so. They skedaddled out of our way into the woods and we crossed over. The river was about two feet deep and we had to ford it. The boys stripped to their waists, and calling it fun, we waded in. As soon as we crossed we started for this place, marching to Leesburg, then turning to the right and following close to the enemy all the way. We got here just after dark, and were pretty thoroughly tired out, for we had marched rapidly all day, and had had but little rest. To-morrow we shall probably follow on after the enemy through Snicker's Gap, where if they make a stand we shall give them all the battle they want. A citizen at Leesburg last night told me that the enemy had left the place but a half an hour before we arrived, that they were 30,000 strong, and told him that they should fight us near here. We hope they will.

———————

Near Frederick City, Md.
Aug. 1, 1864

It is a rare thing now-a-days that a soldier in the Sixth Corps gets a leisure moment to write a letter, or to do anything else. If anyone tries to keep track of us they need not expect to hear from us twice in the same place. We are on the march almost every day, and very often we march all night and day too. It has been continual marching ever since we came into Maryland and from present appearances I see but faint reasons to hope that our task is completed. Probably we shall be on the march again in a few hours. Nobody knows where we shall go to next and some of the boys are of the opinion that it does not matter, so that we keep marching. We marched from Washington, in the first place, to the Shenandoah Valley, then returned to Washington again. After stopping there just long enough to brush the dust off our clothes, and out of our eyes, and get the pay due us for the last four months' service, we started for the Shenandoah Valley again. We left there night before last, and have so far returned on our second trip. It is famed of King Richard, I believe, that he marched his army up the hill and then marched down again; but the Sixth Corps makes *nothing* of such achievements. We have accomplished that same thing twice already, and can do it once a week all summer. King Richard is beaten in his own tactics.

It is terrible hot marching now. The men cannot endure it. Many fell out in our march yesterday, and several died from sunstroke. Straggling may be a serious evil to an army, but under such circumstances as those of yesterday it is as much without remedy as casualties on a battle-field. The first instance I noticed in our last march was coming through the village of Harper's Ferry night before last. The man was alive when he was discovered, but very near his end. Some men found him, picked him up, and sent immediately for a surgeon, but it was too late. He soon died. He could say nothing, and there were no papers about him to give any clue to his history. We carried him into the ruins of an old stone building that was burned at the commencement of the war, and there we were obliged to leave him. He was a middle-aged man, and by no means inferior looking. No doubt a circle of friends somewhere will mourn his loss, but there will be no one to tell where he is or how he died. Stranger hands probably buried him the next day, and there, unhonored and unknown, he will sleep till the resurrection morn.

When I wrote you before, we were on the mountain just west from Leesburg. The next day we marched across Pleasant Valley, through Snicker's Gap, and halted near the Shenandoah River, but separated from it by another smaller ridge. Here we had another day's rest. The rebels held the gap through the second ridge from the other side of the river, they having some pieces of artillery that commanded the road through the narrow break in the mountain. We had some batteries planted on the heights, which were practicing in their behalf as we came up, but with what effect I cannot say.

Tuesday all comparatively quiet, though heavy firing was heard at a distance, on both our right and left flanks. A fight was reported going on at Charlestown, and there were most extravagant rumors of our cavalry gobbling up whole battalions of Johnnies, and recapturing prodigious stores of plunder. Wednesday, the 20th, we waded through the Shenandoah river into the Shenandoah Valley, and Wednesday night we waded back again. We marched all that night, and till nearly night the next day, accomplishing, according to the average of reliable estimate, about thirty miles. We came through Leesburg, and halted near Dranesville. Many stragglers on that march — Vermonters along with the rest. It is a positive fact. I was eye-witness to it and I know all about it. We got into camp at Tennallytown, Saturday noon and the boys say they would have got there sooner, but the officers' horses couldn't stand it.

Our route lay through Dranesville and Lewinsville to Chain Bridge, ground made familiar to us... [A segment of this letter is missing.][23]

...soldier's life. There was the same excavation that we had made for the floor of our tent, the same fire-place and chimney and the same log basement. There was my old bedstead made of barrel staves nailed to two poles, and there was my old stool, which I remember used always to be in the other boys' way and which was always a reproach upon my woeful lack of ingenuity. I found too, the identical cup which has served me with coffee many times — a good one once, but now rusty and half filled with dirt; and there were many other things that I saw around that little spot, uninteresting to others though quite interesting to me. Back of the Colonel's tent, and around the old hospital, somebody had had enterprise enough to mow among the weeds and gather up a small stack of hay. Our parade and drill ground was covered with low blackberry vines bearing a luscious crop of large ripe blackberries. An eventful season of war and strife has passed since we left that ground, and many that were with us then have been laid low by rebel hands; but peace comes not yet. Our regiment was full and strong when it left Camp Griffin, but not one-tenth of those men are with us now.

It was quite a fortunate thing for us that we got our pay while we were near Washington, just as we did, for another such an opportunity may not present itself during the Summer. I think our good luck on this occasion is mainly attributable to the paymaster's unusual promptness. Almost as soon as the men stacked their arms they commenced to receive their pay. Four months of destitution made a ration of greenbacks more than usually acceptable. With pay came sutlers, and they did not forget to bring along all their extravagant prices. Making the largest allowance for the high prices that prevail everywhere I can hardly see an excuse for the bleeding extortion the soldiers were subjected to there. But the men *would* buy their goods, regardless of prices, as if their funds were inexhaustible. Some purchased from necessity, some for pleasure. It was the sutlers' golden harvest and they knew enough to reap it. Many of the boys take no thought of the real value of an article. If they want it they buy it, and the higher the price the more greedy they are to get it. Every sutler's tent that could be found, had its crowd of customers clamoring to be served, and it not only required a pocket full of money to patronize a sutler, but an endless amount of perseverance to get where one could patronize him. The ordinary law which regulates prices according to the demand and supply, is completely upset, and the whole matter is regulated at will by the sutler himself, awed a little, perhaps, by a wholesome fear of the eager crowd who sometimes refuse to submit to the sutler's terms but dictate their own, or take what they want regardless of any terms whatever. But the boys had long been deprived of every kind of luxury, and hence their eagerness when an opportunity presented itself.

We left that camp Tuesday, and marching via Rockville reached the Monocacy Thursday noon. Orders got there almost as soon as we did to go at once to Harper's Ferry, and we lost no time in getting there, unless I except about three hours Thursday night that we rested to sleep. Friday at noon we crossed the pontoon bridge into Harper's Ferry, and about two hours later went into camp some distance beyond. Saturday at four o'clock we left that place, and have marched back to where we are now. We do not expect to stop here long, and I am told that we are under marching orders at the present moment. It is of no use to express any opinion as to where we are going. Ask that question, and no two will answer it alike. The corporal that is with me thinks it is about time we marched the old road through Centreville and Bull Run once more and he says that we are going that way when we march again. The corporal is the most intelligent man in the Vermont brigade, but he knows no more about military matters than I do, and I don't believe we have the slightest notion of going that way at present. Time will tell, and when time tells me, I will tell you.

Near Strasburg, Va.
Aug. 14, 1864

Whoever may have been the first to propose the theory of perpetual motion, I believe the Sixth Corps have been the first to demonstrate its possibility by actual practice. Ever since we commenced our Maryland campaign, marching has been the order of the day, and the disorder of almost every night. Now and then we have a resting day, but this practice of giving us resting days, is fast falling into disuse. It is hard telling whether we counteract the rebels' plans or they ours. The rebel prisoners all complain of hard marching, and their appearance shows that it is abundantly so. I presume Union prisoners make a like complaint to them. The rebels have had a taste of the fine crops in Maryland, and like breachy cattle they continually dodge us and break in there, and all our running does not avail to keep them out. If they are dogged out of one place forthwith they appear in another, and if we drive them away from there, behold they turn up somewhere else! They seem to have the power of ubiquity, and can appear in half a dozen places at once, or else they spring up spontaneously in this valley of Maryland, or wherever they choose. Friday, July 29th, we were hurrying over the road from Frederick City to Harper's Ferry, with all possible dispatch, to intercept the enemy there, as we supposed, and Friday, August 6th, just one week later, we were hurrying over the same road in the same direction and for the same purpose. We only stopped there about twenty-four hours on our first visit, when it was found that some rebel movement on the great chess-board had made a corresponding movement on our part necessary. So to prevent being check-mated, we picked up post haste, and the next twenty-four hours found the troops transporting their knapsacks through the dust and heat back again towards the city of Frederick. Our camp was within two miles of the city. From here I dated my last letter. Some stragglers that fell out near here and remained till we came back saved themselves three days' rest and cheated the government out of about thirty miles' marching. They displayed greater generalship and shrewdness than our commander, but they claim that it is not worth mentioning. The next day we had marching orders, but they were countermanded and we remained there a day longer. We then moved camp five or six miles in a southeasterly direction and crossed the Monocacy river. Since then we have marched to this place, a distance, I should judge, of not less than seventy miles, and orders may come at any moment for us to march seventy miles more. Surely there is no rest for the wicked, not if they belong to the Sixth Corps, as lots of us do.

What an immense cost it is, in labor, on both sides, for Gen. Early to get his supplies in this valley and Maryland. It might be done cheaper and be better for us all around. I heard a fellow explain a remedy yesterday, and I was mightily pleased with it. He would have a detail made out from each regiment and brigade, to gather the crops every season and make a present of them to old Early. The men engaged to do this, would never be missed, and it would really cost nothing except a little sacrifice of pride, which in this age of chivalry we ought to be ashamed to mention, while it would save us an endless amount of marching and the citizens here would be spared so much distress and fear. The crops gathered could be left at Winchester or Martinsburg in charge of a garrison of one hundred days' men, which would be equivalent to delivering them to the rebels at Richmond. This fellow's idea was a capital one, but probably the obtuse War Department won't "see it."

One of the greatest evils we have to contend with is a scarcity of water. On the march, or in camp, we have found it difficult to procure a supply. Day before yesterday on the march, I took a handful of canteens, and started off by the side of the road to find water, if any could be found. I traveled five or six miles, at distances varying from a half of a mile, to a mile and a half from the line of march; and I examined every place where the lay of the land seemed to indicate the possibility of a spring or a creek, and I tried at several houses where there were inhabitants, but could find no water. At one place I found there were some of our wounded cavalry men from the skirmish the day before, and I thought here surely they must have water; but they told me the nearest place where they got any would take me three quarters of a mile further out of my way. Thinking, perhaps, they might have a motive in telling the soldiers they had no water, I felt inclined to examine the premises for myself, but a Union soldier left with the wounded assured me that it was a fact; and he told me I had better not go further from the marching column, as the country was infested with roving guerrillas. Several stragglers had been picked up by them, and no Union soldier was safe beyond our army. Eventually I found some water, and filling my canteens, I hurried to the train, where I was on guard. On my way there, I had many tempting offers for "just a drink," from soldiers half dead with thirst; some offering as high as a dollar, and some a drink of whisky in exchange for a drink of water, but my own comrades needed it, so I paid no heed to the potent inducements urged upon me to give it away.

At our camp near Frederick we pumped every well dry in that near vicinity, and before we left those more remote were beginning to share the same fate. Just before we left, I visited several pumps, but everywhere the guard gave me the same answer — "failed up." At one place there was a little, which was allowed to only a few privileged ones. The guard stopped me, but I told him I wanted to carry it to Gen. Grant's headquarters (I was on wagon guard there). "What," says he, "is General Grant here? when did he come?" I told him Gen. Grant was actually with us — that he came the day before. The guard looked incredulous, but he allowed me to get my water. He probably thought I meant the indomitable Lieutenant-General; but if he pretends to be a soldier in the American army, and hasn't heard of the Vermont Brigade, or our Brigadier General, his ignorance is inexcusable. He deserved to lose a pailful of water.

Our camp near the Monocacy was well supplied. We had the whole river to use from. This might have been one reason of our moving there. Another might have been that our position enabled us better to protect Washington and Baltimore, for under no circumstances must our army uncover those cities. We stayed there just two days. Marching orders came Friday the 5th, and Saturday our corps camped on the same ground, beyond Harper's Ferry, that we had occupied a week before. Here we enjoyed another short respite from marching. We did not leave there till Wednesday the 10th. This gave us an opportunity to draw new clothing, and to wash our old clothes, that had become saturated with dust and sweat. Wednesday we marched all day, and again Thursday. The weather was extremely hot, and the roads dusty as usual. Friday we came up with the enemy on Cedar Creek, near Strasburg. Our cavalry had followed close upon their heels all the way. Our pickets now extended to the town. We are about opposite Manassas Gap in the Blue Ridge, and in the neighborhood of fifty miles from Harper's Ferry. There has been no fighting here with the armies proper, but the skirmishers on both sides have had some lively engagements. The picket line was advanced this afternoon. I hear that Capt. Wales of Co. C, is again wounded. He had just returned from the hospital with wounds received in the Wilderness still unhealed. My informant says that he has an ugly wound in the head, but refused to leave the field till the fighting was over, and he declines leaving the regiment on account of it.

It does not seem to be the intention to attack the enemy here in front. I doubt if any one below General Sheridan himself knows what is intended. Our division has recrossed the Creek, but the picket line is farther advanced. The troops have had orders to march at a moment's notice this evening, but unless we are pressed by the enemy, we probably shall not advance. The cavalry have gone around to attack the enemy's flank. The enemy have got a position here and are evidently waiting for something to turn up. Perhaps they are not expecting it will be Sheridan's cavalry.

Near Harper's Ferry
Aug. 23, 1864

Last night we received orders to be ready to march this morning at daylight; but the order to march has not come yet, and in the meantime, before I lose the opportunity, I wish to record the important fact that we are back again to our old camp on Bolivar Heights. You know it was a little over a week ago that we were here before. Our trips through Halltown, Harper's Ferry, Frederick and other less important places on the route, are generally very regular, but delays are sometimes unavoidable. "Harper's Weekly" is the General's motto; but an occasional deviation in these troublous times is no occasion for surprise, nor should the people withdraw their confidence in our enterprise on that account. When we have added a little more experience to our system we expect to give perfect satisfaction all around. We shall come in "on time" without fail. Whoever intends to join this Middle *Marching* Department must be certain of a pair of legs that will support him in any hour of trial. They will be his main dependence. Unsoundness here will make him a total failure. His locomotion will be suspended at once when his wind and legs fail; and he can be of no further account in this department. At any rate, he will lose one trip, and cheat the Government out of so much marching.

Well, we have been out to Strasburg, and got back again. Coming back was not a retreat, I don't suppose, though it seemed exactly like one. The enemy have followed us closely all the way. There have been no regular battles fought, but considerable skirmishing has been done, chiefly by the Vermonters who are always at it. Gen. Sheridan has marched his army to Strasburg and back again.

How much he has accomplished I do not know. If he was not driven back, he must come back of his own accord, and of course Gen. Sheridan is not such a simpleton as to elect to come back till he had accomplished his errand; that is enough. There is no use in grumbling for more. We certainly have captured a few fat pigs — what we wanted to eat, and collected a little forage — what the horses wanted to eat; but whether the rebellion has gone down or up in consequence of it, I can not possibly say. I suppose it is a main part of our business that we keep watch of old Early, and keep him busy in some place, lest he should move down to help Lee, or turn up somewhere in Maryland. Perhaps Early has some such an idea in regard to Sheridan. If all this marching is in accordance with Early's premeditated plans, I will take off my hat to him. He is an extraordinary genius. He knows his business, and he succeeds in it remarkably well.

Individually, I have been remarkably fortunate on this campaign. My military duties have been to act as wagon guard, at headquarters when in camp, and with the train on the march. We guards have the privilege of putting our knapsacks and haversacks on the wagon, and carry only our guns and equipments. We have to help load and unload the wagons; gather forage, and keep a general lookout for the baggage entrusted to our care at headquarters. It is guard and fatigue duty combined — a little of both, and not exactly like either.

To have our knapsacks carried during so much marching is no small favor. It makes an immense difference, come night after a day's forced march, which a fellow's legs can appreciate very sensibly. It is nothing but fun to march stripped of this load. Getting tired is out of the question. Fortune favors the brave, they say, and if I am indebted to fortune for this streak of good luck, it would be interesting to know what act of bravery I have committed to merit it. I have looked over my diary to find it, but couldn't. I probably forgot to note it down.

We left Cedar Creek near Strasburg, one week ago to-day. Marching orders came just at night. We knew of course that we must be going to the rear, for an advance there would not be attempted, at that time of day. The position of the enemy in our front appeared to be a stormy one, without much chance to flank it; besides we were constantly in danger of being flanked ourselves. And then we were so far from our base that it was difficult to procure supplies. Some of our train had been captured, and our rations had been cut short on that account. It was a long distance for the wagon train to go to Harper's Ferry and return; and it took them longer than the supplies they brought would last; besides they were all the way exposed to capture from squads of cavalry that might come round through some of those mountain gaps and which it would be impossible to prevent. The Shenandoah Valley is a queer place, and it will not submit to the ordinary roles of military tactics. Operations are carried on here that Caesar or Napoleon never dreamed of. Either army can surround the other, and I believe they both can do it at the same time.

Wednesday we halted a little after noon, a few miles this side of Winchester. Before night the enemy attacked our rear guard at that city, and the Jersey brigade stationed there suffered severely. They made a gallant fight, but being attacked by ten times their number, they were broken up and badly scattered. Thursday we marched to within two miles of Charlestown, and halted on the pike road leading to the town. Friday and Saturday we remained quietly in camp. Our brigade had a very pleasant spot for a camping ground. Stately oak trees, with their dense foliage to shut out the burning rays of the sun, made the camp cool and delightful, while good water was abundant, and the country abounded in the good things of all sorts. Besides, there was a large cornfield just at the edge of the woods, where the boys could get plenty of green corn to boil, or roast, — an opportunity that no Green Mountain Boys — or mountain boy that wasn't green — would need urging to improve. I noticed the boys all through our brigade made this no small item of their daily rations, and "succatash" in true Indian style, was served at all hours.

The wagons made several foraging expeditions into the surrounding country, for hay and unthreshed oats. There is always more or less sport in these expeditions. We can generally get some good apples, berries, cherries, or some other good thing to pay us for our trouble. Often we run across a good fat rabbit, and whether its dress is wool or bristles it is all the same to us. Promiscuous plundering, of course, is not allowed, and lays the offender liable to heavy penalties; but when the boys are pinched in their rations, and we are in the enemy's country, our officers are not swift to notice every little infringement of the rules and regulations of war in this regard. The confiscation acts of *ourselves* have made us many a good dinner.

Sunday morning our camp was suddenly attacked by the rebels. While the people at home, were quietly preparing for church, and listening perhaps to the pleasant chime of the Sabbath morning church bell, the boys here, were preparing for the deadly conflict of arms, and listening to the sharp crack, crack, of musketry, as our picket line held the enemy at bay, firing as they fell back. But little was done, however, all day, except skirmishing. The enemy gave our camp a smart shelling, but without causing any great damage. Our brigade was deployed on the skirmish line, and did the principal part of the fighting. The losses were considerable, though not so great as might have been expected, considering the nature of the fighting, and the fact that our men were under fire at pretty close range all day, without any works to protect them. The Second Regiment lost 5 killed, and 11 wounded. They remained on the skirmish line till 3 o'clock yesterday morning, when they withdrew and came to this place. The enemy have followed, and picket firing was heard yesterday and to-day, quite near. The troops are fortifying this position, but at the same time we are under marching orders, so that it is difficult to conjecture whether it is intended to hold this place or not.

Near Berryville, Va.
Sept. 4, 1864

Camp life here in the Valley is growing dull, and so am I. If the reader wishes to partake of the same spirit he can peruse my letter. The medicine is warranted. Early and Sheridan are responsible for this extraordinary state of affairs, and perhaps will devise a remedy before long. They both seem to have been waiting for the other to make the first move. Gen. Sheridan accommodated them yesterday, and last night we had a brisk little skirmish here. We defeated the rebels, capturing quite a number of prisoners, and some of their artillery. The multitude of rumors in regard to it are so much at variance with each other, that in the absence of official figures or official guesswork, it is difficult to tell how great our victory has been. Some say we captured two guns and others say we captured eight. The rebels outwitted themselves. They saw our cavalry approaching, and supposing our force to be only cavalry out to reconnoitre, as usual, they lay concealed, calculating when they passed to gobble up the whole of them. The cavalry passed by them as they had intended, and thus far their plan worked well; but when they turned about to gobble them up, the Nineteenth Corps came up, and the "gobbling" was all on the other side.

We are now about three miles from Berryville, and about half way between Snicker's Gap and Winchester. We left our camp near Charlestown yesterday morning, and marched up the Valley, to guess at it, about ten miles, to this place. We marched over the same road that we did in going to Strasburg, and returning from there. We are beginning to get familiar with this road. This is the third time that we have been over it in as many weeks.

During the last two weeks we have moved camp but twice. We have rested six days, and marched on the seventh. This is reversing the Scripture rule, but I am not sure but that it will have a good effect. It certainly seems better than paying no attention to the divine command whatever. A week ago to-day (to-day is Sunday), we left our camp near Harper's Ferry, and advanced to the same place near Charlestown a week previous. It was here that the battle of the 21st was fought, and we had advanced on to the same ground once more. Breastworks were thrown up here, and artillery got into position as if we intended to make a permanent stand. The rebels had fallen back but not so far but that our outposts had skirmishes with them, and at one time our cavalry was driven in, when the Third Division of our corps went out and made everything all straight again. They didn't visit us after that, although we had made every preparation for their reception, and were anxious to have them come.

Probably they remembered the lesson we taught them in their last attack. That seems to have been more disastrous to them, by far, than it was to us. A rebel prisoner says, that they lost three brigadier generals who were disabled in that fight. Some Georgia regiments suffered terribly. We saw a rebel grave where there were eight buried, and all were from one company. Our boys did not throw away their ammunition in that fight. Some of the 11th regiment got a position in a house, where they were especially annoying to the enemy. The rebels were obliged to shell the house to drive them out. After the battle was over, Gen. Early himself came and apologized to the inmates of the house, for the course he had pursued. He told them he was obliged to do it, for eleven of his men had been shot from there, and our boys were picking off his men with marked precision. He promised them he would make it all up when he got to Maryland. The inmates of the house took refuge in the cellar during the shelling. We had a picket reserve at the place afterwards, and the folks there showed the boys the havoc made by the rebel shot. They smashed up one ancient and venerated bureau, scattered the dirt and plastering over an elegant bed, and committed various rude capers in different parts of the house. The boys carried away the old bureau, nearly the whole of it, as relics, for the bureau had a historic interest, it having as the owner claimed, narrowly escaped a similar fate in the Revolutionary war; but the bed was left untouched, and the carpet unswept, and everything just as it was at the time. They did this to please the curiosity of their visitors.

Our camp near Charlestown was in a very pleasant locality. It overlooked a tract of country the most of which is level. The wide fields showed a fertile soil, and are fair to look upon. They are just such as would please the eye of a practical farmer. In peaceable times this ought to be a rich and prosperous country. Transferred to Vermont, and placed under the control of our Vermont farmers, and many whole square miles of territory would rank next to our best intervale land. Churches, school houses and neat cottages would spring up all around.

The inhabitants are all of them bitterly rebel. I don't know as I saw but one man that claimed to be a Unionist, and perhaps his sympathy for the Union would have been less if we had not come there with a wagon to carry off his hay. He claimed to have about a dozen Union neighbors in town, and he thought he deserved extra credit for being faithful among so many faithless. The old man's hay wasn't so good as we wanted, so we concluded to believe him, and go on to the next house — or barn rather — and see what we could find there. Charlestown has the notoriety of being the place where John Brown was tried and hung. The jail where he was confined, and the court-house where he was tried, have the appearance of being roughly treated from some cause or other. Large holes were punched through the brick walls of both buildings, and from the street they looked as if they had been given over to ruin and decay. When the brigade came through there the last time, the band played the John Brown song, to the edification of that man's executioners. It just suited the boys to hear that air played there. They were determined to give the people there the benefit of it, and if the band hadn't played it they had agreed to sing it, and sing it as soldiers who know how. If they had done so I imagine the citizens would have thought that the ghost of John Brown was actually "marching on."

As the rebels did not choose to attack us there, but fell back, we had to pack up and follow them. Gen. Sheridan is bound to keep track of them at all events. We left camp yesterday morning at four o'clock, and have advanced to this place. There has been some fighting, and there are signs of more. Our brigade has not been to the front yet. I understand that we are going to fortify here, but whether that is to indicate a lengthy stay in this place, or not, of course no one definitely knows.

The glorious news from Atlanta was received in the army yesterday. The troops greeted it with immense cheering. God be praised if the morning twilight of the dark rebellion is beginning to appear.

Headquarters Vermont Brigade
Near Clifton Farm, Va.
Sept. 24, 1864

To-day is a rainy day in camp. It was a rare thing that we could say that all last summer, but it is losing its novelty now. Since the scorching drouth that so long ruled, has at last been broken, it has seemed as if every cloud was surcharged with water, and every one that has happened to float over our heads almost, has sprinkled us more or less. It rains so easy now, that as the Paddy said, "it almost rains itself." Since the month began we have had some unusually hard showers, and some pretty cool weather for this time of year.

Yesterday the corps went out on a reconnoitering expedition to discover where the enemy were, and send them our compliments. They were found in force on the Opequon River, between here and Winchester. Our brigade acted as skirmishers again, and they drove the rebel pickets and skirmishers into their position on the other side of the river. They kept up a casual firing all day, on the skirmish line, on both sides, which, with a little artillery duelling, was all the fighting that was done. There was no casualties in the Second regiment, and but two or three in the brigade, nothwithstanding they were in the very front, and did, as usual, a lion's share of the fighting. At night the troops all returned to their camps.

I don't know why it is that the Vermont Brigade is always used as skirmishers, when skirmishers are needed, unless it is because their skill and courage in this peculiar work has been so often proved, that they can better be relied upon than any other troops. We all know that it requires nerve and reckless daring, to make a good skirmisher. Almost any man had rather stand in the open field and fight, when he knows where the enemy are, and knows that he has an equal chance with them, than to pick his way along on an advancing skirmish line, without knowing when he may receive a whole volley from the enemy, and liable all the time to run upon a line of concealed sharpshooters, or an ambush of lurking foes. Skirmishers have to feel out the enemy's position, and are the first to receive their fire. On a reconnoissance or anything of that kind, when we want to find out where the enemy are, or what they are doing, or how strong they are, skirmishers are almost the only ones that have any firing to do. It requires peculiar courage in the men, and peculiar sagacity and courage in the officers, to do good skirmishing. I always feel uneasy when I am on the skirmish line, in front of the enemy, unless I know that I am being handled by skillful hands. We must not advance upon a superior force of the enemy and expose ourselves needlessly; and we must not break our connection with those on our right or left, or lose our directions and get lost or captured. It is for us more than for anybody else in the world, to "be sure we are right, and then go ahead."

General Grant has the name, I believe, of being the best General in the corps to manage a skirmish line, and everybody knows that he has the best troops in this corps or any other, to make a skirmish line of; so of course, when Gen. Sheridan has a difficult job of this kind to do, he knows whom to call upon to do it. It will be remembered that it was the Vermont troops that advanced the skirmish line at Strasburg, the 14th of August, and it was the Vermont Brigade that was used again as skirmishers on the 21st, in the battle near Charlestown, where they did the principal part of the fighting, and suffered nearly all the loss that was inflicted upon the whole army that day. Again yesterday, it was the Vermonters that explored the way up to the enemy's works, and made it safe for the rest of the army to follow. It is Vermonters on all occasions of skirmishing, everywhere and all the time. With a good General to lead, we can string out the whole brigade of us, in a line five feet apart, or ten if they want; and advance straight ahead without pulling apart here, or crowding together there, keeping a straight line and going straight ahead, until we come upon the enemy's works, and find out all we wish to know, and then we can turn about and go back again without having a man captured, and if it is in the night, without letting the enemy know when it is done, or getting lost ourselves. I don't know but other troops can do this business as well as we can, but I don't believe it, or else why should they be so shy in trying their luck at doing it. Let them prove their right to boast, and we will freely acknowledge it. We make no secret of the pride we feel in our acknowledged worth, and the good name we have won. But it seems to me to be a poor return for valor, that the best troops should *always* have the hardest work to do.

Wednesday, Sept. 21

Well, Mr. Editor, I commenced my letter more than a week ago, but I find that I have not finished it yet. Indeed, I have really had no time. By making several expeditions, scouring the country for forage, by lending two or three days' assistance to the clerks in the Adjutant General's Office, by marching and standing guard, I have found full occupation for all of my spare moments. But to-day as the brigade has gone across to Cedar Creek to make an advance of our line, and perhaps engage the enemy, and a few of us are left back at headquarters, in these quiet woods to guard the baggage, and bring it forward at night if needed, I have an opportunity to finish my very important letter, and I am determined to improve it at all hazards, though it may be a week, and perhaps longer, before I shall have a chance to send it to you.

Of course you will have heard before this letter reaches you, of our fight near Winchester, how we whipped and routed the rebels, drove them pell mell through the city, and followed them clear here to Strasburg, pelting them all the way. It was a glorious victory, but no share of the glory belongs to your correspondent however, for he wasn't in the fight. He was back about two miles to the rear, near the Opequon River, with the train in a place perfectly safe. We could hear the volleys of musketry firing quite distinctly, and by going up through a long piece of woods, we could see the fighting from a distance. Brave soldiers they say, always deplore the necessity that keeps them back when fighting is going on at the front, but I find I can stay at the rear at such a time, and be quite contented.

Down by the creek where the train stopped, they put up the division hospitals for our corps. Ambulance loads of wounded men were continually coming in, and the surgeons had all they could attend to, and more too. Wounds of every description; some in the head, some in the body, some in the hands, arms, legs or feet were constantly being brought forward for attention. It was impossible to attend to them all at once, and many had to wait and suffer a long time with their savage wounds undressed. Amputations at several tables were being made all the time. As fast as one man was removed from the board another was put on. Many poor fellows had to wait for several hours before their turn came. The surgeons, besmeared with blood, and hardened to their business, looked more like butchers cutting up beef than like professional men, adopting the stern alternative of removing a limb to save the life of a fellow man. A hospital on the battlefield always presents a horrid ghastly sight. Surely our national honor ought to be imperishable, purchased at such a cost.

Among those brought in were several of my own comrades. One man struck in the thigh with a piece of shell, which broke his leg, and bruised it badly, was brought in about noon, and it was not till night that any attention was paid to his wounds, except what we could do ourselves. It was not till night that he had any shelter either, and then it was only a fly overhead — a roof without walls. But it was the best they could do, and it is not always at such times, that they can do as as well as that. It was a chilly night, and the men, many of whom had to have their clothing cut from their wounds, leaving them in some instances half naked, had but one blanket for two men. I remember I promised to bring my friend a rubber blanket from the train, but the train moved along, and I could not do as I had promised. Yesterday I suppose he, with the rest of the wounded, were removed to a general hospital. It will be a tedious and painful journey over the rough roads for men with such wounds at his, but I know my friend is a brave man, as indeed they all are, and I know that bodily pain cannot crush his spirit.

Right by the side of the tent where my friend lay was another soldier, mortally wounded, and left there to die. I couldn't help noticing him in particular, though I never had seen him before. Fair looking and intelligent, too young and too tenderly reared, one would think, to endure the hardships of a soldier's life. Alas, he did not have to suffer long. He was wounded in the head, and died that night. I first noticed him a little past noon. He could not speak, but he appeared conscious. A fellow from his company asked him if he knew him. He signified, by a pressure of the hand, that he did. I saw him again at night, he was dying then. Oh what would a brother or sister have given to have been with him then — to have called his name and received back a pressure of recognition? What would his mother give now to drop a tear by his rude grave — a sacred spot that she may never be able to find? And thus have perished thousands since this war began. Verily war is cruel, and none more terribly so than this which the rebellion has forced upon us. God forgive those who started it, they knew not what they did.

The Battle at Fisher's Hill
Headquarters Vermont Brigade
Mount Crawford, Va.
Sept. 25, 1864

The story of the battle of Fisher's Hill will do to be told when it is old, and although I was not an actor there, and saw but little of what transpired, I will take a spare hour to-day and tell you that little, and run the risk of telling you what may have been told you a dozen times before. It was a glorious victory, even more glorious and complete than that of the 19th at Winchester. It was even better I think than Gen. Sheridan himself had dared to hope for. We captured twenty pieces of cannon, and twenty-five hundred well prisoners, exclusive of the dead and wounded left in our hands. It was all accomplished with but few casualties — only about 250 in the whole army — and it inflicted a more discouraging and demoralizing overthrow to the rebel army than any they had suffered before since the war began.

We left Winchester early Tuesday morning the 20th, the day after the fight there, and reached Strasburg a little after noon. We camped by the side of the pike, in the edge of the woods, about half a mile from the town. The rebels were in their old position just beyond, and their pickets and ours were near enough together to exchange shells quite liberally. About noon, Wednesday, the troops were ordered out to skirmish with the enemy, and feel out their position. Not much was done that afternoon except skirmishing, which was pretty lively some of the time, though without doing us but comparatively little damage. We lost a few men, and among them Corporal Thomas Miller, of the 3d Regiment, orderly to Gen. Grant, and Brigade color bearer. He was hit in the body with a chance shot and killed instantly. Our troops threw up breastworks during the night.

Thursday, during the forenoon, skirmishing was pretty lively all along the line, especially in front of the first division. Our Brigade lay comparatively quiet behind the breastwork they had thrown up the night before. About noon we noticed Gen. Sheridan with his staff riding along the line, consulting earnestly with Gens. Wright, Getty, and other officers, and we surmised that they were studying some kind of mischief for the rebels, and pretty soon we learned that there was to be a grand attack. It commenced about the middle of the afternoon. Being loose just then, free to run where I pleased, I thought I would indulge in the rare privilege of witnessing a fight as a mere spectator. It was no common sight. Certainly it was worth a year of soldiering to see the enemy so handsomely whipped, even though I was having no hand in it myself.

Our batteries had an excellent position in front of where our division lay, or had been laying before they advanced, and it was here a fellow "bummer" and myself went out to witness the charge that was going to be made. Crook's command had gone around by the North mountain to the extreme, to flank the enemy, and operate with Averell's cavalry who were around there too. The 19th Corps joined with Crook, and the 6th Corps joined on to the 19th.

Our division under Gen. Getty was down in a hollow pit just in front of us. The rebel works were on the opposite hillside from one to three miles off, and it certainly looked like a formidable and desperate undertaking to storm those works, especially with troops that had been hard at work fighting, marching, or digging, night and day, almost, ever since we left camp Monday morning. Their works were strong, and the rebels had the utmost confidence in them. The citizens said they had been assured by Gen. Early himself, that he could hold that place against any force the Yankees could bring against him, and they confidently believed that it would be our sure destruction to attack him there. They prophesied again and again, that we should be coming back the Winchester and Strasburg road faster than we went up.

But Gen. Sheridan was of a different opinion. There is no timidity about his character. He knew he could whip Gen. Early, and he did it. The attack commenced about four o'clock. While Averell's cavalry and the Eighth Corps were stealing around on to their flank, we had about 20 pieces of artillery pouring shot and shell into their works with marvellous rapidity and accuracy in front. Gen. Sheridan was there superintending matters himself, and Generals Getty, Wright and others with him. The rebels had a battery in a strong position away on our right, and Sheridan at first directed the whole attention of the cannoniers to that spot, throwing the shells into their works with an accuracy that nothing of flesh and blood could stand. Gen. Sheridan was eagerly watching the effect of his work through his glass, and seeing the rebels leave their works, he threw up his hands and says he, with an elation that he did not attempt to conceal, "They're running like hell, They're running like hell." He then sent orders with all haste to have Gen. Crook advance his line and storm the works, while at the same time he told the cannoniers to keep up the firing to prevent the enemy from rallying and coming back to their works again. As Crook's line advanced the enemy uncovered a battery from another point more immediately in our front and opened upon him from there. Immediately Gen. Sheridan had every piece trained upon this new position. God pity them now. Their destruction is inevitable. The artillery fired with remarkable precision. Although the rebels were so far off that you could not distinguish a man from a mule with the naked eye, they would burst the shells over their works every time and scatter the deadly fragments right amongst them. Scarcely a shot was thrown away, and yet it took them less time to sight their pieces than an ordinary hunter would take in aiming his rifle at a woodchuck. Occasionally they sent a shot amongst us, but their situation seemed to be chiefly directed to the line of infantry that was advancing upon them. Pretty soon they began to give away. At first one or two could be seen running with all his might to the rear, then as another volley of our shells was hurled in amongst them, the number would increase, until finally the field was covered with demoralized rebels scampering with all possible speed away from the range of our thundering engines of death, that must have cut them down awfully. Their firing stopped. It was death for them to remain there, and the bravest of them could hold out no longer. Sheridan had ordered Getty to push forward his line and connect with the rest, and now the whole had advanced almost up to their works. They succeeded in getting off with one piece of artillery and tried to escape with another, but in their haste they ran on to some obstructions, and horses, harnesses, carriage and gun, and I don't know but the riders too, were hurled into one promiscuous heap, where they had to remain till our troops came up to extricate them. It was a complete rout. I believe I never enjoyed a sight so well before in my life. Our cheering and shouting must have grated harshly on their tender feelings in their moments of terror, but they could only "grin and bear it."

Our infantry gained the rebel works without scarcely any loss at all, and immediately pushed on after the retreating foe. Our line became badly broken up in pursuing — almost as bad as the rebels did in retreating. It was each man for himself, and each man for a Johnnie. I heard some of the officers say they could not keep up with their men, or hardly keep track of them. The enemy were pursued for some three miles before our troops halted, and then it was only for a few minutes. All night we pursued them, and till nearly night Friday we were on the march up the valley after them. It is the first time that I can remember of our pursuing the retreating enemy close to their heels all night. This time we were scarcely an hour behind them at any time.

Gen. Grant was not with his brigade in this fight. He had a furlough of twelve days, and left for home the day before we were ordered out of our camp on this last move. It is the first fight that he has ever lost. He came out I believe as Major of the 5th regiment, full three years ago, and he has been with his regiment or brigade in every engagement up to the present time. He can afford to lose the glory of one fight. It is doubtful whether we have any more fighting to do here in the valley this season. There is nothing left here to fight.

———————

Headquarters Vermont Brigade
Harrisonburg, Va.
Oct. 4, 1864

We are having a lovely October day to-day, and it is all the more lovely for succeeding several days of wet, drizzly weather. We are lying quietly here near the village of Harrisonburg — a pretty place once, containing some fifteen hundred inhabitants, but now, like almost all of these Southern cities and villages, bearing abundant evidence of the paralyzing effect of war. The camps are spread out on both sides of the city, enlarging its borders and making it tenfold more populous for the tented suburbs annexed.

We seem to be waiting here for no particular purpose, unless it is to pick up what few straggling Johnnies there may be left about here who have become cut off from their main army, or to collect a supply of cattle and horses, what there is left, and forage if they can find any. Day before yesterday a rebel prisoner was brought in from the mountain east of us, and he reported that there were about a thousand rebels, indifferently armed, hid in the mountains watching for an opportunity of joining the rebel army. They had become cut off from Early during the late battles, and were edging their way around us to join him again. Accordingly Gen. Wright was ordered to send 500 picked men from the best brigade in his corps to go out and escort them into headquarters as prisoners of war, and accordingly Gen. Wright, with Napoleon-like shrewdness, selected his 500 men from the Vermont Brigade. They went out early Sunday morning, but the birds had flown. However the Vermonters did not come back bootless. They captured a hundred head or so of cattle, a quantity of horses, some sheep and hogs, besides finding a store of cider brandy — a cheery article that many soldiers love, "not wisely but too well." As they were obliged to return that night they could not pursue these fugitive Johnnies, but there is a report that our cavalry have since come upon them and captured nearly the entire squad. Our cavalry had another little skirmish yesterday out to Mt. Crawford. They were attacked by infantry and cavalry. They repulsed the enemy and drove them back about five miles. We had orders to be ready to move to their assistance at a moment's notice, but we were not needed.

We are now upwards of a hundred miles from Harper's Ferry, and our trains have to work with all diligence to furnish us our supplies. They have no time to play by the way. But the country around here affords us some addition to our rations, otherwise we might quite often find ourselves alarmingly deficient in the wherewithal to gratify the cravings of the "inner man." Here in Harrisonburg there are some 500 wounded rebel soldiers. They have rebel surgeons to prescribe for them, and rebel nurses to take care of them, and certainly they have no reason to complain of their captivity. A great many of the inhabitants have declared their intention of going North to escape the rigors of war which have become almost intolerable. The Government has offered to furnish transportation, and many families are packing up to avail themselves of the offer. Many others are heartily praying for peace, let it come in what way it will. They have tasted the bitter fruit of secession, and have had enough of it. They find that it does not satisfy, that it was a poor remedy for their imaginary grievances. They see the grim determination of the North and they begin to feel that to hold out longer is to fight against inevitable destiny. It is curious how interested they all are in our Presidential election. I haven't talked with a single citizen that did not deplore the probability of Lincoln's re-election. That, they think, shuts them out from any hope. Let McClellan be elected, they say, and we can get together and talk the matter over like men and have our difficulties settled, without prolonging this terrible war. Their reasoning sounds very plausible, but you ask them how peace is to be brought about by the election of another than Lincoln for President, and they will reply, "Why by recognition, of course." They will tell you again and again that they will never yield an inch so long as Mr. Lincoln is President; that they will never make the least concession to *him*. But you find by questioning them a little further that they expect to make just as little concession to any other President as they do to Mr. Lincoln. They only hope that some other President will make greater concessions to them. They know Mr. Lincoln's straightforward iron determination to punish treason everywhere and do it thoroughly, and they know that he will not spare their pride, nor buy them off, nor surrender one iota of the principles that he has avowed. It galls them to the heart's core, that having rebelled against the Government under him, they should have to yield to him finally. Of course we sympathize with them most deeply in their uncomfortable predicament, but we can't quite make up our minds to vote for McClellan to relieve them. They begin to be sick of the war already, but they will be sicker of it by and by, and when they get sick enough of it to throw down their arms against the Government of the United States it will be time to begin to think of talking over the matter together "like men." Does any one say that it is impossible to bring the South to this point? My friend, it is *because* you say so that it will be impossible. How easily you can whip an antagonist that thinks at the outset of the strife he is going to get licked. Only let every man, woman and child in the North feel and know that this rebellion is to be totally crushed, and the thing is done already. The South would see our determination, and if she felt it to exceed her own she would yield at once. The hope of a division at the North nerves them to fight for more than the hope of conquering our armies. *That* hope has pretty nearly faded out. Heaven forbid that we should encourage the other.

For a few days past I have been at work in the Adjutant General's Office, making out for Major Mundee, Assistant Adjutant General of the Division, a list of the killed, wounded and missing in the old Division during the severe campaign of last summer, from May 5th to July 10th, inclusive. The whole loss amounted to the enormous number of 4830, of which the brigade lost very nearly one half.

Our brigade when it crossed the Rapidan, had 3888 muskets that could be called into line of battle. The 11th joined us the last of May with 1490 more. There is now in the brigade present for duty 1687. The 2nd regiment left Brandy Station with 740 muskets available for line of battle, the 3rd with 583, the 4th with 590, the 5th with 491, the 6th with 484. Since then we have had some additions to our numbers, along with our many heavy subtractions, and now the number of enlisted men present for duty in each regiment of this brigade is as follows: In the 2nd regiment, 239; in the 3rd, 174; 4th, 107; 5th, 102; in the 6th, 275; and in the 11th, 683. The number absent from each regiment is — from the 2nd, 233; from the 3rd, 230; 4th, 357; 5th, 214; 6th, 280; and from the 11th, 898. These numbers, it will be observed, include only "the men," niggers, officers, waiters and the like, not being mentioned. Those absent are mostly in hospitals or rebel prisons, and will join us again when they can. There are but 21 reported sick in the whole brigade. Deaths from disease rarely occur here now. As a fellow facetiously remarked the other day, dying off from sickness in this brigade is about played out.

Headquarters Vermont Brigade
Near Front Royal, Va.
Oct. 12, 1864

When I was a boy (which was considerably less than a thousand years ago), I remember at Court time in our little village, when a trial of more than common interest was before the Court, and everybody was eager to know the result, the old bar-room used to be the principal place of resort, where the matter was at all times thoroughly canvassed. All the probabilities were here taken into account long beforehand, the evidence given in, and likely to be given in, and its bearing on the case minutely discussed — and the whole result ciphered out and predicted, long before the case at Court was fairly opened. Loafers, visitors, spectators and the shrewd guessers generally, would have the whole case laid bare and with a marvelous prophetic accuracy render a verdict of their own that would almost always accord with the verdict at Court; and so bar-room gossip achieved an importance of its own, and the "bar-room decision" was looked to as a pretty sure index of the decision to be finally and legally made.

Now we here in the army have no bar-rooms, exactly, nor grocery stores in which to meet and gossip, but we have many places that answer every purpose. "Down to the Spring" is one. Hear a man telling interesting news and you ask him how he knows. "Oh I heard of it down to the Spring," will most likely be his answer. In the summer time a crowd collects at the Spring, because it is a cool place to sit and talk, and at any time the talkers are almost sure to collect there to discuss the topic of the hour, however important or unimportant that topic may be. "Down to the Spring" is a queer place, and I have been amused and interested a great many times in listening to the discussions, arguments, and small talk generally of this miscellaneous assemblage. I believe I never enjoyed a discussion better than I did the other day "down to the Spring" when the parties concerned were discussing the Presidential election and the Chicago propositions for peace.[24] I was so much interested myself that I was sure it would interest others, though it would be impossible for me to give anything like a true idea of it with pen and ink, in the ordinary limits of a newspaper article. Abraham Lincoln had plenty of defenders, and McClellan had a few. The McClellan men were noisy and defiant, and their arguments were of the old stereotyped order, the sum and substance of which usually is "Damn the niggers." Two of the loudest talking McClellanites there would vote for him because they were for peace, and because they liked McClellan. Their arguments and opinions are not worth recording, but we will give them a fair play. One of them would vote for McClellan because he was the best General the world ever produced, and had been so shamefully abused. The President, his General in Chief, his Secretary of War, and the greater portion of Congress, he said, had been "down" on him, because they were afraid of him, and it would do his soul good to see him raised to the supreme control of our affairs. The first thing he wanted to see him do then, was to put old Abe and Stanton and Horace Greeley, and a few other abolition criminals into Fort Lafayette. A long list of other grievances were enumerated, which he hoped McClellan's statesmanship would discover some way to punish, and he wanted he should do it with a vengeance.

The other McClellan man was for peace. All his hopes of our ultimate success had faded out, if indeed, he ever had any. Peace would come if McClellan was elected, and peace was what he wanted. "I have been out here long enough," he said," and now I want to go home and so do you." The war had lasted long enough and it was time to have the trouble settled. He had seen all the fighting he wished to see, and let folks say what they would, he should vote to have the war stopped. A fellow by his side said he wanted peace too, but it was no McClellan peace that he wanted. He had served one three years already, and had begun on his second three. He was as anxious to go home as any man could be, but he didn't want to go till the rebels were whipped out clean and smooth. He said he had always stood up for McClellan, was a McClellan man clear to the bone, but he couldn't vote for him on the Chicago platform. Rather than have peace by surrendering to the rebels, he would let his bones manure the soil of Virginia. "Bully for you," was the response all around. One fellow said every man in his company was for Lincoln and Johnson, and several others said it was the same in theirs. Upon this McClellan man No. 1 declared that more than half of his company was for McClellan, and McClellan man No. 2 said he should vote for him if he had to do it all alone. Another man from the same company told him he would probably have a chance to prove his exclusiveness when election day came.

Just then a well dressed, fine looking Orderly Sergeant, from the 139th Pennsylvania regiment, came along and mingled freely in the conversation. His ideas appeared to be well digested, and being the ranking man, his opinions had greater weight with us than those of any other one in the crowd. He believed the war was about ended, that the South was about ready to yield. They were a proud and obstinate people, and of course would hold out as long as possible. They have studiously concealed from us, so far as they could, their true situation, that we might never know how sorely we had pressed them. "How deeply chagrined we soldiers would feel," he said, "to surrender to the South now, and find that had we held out a little longer, the whole rebellion would have tottered to the ground." He proved that cessation of hostilities could mean nothing less than a recognition of the Southern Confederacy. If we are willing to stop the war for the sake of talking this matter over with the South, we recognize them at once. If we are willing to negotiate with Jeff Davis, England will claim the same privilege, and so will France, and what can suit the rebel President better than that. His government will then be fully recognized, and we can't help ourselves. He thought we had better surrender fair and square, than fool ourselves in that way. A convention of all the States now, he thought, was the greatest absurdity of the age. He believed the South, unless their case was entirely hopeless, would scorn to have anything to do with it. At best, it could only be a scene of crimination and recrimination, of jargon and confusion, and end in a grand fizzle, leaving our ship of state without chart, or compass, or principle, or purpose to guide her. South Carolina would want redress of Massachusetts for the indignity she suffered when black men stormed her forts on Morris Island, and Jefferson Davis would probably ask to have "Beast Butler" hung as a guaranty of our good faith in calling a convention. All the results that could be obtained now, might have been obtained four years ago.

Now, after we have lost 500,000 men slain by this rebellion, he could not call it all a joke and come back to that, and nobody but a coward would think of it.

No sir, said he, there is no use in talking of armistices and conventions. We have got to fight this thing out. There is no other way. The North and South must find out who is master. Timid people might cry peace, peace, but there would be no peace until we had fought and gained it. The South had rebelled against our common Government, and the Government must compel them to cry Enough, or it would be no Government at all. A Government that couldn't vindicate itself, wasn't worth having, and he didn't believe the people of the North was quite ready yet to vote for any such. The Sergeant had lost two brothers in this war, and most certainly desired peace, if it could be had honorably, but he saw no way to end this, only to fight it out to the bitter end — till the last rebel slaveholder was exterminated, if necessary. He did not ask others to do what he was unwilling to do himself; he was ready to practice what he preached.

But the Sergeant had strong hopes that the rebellion would soon be subdued. It made him provoked, he said, that men at the North, who ought to know better, should encourage the South to hold out by talking of propositions for peace. It was only prolonging the war, and killing so many more of our men. He said every man that would vote for the Chicago platform ought to be made to go in front of the whole length of our army drawn up in line, with a board strapped to his back marked COWARD in big letters, and every soldier ought to hiss at him as he passed. Why, said he, to talk of peace is as it was at the battle of Winchester, when the first line of a part of the Nineteenth Corps gave way. The rebel prisoners who were fighting in front of that Corps at that time, all say that they were just ready to run themselves, when they saw those opposed to them give way, and upon this they were encouraged to press forward still harder, thus postponing victory for several hours, and making the task doubly difficult for those who stood invincible during the maddest efforts of the enemy to pierce our line. So if our Government falls back one iota from the principles it has avowed, it only encourages the rebels to hope that we shall finally become weary of the war, and give them all they ask; and every such encouragement prolongs the war so much the more with all its direful consequences.

I cannot follow the Sergeant any farther, for my letter is too long already. As I have had to quote from memory I could not give his words exactly, but his ideas, as they were given during a somewhat prolonged discussion, I have endeavored to follow to the letter, and my word for it, what I have written is as true an index of "what the soldiers think" of the great political contest now pending, as I could have given.

Near Middletown, Va.
Oct. 20, 1864

Tired almost to death, with scarcely sufficient energy left, either mental or physical, to conceive an idea or pen one down, nevertheless I will devote a spare hour, while I have one, in giving you an outline of our yesterday's battle and glorious victory. It commenced a regular skedaddle, and but for the determined fighting of the old Sixth Corps, would have been a most disastrous rout to the whole army. Acting as wagon guard myself, I was back to the rear with the train and saw but little of the fighting, and for that reason any account from me will be rather a tame affair, but I think I have got the reader pretty well used to tame affairs by this time, so I shall persist in writing as usual.

The rebels played a shrewd game on us yesterday, and calculated to make a big thing of it. They thought the Sixth Corps had gone to Petersburg, for we did get started to go last Thursday, and that now was their time. They crept around to our left, and commenced the attack before daylight. The Eighth and Nineteenth Corps, it appears, had no warning of their approach whatever. It is said the rebels entered a sutler's shanty before the sutler was awake, inquired the price of whiskey and tobacco, and then they coolly informed him that they would relieve him of what little he had, and before the sutler had hardly got his eyes open to perceive the condition of affairs, he found himself minus a stock of goods and a prisoner in the enemy's hands. The troops were thrown into confusion before they had time to rally for effective resistance. All was confusion and dismay with them. The plain to their rear was covered with stragglers, panic stricken and running for dear life. Alas for the army here, had there been no Sixth Corps to stand in the breach and hurl back the rebel hordes that seemed to be sweeping everything before them.

The first firing we heard was on our right, then there was a little picket skirmishing on our front, which, however, created no alarm. They were very faint feints. But when the firing commenced on our left it was explained to us very quickly that the enemy was upon us in force, and that they intended no child's play. Orders soon came for us to pick up, and we guards and pioneers had none too much time to load headquarter baggage and tents into the wagons and get out of the way, for in a very few minutes afterwards, the Johnnies had possession of that place themselves. Our camp was about a half of a mile to the right of the "pike," opposite Middletown. That town and road were in possession of the enemy before we had our wagons loaded, and they were coming rapidly down on our left flank. Large squads were streaming back from the front in reckless confusion, totally disorganized, and all the lines of provost guards they could establish, could not check their disgraceful flight. It became evident at once, that the Eighth and Nineteenth Corps were overpowered, and if the staunch reserve Corps, — the old Sixth, could not hold the enemy, all would be lost. Indeed, when our brigade marched out to take a stand against the enemy who were coming impetuously forward, it seemed like opposing a child against a giant, and that we should be crushed at once. The roar of the enemy's musketry, and their hellish yell, was coming nearer and nearer, while through the fog and smoke, we could see but little opposition to their coming. After our brilliant victories at Winchester and Fisher's Hill, were we now to be defeated, perhaps totally destroyed? As things looked then, the very best we could hope for, was that we could hold them till night, and then retreat to Winchester or Harper's Ferry.

Our Corps was pushed back about three miles. Gen. Sheridan was on his way back from Washington, and, thanks to a merciful Providence, was as near as Winchester when the fight commenced. Hurrying forward, he arrived at the seat of action just in time to stay the tide of disaster, and turn defeat into victory. We met him on his way up. There was a look of confidence and stern determination in his eye that inspired the men with more hope and courage, I believe, than a whole corps of re-enforcements would have done. Somehow everybody felt a sense of relief when they heard that Gen. Sheridan was on the ground. We all believed he would accomplish *something,* and he did. Up to that time you could hardly tell that there was any line to hold. Each division appeared to fight and fall back independently, and the best they could.

Things took a different turn, immediately, when Gen. Sheridan rode along the line and commenced operations himself. Seeing some stragglers he rallied them at once, told them for God's sake not to turn their backs to the enemy, and promised them that they should not only get their earthworks back before night, but that they would have the enemy back across Cedar Creek, and Gen. Sheridan abundantly fulfilled his promise.

It was about three o'clock. The Johnnies had had everything their own way. They had captured over twenty guns, almost all of the Nineteenth Corps train, headquarters and all, and a large number of prisoners. But their hour of triumph was at an end. Instead of the glorious victory they had planned, and supposed they had within their grasp, they experienced a most humiliating defeat, worse, if possible, than that at Fisher's Hill four weeks ago. We captured back all we had lost, except prisoners, and twice as much more. Some 4000 prisoners and about fifty guns were taken from them, besides nearly a hundred wagons, and more trophies of victory are constantly coming in. The boys unanimously attribute our final success to the timely arrival of Gen. Sheridan. The magnetism of his fiery energy electrified the army with a kindred spirit, and they fought with just that desperate valor that was needed to turn the tide of affairs in our favor. Sending his cavalry around on their flank, he compelled them to fall back, and then he ordered his boys to up and after them. The retreat soon became a complete rout, and if Sheridan could have told the sun to stand still, as did Joshua of old, their army would never have troubled us again. It will need an immense sight of repairing before it can trouble us much, as it is.

Gen. Sheridan on his way up from Winchester, placed strong guards along the road to stop the skedaddlers, and to take back to the front all soldiers skulking from duty. We wagon guards had to be identified as such, or we were liable to fare no better than the skedaddlers. Once I left my gun on the wagon, and stepped one side of the road to fill my canteen with water, and coming back, I found myself mixed in with a squad of stragglers, and to all appearances, I was as much of a straggler as any of them. Right ahead of us there was a lieutenant with a squad of cavalry, stopping everybody, and sending them under guard to the front. Of course I should be stopped too. I might tell him I was a wagon guard, but just then, both the Eighth and Nineteenth Corps appeared to have turned wagon guards, and if he wouldn't take their word for it, he wouldn't mine. I could have gone up to the front, if duty had required, but to be ordered up there under guard, with a squad of stragglers, I could not. More than all that, I had no business to be away from the wagons. I was responsible for the stuff over which I was guard, besides I must tend the brake on the wagon, for a brake has become an indispensable necessity with our heavily loaded teams over these hilly roads. Now you may laugh at the "fix" I had got myself into, but I was most sorely perplexed to know how I should get out of it. At first, I determined to run by the guard at all hazards, but they were prepared for all such determinations on our part, and when the lieutenant cocked his revolver and held it close to my head, I began to be aware that openly resisting military authority, was rather of an unsafe kind of business. He told me that he would blow my brains out if I passed him, and I saw at once that he was a man not to be trifled with at such a time. Feigning to yield, I watched my opportunity, and dodged between the double line of wagons, and then run for life. I expected a bullet would be sent after me, but for some reason he did not fire. I breathed freer when I got beyond the range of his revolver. I suppose that lieutenant would have been perfectly justified, under the circumstances, if he had shot me dead on the spot, and I thought I was perfectly justified, under the circumstances, in getting by him if I could. The lieutenant endeavored to do his duty, and I endeavored to do mine. If he is satisfied I am.

A little further along, we were all stopped, but the corporal in charge of us managed to make our business known, and we managed to get by the guard in a legitimate way. We reached Winchester about the middle of the afternoon. At night, orders came to go back to the camp we had left. We had heard of our final triumphant success, and tired as we were, we all rejoiced that we were to go back to the old camp from which the rebels had driven us. We now occupy the same place that we left.

There are reported 320 casualties in the brigade, of whom 90 are counted with the missing and may return. General Grant, Captain Amidon of Gen. Grant's staff, and James Gray, mounted orderly and brigade color bearer, had each a horse shot under them. Captain Amidon, and Sergt. Thomas McColley, mounted orderly, were severely, though not dangerously, wounded. H.O. Baxter, Lieutenant and Aid-de-Camp, received a slight wound on his right side. Gen. Bidwell, of the third brigade of our division, a brave soldier and most excellent man, respected by all who knew him, and almost idolized by his own men, was mortally wounded. But you will get in the official report a full list of the casualties.

Strasburg, Va.
October 30, 1864

Dear Bro. Webster:[25] — You asked me to write you a line occasionally after you had left us; and having a moment of leisure this Sunday evening, I will cheerfully comply. We have had a warm, bright Sabbath to-day — just such an autumn Sabbath as one loves to enjoy, and seems really to be designed on purpose to make delightful the worship of God. So clear and warm has shone the sun, so mellow and soft the air, while the crimson tinted foliage adorning the forests on the surrounding hills and mountains, rich as the robes of an Eastern Queen, contrasting most beautifully with the serene blue sky above, all have combined to make Nature more than usually lovely, as if she, too, delighted to worship her Maker, and would lead all men to do likewise. Beautiful foretaste of that Sabbath that shall never end! Where the songs of praise will be heard continually, and where war and desolation will never be known.

The brigade is back again to Strasburg, your regiment very near the same place it was that cold morning that you left us. The 3rd and 4th are encamped on the flat by the railroad near the town. They act as Provost Guard — Col. Foster being Acting Provost Marshal. The 2nd is by the brick church, south of the town, and the 5th is only a little further from the town, in the same direction, while one battalion of the 11th, is further to the right of the town. We are very comfortably situated here. Our duty is to guard the town, that is, those that are on duty, are to keep those that are not, from stealing or making depredations in any shape upon the citizens' property.

Well we have improved the day the best we could. Chaplain Roberts had an appointment at one o'clock, but the funeral of a rebel officer, who died here in town, being appointed at the same hour, the Chaplain postponed his an hour later. Gathering a few singers he attended the funeral. Not having time to organize, the singers took no part in the exercises, and they appeared not to be needed. The friends and neighbors of the deceased made noise enough of their own, and so long as *they* felt inclined to call it good singing, I don't know as it is our business to object. It was easy to see from their manner, that they cared but little for the presence of Union soldiers. Not only on this occasion, but many others, I have thought I noticed a marked desire on their part, to maintain as far as possible strict exclusiveness. But they are civil and polite, taking care to give no offense, and maintaining a respectful bearing, as a general thing, towards our officers and men. I hardly think that Yankees would behave any better to them, under reversed circumstances. But I have not seen any of that violent, malicious, secession disposition said to exist in some places, where the residents, especially the women, delight in spitting their insults upon the Union soldiers whenever they have a chance. The people here have learned manners by their sufferings if no more. And they have had some truly severe lessons.

After the funeral to-day, the drum beat for church, but the Adjutant had neglected to send around the notice of the meeting to the boys, so the drum beat and they were ignorant of its meaning. But the Chaplain nothing daunted, was determined not to give the matter up so, but went personally to the camp, a little way outside of the town and gave notice of a meeting himself, to be held at four o'clock at the brick church in the south part of the town, used as a rebel hospital. The Chaplain had friends and foes for his audience, but the wounded rebels appeared to enjoy the discourse very much, as did also the well Union boys. The attendance was not large however. The regiments were drawing beef just at that time, and you know soldiers, just like all the rest of the world, love the meat which perisheth, a great deal better than they do the bread of life. When the rebels get well and are sent North, where all are sent so far, that have recovered, I hope we shall have the privilege of using that meeting house as often as we choose for religious worship. It is an excellent place, and as the boys say, it seems like home to hear the gospel preached from a regular pulpit in the house of God.

There is another brick church in the opposite part of town, and Chaplain Roberts had intended this as a place to hold his meetings, and we were congratulating ourselves upon our good fortune in having so good a place for this purpose; but one cold morning last week, the boys conceived the idea of appropriating some of the inside work for their own comfort and benefit. Before their depredations were discovered, they had completely torn out the inside of the house and destroyed it for use. The pulpit was entirely taken away, the seats were removed, the doors, windows, casings, and everything that could be used in any conceivable way to build a "shanty," was taken. Nothing but the bare brick walls was left. It was too bad, not only on account of the destruction of property, and spoiling the place that we had intended to use ourselves in an appropriate way for religious worship, but on account of the good name of the troops, for citizens had acknowledged to the General that no troops ever quartered in that place, had been more orderly than the Vermont troops. The General was indignant when he heard what they had done, and would gladly have made restitution, but that was beyond his power.

I was sitting in the office that morning, when an aged and very respectable looking citizen came in, hat in hand, to the General. He appeared to be much aggrieved, and he had good reason to be. He said he had come to plead in behalf of his church which the soldiers were destroying. He said he had helped to build that church, was a member of it, and he seemed to regret most deeply that any harm should have come to it. The General told him that a stop should be put to the sacrilegious work immediately, and sent a guard there at once for that purpose. Everything that was taken away was ordered to be brought back without delay and replaced; but it was too late. It was beyond the power of man to replace the broken up material, or repair the damage. The boys have been so long accustomed to appropriate any unoccupied building near their camp, to any use that their comfort or convenience suggested, that it is hard work to make them respect an empty house, if it is a church, when they need the lumber to make them comfortable "shanties," as they thought they did then.

There appears to be no particular signs of our leaving here at present. I don't know but that we are as likely to stay here as anywhere. Everything is quiet, and no enemy is near. It is hardly possible that the rebels will try to get another whipping here this fall, and it is hardly likely, either, that we shall go very far to chastise them any more. It won't pay now they have no more artillery or baggage wagons to capture. But of this you can guess about as well in your home in Vermont, as you could if you were here. There is nothing of importance going on here now, if there should be, I should be pleased to let you hear from me again.

Strasburg, Va.
Nov. 8, 1864

Election day, to-day, and warm and foggy at that. The boys instead of huddling into their tents, driven there by the cold, are gathered in knots in their company streets discussing politics and other grave questions of the hour, and performing the by no means unimportant duty of casting their votes for men and principles that are to govern our country through another period of four years. Thousands of bits of paper are falling into ballot-boxes today, all over our country. It is a little thing, and can be done very easily, but mighty consequences may hang on the result. It is almost a new thing in the history of the world, when such great results as whether this country shall be governed by one principle, or another in almost deadly hostility to it, can be decided by such simple means. God hasten the day when *all* questions may be decided in the same way, and then war, with its terrible list of horrors, will be remembered as one of the evils buried forever in the grim Past.

The weather, so like an Indian summer to-day, is widely different from what we had a few days ago. It is too pleasant to last long, and by and by we shall have winter upon us, stern and severe as usual. However, it will not overtake us and find us unprepared. Our quartermasters have not neglected us. They have promptly forwarded to us an abundant supply of good warm clothing, substantial for winter wear, and a quantity of good comfortable blankets, not "shoddy" by any means, but thick, stout and heavy ones, just such as we need.

Before these supplies came up, we were very poorly provided against the coming cold weather, especially in blankets. Our summer supply is never sufficient for fall or winter, and especially so after a campaign like this in the valley, when the men have been obliged to dispense with everything they could possibly do without, that they might be able to carry their load during so much marching. So as the season advances, and a cold and rainy day or night happens along, as they always will at this time of the year, it is difficult for a fellow to keep himself warm. I know my time honored woollen blanket, the very one that I picked up on the battle-field of Gettysburg, I have found to be provokingly insufficient to keep me warm a great many times these cold, stormy nights, and my wrath has gone up to the swearing point on several occasions, on account of it. It was for this reason, I suspect, that one cold morning, some friendly rogue in the 4th regiment, very kindly relieved me of any further trouble on account of my blanket. It is possible, however, that he mistook it for his. Soldiers make mistakes like that sometimes, especially in cold weather.

Not only are the boys well provided for now in the matter of clothing, but the most of them have built themselves most excellent quarters to live in. It isn't known of course how long we stay here, but the men never hesitate a moment to go to work in good earnest to build up their little huts on account of any uncertainty about that. They might have to wait all winter if they did. Besides the most of the men like the fun of building themselves good shanties, and they enjoy a lively competition to see which will build the best one.

They can almost get excused from drill if they wish to work on their tent, and where is the old soldier that would not work all day on his tent if he could get rid of a couple of hours drilling by it? Some of the boys made their tents more cosy and comfortable than the citizens have in the village. One fellow I might name has built him a regular brick house of good comfortable dimensions. He has a glass window of four lights in it, which somewhere he was lucky enough to pick up, and with his good fire-place and chimney on one end of his house and his bunk, which answers for a seat in the day time, and a bed at night, on the other, he can sit and talk and laugh, smoke his pipe, and entertain his visitors with all the dignity of a modern aristocrat. All the boys have good comfortable quarters of some kind. They have freely appropriated all the loose boards they could find in the village for building purposes, and some I fear that wasn't entirely loose, and where boards could not be got they adopted the old plan and built with logs and mortar. You never need to fear but that the Vermont Brigade will keep themselves comfortable.

We have been here now nearly three weeks, which is longer than we usually stay in one place. We came here Friday the 21st ult. So far as I can see we are as likely to stay here as anywhere, all winter; and for anything I can see, too, we may move from here before I have finished my letter. Our Division is on the extreme front, and our Brigade is ahead of the rest of the Division. The regiments are detained on different sides of the town, east, south, and west. The picket line is along the north fork of the Shenandoah river, or, as the citizens call it, North river, which bends around and runs east from this place. It isn't a long march for the boys to go on picket from here, the picket line being hardly a hundred yards from camp.

Strasburg is a village that might have contained some five or six hundred inhabitants in time of peace. It can boast of two parallel streets, running lengthwise, and about three running the other way. It has an old, dilapidated appearance, just like all Southern villages, I doubt if a dwelling has been erected here within the last ten years. Many I should judge belong to the last century. Everything looks old and dirty. Perhaps there is an excuse for this now, in war time, there certainly ought to be, but Strasburg never looked like our neat, thrifty New England villages, though many of the houses look much better inside than out. I don't know how the citizens are going to live this winter. They say we have taken away from them everything they have — their wheat, their corn, their cattle, and everything we could find, and now as winter is coming on, they are entirely destitute. Some of these citizens are going North before we leave. The rest I suppose have deliberately embraced the idea, that they are going to starve to death, and become reconciled to it. They say they have, and they ought to know. One citizen told me that he raised crops enough for himself, and two of his neighbors but that our men had taken it all, not leaving him so much as a single bushel of wheat, or corn. He had a field of sugar cane, he said, that would have yielded him six or eight barrels of syrup, but our troops had entirely destroyed it. His mill they had burned for firewood, his cattle and horses had been taken, his pigs had disappeared, and in this situation he was left with two daughters, and a sick wife to get along the best way he could. He said the Yankees would get their pay for all this when Early got into Maryland, and he seemed immensely pleased with the idea. Well, poor man, if he and his helpless family are going to starve to death right off, he can't chuckle long, and we will forgive him. Part of their woes no doubt, are real, but we cannot depend upon all they tell us. Whether justifiable or not, the damage we have inflicted upon them has had its effect in teaching the people to have some respect for Yankee power. They no longer sneer at, and insult "the Yankees," as I am told they did during the first year of the war, in this place. So far as outward appearance goes, they are as respectful, and courteous as we could well expect. The ladies, old and young, do not appear to disdain Yankee soldiers at all, but so far as I have noticed, are quite courteous and civil. Indeed I have quite frequently noticed well dressed, and fashionably appearing young ladies, conversing cheerfully and merrily with the soldiers, as though the best of friendship existed between them. Maybe they will tell you, they hope the North will get whipped, and the South gain their independence, but they will have a coquettish way of saying it, rather intended to please than offend.

The election returns are coming in; the Brigade will stand two for Lincoln and one for McClellan; the whole vote at the latest was 1114. There was 764 for Lincoln, and 350 for McClellan. The McClellan men complained bitterly, because they could get no printed McClellan votes. They seemed to think the Lincoln men were very partial, distributing only their own kind of votes. With the experience of the September elections before them, they ought to have known that the Union men were too selfish, to print and distribute tickets for the opposite party, and sought out some way to furnish their own. The 10th Vt. promises to be the banner regiment. I have it on good authority, that their vote stands 175 for Lincoln, to 7 for McClellan; just twenty-five to one. Soldiers don't generally believe in fighting to put down treason, and voting to let it live.

Headquarters Vermont Brigade
Near Kernstown, Va.
Nov. 16, 1864

Another lovely day is given us to-day. The sun shines down upon this camp, this city of tents, without an intervening cloud. "Sunshiny" days are always pleasant after several days of raw, windy, uncomfortable weather. Everybody looks better natured than day before yesterday, when the cutting northwest wind wouldn't give a man a moment of comfort, or a moment of release from its unceasing torment. Everybody is busy, too, for such days are rare now, and men that have work to do, snatch at the golden moments. Let a stranger come into the brigade to-day, and he would find but few idle men. They are all at work at something, the most of them building quarters for winter. The clatter of axes is heard all through the woods surrounding our camps, and the crashing of falling trees greets the ear continually. Nobody knows how long we are going to stay here, but we have been here nearly a week already, and there are no signs in particular of a movement; and now, after this biting cold weather, a pleasant day like this is too much for the soldiers to lose in speculating upon probabilities, so they very naturally follow their old instinct, and commence at once and in earnest to build good, warm houses, that will be comfortable in spite of northwest winds, or winds and storms of any kind. We have had to leave our good quarters at Strasburg, but we are not going to be discouraged from building more on that account. It isn't our way of doing business.

We left Strasburg the morning of the 9th. We were not *driven* away by any means, nor did we leave because we were afraid we should be at some future time. We were far away from our base of supplies, and it was difficult for our horses and other animals to get sufficient forage, either from the country or the government. More than that, we were giving the rebs an advantage over us for nothing. So long as we were so far from our base of supplies, the guerrillas could always annoy our trains. There was the North Mountain on our right, and the Blue Ridge on our left, affording excellent passage ways for rebel cavalry to crawl through, and pounce unawares upon our train, capture and destroy what they could, and then skulk back through some of the gaps again, leaving a guard to shut the gap behind them. Now we are where we can have our flanks protected by our own cavalry, and can hold the valley just as well here, I suppose, as at Strasburg, besides being about twelve miles nearer our supplies.

We left the next day after our Presidential election. For two mornings previous to the 8th, the troops were got under arms at daylight, in expectation of an attack from the enemy. Monday morning at four o'clock the boys had everything packed ready to fall into line at a moment's notice, and so again Tuesday morning, but no movement was made, and the enemy did not attack us. It was known that Early was receiving re-enforcements at New Market, and though the boys would have liked nothing better than to have given him another whaling, they did not wish to be disturbed in their privilege of voting for Uncle Abraham, Tuesday, a thing that Early would have given, nobody knows how many pieces of artillery and baggage wagons, to have accomplished.

We marched back through Middletown and Newtown, and took up our position on the right of the pike, about two miles from the latter place. Friday there was firing on the picket line. The rebs had found out that we had left, and followed us. Friday morning the troops were under arms again, and all day held in readiness for an attack. There was quite lively skirmishing at times during Friday and Saturday in our front, but they did not venture up to make any serious attack. Before night a gratifying order came in from head-quarters, stating that Gen. Powell with his cavalry, had driven Lennox's Division two miles beyond Front Royal, capturing two pieces of artillery, — all the artillery he had, — his caissons, ammunition train, and one hundred and fifty prisoners. Since then everything has been quiet here, and the troops have commenced building breastworks and throwing up fortifications.

The army left some very good works at Strasburg. Our brigade occupying the town, was in position to fortify, but the rest of the division on the crest of the hill in the rear of Strasburg, had built a good, substantial breastwork, and placed an almost impenetrable abattis in front of it, at good fair range from the works. Woe to the rebel line of battle that had attempted to charge up that hill through the craggy, snarly abattis on to the 2d Division of the 6th Corps, behind those breastworks. One would think that no rebel could get there alive. It is very seldom, however, that we have a chance to use our works in that way. More commonly the positions are reversed.

The New York boys had built good winter quarters, as well as we. Some of their houses showed a skill and ingenuity, on the part of the builders, of no inferior quality. On the western prairies, no doubt there are many log houses, not one whit more comfortable than some I saw by the side of the road as we were coming along from Strasburg. And this, too, where the timber to build of had to be carried by hand upwards of half a mile, from an adjoining woods. One fellow in the 49th regiment had a house that a prince, endowed with the faculty of appreciating the good things of this world, might have envied. It was built of large, straight cedar sticks, from three to five inches through, hewn smooth on the inside, and papered with newspapers. He (or they) had a board floor, brick hearth, glass window, and as good a chimney for its purpose as ever was built. It had a capacious fire-place, and crane, and pot hooks, and all the conveniences for cooking annexed. No doubt the owner of that house enjoyed his work, and the comfort it bestowed, with as much heartfelt satisfaction as half the wealthy occupants of those princely residences that may be found on Fifth Avenue in the city of New York. It was too bad that he should have had to throw away so much labor, and leave so good a house to fall into rebel hands; but I don't suppose that the army stayed there a moment longer on his account. On a scrap of paper that I picked up from his bunk, addressed "To the first Johnnie that dares step into my Sanctum," there was the following directions: "You will please burn this hut in retaliation for the wheat stock, Ed and I burned, near New Market. Get as mad as you can and then apply the torch."

I guess the New York boys all felt pretty well that morning, notwithstanding they were leaving their comfortable quarters. In another tent I saw another inscription to the rebels after this fashion: "I, a Yankee of the true stock, give and bequeath this house into the first rebel's care that wishes to occupy it. Come right along in; you need not be afraid, the Yankees are all gone. I have left two of your wounded at the residence of Mr. Bowmans. Give them my last respects, and don't starve them to death. Yours, for Abe Lincoln and the Union." On other pieces of paper I saw all sorts of advice for the rebels, some of which they would do well to heed.

Scattered about the camps were quantities of blanks such as the soldiers had used for voting in New York. Their balloting was carried on on an entirely different plan from ours. Their ballots were made up and sent home to some elector in the same town or county where the soldier was a resident and a voter before enlisting, who by a power of attorney given him by the soldier could cast for him his vote the same as if he were himself personally present. In the Vermont regiments we did our own voting. The three ranking officers were the constables of election. Every man's vote had the name of his county written on it. The constable would take each ballot, examine it to see that it was right, then drop it into the box, while the the clerk would take down the name of the voter, his county and town, These votes were counted by the constable, and a statement made of the result in writing, which, with the ballots cast, and poll lists, were sent to the Governor and Secretary of the State. Any voter could challenge another whose right to vote he had reason to suspect. There was no chance for fraudulent voting. It was a very simple and fair way of holding an election, here in the field — the best I think that could have been adopted.

The day after the election we were drummed up at four o'clock, to be ready to move at daylight. We knew we were going to the rear, for the Vermont Brigade was assigned its accustomed position, as rear guard for the army. We took up our position here, about five miles from Winchester. There is a rumor that we are going to fall back still further, to the line of the Opequon before we go into Winter quarters. If we keep moving about, we shall by and by have the Shenandoah Valley full of Winter quarters, and then it will be immaterial with us where they move us to.

Camp Russell, Va.
Nov. 25, 1864

Returning to my company on Saturday, it was my privilege to take a tour of picketing during the twenty-four hours commencing yesterday morning.

Picketing Thanksgiving day was not particularly different from picketing any other day, and I don't know as I have anything new or marvelous to say about it. Dear Mr. Editor, I shall only weary your patience with commonplace repetitions, notwithstanding your compliments, if I attempt to tell you anything about what we boys are doing here now, for camp life has become an old story, and camp life is always dull to make the best of it. But I have a leisure day on my hands which I must pass off some way, and my old habit of writing for the *Freeman,* is the best I have ever invented for that purpose. So with your indulgence again, kind reader, we will have a little chat in our old fashioned way, telling our thoughts as they come along, and we won't reject any as unworthy, for fear of having none left, but we will give all fair notice that what we chat about shall be of no consequence whatever.

Pickets have usually remained on duty three days at a time, but according to the new arrangement, they stay out but one. The change was made in consequence of the cold, tedious weather we are having the most of the time this fall, and will probably continue until the extra clothing that we sent away to Washington last spring, is returned to us again, when we shall probably go back to the old three days system once more. Picket guards, camp guards and all other guards in the whole Division, assemble and have guard mounting together on the parade ground in front of brigade headquarters. It is a new style, but we here in the army are prone to invent new styles, just like all the fashionable world outside. Yesterday morning at 3 o'clock precisely, when the drums beat for the guards to assemble, your humble correspondent might have been seen, and doubtless was seen, with eight other men, I believe, and one corporal from the 2nd Vt. Regiment, making their way to the ground where the ceremony or whatever you would call it, of guard-mounting, was to be performed. Well, guard-mounting isn't a very important, or a very imposing affair, but I suppose it is one of those little things that are necessary to keep up a wholesome state of discipline among the troops. We were arranged in line in open ranks, our arms were inspected by the commanding officers, the band playing meanwhile, and after this we passed in review before the highest ranking field officer of the day, when we were ready to start for the picket line. All the officers of the day from each regiment, brigade, and the field, in the Division, were arranged in line in front of the pickets, at distance varying according to rank. Quite a splendid line of them there was there, with their red sashes on, and their dainty little swords hanging by their sides.

Speaking of swords, I cannot refrain from wondering at the magic charms which it always seems to have for the wearer. All the virtues imaginable seem to be concentrated in this little, useless weapon of war, and all the soldiers are half mad with eagerness to wear one, all I mean except myself. It is always a sure passport to the most select society, and we privates esteem it our highest delight to render homage to the wearer, no matter who he is, or what are his antecedents. Now I am loth to speak irreverently of what all the world worships, but I have pondered long and deeply on this subject, and so far, have been wholly unable to comprehend the practical utility of this same pretty, harmless weapon that everybody loves to see. It is all owing to my own obtuseness I admit, for almost anybody can see that there is a potent charm to them somewhere. Why, I have seen men of no sort of consequence above the average of soldiers generally, suddenly raised to vast importance in this little world of ours, upon getting the privilege of buckling one of these swords around their waists, and dragging it dingling along after their feet. I have seen young men elevated by it to such a high standpoint (I am taking their own opinion for this, dear reader) that it has seemed a long ways for them to look down to where we poor sinners in the ranks live and move and have our being — so long indeed, that they are seldom ever inclined to look this way. What wonder then, that every soldier is ambitious to get one of these swords to wear. What wonder that they will fight with desperation, "treat" with liberality every superior officer whose influence will in any way help them to gain their object, and what wonder that they will try their utmost to be "hale-fellows-well-met" with everybody, that if possible they may win popularity, and in this way be helped to gain the coveted prize. Of course soldiers will do so, and it is no use to dispute taste, or quarrel with human nature. Doesn't a soldier know that with a sword by his side, he is free from a thousand vexations that a soldier with a musket is subject to? that it gives him a thousand privileges from which a private is debarred? Don't they know that newspapers will speak of their services in longer paragraphs if they live, and give them a longer obituary if they die? Don't they know, too, that the ladies will smile upon them more sweetly, and welcome them more cordially if they wear a sword, than if they carry a gun? For ladies have stimulated this sword mania, and some of the more thoughtless ones imagine (oh foolish absurdity!) that the salvation of this Union depends upon the use of the sword simply and literally, rather than upon muskets and cannon, and the more common implements of war. Well, I have my own opinion of these swords, which I suppose is different from that entertained by all the rest of the world, and yet my opinion is right, and all the rest of the world are wrong. I regard them as a child's plaything, of no consequence whatever in the bloody, earnest work of fighting this rebellion. When such formidable arms for accomplishing death and destruction are being invented and made, as this war has called into being, it seems not only passing strange, but ludicrous in the extreme, that officers should be made to go into a fight with such perfectly harmless arms for offence or defence, as a little polished sword. The boys have rather irreverently nicknamed them "toad-stabbers," and it is not an inappropriate name. I certainly would as soon think of going out here to fight the Johnnies with a little boy's pop gun, as with one of these harmless swords. I don't know as you ever thought of it, my proud fair lady, but it was the muskets of private A and private B that killed and wounded so many of the rebels, and that drove them before us in such wild dismay. That dashing captain or lieutenant that you think so well of, never hurt one of them with *his* weapon. His courage was good enough, but the simple reason was, poor fellow, he had nothing to hurt them *with*. I am not writing this to hurt your feelings or his, nor to magnify my own office, simply, but you have heard doubtless, that facts are stubborn things, and you probably know that stubborn fellows delight in telling them.

But I have wandered a long ways from my story of picketing, and, begging the reader's pardon, I will return, immediately, to my narrative.

Guard-mounting was soon over that morning, for it was a cold, uncomfortable morning, which made the pickets all eager to get on to their posts, and the officers all eager to get back into their tents. Soon we were on our way to the picket line, and soon after we were all distributed along the line, to the several posts, there being about four men to a post. From each of these posts, there was sent out one man, for vidette, as we call them, about twelve rods, more or less, in advance of the post. After the first man had been out as a vidette for two hours, he was relieved by another one, at "the post," who exchanged places with him. It happened to be my turn to go on the first thing. The post where I was to go was pointed out to me, and I assumed the responsibility of going to it, without being conducted thither by a corporal. It was on a little knoll, about one mile and a half to the right of the village of Newtown, which was in sight, from a point just a little distant from my post. The fellow that I relieved was sitting and shivering over a few coals, that he had been allowed to have on his post after daylight, and he appeared to feel genuine satisfaction at seeing me come. I commenced to walk my beat, at once, back and forth, with all the dignity of a man terribly in earnest in putting down the rebellion. I was told to keep the fire burning on that post, but, I became so absorbed in my occupation that I forgot it, and the fire went out entirely, But the day grew warm and pleasant, and no fire was needed.

Three years ago this very day I was doing the same business, just beyond Lewinsville, when the regiment was at Camp Griffin. I remember the time well. Alas! what changes have been made to our ranks since then. Seventeen men from the little company of which I am a member, have been killed outright by rebel bullets, during the past season alone. Scott used to say that four men perished from disease on a campaign, to one from the enemy's bullets, but Grant reverses the order, and kills four men on the battle-field, to one that perishes from disease.

Three years ago I remember having a long dispute with the fellow on the post next to mine, as to the probable duration of the war. My opponent was willing to admit, that it was barely possible for the war to last till the next Fourth of July then coming, but he thought it preposterous to suppose the war could last longer. Half for mischief, for I didn't believe it myself, I argued that we should all have a chance to serve our time out, if we lived. He finally refused to argue with a fellow who used such unreasonable opinions. But he was killed on Marye's Heights, near Fredericksburg, and I am not allowed the poor enjoyment of triumphing over his opinions.

My Thanksgiving that day consisted mainly of a few cold biscuits that an old woman brought out to the picket line, and sold us; yesterday our Thanksgiving consisted of turkeys, sent us by the Sanitary Commission, from New York. The *Baltimore American* said that there was sent to Sheridan's army, and other armies, 50,000 pounds of turkeys, "besides fabulous amounts of apples, cakes, doughnuts, cheese, butter, cranberries, canned fruits, pies, and all that goes to make a thanksgiving dinner," but this must have been a mistake, certainly so far as this army was concerned. Gen. Sheridan acknowledges, over his own signature, having received 6000 turkeys, which he promised should be equally distributed among the men in his army, and I think they were. Out there on the picket line it was a rare luxury, and seemed all the better being sent us through the kindness of the people at home. We ate it thankfully, and hoped that when another Thanksgiving day should roll around, there would be no picket lines in these Re-United States, and that we could celebrate our thanksgiving around our own firesides, and in our own homes. May God bequeath to us this priceless privilege.

Camp Russell, Va.
Dec. 1, 1864

   Yesterday morning there were pretty strong evidences that we were going to break up our new camp here and move to parts unknown. Signs, plainer than we wished to see, indicated that we had got to leave our good quarters once more, pack up our little pile of goods, shoulder it, and start out, perhaps, for another long, rough campaign. We soldiers love our ease as well as anybody, and the greatest share of the men had quite as lief remain here, and call it that our work for the season is done, as to start out, and on new expeditions which, of course, would involve fatiguing marches, and tedious hardships, at this cold and every-way uncomfortable season of the year. But the signs of the times we thought to be unmistakable. Various rumors had been circulated in camp about our going to Tennessee City, Point Savannah, and several other places, which seemed to be in need of a Sixth Corps to put things in order. So Thursday morning, long before light, when we saw great bon-fires burning in the camp of the first division, such as soldiers always build when they leave a camp which they have occupied long enough to accumulate the material for a bon-fire, and heard that the division had actually started for Washington, and that we were to follow as soon as transportation could be furnished, we considered our leaving this place a foregone conclusion, and began to make up our minds accordingly. All sorts of conjectures were indulged in as to where we should go after reaching Washington, but the best guessers amongst us couldn't agree upon any one point. Indeed no one was sure that we should go to Washington at all. No drilling was required of us yesterday, on this account, but before night the order was countermanded, or postponed, and we have yet a few days further lease upon the good quarters we have built here, and there are but few but that would be quite willing to have it last all winter.

   News is extremely scarce here, now, and gossip immeasurably dull. We are getting dull, too — dull for want of excitement. To be sure, we have a drill once a day, and sometimes more, but drilling is the dullest business that ever was invented, especially for "we veterans," and after all the new recruits will get ahead of us at it. We usually have a brigade or battalion drill in the afternoon, of an hour or two hours duration, and that is generally about all we have to do, except our usual guard duties, which, however, have called us out pretty often of late. The weather — a topic that all sensible people can fall back upon when others fail — has been very pleasant and Indian summer-like for the past week, and the boys have improved the weather by improving their shanties in various ways. A board fence that was discovered out beyond the picket line has added quite a stimulus to the architectural inclination of the boys. They added new improvements to their shanties, and improved those already added. We had to go three miles nearly for these boards, and back them into camp, but that was not the worst difficulty. The boards were beyond the picket line, and no one was allowed to go through. But the boys planned a way of smuggling them through that I suppose was perfectly satisfactory all around. The pickets themselves could almost always get permission of their commanding officer to go outside of the lines for a few boards, if that officer could be made to believe that they were urgently needed, and these pickets would generally, of course, remember to bring along a few for their friends, who would be at the line waiting to receive them. In this way the boys kept at work till they had got all the boards they wished for, or till the fence posts were completely stripped of every piece of board and nail that was attached to them. In this way, and many other ways that would be too tedious to explain, we have fitted up most excellent quarters, and "all we ask is to be let alone." We will live here as comfortable as a nest of mice this winter if Sheridan will only agree not to disturb us till spring. As for Early we leave him out of the account.

I had almost forgotten that we had a corps review a week ago last Monday, by "Little Sheridan." It was forcibly brought to mind, however, by a vivid account in the N.Y. *Herald*. That correspondent made a pretty big thing of it, but he didn't (begging the fellow's pardon) tell the truth; and some of his statements, though of no particular consequence, are rather amusing in view of the facts. For one thing, he said, Gen. Sheridan rode *slowly* along the lines. Slowly! Shades of John Gilpin! what must fast riding be then? Gen. Sheridan is a man of too much energy to do anything slowly. He ran away from everything when he came up to the fight October 11th, and on this occasion, he hardly seemed to ride but fairly flew. We were in line by brigades, and the General halted in front of each brigade, raised his hat to the troops and then dashed on to the next brigade to do the same. His body guard, who had halting or saluting to do, were left far in the rear. The General rode along the whole length of the line in our front, and back again to where he started from in our rear, and he accomplished it in an incredibly short space of time. Only a few of the General's staff, who accompanied him, were able to keep pace with Sheridan's fiery steed and its fiery rider. His body guard were scattered all along the way clear back to the further end of the line. If the correspondent of the N.Y. *Herald* considers that slow riding, he could please a large audience by exhibiting what he would be willing to consider a specimen of riding that might be called fast. He said the troops rent the air with cheers, as Sheridan rode "slowly" by us. No doubt, the boys *felt* "cheer-ful" enough to have rent the air with shouts of applause to the hero of the Shenandoah Valley, although we were standing in a pelting rain which had already wet us to the skin, but on a review there are special ways prescribed for showing our respect to a beloved General, but cheering is not one of them. When a reviewing officer at any review, halts in front of us, we may, at the order, present arms to him, and this is all the demonstration of respect that he wishes to see or allows to be made. We should go through the required manual of arms in a ludicrous manner, if every man was swinging his hat and cheering all the while the General was riding by. No, we did not disturb the equanimity of the atmosphere with serious rents for the occasion, nor are we apt to on reviews, any more than a congregation is apt to rend their meeting-house with cheers when a respected minister comes in. The correspondent of the N.Y. *Herald* must not think that soldiers are all wild school-boys, if he does he will be liable to commit some very ridiculous mistakes.

The general health of the troops here is good. There have been some changes in our commanders within the last few days. Gen. Wright, who has command-ed our Corps ever since the death of Gen. Sedgwick, has been assigned to another command, and Gen. Getty, of this Division, commands the Corps in his stead.

Gen. Grant takes Getty's place, and Col. Geo. O. Foster, of the 4th Regi-ment, commands the brigade. Our regimental officers now are mostly those who have come up from the ranks. They understand the nature of their business from its foundation, and are every way qualified for the trusts they have won. They have all been weighed in the balance a great many times, and in the hour that tries men's souls have never been found wanting. The com-mander of the regiment, Lt. Col. A.C. Tracy, is absent again, wounded. Maj. Johnson has been absent on a short leave, and during his absence the command has devolved upon Capt. Ballou of Co. K, who has, but a short time since, returned from the hospital, where he has been for a long time confined in con-sequence of very severe wounds received in the Wilderness last May. There is a rumor that he is to be one of our field officers, and all the boys are in hopes the rumor will prove true.

Our regiment is still small. We have had a few recruits added, but not much more than enough to balance our continual losses. We barely hold our own. The Old Brigade does not receive so many recruits in proportion, by far, as do the other Vermont organizations in the field. This ought not to be so, and yet it is best that only those recruits should join us, who have a soul to dare the worst perils of the service. We shall not hold out that we are a favored brigade, to tempt recruits to join us, for we are not. We always have an honorable share of the sternest work to do, and we believe that we have earned a choice reputation in always doing this work creditably.

We would welcome gladly all recruits who were willing to sustain the reputation we have gained, and who would cherish, as a sacred trust, the honor of this veteran Brigade, and feel proud to share it with us, but all others are warned that if they enter the army this Brigade is not the place for them to come to. Our record is a record of blood as well as of honor. Our roll contains the names of many of Vermont's truest patriots, and our chief reward, when the war is over, will be a consciousness of having belonged to the old Vermont Brigade, and having borne an honorable part in their many hard fought battles. But there is room for many more here, and the country needs you. The question is, Will you come?

In Front of Petersburg
Dec. 15, 1864

We are finally back here on Gen. Grant's line fronting Petersburg.[26] We have expected this change for a long time, and on several different occasions have come very near making it, and now the thing is done. We had hoped to have been sent somewhere else, or to have remained in the Valley; for to be honest about it, this was the least desirable place to which they could have sent us. We had rather have been sent to Savannah, and fought with Sherman through thick and thin until we had cut our way through, and gone in at the back door of Richmond, or have stayed in the Valley and fought Early as often as he could have raised an army big enough to make it pay, than to have come back into these dirty trenches again. There is nothing desirable about this place It is all fighting and no fun. We neither whip nor get whipped here. It is regular cold blooded duelling, day after day, with no decisive result on either side, and fellows no braver than I am, get tired of it after a while. I suppose those that *are* braver have a keener relish for this continual skirmishing and picket firing, but I own I haven't, and a man that writes must tell his own feelings and speak his own thoughts. But they have got us here now, and we will make the most of it.

Somebody must do this work, and they probably thought it might as well be us as anybody. We know how it is done.

Our Division left Camp Russell, in the Shenandoah Valley, Friday, December 9th. I would like to tell you a long story of our march and ride from that place, for I call it the roughest experience I ever knew, and I believe I have known some that were pretty rough before, but we will be brief and give a cursory description of it. To do it justice would be impossible.

It was a bitter cold morning when we packed up to leave our old camp and start for Petersburg. The ground was frozen stiff, and the water that we took in our canteens froze as we carried it along. But we were warm enough while we were marching. We marched through Winchester and on to Stephenson's Station, about five miles this side of the former place, and there we waited till between three and four o'clock in the afternoon, for the train that was to take us to Washington. We got to the Station about 11 o'clock, stacked arms, and then employed ourselves in killing time, and in keeping ourselves warm until the train started. The delay of the train made the boys impatient, and the cold weather made them full of mischief. Finally we got aboard the train, and then we had to wait another hour. The boys could stand it no longer, and their mischief found vent. They "rallied" on one sutler and distributed his goods among themselves, — the eager crowd getting, each man, all he could. After that they attempted to rally on another, but Col. Foster happening to be present at the critical moment, scattered the boys to the right and left as a wolf would scatter a flock of sheep. He used no sword and exerted no authority, except what was in his very muscles (and they are of no mean calibre), but he used authority enough to save the sutler's goods. Had he been two minutes later, there would have been a crowd around that sutler's shanty, that all the authority in the place could not have controlled. One fellow stole a barrel of commissary whiskey from the platform, rolled it down among the boys, and knocking out the head commenced to treat them on a pretty liberal scale. We should all of us probably had a good drink apiece, of that whiskey, but the boys saw the ubiquitous Col. Foster coming again, and knowing right well that their fun would be ended straightway, they tipped the barrel over and spilled the vile poison on to the ground. Col. Foster would probably have been quite willing that the boys should have had a little to cheer their spirits during the coming night, but there are so many indiscreet men in an army, to whom an opportunity to drink what whiskey they wanted would be a ruinous privilege, that there is no telling what disagreeable consequences might have followed had it not been for our stalwart but good natured Colonel who commanded the brigade.

But the time came, the whistle sounded, and the train moved along. Long before morning the boys got thoroughly sobered down. The northeast wind was blowing keen and sharp, and the velocity of the train made it doubly severe. It was hard work to keep from freezing and quite impossible to keep comfortable. The most of our brigade were crowded into open cars, that had been used for drawing coal, and the floors of which were covered with crocky coal dust. The body of the car was a box about a foot and a half high, and into these we put our guns, our knapsacks, and ourselves. There was room enough for us all to stand up, but not half room enough for us all to be down. The leaden sky threatened a storm, and at night it came. If we had been in covered cars, or even if we had all had a chance to lie down where we were, we should have been spared a great deal of unnecessary suffering. But as it was the boys huddled in together the best they could lying lengthwise, crosswise, under and over each other, and in every imaginable shape, all endeavoring to keep warm, but making a most miserable failure in the attempt. The train moved provokingly slow — so slow that the boys would sometimes jump off and run along afoot beside it, as they were going up some steep grade, and then when the speed increased, jump on again. In this way the boys kept from freezing till night, when in the storm and darkness it was no longer safe for them to do so.

Night came on and the storm came with it. It is impossible to convey any sort of an idea of the misery we suffered during that miserable night. I doubt if real physical torture was ever reduced to a more concentrated form, or ever was doled out in a manner more excruciating. It was the very essence of misery, doubly distilled and long drawn out. Just give me your imagination, dear reader, and I will give you some idea of my own predicament, and the kind of time I had during that twenty-four hours which was neither better nor worse, but a fair sample of all the rest.

Imagine yourself on the top of a platform car, which has a rim around the border, making a box several inches high, with a floor covered with fine coal dust, dirt, ashes and cinders. A crowd of other soldiers are there with you, with all your knapsacks, haversacks, guns, equipments, and so forth. It is cold, windy, and as tedious as you can imagine. You have no overcoat and are at best but thinly clad. You have been standing up until you are tired of it, and now as night comes on you very naturally begin to seek for an easier position. You can lay your head on the rim of the car for a pillow and have about two feet of the floor. You double one foot under you and stretch the other a little farther out, but not much, for there is a man there in a worse position than you are in, and you do not wish to disturb him. You pull out your woolen blanket and put it over you to keep out a little of the pinching cold, and prevent if possible, your hands and feet from freezing and your body from becoming chilled through.

You have no hopes of keeping comfortable, but you hope to live, and you determine to submit to your lot and suffer for your country's sake as manfully as possible. But your discomforts are not all enumerated yet. It begins to storm, and the snow sifts down with a rapidity seldom ever known in Virginia or Maryland. Your blanket gets covered three, four, five, six, inches deep, and still it keeps coming. The snow melts on your blanket, and you feel it wetting you through to the skin. It trickles down on to the floor of the car making a nasty mud, with the coal dust, dirt and soot, as black as ink, and as cold as ice, and you feel this mud soaking through your clothes and making your flesh cold and benumbed. But you must not stir. Every movement rattles down more snow on to your bed and makes your position so much the more intolerable. And if you get out of your position where will you go to? There is no place on the platform for there is no platform and if there were, you could not stand or sit there and survive an hour without an overcoat and with your clothes wet and frozen. When Napoleon marched his wretched army through the snows of Russia on his retreat from its ill-fated capital his soldiers had at least the simple privilege of keeping themselves warm by exercise but no such privilege was ours here. Yet this is not all. You are supposed to be made of flesh and bones and nerves, and though you may be willing to lie in an unnatural and cramped up position, they will not. They demand a change, and their demand must be heeded or your torture becomes absolutely insupportable. But if you are held as in a vise and *cannot* move, what then? Could the Spanish Inquisition have produced anything more exquisitely tormenting? This is no fancy picture. It is every word true. I am told that two men on that train died during the night. I know many of the boys had frostbitten hands and feet, and some were so chilled through that they did not get over it for several days. Some have not recovered from the effects of it yet.

The train was heavy and moved very slowly. Going up the grade at Mt. Airy a few miles east of the Monocacy, it stopped entirely. The willing engine puffed and his wheels revolved but the train budged not an inch, and they had to go for an extra locomotive. While waiting here some of the boys got off the train, built them up a fire and stayed by it till morning. They swore they would stand a court martial before they would stand such treatment any longer. Some were so chilled and benumbed they could neither stand nor walk.

I call that the longest night I ever knew. I have read somewhere a story of a night, said to be the longest on record, because a man found himself shut up with a ghost, or an apparition, or something of that sort, and had to remain in mortal terror till daylight; but I doubt if there was a man on that train who would not have exchanged his place for a dungeon filled with all the ghosts, apparitions or hobgoblins, that a live Yankee ever saw, if that dungeon had only been a warm one, or had a good bed in it. But morning came at last, and the air grew warmer somewhat, but the storm did not cease entirely. It changed to rain and sleet. At a station where the train halted just at daylight to supply the engine with water and coal, as I was trying to warm myself up by the engine fire I was amused to see the astonishment of a railroad official of some sort, who came out to inquire of the conductor in regard to some express matter, when he saw the train was loaded with soldiers, riding in that kind of weather and in that kind of style. "What kind of a load have you got this morning, Conductor?" "Soldiers, sir." "But what have you got on those open cars?" (It was hardly light and the boys were covered up with their blankets.) "Soldiers sir, nothing but soldiers." The gentleman was completely bewildered. He seemed at a loss to comprehend what sort of material soldiers were made of that they could live under such exposure. "Good God," says he, "what a shame!" and it *was* a shame. This is no excuse for it. The conductor said there were plenty of box cars that might have been provided as well as those open cars. As he not very mildly expressed it we were a pack of —— fools for allowing ourselves to be so meanly cared for.

The train increased its speed as it passed along down the Patapsco river towards the Relay House, much to our delight, for we were getting impatient to have our dreary ride concluded. It was not really so very cold during Saturday forenoon, but our clothes were wet and we were tired, hungry and cross, and we had no stamina to withstand the little cold there was. Through many of the little villages along the route, the ladies waved their handkerchiefs and little flags to us as we passed, but the boys were in a poor humor to respond, and we passed along in grim silence, taking no notice of their kindly meant homage.

After many delays we finally got to Washington. It was between three and four o'clock in the afternoon. Here we hoped, at least, we should have the privilege of going into barracks at the Soldiers' Retreat, and drying our clothes and warming ourselves, getting us some coffee, and perhaps a little rest, but we were not granted even this. The train moved right by the Retreat, by the depot, across Pennsylvania Avenue, along in front of our grand and majestic Capitol, and so on down to the wharf. Congressmen were standing at the gateway entrance to the Capitol yard watching with curious interest the soldiers as the train moved by. Wonder if they gave us credit for what we had just endured for country and freedom? We got aboard the transport Massachusetts Saturday night, and Monday about noon we landed at City Point.

It is said that the reason why we were not allowed to stop at all at Washington, was because the behavior of the Sixth Corps was so "rough," the authorities dared not trust us. Perhaps it is true, and what wonder? Treat men like brutes and they will become like brutes, but you treat them worse than brutes and there is no telling what they will become. And we were treated worse than brutes. The horses on the train were sheltered from the storm, but we were not. However, I saw no acts of lawlessness in Washington worthy of record. As we were waiting for the boat I saw one fellow who had lost his hat on the train, supply its place with another from a daintily dressed darky's head, because, he said, he was fighting for the nigger, and he thought they could afford to replace his lost hat; but that was all I saw. But I will make no further comments, I have made too many already.

Near Petersburg, Va.
Dec. 22, 1864

Pity the pickets to-night. It is windy and cold, and so stinging is the air that veterans of three years and more, have to walk their beats with more than usual briskness, to keep themselves warm. But the picket who must curl down behind his protection, lie quiet and still, fares the worst. His two hours seem long to him, and sometimes he gets a frozen finger or toe, as he watches the enemy in silence on such a night as this. How clear the air is, how cold and how sharp. Yesterday, it rained; we had a furious storm. To-day, the wind has changed and the weather too. The keen air comes from the chill north-west, comes straight from the Polar regions, comes like a traveller in haste and pinches your cheek as he passes you. Vermont can boast of her tedious weather in Winter time, but just now we would place our own weather in no mean rank in Vermont's Winter calendar. Hope that it is warmer where Sherman's boys are marching and fighting and where Thomas's braves are crushing the life and soul out of Hood's forlorn army. They certainly have warm work and they ought to have warm weather. It would be cruel campaigning here. Now and then, as I write, I can hear the crack, crack of a rifle out on the picket line, — either ours or the Johnnies', — and I know some good soldier is getting belligerently inclined, but that good soldier isn't I. I am sitting by a good fire of pine knots and limbs, taking delicious comfort and endeavoring to carry out my very benevolent intention of telling the readers of the *Freeman,* of our life here in our homely way. Nothing could possibly be further from my inclination, just now, than the idea of leaving this warm fire and being hurried out to the picket line to repel an attack or to make one. But we won't worry about the picket line, for there are brave boys out there; but we will give them our sympathy and remember them. Perhaps the next cold night we may be there ourselves.

A few nights ago there was a brisk little skirmish on the picket line in front of the Second Corps, just to our left. The enemy charged out and captured three posts taking the pickets prisoners, except one or two who escaped in the darkness. It was a very dark night and the rebels were clear to our line before they were seen. Our men were overpowered at once and had to surrender. Before assistance could reach them they were back again to their own line. One man was killed and one wounded. Eleven or twelve were taken. These sallies are frequently made, but they seldom amount to anything, on either side. A few men killed and wounded and a few pickets taken is all. The pickets are within speaking distance at some points and at others they are not. At night the videttes of both armies are advanced, in some places, to within fifteen or twenty rods of each other. The rebel patrol came around last night, — so I heard one of our pickets say, — within a few feet of him in front of their videttes, riding along as carelessly as if they were not within a thousand miles of an enemy with a loaded musket, instead of being within a stone's throw of one. Our pickets had orders not to fire unless the enemy came upon them in direct assault; and the rebel pickets say they have the same orders about firing on us.

We occupy the old quarters left by the Fifth Corps. I haven't yet ascertained our exact geographical position, but to make a headlong guess, I should say that we were about half a dozen miles from Petersburg, in a southwest direction and between the Weldon and Southside Railroads. Off to our left the line bends around to our rear so that the enemy are on three sides of us and but little ways off. But a few rods from here the rebel camp can be seen in plain view. They are within good shelling distance of Fort Wheaton. Directly in front of us a wood intervenes and shuts them out from view. The opening where they are seen is on a direct line with our own army here, and at first sight one would suppose that they were another corps of our own army. I don't believe that I am the only fellow that inquired what corps that was out there, before I had become acquainted with "the situation here," or that I am the first one that was surprised to hear the reply that it was one of "General Robert E's." I might have noticed the lines of smoke curling up from the rebel picket line and ours, at intervals along between us.

We have been here now about ten days. We landed at City Point, off the boat, a week ago last Monday. City Point has become remarkably settled in her habits, during the last five months. Everything there is now done quietly and in order, and the amount of real business is not small. There seems to be no particular hurry or bustle, but everything goes on in regular clock-like order. You feel at once that there is a master mind there, somewhere. The transports come quietly into dock, and are met by the railway train which runs along the wharf, so that supplies can be taken from the transports and loaded directly on to the cars, and then they are ready to be sent up to the front. Immediately the engine whistles, and off goes that train to give room for another.

We rode up on the train from City Point to near Hancock's station. This station is on Grant's new military railroad, which branches off from the other, about five miles from City Point. Gen. Grant has a network of railroads, which connect with every corps, and almost every brigade. In a short time I expect they will issue rations to us on the picket line, from the cars. They run almost out there now. Railroads are made very easily here. About all there is to do, is to lay the sleepers, and pin down the rails. I always supposed an iron horse was very particular about the evenness of the ground over which he had to travel, but he seems to have become like the rest of us, by military necessity, adapted to almost anything. I have seen him climb up a pretty steep hill with his load, and go steadily down it as well. To ride over these roads on a long train, would be hardly pleasant for fastidious people, where the swells and depressions in the roads are continuous, and where the cars will settle together, and the next moment fetch you a jerk that will pretty nearly throw you out of your seat. But these railroads are not made for fine ladies or fine gentlemen in particular, but for supplies and forage; and barrels of pork, or bales of hay are not supposed to be very sensitive about these things.

We halted Monday night by the railroad, and staid there long enough Tuesday to get paid off. We had not been paid anything, since we were at Tennallytown, last July, just five months ago. The boys had been out of money for a long time, and the officers were about equally as destitute. The sutler had trusted many of them all he had a right, and more too. Long before we left the Valley the boys thought surely, if we were called away upon any expedition, or sent to Petersburg, if we passed through Washington we should see our dilatory friend, the paymaster. Well, some of the boys *did* see him there, but none of them got any pay. But we were comforted with the assurance that the paymaster would follow us, and he did. Five months and a half were owing to us, but of course we should get but even four. And then the boys must settle their clothing accounts at this payment. I suppose everybody knows that a soldier gets $42 a year allowed him for his clothing, and at the end of the year he squares accounts with Uncle Sam. If the cost of the clothing he has used during the year, including camp and garrison equipage, gun and equipments, if any are lost or destroyed, as they sometimes will be in spite of us, exceeds the forty-two dollars, the balance comes out of his pay. If it falls short, the surplus is paid to him. During such a tough campaign as the one we have had the past season, the wear and tear of clothing has been great, and when the prices of everything run so high without any corresponding advance in the money allowed, it is a pretty difficult thing for a soldier to come out even with the Government. Sometimes it takes the whole of two months' pay to make it even, and quite frequently it takes more. It is apt to dim a fellow's bright anticipations of pay-day somewhat at the year's close, if he knows that he has made liberal drafts upon the quartermaster's department during the year.

But we had another drawback upon our expected feast of greenbacks that we had not counted. When we came to sign the pay-roll, instead of finding the amount carried out for four months, we found it was only two, the other two being retained. But this was not all. The sutler, who had been trusting the boys from time to time during the past five months, had his *whole* account on the pay-roll. The paymaster, of course, subtracted the shrewd sutler's account from what there was left to the soldier, leaving him only the pitiful remainder. The boys begin to think that their little pay is held in light esteem by those to whom they must look for it when it is due. By and by they will learn to dispense with a paymaster entirely; we are having most excellent lessons. But I am not writing this from any personal motive, for I myself was neither owing the Government nor the sutler. But many of the boys were, and I took the liberty to express myself as I had heard them. There may be good and substantial reasons for all of this of which I have been speaking, but they are not told to us, and so of course we do not see them.

But better than pay-days, paymasters or greenbacks, is the glorious news that is continually coming in from the armies all around. One hundred guns were fired Sunday morning in honor of Thomas's victory over Hood. The war news from all points is good. Victory — complete, decisive and glorious victory greets our armies everywhere. The rebellion is toppling down. Slavery's champions, vanquished in the field of open discussion, are being vanquished in the field before the bayonet and the cannon's mouth. The day-star of Freedom, dimmed by the smoke of battle, seems about to shine brighter and more beautiful than ever before. We have reason to rejoice, thank God and take courage.

Retrospect
Near Petersburg, Va.
Jan. 1, 1865

Another year of the world's history and ours has gone with its records into eternity. Every man as he stands on the threshold of the new year, naturally, almost involuntarily, reviews the year just past, and examines to see what its records are, to see what he has done, and what he might have done, and to see how stands his account in Time's great ledger. How stands the work accomplished with that laid out for accomplishing one year ago. There being no particular news to-day, I propose to give a brief summary of the work we have accomplished during the season just past, as well as I can from the data I have, trusting that it will not be without some interest to the readers of the *Freeman*.

Last year our gains had been great, this year they have been greater. Sanguine people predicted the immediate close of the war one year ago, because so much had then been accomplished in the field, but more has been accomplished in the field since then than ever before, and still the war lingers. The past year has been an eventful one — full of war's severest hardships.

It was May 4th that we left Brandy Station with full ranks and hopeful spirits; the next day, in the Wilderness, how terribly those ranks were thinned. There in that thickly timbered wood as we advanced in line of battle we came suddenly and unexpectedly upon the enemy, who, as General Grant thinks, were advancing upon us in the same way, a remarkable coincidence, of which there are but few on record. About one-third of our brigade fell there. The next day we fought over the same ground again. The third day our brigade did but little fighting except a little picket skirmishing, and at night we commenced the series of flank movements, which have brought us finally to our present position. We marched all that night, or tried to, and during the next day. The succeeding night we came up with the enemy, but had only a meagre opportunity to rest. Early the next morning, May 9th, we commenced throwing up breastworks.

May 10th we moved around to the left, and made a charge with Upton's brigade of the first division of our corps. That charge was splendidly made, but failed because the line on our right broke and fell back, and we had to do the same or be flanked. We had formed in a ravine, the other brigade ahead, and ours in the rear for support. At the signal, Col. Upton with his three lines of infantry, jumped to their feet, and rushed ahead across the open field, to the enemy's works, while we cheered as lustily as we could to heighten the effect, and help create a panic among the enemy. How terribly the bullets swept that plain, and rattled like hailstones among the trees over our heads. The boys could not be restrained in their wild excitement, and without waiting for orders (for I certainly heard no order but "halt," and I know of no one that did) they rushed in after the other brigade, and we drove the enemy from his first line of works. But here we had to stop. The left of the line had been repulsed, and we must now fall back too, or be captured. It was too bad. Had we succeeded there, it would have saved us that bloody fighting two days later, at what is generally known here as "the slaughter pen."

But on the 12th we forced them from their line, enabling us to move again to the left. The enemy confronted us again between the rivers Ny and Po, near Spotsylvania Court House. May 15th the Eleventh Regiment joined the brigade. May 24th we crossed the North Anna river at night, and at midnight the 26th we crossed back again to make another "flank movement." May 28th we crossed the Pamunkey near Hanover Court House, and June 1st we came upon the enemy near Cold Harbor. We charged upon their works there and were fairly repulsed. We have to acknowledge that here we did not get even the first line of the enemy's works. There was a larger force there than we expected. We took up our position in a woods near there, and night and day we worked busy as beavers, building works that the Richmond *Enquirer* pronounced after we had evacuated, to be of the most formidable character.

June 12th we left our works there, and moved to the left again, flanking the enemy once more. June 16th we crossed the James river, and the 18th found us on the skirmish line in front of Petersburg. June 23d, being on the extreme left, a large share of our skirmishers, from the 11th and 4th regiments, were fiercely attacked and many of them captured. June 29th our corps made a reconnoissance to Reams' Station, destroyed several miles of the Weldon railroad, and July 1st returned. At 11 o'clock on the night of July 9th, we had orders to pack up and march to City Point, and the next day our division embarked from that place for Washington. We had been in the forefront of battle from May 4th to July 10th, from the Wilderness to Petersburg, and now when the nation's capital was threatened, we hastened to Washington. We drove the enemy away from Fort Stevens, drove them out of Maryland, drove them through Snicker's Gap, and up the Shenandoah Valley, and then we returned to the defences of Washington.

Again Maryland was threatened by the rebels, led on by Gen. Early. After resting at Tennallytown from Saturday afternoon till the Tuesday following, from July 23d to July 26th, we started after them. We marched to Harper's Ferry and back, then to Cedar Creek and back to Harper's Ferry, with no fighting except a severe skirmish Aug. 21st near Charlestown, the place where the famous John Brown was hung. We advanced up the Valley again, and September 19th fought the battle of Winchester, our corps charging several times, and every time successfully. September 23d we fought again under the brave Sheridan, and drove the enemy from Fisher's Hill, drove them up to Staunton and out of the Valley entirely, and came very near doing what President Lincoln once said Meade's army would ultimately do to Lee's, drive them out of existence. Oct. 19th we fought the rebels at Cedar Creek. Here we claim especial credit for the old Sixth Corps. When the enemy, re-enforced, fell suddenly at early dawn upon the Eighth and Nineteenth Corps, creating a wild panic almost, and disorganizing them to a great extent, our corps held in reserve stood firm, and when the enemy came exultingly on with their hellish yell, expecting sure victory, they found only sure defeat. In turn we drove them back completely routed, changing defeat into victory for us, and victory into defeat for them. The material fruits of that day's work were great, but its moral effect upon the nation's welfare at that critical time, just on the eve of a Presidential election, is beyond the power of figures to estimate. Just imagine the result had our corps been sent to Petersburg, as we thought we had got started to go Oct. 13th, leaving Early to defeat the remaining portions of the army, and cross once more into Maryland and Pennsylvania, to wreak his vengeance for the property we had destroyed in the Valley. How many timid men would have been frightened to cast a vote for peace, that ever afterward they would have been ashamed of, though ashamed too late to do any good? Can there be any doubt on whose side God's Providence was there?

This was our last fighting of any consequence. Our record if it could be fully written would make an interesting page in history. It is dyed deep in the blood of our bravest men. The Sixth Corps has suffered terribly. Our losses have been heavy. Take our brigade for example. We left Brandy Station with 3899 men for duty. The actual casualties since then are reported to be 3086. The Eleventh Regiment joined us, and adding their number makes not far from 5500 men all told, now we have only about 1500. Such figures need no comment. They speak for themselves.

We are now in front of Petersburg. A year ago Grant had severed the Confederacy in twain and opened up the Mississippi river, now Sherman has divided it a third time, and their total destruction is only a question of time. Who can despond now? Looking at what we have done, and the cause we had for doing it, can any man wish to say to our enemy: We will let by-gones be by-gones, and unite again under some sort of treaty or compromise? God forbid.

Blot out our record and count it as nothing! Give us death rather than that. If, over our graves, any are so craven-hearted as to wish to see it done, let them do it. We shall not be alive to see it, nor wish to be.

But we have no fears. A revolution against such a Government as ours is too foul a thing for God to permit. The Confederacy is doomed. Cut asunder now in two vital points, their armies pent up, they can only struggle and die. Their victories, if they have any more, will be few and feeble, and may possibly lengthen out the contest a short time, but not long. Trusting in God we know the issue cannot be doubtful, and we commence the new year with the firmest determination and the highest hopes.

> Sixth Corps Hospital
> City Point, Va.
> Jan. 16, 1865

You will see by the above place of dating my letter, that I have changed my location once more. The scenes in a soldier's life are continually shifting, sometimes for better and sometimes for worse, and we soldiers get to be nearly as indifferent about the matter, and care as little where we go, as a horse cares where his driver may see fit to drive him. And we have just as little voice in the matter as a horse has. One day a soldier may be in his tent comfortable, contented, and happy, and the next day on a march with but few of the world's comforts and but little cause of contentment except what he finds within himself. A soldier's time and services are not his own, they belong to the Government which he has sworn to defend, and it is his duty to be ever ready and obey with alacrity whatever the Government calls upon him to do. Sometimes a streak of good luck will turn up to a soldier whether he deserves it or not, and sometimes they won't turn up though he may deserve it ever so well. It would be easy to mention a great many good boys in the ranks who have been doing duty at the front since the war began, but to whom no soft detail has ever been given, or any particular favors shown. To have followed the regiment through thick and thin from the commencement till now would be a glorious record, but your humble servant comes a long ways from possessing it. Just now, in the shifting panorama he finds himself doing guard duty at the hospital, where he may be seen watching over the property here with paternal solicitude, two hours out of every six, day and night.

A week ago last Saturday, 21 men were detailed from the front out of the Sixth Corps, for guard here, and about twice as many more of musicians for light fatigue duty. Seven men for guard were detailed from each division, and of the seven details from our division, one of them was kindly given to me. Without five minutes' notice we packed up and went to Corps headquarters, where we found those from the other divisions awaiting us, and at night, under the charge of Lieut. Percy B. Smith, of the 5th Wisconsin, we took the train for City Point. We were soon on the ground, and without so much as a finger scratch for an excuse, we find ourselves at the hospital, and enjoying the full rank, title and privileges of a "hospital bummer." Our duty here will be light, or at least it will be regular. We shall have good comfortable quarters, good beds to sleep on, and be accessible to a great many other good things that are rarely known at the front. There will be no marching, fighting or picketing to do, and so long as the country's good shall excuse us from these we shall not have the remotest disposition to complain. Usually for such work convalescents from the hospital are detailed as soon as they are able to perform the duties required, but this system of detailing seems to have been generally attended with vexatious difficulties, and not at all satisfactory, so they have resorted to the method of detailing able bodied men from the front. Commanders of regiments are always eager to have every man at a hospital returned to his regiment as soon as he is able to be, for they like to have a full command, and report as many men present for duty as possible. Besides, the more men he has the more officers can be made, and hence, when they knew a man at the hospital was fit for duty and detailed, they would send for him at once and if the surgeon should refuse to return him to his regiment upon the Colonel's order, the Colonel could appeal to authority that would send him there in spite of the surgeon. Thus constant details of inexperienced men must be made. The idea of retaining one's place could not be held out as an inducement to faithfulness, so long as they could be ordered to the front by another than the surgeon's authority.

And then convalescents in a hospital, if they dislike menial duty, as they are sure to imagine they do, will raise a thousand objections to the surgeon's authority in calling upon them, and say if they are fit for duty here they can do it at the regiment, when really a little light duty here would be rather a benefit than an injury, and the man at the same time wholly unfit to take the duty as it comes in his regiment. Of course the surgeon in charge has authority, and can enforce obedience by a wholesome dread of the guard-house; but it is disagreeable always to force work out of unwilling men, and usually officers of high rank take no pleasure in having their men under confinement. But we are detailed by as high authority as the Corps commander himself, at the instance I am told of the Lieut. General, and for this very work of guarding, cooking, chopping, building barracks and so forth, and it will require the same authority that detailed us to send us back to our regiments. Our duty is here, and we take hold of it accordingly. The surgeon said that the men he had detailed from the front had occasioned him less trouble since they had been here than his light duty men did in a single day. So the light duty men were sent to their regiments where they so anxiously claimed that they wanted to go, and we have taken their places.

We guards have taken possession of one of the hospital tents, which furnishes accommodations for eighteen men. A hospital tent, such as are used here, and at almost every other hospital, is really three tents joined together. They are large wall tents, made of the best material, and large enough for two rows of beds. Each bed has a good mattress or tick, filled with straw or hay, and plenty of blankets. Each component part of the triple tent usually has in it six beds, three on a side, with a space between almost as wide as the bed itself, but we guards double two together and in this way have plenty of room for eight beds in each part of the tent, and leave room for a good coal stove in the middle. So at present we have no excuse for grumbling, and if they will feed us well we will be contented.

Beside standing guard, we have occasionally to go away with a squad of convalescents — as often as they find a squad well enough to be sent to their regiments. The other day a squad of black men were returned to the front at Bermuda Hundred. Part of them were hospital patients, and part were armed men, who had done the guard duty here till we came. There were between eighty and ninety of them in all. A pretty jolly set there was of them, full of fun and wit, and apparently enjoying themselves the very best. Now and then there was a sober face among them, and one smart little fellow, who had been a nurse in one of the wards, seemed to take a more sober view of the matter. I imagine that he felt that he was leaving a place more suited to his liking than service in the field, but he had too high a sense of honor to show any reluctance about going. Another, a great brawny negro, exactly his opposite seemed to regard his getting out of the hospital as an escape from prison. He shook hands with the officers, and bid them good-by with much politeness, as did several of the others, thinking, I suppose, that it must be an occasion of affecting importance to them. All the way down to the boat they were greeted by their comrades of the same hue. Every colored teamster that we passed by seemed to know one or all of them. It was "Hallo Sam" and "Hallo Tom" and "Where are you going Jack?" all the way down there.

Talk with the negroes and you will find that they are not at all lacking in a general knowledge of events that are transpiring, and they are far from being wholly indifferent in regard to them. There would be many strange histories if each man should tell his own story. One man said he had been a slave in Richmond, and had a wife there now. A son and daughter had been sold south nearly twenty years ago, one was sixteen and the other eighteen years of age. The man came into our lines on the Peninsula two years ago. He was an old man, and to me looked hardly fit to shoulder a musket. I asked him if he would know his children if he should see them now. "O yes sah," he said, "I'd know 'em, 'deed I should," as if there could be no doubt about it.

The negroes certainly possess general intelligence sufficient to make as good soldiers as anybody, but as to their bravery, of course no one can tell, not even the man himself, perhaps, till it is tried. They say that they are put under pretty rigid discipline. With white men for officers it would be an easy matter, under the cloak of military discipline, to impose upon them a slavery more severe than that from which they have escaped. It is about two miles from the Point, over across the mouth of the Appomattox, where we left them, under the charge of other officers, every man being "present or accounted for."

Sixth Corps Hospital
City Point, Va.
February 3, 1865

Last night we were routed out of our sleep suddenly about ten o'clock, just as we had fairly commenced our slumbers, not by an alarm or picket, nor by the order "fall in," but to provide places for more sick men, who were coming in from the front. Three hundred patients for our Corps Hospital they said would be here, some of whom were already on the ground, and the poor fellows must have quarters somewhere. Every man was wanted to help, and every man was willing to lend a helping hand in such a case, and all that were able did. The guards were relieved from their posts for the time being, and joined with the rest to assist. All hands worked with a will, for sick and wounded men must not stand and suffer for want of quarters, if anything we could do would prevent it.

The first thing we did was to clear out a long barrack that had been used for a carpenter's shop. It was full of benches, window-casings, door-frames, and half made bunks, besides a large quantity of pine boards stored away in there, which had to be all carried out. All this stuff was soon in motion towards the door, and what couldn't get out at the door, was handed through the windows into the street. The boys worked lively, for it was a work of mercy, and we soon had the barrack cleared out. The next thing was to place the beds in there. Away we went to the storehouse for the iron framed bedsteads, such as are used in all of our hospitals, and soon we had two rows of them, one along each side of the barracks. Now the ticks must be filled with straw which is kept for that purpose at a shanty near by, which done, we have accomplished our part towards preparing accommodations for about fifty men. Blankets and sheets must be furnished, and the beds must be made, but the stewards, wardmasters, and nurses will take care of that. Other squads were doing in other places what we had been doing there; but still we hadn't made provisions for all that were coming. One room in the "light diet kitchen" had to be appropriated for this use, and here we made beds for eighteen more. At last all were provided for, and our work for the night was done. It was after twelve o'clock, and the boys thought they deserved a "treat." It wasn't whiskey nor gin they said they wanted, but substantial bread and coffee. But we don't draw our own rations here, and have no control over them, except to eat them when they are cooked and placed on a table before us. We went to the cook but he had no authority to give us an extra ration; we went to the steward but he appeared to have no inclination to do so, so we had to go to our quarters minus our "treat." Over in the Fifth Corps they appeared to be less prepared for this sudden arrival of sick men than we were. They had to put up again some of the tents they had taken down, to send away and give place to the stockades or barracks that are being built all around here. They were busy a long while after we had gone to our quarters, and lanterns were flitting about to and fro, nearly all night.

The reason of this deluge of sick men was in consequence of an order at the front to move, and the sick had all to be sent away. The 2nd, 5th and 6th corps were under orders to move day before yesterday morning. They drew five days' rations, and were ordered to have everything packed up ready to march. Nobody knew where they were going, though as usual there is a multitude of rumors about it. Some thought they were going out to try and possess the Southside railroad, some thought they were going down to co-operate with

Gen. Sherman, and others thought it was only to prevent Lee from sending away troops to oppose Sherman's march. Whatever may have been the plan it has been found unnecessary or inexpedient to execute it up to the latest accounts, and the troops still remain in their old quarters. These sick will, a large share of them, be sent immediately away to general hospitals at Washington, Baltimore, or some other place. Some of the worst cases will doubtless find their way to their native state. The order to move will be a lucky thing for such.

These sick men coming and going has added new activity to the business of the hospital for the time being, but otherwise it is as dull as it usually is in our hospitals generally. News items are always scarce here. Day before yesterday though, a woman called at the office and inquired for the name of her brother. Surgeon Elliott looked over his books but couldn't find it. At length he found it among the names of the dead, and he died but the day before. The poor woman was boisterous in her grief, when she found after so much trouble in getting here, she was too late to see her brother alive, and could only know that he was buried forever out of her sight.

There was another execution a week ago. Private Newell H. Root, alias George Harris of the 1st Conn. Heavy Artillery, was hung for deserting to the enemy. He left his regiment at Dutch Gap last summer, and gave himself up to the enemy as a deserter from the Union army. According to an order issued by the enemy to encourage deserting from our army, he was sent to Kentucky, where he found his way to our lines. There were other deserters with him, and one or two bona fide prisoners of war, who had adroitly managed to get mixed in with them and sent there too. Of course as soon as they found Union men they all claimed to be wonderfully deserving of charity and sympathy, either as deserters from the rebel army, or as long suffering much abused prisoners of war, just escaped from rebel tyranny worse than the grave. As the story was told me those who were actually suffering prisoners of war, were indignant to see kindness and charity thus imposed upon by a class of men the most unprincipled in all the world, and as soon as they had a chance they told who they were. They were arrested, and this one was taken here, tried, condemned and hung. Pity he hadn't heeded the voice before, "Be sure your sin will find you out."

I am in luck again, Mr. Editor, and must tell you about it. We soldier correspondents who have but little else to write about, have to presume largely upon the forbearance of our readers and write a good deal about ourselves. The fact is, we know but little of what is going on in the world beyond our own range of vision. We know what *we* do, and that is about all. I suppose I ought to write a remarkably good letter this time, for I have got a remarkably good place to write. I am not sitting on a knapsack, nor curled upon the ground, to write this letter, but I am sitting up to a genuine table, and writing as dignifiedly for anything I know, as anybody would sit up to a table and write letters. There is a coal stove not six feet from my elbow, which I can make as warm as I please, and then the room is eighteen or twenty feet square, has a good board floor, and looks so neat and comfortable that a fellow can feel it clear to his fingers' ends. This is the quartermaster's tent, and I being his clerk have the privilege of occupying it. My business is chiefly with the pen. They say the pen is mightier than the sword, and between you and I, Mr. Editor, I had a mighty sight rather use it. To be sure I may be sent to my regiment to-morrow, and if I am, why I will shoulder my gun and trudge along, and make the best of it, as I have done a thousand times before, when duty lay in that direction.

My immediately superior officer is from Co. E, 5th Wisconsin regiment. He is lieutenant of the guard, and quartermaster of the 6th corps hospital. Lieut. P.B. Smith is a young, energetic officer, who was selected for this place by Gen. Wright who commands our corps. It is a double duty and a responsible position, and Gen. Wright wanted a man, he said, who was well posted. To be quartermaster of a hospital requires that qualification in an eminent degree. We have to make out papers for every different company and regiment that are represented by the men drawing clothing. In our last issue there were eighty names, seventy-six different companies, and thirty-one different regiments, to which the clothing accounts had to be sent. Every article of clothing issued must be accounted for on paper, by the proper authorities and in the proper manner, or the quartermaster is responsible, and will have to pay for it himself. The quartermaster who issued the clothing to Lieut. Smith, assured him that his were the only papers he had seen here at the hospitals made out correctly in every respect. This assurance coming from such a source is no mean compliment. This, however, was mainly owing to his having a good clerk, for anybody can see if I hadn't made out the papers exactly as he told me to, they wouldn't have been right.

Lieut. Smith was once a private in the 7th Wisconsin Battery of the western army. Once he had a rope around his neck by Gen. Forrest's guerrillas, into whose hands he had fallen, and was about to be hung, but was recognized and saved by a rebel surgeon who had once been a guest at his father's house. Yet the spirited youth would not be frightened by the prospect of death from his contempt of rebel authority, and for this reason they intended he should feel their power. This war is making many heroes — earnest men with abiding faith in themselves. Let them have a laudable ambition to acquit themselves well, and rise as high as possible in the scale of promotion, for the country will need just such men, and need all she has.

———————

A Trip to the Front
City Point, Va.
Feb. 8, 1865

Last Saturday I was up to see the boys in the brigade. This, of course, isn't a transaction of any very great importance, but I thought perhaps some of the boys who read the *Freeman,* but are not old enough yet themselves to be soldiers, and some of the little girls too, perhaps, who never can be soldiers, but who almost wish sometimes they had been born boys so that they could, would be interested to read all about the little affairs in a soldier's common everyday life, and having nothing else to do to-day, I thought I would write you about this visit to the boys up in front of the enemy. So if you will give me your imagination my little friend, we'll go up there and see what we find that is worth talking about there and on the way.

But in the first place we must get a pass. This is an important prerequisite, as indispensable as the first direction in that famous recipe for dressing and cooking a hare. First catch a hare. We must bear in mind that passes are not always given, and to everybody, merely upon the asking. Some good reason must be shown for wanting a pass, aside from the simple pleasure of making a visit and having a good time. But pay-day is coming (sometime, we hope, in all conscience), and we want to make some arrangements to have our pay drawn by somebody, if we are not there ourselves when it does come, besides we have several little debts among the boys to pay, and several to collect, all of which business needs our personal attention. These are our arguments, and armed with these, we go to one of the assistant surgeons and ask if a pass can be granted us. He asks us a few questions, but being busy tells us to call at his office again. So at the appointed time we are there, and finally get our pass written and signed by him. Now it must go to the surgeon in charge of our corps hospital. After he has approved it, it has still to go to the surgeon in charge of all the hospitals. We want to start early Saturday morning, and we

must have our pass ready the night beforehand. It is all right so far, and now
we will take it up to Dr. Dalton's office for his approval. After knocking, being
invited to enter, taking off our hats and so forth, we hand our pass to the first
man we see. Of course it isn't the right one, but he tells us who the right one is,
and that is what we want to know. He takes the pass, reads it, turns around to
us and wants to know *why* it is necessary for us to go up to the front, at the
same time giving us an uncomfortably searching look that would freeze our
tongues still, if we had the least disposition to equivocate. We attempt to say
something about pay-day, debts, and to explain the matter more fully, but he
breaks us off short and puts the whole thing in a nut-shell. Money matters is it,
sir. We reply in the affirmative, and he makes a few rapid marks on the paper
with his pen, which, we have no doubt, answers for his signature, and now we
are all right so far. But after all, this only gives us permission to be absent from
the hospital that day, and to apply to the Provost Marshal for a pass to go to
the front, so there is still another chance to be cheated out of our fun yet. But in
the morning when the Provost Marshal reads our pass and stamps it, we know
we are all right. We climb up to the top of a loaded train and are soon whirling
through the bright morning air, on the old railroad between City Point and
Petersburg. A little over five miles from City Point, the railroad branches off to
the left, through a piece of woods and around the city of Petersburg, it not
being considered safe at present for the Yankees to run their trains through it.
The grade is pretty steep where we first turn off, and it seems more like a wood
road than it does like a railroad. Presently we get around opposite the city. We
can see the rebel works, and ours too, from the top of the train as it moves
along. There is the great brick house where army headquarters were when we
first came up to Petersburg, calculating to capture it the next day, and there is
where our regiment stopped when the few lucky men who had served out their
full three years, were told to fall out and GO HOME. I could point out several
familiar places, and it didn't take long to make them familiar, as we pass along.
I shan't need to call your attention to the city of Petersburg itself. The hill partly shuts it out from view, but the tall spires here and there are plain to be seen,
and occasionally you get a glimpse of the buildings. They don't look to be more
than a mile and a half from the railroad, and you wonder if that can be the
place where so many shells have been thrown when Grant has celebrated his
victories, and at other times, and yet so little damage is done. How pretty it
looks in the warm sunlight this morning. Everything is so quiet and still that
you hardly believe that between you and that city, there are two hostile armies,
who have been seeking to destroy each other all they can for almost eight
months. Awful tales of desperate charging and bloody fighting, that line along

there by the crater Fort Hell,[27] and those formidable works could tell you, and we fear more yet to come.

But we must hasten on. We shall find now a city of camps all along the way till we get to Patrick Station, which is at the extreme end of the line, and about fourteen miles from here. Near this station we find the Vermont Brigade. We find them about as we left them, only they have improved their camps and made them look more neat and comfortable. Old brush, logs and rubbish has been cleared away and the ground has been swept over and everything made to look tidy, cheerful and pleasant. The boys appear to be enjoying themselves well, as well for anything we can see, as the average of human nature anywhere in this discontented world. Everything is as quiet as usual. They had been under orders to have their things packed up and ready to move, and for two days fatigue work and everything not positively necessary to be done had been suspended, but at that time everything was going on as usual in winter quarters, with no signs of a move. Men were out in the woods after wood for fuel and lumber for building. On the plat of ground between the 6th Corps and the 2d, they were building a high "lookout," which has already reached an altitude of 140 feet. How much higher it is going up isn't known, but already an observer on the top of it can overlook a large tract of the enemy's country. The rebels had honored it by sending one shot plunging over into our camp, but that elicited no reply and did no damage. There is a new chapel tent near the Eleventh Regiment, and one near the Fourth, but the Second has none as yet.

But time flies swiftly. We can't see half the boys we wish to. We must do our business and hasten back, for it is night already. The freight cars have all gone down, but there is an officers' alias passenger car going from this station and it will be empty till we get to the next station, at corps headquarters. So, unless we are prevented, we will jump on to the platform and ride to there, where, perhaps, they will attach a freight car, and we ride the rest of the way in a more legitimate manner. But we are disappointed. The train receives no addition at Yellow House Station except an officer and his lady, and that cuts us off from all hope. There are some twenty other fellows on the platform there, in the same distressing predicament, some swearing at their accursed luck, and others laughing and calling it a good joke.

The train starts. One of the railroad men sitting on the platform, whom we had just been talking with, gives us a wink which we interpret in an instant. We are just in time. The platform is crowded with railroad men, and they are all negroes, but we won't mind that; our object is to get to City Point some way. We get barely a foothold on the lowest step, and hang on by main strength. The train jumps along over the rough road at an awful rate, and we wonder over how many rods of ground our remains would be strewed if we should happen to lose our hold. The negroes make all the room for us they can, and offer to take our bundle, but we decline the favor, though we can't help noticing how differently they act toward a white soldier, than white soldiers sometimes act toward them. At the next station there was a freight car back on the switch that was to be taken to City Point. These negroes don't neglect to apprise us of this, and to tell us, furthermore, that we must use our legs nimbly in getting to the car, and getting on to it, for they won't wait for us an instant. In spite of our vigilance we should have been left there if it had not been for these negroes.

We mount to the top of the freight car and ride with our black comrades the rest of the way to City Point. Don't be alarmed, my friend, nor disgusted, I pray you. We have found these negroes to be civil and obliging, and we have been favored at their hands, and now it would be the essence of meanness to show contempt for their persons. They won't thrust themselves upon you, yet if you ask them a civil question you will get a civil answer, and if you ask for information they will impart willingly all they know. Rude soldiers sometimes abuse negroes without provocation; here now was a chance for them to retaliate, and why didn't they do it? It couldn't be because they were afraid to, because they had the coward's opportunity, and had a half a dozen against one. They were in no wise duty bound to show me respect. Pollok may be right after all when he says:

> "That not in *mental,* but in *moral* worth,
>   God excellence placed."

But he hurls man's pride of intellect into the dust. I wonder if some extremely respectable Christian people, who would consider it a sore punishment to be compelled to sit in the same pew, or ride in the same car with a black, however worthy, will now wish they could hear in that great day which is coming, the Saviour pronouncing to them the sweetly welcome words, "Inasmuch as ye have done it unto the least of *these,* ye have done it unto me." They may have given now and then a dollar for the "Freedmen's Aid Society," or for some such purpose, which they suppose is to go to improve the spiritual condition of the black men in some sphere and in some way, though how they hardly know, but will that make everything all right *then*? Perhaps it will, I cannot tell. One thing however is obvious. The Almighty who made mankind in the first place, knows how to classify them, and we have no certain account that he ever made but two distinctions, the righteous and unrighteous. Will it not be ill then with that man who shall unwittingly despise whom God delights to honor?

But I am making my letter too long. About half past nine we got back into our old quarters here again, having had I trust a pleasant and profitable time, and enjoyed our ride and visit well. Isn't that so my young friends? If it is, perhaps we will renew our acquaintance again.

Sixth Corps Hospital
City Point, Va.
Feb. 25, 1865

It is winter time, but this season of the year seldom brings any storms but those of rain, and rain storms we have in abundance. Drizzling, disagreeable weather at this time of the year, the man must expect to find who lives in this part of the country. It is disagreeable, not simply because rain clouds shut out the sun and veil everything in a misty gloom, but because it converts the earth underfoot into a nasty, sloppy mortar-mud, that becomes universal, and cannot be flanked nor dodged. No matter where you go, or in what place you step, you are up to your ankles in mud and may consider yourself lucky if you go in no deeper. Blacked boots and clean floors are having a sad struggle to maintain a respectable appearance in these regions just now. A Vermonter to appreciate at least one very meritorious excellence in the soil of his native state, needs to come and spend a year here. In place of deep snows and piling snow-drifts, which are sometimes bad enough, he will have an eternal slough that is at all times insupportable. He may have seen muddy soil before, in the thawy days of April, but such unlimited extremes as Virginia produces probably never entered his wildest calculations. And when he has seen one extreme in the winter season, the transition to the other as far the opposite, in the summer, is as rapid as it is wonderful. Instead of mud he will have dust, which is hardly less annoying. This dust will find its way through the smallest crack or crevasse, and sprinkle itself over everything. Neither his clothes, body, nor food will escape, and if he is in the open air, clouds of it will well nigh suffocate him. Vermont preserves the happy medium. Either Vermont soil is very peculiar, or that of Virginia is remarkably so.

This evil is remedied around the hospitals, so far as possible, by ditching and other methods. The barracks are built on a line facing each other in two rows, one on each side of the yard. The entrance to the barracks is at each end. The sidewalks along by the door of the barracks are raised and covered several inches with sand, which will not hold the water, while the ditches on each side are made to offer especial inducements for it to keep out from under foot. Inside of the barracks there is no floor except the ground, but the same peculiarity which makes the ground soft when it is wet, makes it hard when it is dry, and in the barracks where it is kept smooth and cleanly swept, it has almost as neat and tidy an appearance as if it were a good board floor, instead of a floor of mother earth.

There are between three hundred and four hundred men here now. These are mostly sick. But few wounded men are here. Our Corps didn't get into the last fight, up on the left of Petersburg, but very little, only a portion of the first division being engaged. There is something very strange about this fact. Evidently "somebody must have blundered." The Fifth Corps had a large number of wounded men brought to their hospital. Three trains of about a dozen cars each loaded with the wounded, were brought here to them. It was during a bitterly tedious storm of rain, snow and sleet that they came, and their sufferings were great. Several died on the way. It was a glad privilege for these wounded men to find here good comfortable quarters and warm beds ready to receive them when they arrived. All that can be done for their comfort will be done. Not only the Government, but the Christian and Sanitary Commissions endeavor to leave nothing undone that can contribute to the relief of the men who are wounded and brought here from the front.

The hospitals of the different Corps are all here together, but they act independently of each other. Each Corps has its own staff of surgeons, and is a unit by itself, but no further distinction is made as regards Division or Brigade.

We have a large force of nearly one hundred fatigue men to do the work of the hospital, which is almost endless in its variety, and about twenty guards, half of them on duty one day, and the other half the next. This is sufficient to guard what property it is necessary to have guarded, and to enforce discipline and good order. Our hospital stands on the south-west part of the hospital grounds. South-west of all the buildings save one, and that is going to be the wash house when they get it done, stand two little barracks, each twenty feet long, and ten wide, covered with shelter tents, and here is where the guards stay, of which your humble servant is nominally a member. Although I was busy elsewhere, and didn't have a word to say nor so much as lift a finger about building them, yet somehow they got up real nice, comfortable ones for all that; and if they did pass a unanimous sentence upon me for my delinquency, that I should be forever prohibited from entering their quarters upon any pretence whatever, I nevertheless, contrary to all rules of etiquette, when business drags and times are dull, find myself there, asking some one to beat me at checkers, dominoes or some other game, and I do not find myself refused, nor do they find the task imposed upon them at all difficult to accomplish. One evening we had a delicious feast of good, mellow apples, which is a rare treat nowadays, since our paymasters have deserted us, and there is such a dearth of money throughout the army. The boys said we must thank Mrs. Portus Baxter,[28] who was here on a visit to the hospital at the time, for the apples, for they were a gift to us from her, but I didn't see Mrs. Baxter, and therefore, had no opportunity to thank her. If I knew she would see this letter, I would like to tell her that she has not only the thanks, but the hearty good will of the boys here, for this token, with many others, of her kindness to us, and interest in our welfare.

We are beginning to feel a little misused because we don't get our pay. The most of the boys have received none for nearly five months. To say that they submit heroically to this, and without grumbling, may be partially true, for what is the use of grumbling about a thing that can't be helped, but where is the heroism of submitting when there is no other possible alternative but submission; but to say that we submitted resignedly, would be manifestly untrue, for it would make us out to be either less than human, or else a great deal more, I don't know which, and this the practical facts of the case will hardly warrant. Senator Wilson[29] said in the Senate, not many days ago, while speaking in opposition to the bill to raise the salary of clerks employed in the different Departments, that the Government was sorely embarrassed for funds, and he seemed to think the army deserved their first attention. Officers, he said, were resigning that they might go home and take care of their families, and this added to the embarrassment; and he thought in justice their pay should be raised, rather than the clerks at their comparatively easy labor. From this eminently logical statement we see that officers, even, are not in all respects contented with this state of things, and when they with their hundred dollars and upwards per month complain, we certainly cannot be blamed if we feel a little cross about it once in a while. Recruits who can enlist now and leave at home the large bounties offered, doubtless, are well enough satisfied as far as money is concerned, but many veterans who are receiving less bounty for their six years' service than these recruits have given them for one year, and who are dependent almost entirely upon their monthly pay to support their families, if they have them, find sometimes that it is hard work to keep their patriotism in working order. The philosophical editor of the *Tribune* said, when he raised the price of his paper, it was only adjusting the nominal to the actual value, for with the increased prices of labor and produce, the mechanic and the farmer could pay for his paper as easily now as formerly, but with us sixteen dollars a month would be only sixteen, though gold might go up to ten dollars for one, and everything else accordingly. What would Uncle Sam say, I wonder, if we soldiers should "strike" for higher pay, as laborers generally do when wages are oppressively low? I don't suppose he would tie us up by our thumbs as our officers sometimes do when we misbehave, but he might tie us up by the necks, and if he did he would be likely to keep us hanging until he was sure beyond a peradventure that we wouldn't give him any more trouble in that direction. After all, it isn't because they pay us so little that we complain, but because they are so abominably slack about paying us that little when it becomes due. But the newspapers say the whole army is going to be paid off soon, and that they have commenced to pay already. This last paragraph of my letter will rank, I suppose, as first class grumbling, and I hereby most respectfully dedicate it to Uncle Sam, but if he will pay me all that is due within a week, I will agree, honor bright, to take back every word of it.

Sixth Corps Hospital
City Point, Va.
March 13, 1865

We are having genuine March weather here just now, and its drying winds are having a salutary effect in relieving us of mud and the surplus water with which the ground is abundantly saturated. The wind is blowing in a very becoming manner to-day, considering what it has to do, and the sun "pours his full radiance far," as if to help in the benevolent work. The mud is rapidly drying up, and our military city here is already looking considerably more summerlike. The mud isn't over shoes now in many places, and a man wearing government bootees will find it perfectly safe in attempting to cross the majority of our streets. By next week, unless it rains, he can go anywhere.

About a hundred men were sent to-day from this hospital to their regiments at the front — convalescents pronounced by the surgeons fit for duty. Yesterday was the day for examination, when the surgeons passed their judgement upon the physical soundness of the men under their care. Not every man, however, gets a formal examination, that is returned to his company for duty. The surgeons of the respective wards examine only such of whose condition they have some doubts; of the majority they have formed their opinion before. But if a man imagines or tries to imagine that his surgeon is hurrying him off prematurely, and asks for an examination, unless his plea is too frivolous to notice, it is given him. Not many, however, have the disposition to ask for this, and of those that have, the majority keep it entirely to themselves. Most generally a fellow that has been a patient in a hospital for any length of time, when he gets well so as to be back again with his regiment is pleased beyond measure when the time comes for him to go. It is like getting out of prison. It is as dull as death confined here, and a man with any life in him, so to speak, likes to be among his own boys again and doing his regular duty at the front. Very many when the surgeons come around taking down their names, and they suspect what it means, will plead to be reckoned with the number, but the surgeon will be obliged to refuse their request. And there is once in a while one with a weakness about him somewhere, which the surgeons have persisted in ignoring, and which it would be hard work to reconcile with his other symptoms of health and the science of physiology, who will plead the other way, but if he attempts that and gets off without giving the wits and lovers of fun a cruel advantage over him, he may consider himself a lucky fellow.

Each man's effects, his knapsack, haversack, gun and equipments if he has them, as every soldier is supposed to have, are kept for him in a store-room for that purpose under the charge of a trusty man detailed for that business, while he is a patient here, and when he returns to his regiment they are given up to him. But before they leave the hospital, however, they have a sort of inspection, and if any hospital blanket, underclothes or anything of that kind, is found in the knapsacks which the soldier cannot establish his claim to, it is taken out and left. I noticed this morning when the steward was inspecting the knapsacks, the sergeant that followed him had quite an armful of confiscated plunder of one sort and another, which the steward had extracted from the various knapsacks. The boys thought it was hard that the steward wouldn't let them have a little something to remember the Sixth Corps Hospital by, but he wouldn't.

This reduction of our numbers makes quite a sensible difference in the appearance about the hospital. There isn't so many of the inhabitants walking about, and many faces that had become familiar are among the absent. New ones will come and take their places, and thus change is going on continually — changes such as a man would notice in any quiet, little village, after an absence of some years, while here it requires only a few days. The Ninth Corps had an addition to their number day before yesterday. Two hospital cars came down from the front in the afternoon, loaded with sick, the most of them very bad cases, I judged by the care with which they had to be handled. These hospital cars are used for the express purpose of carrying very sick and wounded men. They are passenger cars, but instead of seats on each side, stretchers are strung up, and in this way sick men can be transported from one place to another, as comfortably as it would be possible to transport men by land. There are five tiers of stretchers on each side of each car, and three in each tier. These stretchers are held up by large India rubber straps, and can be taken down or put up, with the individuals that occupy them.

We are having some very excellent religious meetings here at our new chapel. Last evening there was a crowded house, I should think there was nearly if not quite 500 men present. There were several of the Christian Commission delegates, who spoke briefly; three of whom I believe were from Chicago. The interest and feeling appeared to be deep and earnest. The last speaker's remarks abounded in incidents, illustrating the power of prayer, and the interest felt by the people at home for the spiritual welfare of the soldiers. He spoke of one little girl in Chicago, the daughter of a poor widow, only six years of age, and some of the incidents he mentioned of her simple faith, were very touching and beautiful. I wish I could tell the story here, as it was told us last night. But that would be impossible, and I haven't room. But I can give the bare circumstances of this little incident, if you will pardon the digression.

It seems they were very poor and had suffered much as, alas! many do in our great cities. Three years ago this woman, with her two little children, had been threatened by their landlord with being turned out of doors, because their rent had been long unpaid, and there appeared to be no prospect of their being able to pay it. This little girl, then only three years of age, asks her weeping mother one evening, "Doesn't God hear us when we pray?" "Yes," says the mother. "And won't he give us what we need if we ask him?" "Certainly my child." "Well mamma don't we need a house?" "Oh yes," says the mother, "we need a house," and the poor woman wept, when she thought how great was that need. Not for herself simply did she shed those tears; ah! no, but the sufferings that must come upon her little babes, were more than a mother's heart could bear. "Mamma," says Fannie, for that was the child's name, "I will go and ask God to give us a house." She went into the bedroom to pray, leaving the door ajar so that the mother could see, and there kneeling by her cradle with her hands clasped together, her little curls drooping down on her shoulders, and looking up to heaven with such love and trust that she seemed more like a being from a purer world than an inhabitant of this sinful earth, she offered her simple prayer. "O Lord, please lend us a house. It is cold out of doors to stay on the door-stone, please lend us a house." Simple as her prayer was, the Lord heard it. Coming from the bedroom she threw her arms around her mother's neck and kissing her, plead with her to cry no more, for says she, "God will give us a house, I know he will." And so it proved. Her rent has been paid for by some one, from that time to this. When the speaker left Chicago about a week ago, this little girl and her sister came to him and wanted to know what they could send to the soldiers. They had prayed for us, but they wanted to send us something. Finally Fannie's face brightens up and she says, "I will tell you, Mr. Moody,³⁰ what we will send them. I have got pennies enough to buy them a testament, and I will give it into your hands." This litle girl, her sister and mother, contribute in all two dollars, a widow's mite truly, for the speaker thought it must be the last cent of money they had in the house, and perhaps all they had seen for many days. Before the speaker closed, he asked us what word he should carry back to that little child who had contributed her all for us. He said he should tell her to pray especially for all that arose for prayer that night, "and now," says he, "how many of you will rise." About fifty rose to their feet, saying by this that they wanted the prayers of this poor widow's daughter, this sweet little child of faith, only six years of age. It was a singular and affecting sight.

The guards that went up with the convalescents this morning have just returned. They say a squad of rebel pickets came into our brigade the other night. They said their officers never tried to hinder them from coming in, but purposely looked the other way that they might not *see* them, nor appear to have connived at their coming. The officers seem to have given up all hopes of the Confederacy, and though they do not want to compromise themselves, they are perfectly willing that others should contribute what they please towards the final event of peace, in the only way in which they now know it must eventually come.

Sixth Corps Hospital
City Point, Va.
Mar. 24, 1865

The mud here at City Point is rapidly becoming dried up, an important event that it would be inexcusable not to mention. The streets are not only dry, but some of them are actually dusty. Everybody was made sensibly aware of this in the gale of yesterday, for the clouds of dust, at times, completely shut out the horizon from view, and well nigh blinded the man who had the temerity to face it. I don't know as I ever saw the wind blow more steadily or more furiously than it did yesterday, and it isn't done yet. It would almost raise a cloud of dust from the veriest mud-puddle, as I believe it must have done in many instances. I know it raised particles of dust nearly as big as robins' eggs, and sometimes hurled chunks of wood from one place to another with a spitefulness, quite amusing to witness.

This is the third day that the wind has blown with almost unexampled fury. Yesterday afternoon at one time one would have thought the seven furies were let loose. It made sad havoc among the tents of the hospital. Some have stood it thus far heroically, but many have not. It was impossible for the ropes and fastening to sustain the pressure, and woe to the unlucky tent that begins to yield. Let but a corner of it get loose in this wind, and it would be torn in shreds without mercy. I saw several of them torn in twain from top to bottom, and some were prostrated entirely. I pity the poor fellows that were sick in the tents that were blown down, if there were any such, and there must have been in some of the hospitals. The men had to work for life, almost, in some parts of the hospital grounds fixing guy ropes, and fastening the tents in every way that could be devised. It seemed as if the winds had conspired to sweep every tent off from the ground. It was more moderate last evening, but at midnight it repented of its moderation, and since then this invisible element has kept us apprehensive of its power. Up to the present moment, however, my own tent stands, and I hasten to chronicle it while it is in my power to do so. One rope at the windward corner has given out already, leaving a gaping rent. I should grieve exceedingly to be obliged to tell you of the ruin of this tent, for from its dilapidated and mildewed appearance it is a veteran of many a stormy hardship in its country's service, and I think it deserves a better fate.

Aside from this, everything is quiet here at the hospital, and the news market is uncommonly stagnant. Even the guards grumble that there isn't anything going on, not so much as a drunken man to arrest, and they are spoiling for a little fun. The other night, though, they had all the fun they wanted. A drunken vagabond from one of the hospitals (not the Sixth Corps by considerable), came to our contraband here of negro families, on an errand worse than contraband. The guard of course ordered him away, but the miscreant had a loaded revolver, while the guard's musket was unloaded, and therefore he had the guard to advantage. But the guard feigning to yield the point managed to gain time, load his gun, and get help. Overpowered, he gave up his belligerent intentions, and attempted to use his legs and escape. The guard's gun was now loaded and under the circumstances it was his duty to use it rather than allow so dangerous a person to escape, but it wouldn't go off. He snapped three caps on it at the fellow, either one of which, he said, would have sent him into the other world where we suppose they have better conveniences for such characters; but the piece refused to go off, and no blood was spilled. They finally, after considerable "fun," as they called it, got him arrested and into the guard-house. Our guard-house here is a miserable affair, being seldom used. It is seldom fit to use, especially to secure such a prisoner as we had on this occasion, and this defect gave the guards some more of their "fun" before morning. The prisoner watched his opportunity, and when the guard's back was turned attempted to ecape. But "Sherty" was too smart for him. He didn't get far before he was overhauled and brought to the guard-house again. The rascal came back with a broken head, and "Sherty" came back with a broken gun, and as I understand it there is a very intimate connection between the two. The prisoner gave the guards no more trouble that night, and in the morning was turned over to the authorities where he belonged. The guards relished their "fun" exceedingly well, and on this occasion, doubtless, they considered the allowance sufficiently liberal. Last Saturday there were two more deserters shot here. These deserters had played a double game. They were formerly rebel soldiers belonging to a North Carolina regiment. They got their bounties, and that was all they wanted. They tried to pass themselves as rebel deserters and escape, using the papers given them in the first place as such, but they were caught in it, and this was their fate. As a general rule a rebel deserter is not to be trusted in our ranks.

We have been expecting every day to hear of fighting at the front, but as yet there has been no movement made, though the troops are held in readiness for a movement at a moment's notice. Over a week ago all the sick and wounded from the Division Hospitals were sent here. Stirring news may be expected at any time. The rebellion is reduced to such a compass now that the coming conflict *must* be "short, sharp and decisive." But little doubt is entertained here of the result. All are confident of returning peace, and that right speedily. This is well, but we must bear in mind that we have not yet rendered it impossible for

Gen. Lee to win another victory. By concentrating all his available forces upon one part of our lines, or upon one of the armies now encircling Richmond, he might possibly postpone the downfall of the Confederacy a few weeks or months, but it is difficult now to see upon what reasoning an opinion can be based, that its downfall may be postponed altogether. On the other hand a bloodless victory may not be impossible. Bitter as the rebel leaders may be, they will not fight when there is no hope whatever. Dying in the last ditch looks very well from a distance, but on a nearer approach it becomes less desirable. With all the supplies for Richmond cut off, the armies of Sherman, Schofield, Grant and Sheridan connected, if they shall attack our lines and fail, our armies increasing while theirs are diminishing, Jeff Davis or Gen. Lee will hardly be justified in the eyes of the world if they prolong the slaughter simply because they had rather fight than surrender. Our Government will, doubtless, offer them better terms, than in the same circumstances any other Government on earth would offer them, and much as the world may admire the heroism that would rather die than surrender, so far as one's own individual self is concerned, it would not justify men in the position of Davis and Lee who would compel men to die, that they may not be caught in a trap of their own setting, and these gentlemen will understand this. Therefore, while we prepare for the worst, we have much reason to hope for the best.

The Rev. Dr. Vincent, who was Gen. Grant's former pastor, said last evening at the Chapel of the Christian Commission, in the course of his remarks to the soldiers, that within three months in all probability, and within six months beyond doubt, this country would be cemented together in stronger bonds of union than ever before. He said there would be a fraternity of feeling between the masses of the people, both North and South, that did not exist before the war. Slavery, the bone of contention, would be removed, and both parties would understand each other as we have never yet done. The veteran soldiers of both sides were ready to grasp each other by the hand in the kindliest manner when free to do so, and there seemed to be not a particle of personal ill will between them. And here I might remark what I have often heard our boys say, that if they were ever taken prisoners and kept under guard, they hoped above all things that they might be guarded by the men who had opposed them on many a field of battle, and who had learned in actual war how to treat a soldier. But those unhuman bipeds who guarded our prisoners at Andersonville, Salisbury, and other places, had doubtless never smelt gunpowder on a field of battle, and never fired a gun at any man except unarmed prisoners. There is no such thing as coming to an understanding with such men; but in charity let us hope that all are not like them. And in faith let us pray that this war which has cost us so much sorrow, may be brought to a speedy and triumphant close, and this nation have a unanimity of feeling from Maine to Texas that nothing shall ever again disturb.

> Sixth Corps Hospital
> City Point, Va.
> April 9, 1865

The glorious news of the past week is known all over the North, and thousands of hearts long burdened with hope deferred (which maketh the heart sick), both there and here, now leap anew for joy. The nation rejoices, though there are individuals who are called to mourn for the fallen; for the victory was not purchased without blood and life. Three long arduous and bloody campaigns have before been made by the hard fighting, but luckless army of the Potomac, with Richmond for its object; but up till now, that city remained impregnable, and mocked at our efforts. This fourth campaign, less bloody than any of the others, commenced but a few days ago, and now Richmond is ours. In a few days more, with the capture of Lee's army, which every one now believes to be as sure as human events can be, this campaign will be virtually ended. We can then shake hands with our Western comrades without feeling reproached, as if our ill luck had left the burden of the work for them to do. We shall have shown them, that we can do something besides retreat, fight and die; we shall have shown them that we can win victories as well.

Richmond was evacuated last Sunday. At three o'clock on that day, the old Sixth Corps had made Lee's strong line of no use to him — charging through rebel fort, after fort, and killing rebel soldiers with rebel artillery, in a terribly unceremonious manner. At three o'clock on that day Mr. Jefferson Davis (unhappy man) was obliged to read a telegram from Gen. Lee, his chief hope and reliance, announcing that Richmond, after four years of warfare to hold, could be held no longer, and that he must leave his throne to fly for safety; for the Yankees were coming in to possess the city. At that same hour, in every Northern city, the telegraph carried the news of our successes, and its probable result. The same joy was felt here, and at the same time, and I think we rejoiced as much as anybody. At the close of the afternoon service, at the Chapel of the

Christian Commission, Gen. Patrick himself read the latest dispatches he had received from Gen. Grant. There was no cheering when he read them, nor any outward demonstrations of any kind; but the feeling was deep and intense. You could almost have heard a pin drop when Gen. Patrick stepped upon the platform beside the pulpit to speak for a moment. The General wears a long white beard, and his looks and bearing, as well as his stern voice, are particularly impressive. All the soldiers watched him eagerly, and not a word was lost. We knew that a terrible battle was then raging, and every one was feverishly anxious to know *how* terrible, and what was the result. The camp and hospital were full of tantalizing rumors, too absurd to believe, and not daring to believe them we forbore to believe anything. Gen. Patrick did not know that Richmond and Petersburg were ours, or that they would become ours so soon; but he knew what we had gained up till nearly noon, and he considered the battle then raging the turning point with us. He told us to pray every man of us to the God of battles, for the men who were fighting at that moment, as it was not only fitting, but our solemn duty to do so. He called upon the Rev. Mr. Vincent to lead in prayer, but the leader of the meeting asked *him* to make the prayer, and he did pray before us to God, in a manner not easily to be forgotten. The General didn't choose soft words at all. He took it for granted that the Almighty regarded the cause of Jeff Davis and that of Satan in the same light, and he prayed for the complete overthrow of the rebel army, and their utter annihilation as a military power. Many felt then, if never before, that the cause for which we were fighting is no selfish or trifling matter.

The next day, and the day following, the news of our successes continued to come in, more and more glorious still. Petersburg was taken, Richmond was taken, and guns and prisoners to an immense number were captured. It seemed almost too good to believe. One fellow said, he tried as hard as he could, but it took him all day to believe, that Richmond was actually ours after it had been announced officially, and this fellow wasn't a copperhead either.

Large squads of the prisoners were taken by here, and of course every fellow that could leave his bed had to go out to the road to pay his respects to the Johnnies. I thought they looked remarkably well, considering what had been said of their condition. Their faces looked grim and dusty of course, but I couldn't see any sign at all of their having suffered from starvation. And their clothes and general appearance were as good as ours generally are, after we have been marching and fighting for some length of time. Great, long legged, hearty fellows — they looked as if they might fight with a vengeance, if they were where they could, and thought it would be of any use.

Our boys couldn't keep from asking them about the latest news from

Petersburg, Richmond, &c., and what they thought about going to Libby Prison, Andersonville, Salisbury, or some such place — to which they replied or not, as they thought most convenient. The most of them appeared to be good natured about it. "Damn it" says one, "you needn't laugh, you ought to have done this before." Another said the Sixth Corps rapped at their door Sunday morning, before they were up. "Well," says one of our boys, "did you let the Sixth Corps in?" "By _____" says he, "they *did* come in and we are here, that's what's the matter."

But I ought to speak of the wounded, who were brought in here in such quantities, to be cared for and healed if possible. I have described such scenes so often, that I have no heart to do it again. God grant that it may not have to be done many times more. Where war is, such things must be. It is the price alike of victory or defeat. While we were rejoicing at the good news of our successes, there was a tinge of anxiety to know who of our comrades were wounded, and who had fallen. Among those from the Second Regiment, I hear that Capt. Charles C. Morey, of Co. E., was killed Sunday afternoon by a grape shot, while charging the enemy's works. Capt. Morey had been a soldier almost four years; he came out with the regiment, and has been with it through everything since, except for a short time that he was absent in hospital, from a wound received in the Valley. He was faithful and fearless, and always rigidly abstained from every appearance of dissipation. He came out as a corporal and had risen to captain, and at the time of his death was considered one of the most reliable officers in the regiment. It seems a hard fate to perish in the last struggle, after having passed safely through so many.

President Lincoln was here at the hospital to-day to visit the boys, and shake hands with them. It was an unexpected honor, coming from the man upon whom the world is looking with so much interest, and the boys were pleased with it beyond measure. Everything passed off in a very quiet manner; there was no crowding or disorder of any kind. When the President came all the men that were able arranged themselves by common consent into line, on the edge of the walk that runs along by the door of the stockades, and Mr. Lincoln passed along in front, paying personal respect to each man. "Are you well, sir?" "How do you do to-day?" "How are you, sir?" looking each man in the face, and giving him a word and a shake of the hand as he passed. He went into each of the stockades and tents, to see those who were not able to be out. "Is this Father Abraham?" says one very sick man to Mr. Lincoln. The President assured him, good naturedly, that it was. Mr. Lincoln presides over millions of people, and each individual share of his attention must necessarily be very small, and yet he wouldn't slight the humblest of them all. His wife, accompanied by Senator Sumner, and other ladies, officers and eminent men were with him. The men not only reverence and admire Mr. Lincoln, but they love him. May God bless him, and spare his life to us for many years.

———————

Sixth Corps Hospital
City Point, Va.
April 20, 1865

The sad calamity which the nation has suffered, here, as elsewhere, is the all absorbing topic of conversation and of thought. The fountains of feeling have been so deeply stirred by this horrid event, that other events scarcely stir them at all. Scarcely anything else seems worth talking about, and all other news has lost its interest beside this. Less than two weeks ago Mr. Lincoln came here and shook hands with us, and we all wished that for many long years yet "Father Abraham" might be spared to this nation, which he, humanly speaking, has saved. But President Lincoln has been murdered — murdered by the same fiendish spirit, begotten in hell, and fed by slavery on earth, that has brought forth this rebellion. If I write a letter to-day I must write of this event. I should mock my own feelings if I did not. Never has sadder news been brought to us than this. It seemed as if we had lost a father. Mr. Lincoln was different from everybody; so sagacious, so straight-forward in all that he did, so apt in all that he said, and withal so kind-hearted and honest, he was winning the admiration of the whole world. When he was here a week ago last Saturday, some of the surgeons told him that to attempt to shake hands with so many thousand men would be more than he ought to endure, but he overruled them, for he said he wanted to shake hands with the brave boys who had won the great victories which gave him, with all the rest of the nation, so much cause to rejoice, and had been wounded, many of them, in so doing. The President appeared to take delight in it. I believe he took almost as much pleasure in honoring the boys, as the boys did in receiving the honor from him. But Abraham Lincoln is dead. As we think of this mournful calamity we can hardly keep from asking, Oh why did a just and merciful Providence permit this thing to happen? Why was not the assassin's hand stayed before it had stricken down the man we all so much loved to honor, and the leader in whom we could place our fullest confidence. But we must quote, in view of this event, the same words that Mr. Lincoln quoted in his second inaugural, "The judgements of the Lord are true and righteous altogether."

Last Sunday was a day of mourning here at City Point. The people were startled when the news came. Abraham Lincoln dead! oh no, it could not be. Rumor had outdone itself. We could not believe it. The doctors saddled their horses and rode to the Point, before waiting for the official news to come to the hospital. Alas, the news was confirmed. Not only the ladies wept, but the soldiers many of them shed tears tenderly like women, for all felt this to be no common grief. We felt as you did, dear reader, too much grief and indignation for words to express. For four long years we had been at work fighting the rebellion, that our lawfully chosen Chief Magistrate might administer the laws in every one of our United States, and now just as the war was about to close, and our object be accomplished, the hand that has lead us and the heart that has beat in sympathy for us in all the struggle, are still and cold in death. A rebel has done it — a stealthy cowardly rebel. The boys swore eternal enmity against everything in sympathy with that spirit of secession that has committed this crime, unequalled in atrocity in the history of the world. I have seen the men look grave and sad before when we have heard of defeats, of losses in battle, of comrades killed, but I have never seen that which moved every one with sorrow as did this. I remember last May at Spotsylvania, when the brave and much loved commander of our corps was killed, and what a feeling of depression there was when it was told us that our almost idolized general was shot and mortally wounded; but General Sedgwick was killed in the accepted danger of honorable warfare, and we bowed to fate's decree. Mr. Lincoln was killed by an assassin, and it seemed almost impossible to submit to it as a dispensation of Divine Providence. A man from the front told me that he never saw such a feeling manifested among the troops, as there was when the news of the President's murder was received. The indignation of the men knew no bounds. Had there been fighting going on, and more rebel prisoners captured, he thought that it would have been difficult to have restrained them from indiscriminate carnage. They swore if it came in their power to take a rebel's life they would take it, no matter what the risk might be to their own.

Over in the Fifth Corps Hospital a wounded rebel indiscreetly dropped a word expressing his satisfaction that Abe. Lincoln was murdered, and his indiscretion liked to have cost him his life. The boys in his ward would have torn him to pieces had not the authorities arrested and confined him. Even then he would hardly have been safe if the officers had not assured them that he should be sent to the Point in the morning and taken care of — taken care of being supposed to imply a punishment of a magnitude commensurate with his crime, as they regarded it.

There was a singular rumor afloat here Sunday evening, which shows how easy it is to catch at and believe what we wish to believe. It was reported that the whole story was a hoax. Some rebels had tapped the telegraph between here and Fortress Monroe and sent us up this news just for a sensation. Some of the men doubted this, but others believed it fully, and laughed at their former fears. "A pretty big fright we have had to-day," says one. "Yes," is the reply, "I never felt so bad in my life." But this rumor stilled our fears only for a brief moment. The booming salute in the morning gave us no longer any room to hope.

I believe I have never seen newspapers in such demand as they have been since Sunday. The details of this appalling tragedy, and the movements of the authorities to arrest the perpetrators, excite more interest now than the details of the last battles, or the movements of our armies in pursuit of the foe. Every other interest is swallowed up in this. We want by all means that the remainder of the rebels should be caught, but to-day we feel a livelier interest that Mr. Lincoln's murderer shall be brought to justice.

Just now, however, there isn't much of interest going on. There are all sorts of rumors as to the disposal that is going to be made of us. The Ninth Corps Hospital here commenced to break up yesterday. They were to take transports for some place, but they had no certain idea where, though the most of them supposed it would be to Washington. Part of the Ninth Corps itself passed here to-day to go on board the boats waiting for them at the wharf. They seem to think, the most of them, that they shall be sent to Washington, and from there sent home on discharged furloughs, that is, they are to be left to shift for themselves in the world without Uncle Sam's pay or his rations, but to be ready at any time, if needed, to fall in and enter active service. The Government is not quite willing to let go of us, nor quite able to bear the burden of our support, and hence this compromise. However, the boys will be abundantly willing to accept their liberty on these terms, if they are the best the Government can give. If this is true of the Ninth Corps it will probably be true of ours. The surgeon in charge expects the whole thing to be cleared out here in a short time. A fellow applied to the surgeon for a furlough, the surgeon told him in three weeks we would all have furloughs. He might have been in earnest or in fun, but his remarks made an excellent foundation for a camp story, and it has been given a pretty wide circulation.

Our Corps they say is in camp out to Burkeville Station. I understand our boys have got them a fine camp out there in a pine woods, and are resting on their laurels. They have but little to do now, and nothing to hinder them from enjoying themselves to their utmost. There is no enemy in front of them, and they have no picketing of any consequence to do. The boys think it a little odd, for it is something new in the experience of the Sixth Corps. We shall be expecting them this way now soon. Rumor has had them on the way every day since the surrender of Lee.

The hospitals here have been filled to their greatest capacity since the late battles, and many new tents added, but they are sending off to the general hospital every day, almost, many of the worst cases. None are sent to their regiments. I suppose they are waiting for the regiments to be sent here. There can be no doubt but that we shall be on our way to Washington before many days, and then *home,* we hope.

Sixth Corps Hospital
Near Alexandria, Va.
May 19, 1865

The war being over I suppose "war correspondence" will play out, as we boys would say, now directly, and I shall have to give up my favorite pastime of writing to you, but I will venture to write you a few words to-day, war or no war, though I shall have to ignore the fact that I have nothing of particular interest to communicate. Indeed war news in our country of late has been on a scale so grand and glorious that a new cause for jubilee cannot be produced. It is hardly possible for anything to take place now that will compare with what has already taken place. Few nations at any period have had such a succession of important and startling events transpire within so short a period of time, as we have had in ours for the last few months. When Gen. Sherman cut loose from Atlanta, and plunged with his invincible army through the heart of Georgia, we watched him eagerly, almost apprehensively, but when he arrived safely on the Atlantic shore, and gave to the Union the captured city of Savannah as a Christmas present, we were delighted and astonished. Then came his victorious march through South Carolina, capturing their strongholds including Charleston, that vile nest of treason, and disposing every force that opposed him like chaff before a hurricane, and our delight knew no bounds. Next

came the great and glorious victory of Gen. Grant with the army of the
Potomac, which resulted in the complete overthrow of Gen. Lee and his rebel
host, that had so long withstood us, and we knew that the great serpent of
secession whose poisonous fangs had been struck at the nation's life, was about
to lose its power for evil forevermore. That power as a power, is dead, but it
was true to its ruling passion to the last moment. It did not die until it had exhibited to all the world, the infernal spirit which has ruled its every action, by
committing a crime, the atrocity of which shows a depth of depravity and
wickedness without parallel in modern history. It did not die until it had
murdered America's most illustrious citizen, and (if they had known it) their
own best friend. So sad an event as this was never known before in American
history. Abraham Lincoln was killed, but his spirit is still with us, and though
dead, he yet speaketh. Following that most sorrowful event, came the news of
the surrender of Johnston's army and the remainder of the rebel forces, and
finally the capture of the rebel president in his wife's petticoats,[31] ingloriously
endeavoring to flee from justice. Now the government is discharging as fast as
they can the men who have fought and conquered, and is sending them home
to their families and friends. Surely the United States will have cause to long
remember the months of March, April and May just passed, and the year 1865
will forever form some of the most interesting pages of our history.

Just now with us soldiers, everything else is swallowed up in the idea of being
soon discharged and sent home. Our army is fast dissolving. Sheridan's cavalry
passed through here last Tuesday on their way to Washington, they said, to be
discharged. Part of the army of the Potomac is at Bailey's Cross Roads, and the
remainder of it will doubtless be there soon. Sherman pitched his headquarters
about a mile from here, day before yesterday, and his army cannot be far
behind. They will be reviewed next week, and then a great many of them will be
allowed to go home — some think the whole force will be disbanded. Meanwhile, mustering out is going on continually here in the hospitals. The mustering officers have already been at work at the Fifth Corps Hospital, mustering
out all that had less than one year to serve — the others will be reserved to the
last. To-day they will commence in the Second Corps, and then most probably
at this hospital.

But our Corps Hospital is not all here. Only about a hundred of us in all left
City Point last Saturday to establish a hospital here, taking with us a few
stewards and doctors to give dignity to the undertaking. Not being in the secret
myself, I cannot tell the precise object of our mission, but have no doubt but
that it will result in much good. I presume Uncle Sam had as lief feed and pay
us for staying here as anywhere. We expect the rest here from City Point soon

but they were sending all the sick away to general hospitals, so that there can't be but few left to come by this time. I suppose it is thought when the corps itself gets along here, there will be some "played out" soldiers among them, who will need to come here for treatment. If there is none it can be of no object whatever to keep us here. The Fifth Corps came here several days ago, and they say when the hospital was established, more ran away to their regiments than came from the regiments to the hospital. The boys had the story that they had only three patients left in the hospital then, one of whom has since deserted to his regiment, another has died, and the third having the whole corps of surgeons to attend him, is expected to die soon. Besides these patients, they have their "light duty" men, and all the men that have been detailed for hospital duty. Those that are detailed cannot return to their regiments if they wish to. We have no sick men at all here! only detailed men, and men on light duty. We have seventy-six light duty men or convalescents, but if you should see them when their "light duty" was done, frolicking and scuffling, and matching their strength against each other in a thousand different ways, you would doubtless consider it a pretty healthy army that could turn out such robust convalescents as these. Our quartermaster at City Point left us and went home on a furlough, and being promoted to Major did not return again, and my position as his clerk became vacant. I am now in the Commissary Department, and have a portion of the responsibility of drawing the rations, and feeding these hundred men. I came very near forgetting to mention this important fact.

We are situated near the three mile post on the Loudon railroad from Alexandria, and near the old Convalescent Camp that has now been turned into a general hospital. We have a pleasant place here, unlike that at City Point in many respects. We are in a quiet little valley that opens out on to the Potomac a little distance above Alexandria, and as it recedes from the river it hides itself from Washington behind the ridge of fortified hills which overlook that city. Opposite these hills is another ridge, abrupt and steep, and beyond this the valley of the Orange and Alexandria railroad which unites with this railroad at Alexandria like the two parts of the letter V. Once these hills were covered with forest trees, but there is scarcely one left now to remind us of their former glory. Soldiers' axes have swept them away, and soldiers' camp fires have consumed them all. Nature, however, not at all discouraged, is vigorously reproducing what she has lost. Already a second crop is springing up, and this uncommonly thrifty forest of little trees has clothed these hills again with verdure and beauty. We are not troubled here with dust as at City Point. Instead of being on a plain which army wagons innumerable have made like one vast highway, where every passing breeze can catch up a cloud of dust and hurl it into our faces, we have a pleasant hill-side, carpeted with green turf for our camp, which makes it seem not only pleasanter but cooler and better every way.

We had a pleasant trip from the Point. Just as we left on the transport Prometheus, the hospital boat Connecticut — that giant among transports — came up to the wharf to convey away the sick from our hospital. We left about 4 o'clock Saturday evening, and anchored that night on the James some forty or fifty miles below the Point. Sunday about noon we passed Fortress Monroe. I couldn't see but that the old gray walls of that stronghold looked exactly as they did three years and more ago, when we first landed there — the "Grand Army of the Potomac," which we had no doubt was capable of subduing the world. The old light-house stood in the same place and had the same look that it did then. The sand at its base has not changed its appearance at all since that night of our first landing, when we spread our blankets on it and slept there and dreamed of conquest and glory. But the monster gun that stood then pointing towards Sewell's Point was not there. The boys told me it had been removed to a new position, and pointed out a dark speck back from the shore and farther up the Bay as its present site. And there were no officers about there, as there were then, with their glasses looking anxiously across the water to Sewell's Point where the masts of the rebel shipping could then be plainly seen, and among which some of those officers affirmed they could see the grim outline of the Merrimac. Three years have made a great difference in the association of objects. Then the shipping was all huddled close to the shore, especially the smaller craft, and outside of them all stood the Monitor itself as a sentinel to protect them from the rebel fleet; now the vessels ride lazily at anchor anywhere, gunboats and monitors mixed promiscuously with others, and no danger was felt or thought of. We didn't reach Alexandria till Monday afternoon, and it was not till Tuesday night that we got our "cargo" moved up here. Since then the light duty men have been busy in putting up tents and fixing things as nice as they can, for they are old soldiers the most of them, and they know that the nicer they fix up things here the surer they will be to leave, and to leave now means to go home.

Sixth Corps Hospital
Near Alexandria, Va.
June 4, 1865

It is more than a warm day to-day, it is *hot,* and that hardly expresses it. In spite of all you can do or all you refrain from doing, you find it impossible to keep cool. A canvas tent is no protection from such a sun as is burning down upon our heads here. However, this weather so uncomfortable to us, is just what the country needs at the present time and we won't complain. We are going home soon, we hope, and there isn't one of us that has the remotest idea anything uncomfortable or inconvenient will ever happen to us there.

We are getting dreadfully out of patience at the delay that keeps us here doing nothing, when we are so anxious to get to our homes at the commencement of the season. The only men that have anything like business here to do, are the clerks, and as is usually the case, they are continually reproached because they work no faster. We want our papers, that we may be discharged and sent home. Doing nothing is a sort of business that never was calculated to put a man in a cheerful temper of mind at any time, and this is doubly true just now as we are expecting to go home. It is impossible for Uncle Sam to discharge everybody at once, and we must wait our turn, but we are decidedly opposed to waiting any longer than that.

There has been for several days a rumor afloat very discouraging to the prospects of your humble correspondent and his comrade "vets." They say Uncle Sam is going to keep us, to make up an army after the rest have gone home. The argument is, that we have a longer term to serve, besides the old fellow is paying us more bounty, and so he concludes to keep us while he dismisses the rest. In such an event the prospect opens before us of being sent to Savannah, New Orleans, Texas, or some other place, and put into a dull garrison, where we shall have to do our stupid round of duty for our full "sentence," as the boys call it. There may be some veterans who would like such an arrangement, but if there is, I haven't seen one of them. All are anxious to be discharged at the earliest possible moment. Such an arrangement as keeping a part of the men till their time has fully expired, and discharging others before, would be hardly fair, and it seems to me to be altogether improbable. Those whose term expires on or before the first of October next are to be discharged first. When these have been disposed of, doubtless the time will be extended from October first to another date, and all those included will form the second class to be discharged, and so on until we are all disposed of.

The luckiest fellows in this war appear to be those who enlisted previous to October 1st last year for one year. Many of these get enormous bounties as substitutes, reaching as high as $1500 in all, and in some instances that I have known to two thousand. Now these fellows happen to come among those who are to go home first, before they have hardly found out what real soldiering is, or become hardened to it. One of the clerks at Dr. Parker's headquarters was telling me, since I commenced this letter, of one with him who got his discharge day before yesterday, and is now on his way rejoicing. He got sixteen hundred dollars bounty for coming out here, and was with his regiment only three weeks when he was taken sick and sent to the hospital, and here he has been ever since. By some skillful diplomacy, which the rest of us cannot equal, he managed to get a *bona fide* discharge from the hospital, enabling him to go home at once. We don't blame a man who intends to be a soldier for taking whatever of money may be given him as bounty, for a man can't live in this world without his bread and cheese, and it takes money to buy these; nor is a man's good luck in getting his discharge and getting home a thing to be censured, but it seems decidedly cool, on the top of all this, to tell the veterans that they must stay a year and a half or two years longer because they are paid more. If they are going to keep us that long, why don't they say it is because we are the best soldiers, and done with it.

The *unluckiest* men in all this war are the drafted men who have got a year or more to serve. These will probably have to stay with us to serve out their time, if we do ours, and so far as big bounties go, many of them get none at all. They were forced into the service, in the first place, against their will, or at least against a will strong enough to enlist, for we all know it costs some men a greater sacrifice of feeling to become soldiers than it does others, and it seems a little hard, now that the war is over, to disappoint their expectations of going home. It really seems as if there was no need of this. There will be a plenty of soldiers, by and by, who will want to enlist in the regular army, and the Government can get all the men they will need without asking any one to stay who does not choose to do so. It is very likely some plan like this will be adopted. The regular army will be increased and the volunteers dispensed with. Good policy, as well as justice, would seem to require this, but we must be patient, the Government cannot do everything at once. They have some 250,000 loose men to dispose of in the army of the Potomac and Gen. Sherman's army, and this will require no small amount of work. Meantime, some troops must be kept, and somebody must be those troops. But before the summer is out, it is the opinion of many competent persons, that all except the regulars, colored soldiers and those who wish to remain, will be at liberty to go and come as their hearts incline, unrestrained by military discipline.

We have sent to the regiment from this hospital nearly 200 men to-day. The 2nd Corps Hospital and the Fifth broke up a week ago, and the men were sent to their regiments. The men had all been expecting to be discharged, direct from the hospital, which in justice ought to have been done. This would have been much more convenient for the men and saved the most of them a great deal of trouble, but the men's wishes in such matters are never taken into account. It has leaked out that our surgeons had orders some time ago empowering them to discharge every man that did not belong to the Veteran Reserve Corps without distinction as to veterans, drafted men or any others, and this order has been wholly ignored. It saves time and trouble to send the men to their regiments, and the surgeons plead that it will make no difference about their being discharged. We will get home just as soon, they say, if we go to the regiment as if we stayed here, but it is not so. Very many who might have been discharged weeks ago, will now have to wait for days and perhaps months. The only excuse for this is that the records of the hospital, and other business that has to be done in the office on paper, was behindhand, and it would take some days to get them made up to date. All along it has been contrary to the rules to send any one to his regiment, let him be ever so well; but now by some red tape maneuvre which we know nothing about they have found a way to send the men to their regiments, and thus spare themselves a vast amount of labor. We have to commend the surgeons for their shrewdness, for we well know that to make up each soldier's account with the Government in discharging so many is no light job, but at the same time we are exceedingly loth to remain in the service weeks or months and perhaps longer still, just to save those headquarter gentlemen a little extra writing. If the War Department has opened a way for us to get out of the service, we cannot see our surgeons close it again without indignation and concern.

The remainder of the hospital left back at City Point came along last Monday. Nothing now is left at the Point except a few guards and these will be along by to-morrow. All have been sent away from here, too, now, except such as were needed to the last. In a few days we expect the hospital to be broken up entirely. All the hospital stores are being turned in, and to-morrow morning there will be forty wagons here to take them to Alexandria and Washington to a government store house. Tents, bedsteads, blankets, sheets, pillows, and everything that belongs to the hospital has been picked up and are now ready to load on to the wagons, which are ordered to be here in the morning. By the next day, or the day after, we expect the approaching hour of dissolution, and then we that are left will be sent to our regiments if they are near so that we can, otherwise we may be turned over to the Provost Marshal General, or Adjutant General, to be disposed of according to his will and pleasure.

The Corps itself lays up here near Bailey's Cross Roads, about four miles from this place. They came in last Friday. They expect to be reviewed next Thursday, and then those regiments whose term of service expires before the first of October will be sent home immediately. The boys are in excellent spirits, although they had been doing some pretty hard marching. They were short of rations and out of tobacco. They marched in the rain and had two days' rations spoiled, and as for tobacco they had no money to buy it. They were too late at Richmond to get any without buying, but they expect to be able to triumph over these difficulties soon.

Second Vermont Regiment
Camp in the Field
June 21, 1865

I see I am getting slightly behind the times. I meant to have written you several days ago, and I did get started to do so once, but was broken in upon by circumstances, and the thoughts I had noted down, as well as those I had ready to note down, are lost now, I am afraid, forever. It is too bad, but it cannot be helped. I shall have to commence anew, but it is hard work at this particular time and only for its being out of fashion, I would make several very excellent apologies about it. In the first place, I could tell you I was on guard yesterday and last night, and this blessed minute I haven't been relieved more than a half an hour. You call a fellow up twice during one of these short nights, and make him walk a beat two hours each time as they did me last night, and you need not expect his meditations the next morning will be of the profoundest kind, unless they are profoundly dull, as mine are now. But there is no possible help for it. To-morrow I expect we fellows that came off guard to-day will have to go on again, and so on every other day indefinitely, for anything I can see now, unless we have more men or less duty. But I have taken my portfolio, pen and ink-bottle, and come away from camp out here under the shade of a little oak bush, and I am determined to write you something which I shall call a letter before I go back, if it takes till night. If this desultory scribbling fails to be highly entertaining and instructive please bear in mind that I have various other apologies I can give when called upon. One thing is certain, I shall have to keep wide awake in order to fight this innumerable army of mosquitoes. They appear determined to bore my face at all points. They act as if they belonged to a petroleum company, and thought my face was an oil region. Unless I am pretty vigilant in self-defense, they will make their business pay, and bore their living out of me in spite of my teeth. We had a terrible thunderstorm yesterday afternoon, and I suppose these torments rained down then. I have heard old women say they rain down on such occasions, and I don't know where in the world so many of them could come from if they didn't.

You notice I am back to my regiment again. The ups and downs of military life has brought me back into my old place in the military marching of the United States. June 7th your humble servant, along with several other of the country's servants, supposed to be more or less humble, left the hospital near Alexandria and returned to our companies. We are now ready as we have been all along heretofore, to do whatever duty this Great Republic requires at our hands. If they want to have us walk our beats as guards every alternate day and night, we are willing to do it, or if they want to appoint us provisional governor of one of these southern States or something of that sort, we are willing to do that. It makes no particular difference with us, only we would a little rather be a military governor because walking a beat so much, especially nights, is very tiresome, and makes a fellow feel so sleepy in the morning. We would like to have a little easier time now for a while, but we will not be particular. We would like a change first rate now for a year or so, but we have imposed no conditions upon the country for our services, and we are just as patriotic to-day as we were the day we enlisted. We have got just enough of that quality on hand to last us till our times are out, if we are kept so long, and no more; but if we are let off before that time we shall doubtless have some to spare for future emergencies. Uncle Sam will please take the hint.

The Sixth Corps Hospital is now hopelessly defunct. Almost all had been sent away before we came to our regiment. We were about the last dregs of the hospital, only a few stewards and doctors being left till the next day, with three or four light duty men under a sergeant to see them safely off. Now there is nothing left there to show hardly that a hospital had ever been there. We didn't stay long enough to collect a very large pile of material, or do work sufficient to leave any very lasting ruins. There was a little of the commissary goods left which the negroes appropriated, otherwise it would have been wasted. I was passing there a day or two after we left, and just for the fun of it I went on to the ground to take a farewell look at the spot. At the place where the commissary tent had stood, in which I had pretended to officiate for a little while, there was an old negro filling his bag with coffee from a barrel that had been left partly full. The old man thought he had found a mine of wealth. From his appearance I should judge he had suffered much from destitution. He had nobody to care for him now, he said. His former master was gone, and government had taken possession of his master's property. There was another young, stout-looking fellow there, that had been at work at the hospital all along, but now had nothing to do, and hardly knew which way to turn for a living. He said his former master had asked him to come back and live with him, but said he "I would sooner starve to death right here than go back to him." He said he had worked enough for that man, and had suffered enough from him. He said he had worked for him day after day, from earliest light till dark, with only fifteen minutes rest at noon for dinner, and on several occasions he had been whipped without mercy. "I haven't forgotten him," said he, "and if I ever meet him again I will have satisfaction, I am a free man now, just as free as he is, and just as good, and if he refuses me satisfaction I will take it." He was vehemently in earnest. When I noticed the broad chest, fine physical development of limb and muscles, and the energy and apparent vigorous will of their possessor, inspired by his wrong, I thought I should have felt a trifle ill at ease if I had been the master in question at that time. His master had owned 130 slaves, and lived on the York river. Nearly all his male slaves had left him — all that could. If slaveholders generally here in Virginia have gained the antipathy of their slaves in this way, no wonder it is a death blow to them to abolish the system. It must require the most prudent legislation to prevent unhappy collisions in this new state of things which has been introduced. Though they may not in many instances resort to violence, they will hardly be induced to go back to their former masters for employment. But necessity will soon provide its own inexorable laws, and master and slave will find that, as President Lincoln in his "little story" to the rebel commissioners said, they must "root hog or die." If they won't work for their former masters they must work for some others. Employment must be had, and work must be done, and these two wants must meet each other some way. In the nature of things it can't be otherwise.

Our camp here is about seven miles from Alexandria, and five from Washington. We are just about opposite Georgetown, on the Loudon and Alexandria railroad, and near Falls Church. We appear to be simply camped here without order or system, just to stay till some proper disposal is made of us. I don't know which way the army pretends to front, or whether it pretends to have a front. There is no picketing done, and no watching for the enemy.

There is nothing whatever going on except camp duty, and that just now, is quite enough. The whole brigade is camped here near together. From Gen. Grant's Headquarters you can see Washington, with its snow white capitol and lofty dome, towering in its majesty of strength and beauty for above all other buildings in the city. The view from this height is really delightful. I have been told that on this eminence, rebel cannon were planted in the summer of 1861 — the nearest they ever got to Washington. How confident they were of final success in their cause; but how great has been their failure. They had no sort of an idea what kind of stuff Yankees were made of but they have found out to their abundant satisfaction.

The men whose term of service would have expired before the 1st of October, were mustered out of the service night before last, and yesterday they went home. There were I believe, 168 men discharged from this regiment in all, 115 of them being present. It was just one year since the original regiment went home, and as many went this time as then. The veterans, drafted men, and substitutes are all that is left, and there is hardly enough of them to call it a regiment. Less than a hundred men for duty is all there is now. It took twenty-four men yesterday for our police guard, and the sergeant major wanted one or two more for supernumeraries but he couldn't get them. He had detailed all that was detailable.

The men that went home yesterday were a happy lot of fellows. They went over to Division headquarters and got mustered out the night beforehand. They considered themselves free citizens when they got back. No more guarding, no more picketing, no more watching for them. They were free men, free to go home and stay as long as they pleased, and no dreaded penalty of being considered deserters would hang suspended over their heads. A sweet thing is liberty; but a man if he becomes a soldier, must for the time being suspend his claims to its privileges, and surrender himself to the requirements of military life, absolutely and entirely. Their hold on him is ironlike, and at the same time it is necessary. No wonder the boys could hardly contain themselves for joy at the thought of release, no wonder they shouted and cheered. They couldn't help it. It was in them, and it would come out. Mock orders were given to each other till late in the night. "Joe I want you for guard in the morning," says some pretended orderly sergeant, with mock gravity. Joe has always had a mortal dislike to that order till now; but this time he hears it unmoved. "Pack up and be ready to march immediately," has been obeyed by them for the last time.

Yesterday morning at five o'clock, they started. Those that chose to, had the privilege of taking their guns, by having six dollars deducted from their pay, not many chose to. They never wanted to see one, again, they said. What is to be done with the rest of us isn't known, though it is generally believed that we shall soon be mustered out in the same way. Something will doubtless have to be done. Every regiment in the brigade except the eleventh, is left a mere skeleton, all bones and no meat, all officers and no men.

Orders are being circulated offering inducements for soldiers in the regular army. That is what we like to see. Fill up the regulars, and let us go home. I have heard today that preparations were being made, so that men already in the field, can enlist in the regulars. With suitable inducements, there are large numbers that would do so. I hope it is true, for it is a consummation devoutly to be wished. Meanwhile we wait with martyr-like patience.

Second Vermont Regiment
Camp in the Field
June 30, 1865

Notwithstanding it is so awful hot here to-day, I have determined to snatch a few spare moments again, and drop a line to you. I believe it would be impossible for the most eminent scribbler on earth to get anything very eminent on to paper in this terrible furnace-like heat. It melts a man completely. His energies, mental and physical, droop in this hot sun, like a wilted cabbage leaf. Perspiration actually rolls off in streams from a man's face and body, as if each pore had become an exhaustless fountain. The ground, as you walk over it, feels as if it had been heated in an oven. I don't know as it is precisely known how hot Virginia *can* get, but if it can go much beyond this, I should hardly blame the inhabitants here if they become predisposed to believe Miller's doctrine of the world's burning up immediately. The elements are almost melted with fervent heat now..

The boys are quite willing to keep under their shades. Our camp is protected from the sun as well as the ingenuity of the boys could make it, and the most of us have learned considerably of the art of keeping cool since we have been here. We have abundant need just now of all that we have learned. We have fitted up our camps in the old style, plus all the recent modern improvements, so, if the Government ordains that we shall stay here this summer, we mean to enjoy ourselves as well as we can. There is no particular danger of our being driven out of our camp by the rebels, or of our being called upon to drive the rebels out of their camp. We can make ourselves just as good houses as we please, and if we are ordered out it will most likely be to go home. We could obey that order without the least reluctance under any circumstances. I believe we worked all the harder because we knew, as I have often told you before, that the nicer we make our camp, the more likely we are to leave it. We had plenty of shelter tents when the last detachment of men went home, and when we have these we can very easily provide the rest. We covered our tents all over with evergreen or other boughs, raised up on poles and fastened to posts, and this, extending in front over our door, makes a very cool bower. Our camp is pitched in an old bush place that has grown up since we cut the trees in Camp Griffin times. Trees grow remarkably fast here. Since we cut down the old stock, these new ones have grown up, eight, ten and fifteen feet high. These we have swept away except where they benefited us, and have made the ground, that was but a short time ago covered with bushes and briars, fit for the abode of rabbits and snakes, clean and smooth as a parade ground, and quite fit for the abode of the Second Regiment. Almost any time, reader, if you should happen along here, you would see us under our bowers, smoking our pipes, or telling stories about the late war — how we charged up such a place, and drove the rebels here, and got drove there, mixing in a thousand little personal reminiscences that will never find their way into print, though not in time nor eternity can they be forgotten by us. Perhaps you would find now and then a fellow looking over the New York *Herald,* trying to find where it tells of the Army of the Potomac, to see if it says anything about when we are to be discharged, but the most of them would be as careless and easy as if it were a matter of perfect indifference to them whether the "school kept or not." We don't have to go out on picket nor on drill. We have simply to do our guard duty regularly, eat our rations promptly, appear on dress parade punctually, and sweat all day most abominably. Please call up here some day and see if it isn't so.

The boys got pretty mad the other day when the order came to muster out the 5th, 6th, 8th and 11th regiments, and leave the 2d, 3d and 4th till the last. They thought by right the oldest regiments ought to go first. To have the 6th or 8th go and leave the 2d, seemed like giving them the rights that belonged to us. Somehow the story got around that it was the work of the officers who had voted to stay, by this means cheating the men out of going home when they might otherwise have gone. Probably the officers had nothing to do about making the selection, but they thought they had, and to see if there wasn't some remedy they made arrangements among themselves to go up to Corps

Headquarters and lay the matter before Gen. Wright. They beat the drum and fell into line, but Col. Tracy hearing what was going on, gave orders that not a man should leave camp. The boys, after the good name they have won, were hardly prepared for mutiny, indignant as they were at their grievances, real or supposed; so they quietly withdrew to their quarters. Col. Tracy explained the matter to them and corrected the misunderstanding, and doubtless the most of the boys are now satisfied that the officers had nothing to do with their staying. I have heard that regiments, in some of the other Divisions, did go up to Corps Headquarters to see about this same matter of going home. They were veterans, most of them, and felt indignant that others, who had done less, should be privileged above them. In one instance, they went up under lead of a non-commissioned officer one night, in a sort of torch-light procession, carrying flags and devices of various descriptions relating chiefly to veterans, what they had done, and how they were treated. "Who saved the country? Veterans." "We have served our country four years; we have done our duty; now, sir, we entreat you do yours and release us," and scores of others of similar import. Gen. Wright told them that they could be discharged only by order of the War Department, that it was not his fault that they had not been discharged before. He did not select which regiments should go, nor which shouldn't. It wasn't the fault of their officers, neither, he told them, that they had been selected to stay, and others had been selected to go home. He told them that we should all go home soon, and he hoped that as they had borne an unstained record so far, that they would bear it bravely to the end.

The 5th, 6th, 8th and 11th regiments all left here last week. The camps begin to have a deserted look along the line here. There is only now and then a stray regiment, and these are very small. Brevet Maj.-Gen. Grant took leave of us last Monday. He has gone home on leave of absence, but does not expect to return.

———————

Burlington, Vt.
July 20, 1865

Long before this letter reaches you, it will doubtless have become known that the Second Regiment has at last been mustered out of the United States, and arrived in the State of Vermont. We arrived here at Burlington yesterday morning. The Seventeenth, Fourth and Second Regiments are here now at this present writing, waiting to be paid off and discharged, after which they will disperse to their several homes.

We left our camp in Virginia Sunday morning, but it was not until nearly night that we started on the cars from Washington. About noon the next day the regiment arrived at Philadelphia, and were treated to another excellent meal at the Union Volunteer Refreshment Saloon, — a place that many a soldier will long hold in grateful remembrance. The boys think there is no place for a soldier like Philadelphia, and indeed, we have good reason to think so, for their hospitality has often entertained us, and there is nothing in the world that will make a hungry man so grateful as to give him a good dinner. As our transportation is never furnished us by the Government between New York and Washington, only on rickety cars fit for nothing else only to carry soldiers, and as we are almost always at least forty-eight hours getting over the distance between these two cities, we are usually tired enough and hungry when we get to Philadelphia, going either way, to appreciate to the fullest extent, the kindness of the ladies and gentlemen who have, during all this war, contributed so bountifully for the comfort of soldiers passing through there. Besides the table spread for us, there is a glorious place for the men, sweaty and dirty as they have become riding in those close, dusty cars, to wash themselves, which is of itself a treat of no small consequence to a soldier. The pure Schuylkill water which spouts from the sides of a long horizontal pipe in scores of cooling streams, would almost inspire a man with an appetite when everything else had failed, if a man's appetite needed any such inspiration, which, however, in that place is seldom ever the case. I saw on a card they gave us, the statement that their committee had furnished seven hundred and fifty thousand meals to the soldier through the liberality of the citizens of Philadelphia, without any help whatever from the City, State or General Government. They have also a hospital to receive any sick or wounded soldier who may get so far on his journey and be unable to proceed further. They claim it to be the first one of the kind established in the country. From 15,000 to 20,000 have had their wounds dressed there, when otherwise they would have been thrown helpless among strangers. They also make it a part of their duty to care for and obtain employment for refugees and freedmen when they come among them.

Their work there is about done. They have fulfilled their benevolent purpose during this long war, without slackening their hands for an instant. No regiment has ever been sent empty away, and their arrangements have been so complete that no regiment has had to wait for their refreshments, but on the contrary, they always found the refreshments ready and waiting for them. They had only to telegraph forward that they were coming, and Mr. Brown, the head man of the committee, would announce the fact to the rest by firing a big gun which they have in position there for that purpose, and which is used as a signal to commence preparing a meal at any hour in the day or night. The country is full of just such benevolent institutions, though perhaps there are none of this kind placed where they have had such an opportunity of aiding and feeding so many as this at Philadelphia. Americans may well be proud of their nation when the common people will show a spirit like this, through a long relentless war.

We left Philadelphia Monday afternoon, and early Wednesday morning, July 19, had the pleasure of finding ourselves in the city of Burlington, in our own native State. We arrived here, so they told us, two hours before we were expected, but they were not long in finding out that we had come. The band escorted us up to the City Hall, where they had provided us a breakfast of all the rare luxuries of the season. Pies of all sorts with cakes and sweetmeats in abundance were set upon the table, and the ladies waited upon us, and we thought they appeared sweeter than all the rest. The boys all called that decidedly the best entertainment of the kind that we have had since we have been in the service.

So in the good Providence of God we are permitted to breathe the sweet air of Vermont once more. Old Vermont looks about as it used to, only they have closed the hills up nearer together and made them perhaps a little more steep and abrupt. We miss the large plains of Virginia. I suppose Nature thought Vermont so good that, as I heard a man say once, she set the ground up edgeways to make more room. Vermonters ought to fight well, raised among these rugged mountains so wild and free, and breathing such pure, delicious air. From the hospital barracks here, where the boys can stay at Uncle Sam's expense, if they prefer doing so to staying down town at their own, we can see a large portion of the surrounding country. I had the good fortune, too, to find comrades of my school boy days at the University, who, besides gratifying my curiosity with a sight of all the College Museum contains, treated me to a view of the place from the College belfry. I don't know of anything that could be more delightful to a four-year-old soldier than to stand upon the tip top of an institution like that in his own native State, which he has not seen in its verdure and beauty since the day he first left it for the war, and look at what he has so long wished to see from a standpoint like that. Quite a respectable portion of the country that a man may be proud to say he was born in, can be seen from there. The smooth lake on one side, pent in by rugged mountains all around and on the other side the hills and valleys, fields and forests, entertain the eye for miles around, while Winooski and Burlington seemed almost under our feet. If anybody should tell me that a man could live in that beautiful region and be a copperhead, I should want to tell him he lied.

The boys are only impatient now to be paid off and discharged. Some have gone home without waiting. We expect to be paid Saturday. What we most desire to see now is that paper with a spread eagle on it which says, "to all whom it may concern," that the owner is a free man.

[Tunbridge, Vt.]
July 26, 1865

Home at last. The Second Vermont Regiment was not paid off till yesterday. Now the most of the boys are at home, and have become citizens instead of soldiers of the United States. Our old regiment no longer exists as an organization among the powers that be, but must henceforth be reckoned as among the powers that were. There have been great changes in our ranks since their organization four long years ago, and so, too, we find among these hills and valleys great changes have occurred among the inhabitants with whom we used to delight to mingle. Some have removed to other places, but many have gone, alas! to return no more. How well I remember my parents' anxiety when we parted four years ago, but since then they have followed two of their dear children to the grave, while their soldier son still lives. Here are the same hills and the same fields that we saw then, but they have passed into other hands, and somehow there seems a loneliness in contemplating them, which forces the impression that this world cannot be man's abiding place. We have seen home so often like a fairy vision in our imaginings and dreams, and so often have wondered whether, in the good Providence of God, we should be permitted to return and find it as we left it, that now the ideal is realized it almost seems as if we were dreaming still. To look back upon the campaigns of the Peninsula, of Maryland, of the Wilderness, Shenandoah Valley and others, it seems almost impossible that all the events which our recollection can recall, should come within the range of four years. A lifetime of experience has been crowded into this fierce term of war. If I was asked "how it seemed" to be a free citizen once more, I should say it seemed as if I had been through a long dark tunnel, and had just got into daylight once more.

Soldiering is a hard life, and a very undesirable one at best. I don't know what an army *might* be, but certainly take them as they *are,* a man to become a soldier must lay aside almost everything that makes life worth the having. All the tender endearments of home, and all the refining influence of good society are almost wholly sacrificed for the time being, or most certainly a man gets a miserably poor return for these, when he becomes a soldier. Still if a man loves adventure he finds a wild, reckless freedom in soldiering that has a charm for him, and leads him to drop his soberer reflections till a more convenient season. There are many such take delight in the fierce excitement of a campaign. But so far as I am myself concerned, take it all in all, though I hope I shall be ever ready when enemies threaten the Government, and thousands spring to arms to join with them, but to become a soldier, simply as a means of earning a livelihood, I say it in all candor, I would only do it to save myself the necessity of begging my bread from door to door, whether it was a time of peace or war.

Now that the war is ended, it is pleasant to reflect that we had the honor of bearing some humble portion in it. If I had been constantly on duty in the ranks during the whole war, as I could name many that have, I would not exchange such an experience for the noblest fortune in the land. That honor, however, is very far from being mine.

One meets all sorts of men in the army, and he often finds himself in a crowd of the very roughest of the human species. But human nature is very much the same everywhere. No matter how "rough" a man may become, or how wicked, he naturally admires the excellent qualities of others, and condemns their faults very much the same as do those more cultivated and virtuous. To be popular with such men, it is only necessary to be unselfish. A selfish man is popular nowhere. His ill nature will creep out in a thousand ways in spite of him, and bring all his virtues into contempt.

Now that the war is over and I am no longer a soldier, I can not well inflict upon the reader any more "soldier's letters," but hoping that I have furnished some entertainment in my rough way to others, while I have found a pleasant occupation for my own idle hours, I bid you a kind adieu.

ANTI-REBEL

APPENDIX

Three Speeches by Wilbur Fisk

Wilbur Fisk's Decoration Day orations of 1891 and 1894, both in Alden, Minnesota, and a talk before the Grand Army of the Republic gathering near Albert Lea, Minnesota, in 1894 provide a fitting epilogue to his Civil War letters.

These addresses, which have not been published before, were transcribed from Wilbur Fisk's handwritten notes for these occasions. Fisk's writing is fine, small, and clear, having a quality of copperplate script, but occasionally his words are pushed to the end of his note paper or an additional thought, couched between lines and words, becomes difficult, if not impossible, to read. In the case of illegibility we have "guessed" strenuously, conceiving of the word Wilbur Fisk intended to use. These words are bracketed. Fisk often abbreviated in his notes, and where we have been able we have written out words and titles. Where words are apparently omitted (and, but, the, etc.), we have simply added the missing words.

In these notes for his orations Fisk did not punctuate in a consistent, formal manner. He probably felt that his pauses, inflections, and gestures would punctuate and clarify as periods and commas and other marshalling signs help clarify and separate thoughts in writing. We have introduced some punctuation for the sake of increased clarity and emphasis. These minor changes will not, we think, impose on or change Wilbur Fisk's message.

The Decoration Day address of May 31, 1891, is indeed an oration, in spite of Wilbur Fisk's modest but humorous assertion that he is incapable of an oration and its implied dignity and solemnity. But if purpose and feeling, solemnity and occasion are expressed in an oration, then Fisk's effort in this address warrants the term. Fisk sees the "strewn flowers" of Decoration Day as personal and national mourning and gratitude for those who fought and died in the cause of the Union. In the healing sense of union Fisk does not forget the Confederate dead. But the cause of the Union is emphatically present in his thoughts. Here there are recollections of battle, death, and rushed, expedient burial. But this is Decoration Day, and those in the rushed and shallow and expedient graves are hallowed in national tribute. Fisk's words are strewn on these graves.

"Time flies," states Fisk in his 1894 Decoration Day address, when he sees the graves of the Civil War veterans increasing. Now there are fewer men of the Grand Army of the Republic left to decorate the graves of their comrades, the comrades who were part of the critical years of American history of 1861 to 1865, when the men who stood for good, for the liberty planted in early seventeenth-century America, fought in fierce Armageddon against the men who stood for the evil of slavery, also planted in America in the seventeenth century. The soldiers of the Union saved this seed, this tree of liberty.

Fisk brings forward the political strife between North and South, describing the South's reckless decision for war and the long, cruel military contest between the North and the South that destroyed fields, farms, and homes and brought bitter suffering to soldiers and their families.

Fisk's address to the G.A.R. on August 22, 1894, does not have the solemn national review of the Decoration Day statements. It is indeed more a narrative than an oration. Here Fisk deliberately does not consider a long, solemn retrospect of our history or the gruesome conflicts of the war. Here is a story for the boys laughing in bivouac, the story of the pursued and slaughtered pig monopolistically devoured by Wilbur Fisk of Tunbridge, Vermont, and Nelson Fassett of Jericho, Vermont. This is a story for the inner circle of veterans, for the boys in reunion.

These three orations were made by Fisk twenty-six and twenty-nine years after the Civil War, and in his statements we return to the young soldier who wrote his letters to Vermont and ultimately to the world. We see the soldier in bivouac, on the march, on picket, and on the battlefield. And then we see Wilbur Fisk past his fiftieth year recalling his life and America's history and attempting to interpret and judge, asking what happened in our history and what was this fierceness in battle. Was there no other resolution in the name of Union and Freedom? Here we have Wilbur Fisk, then and now.

Emil Rosenblatt

Oration
Decoration Day, Alden, Minnesota
May 31, 1891

Mr. President, Ladies and Gentlemen,
Fellow Citizens and Comrades—

I told your program committee that I would not make an oration to-day. And I think I will keep my word. There are some gifted people who can talk about the deep principles which underlie the events which have called us together to-day and they can do it with language so clear, so forcible and so eloquent that what they say may fittingly be called by so dignified title as oration. But I have not the ability to do that and if I had the ability I have not the time to prepare anything which might properly be called by such a name. But I am pleased with the honor you have put upon me in giving me the first place among all those who are to follow me in speaking to-day. It is very easy for an old soldier in the presence of his comrades to talk—in fact they cannot help talking. If I bring into my remarks any personal reminiscences, it is not because I think my experience any more remarkable than others, but because I know the experience of one is the example of all.

It is a beautiful custom which has sprung up of decorating soldiers' graves, not because soldiers are any braver or better than other people but because it calls to mind those days which can never be forgotten and because it has become a tribute to the memory of those who sacrificed their lives for the country's welfare. Law does not compel us to observe the day but all over the land the wheels of business are stopped and the people gather to-gether to suitably commemorate the day. It is a spontaneous act which shows the patriotism and loyalty of the people to the country they love and their gratitude to those who have helped to preserve it.

The custom of decorating the soldiers' graves we are told began with the South. Immediately after the close of the war, the Southern ladies went out and strewed flowers over the graves of the Confederate dead, and it was flashed over the North that flowers were distributed impartially over the graves of the Union soldiers as well as Confederate, many of which were unmarked and unknown. This touched a tender chord in the hearts of the North. It did much to allay sectional strife and animosity. Many a bereaved household where a son, a father or a husband had gone forth to the war to return no more and whose final resting place was not definitely known, heard of this and the thought came to them, "Perhaps it was our darling." Then the North said, "We will do the same." So upon a set day the soldiers' graves in the national cemeteries were strewn with flowers, and the Confederate graves were not neglected.

A large number of those gathered in our national cemeteries are marked unknown. Forty-six per cent of the whole number could not be identified. In these cemeteries there are 318,176 and of these 146,874 are unknown. It was the original design to strew flowers upon the graves of these men who perished in the war, but the generosity and patriotism of the people have extended the custom until it includes all soldiers who have died not only in the war and because of the war but those who have died since. And the day is not simply for those who mourn; it is the common heritage of all.

But we do not make this a day of funeral solemnity. In the army when a comrade died we marched with slow and solemn step to the grave, but as soon as the hollowed earth had been filled we went back to our tents keeping step to a lively tune. Not that we had ceased to remember our comrade but there were duties before us which demanded that we should not [be] depressed by sorrow but that we should take them up heartily and cheerfully as our deceased comrade would have done if he were living. So to-day while we in a suitable manner pay a tribute to the memory of those who by their sacrifice and heroism have given us the national blessings we possess, we will enter into the enjoyment of these blessings in an appropriate and becoming manner but heartily and joyously.

The strewing of flowers upon the graves as we have done to-day reminds me of some things which I wish to speak of. In the first place I am reminded of the fact that every great and important blessing we enjoy has been purchased at a costly price. Great sacrifices have been made for every liberty secured. Go back to the time of the securing of the great charter when kings were compelled to rule by some sort of law instead of according to their own despotic will. It was a bloody struggle which the Barons of Runnymede had with the reluctant King John before that right to the people would be acknowledged. Our forefathers came to this country to find an asylum from religious persecution. Driven from England to Holland and finding no congenial place there they set sail for America in summer of 1620. They landed at Plymouth Rock in December. Their sufferings and privations were great—how great they were may be known from the fact that just one-half of their number perished the first winter. Out of 102, 51 died and their graves were leveled down so that the Indians might not mistrust how weakened the colony had become. Afterward came the War of the Revolution when the feeble struggling colonies fought for and obtained their independence and we became free from a foreign [power]. Still the question whether we were a nation or an assemblage of nations had yet to be decided and the deeper moral question whether human slavery should be perpetuated as a national institution. To settle this question for all time and give us that place among the nations which we now occupy and the blessings of liberty which we all now enjoy, more than a million men have laid down their lives on one side or the other and more than $12,000,000,000 worth of property destroyed.

Another thing I am reminded of by the strewing of these flowers on the soldiers' graves and that is whenever this nation has called for help the help has come—when men and money have been asked for, the men and money have been forthcoming. When Abraham Lincoln called for troops to put down the rebellion, the men enlisted for the war faster than the Government could equip them. And it was bloody work to which they went. Now I see before [me] a large number of children who cannot remember back to the days of the war. I want to tell you of the first soldiers' graves I saw dug—that is the first I saw on a battlefield on a very large scale. There had been skirmishes before and some of our boys had been killed and I had seen them buried, but this was at the first great battle where a large number were killed and had to be buried right there. It is called in your history the Battle of Williamsburg. It is on the Peninsula. I suppose these children know what a peninsula is—a portion of land almost surrounded by water. This is a strip of land between the York and James Rivers and these rivers are so wide at the mouth that they call the strip of land between them the Peninsula. At the extreme end of this Peninsula is Old Point Comfort where Fortress Monroe is situated. In the spring of '62 our army marched from their winter camp towards Richmond by way of Manassas, but the difficulty of taking the rebel capitol that way seemed so great that General McClellan determined to go by the way of the Peninsula. So the whole Army of the Potomac went to Fortress Monroe and advanced up the Peninsula. We first met the enemy at Warwick Creek which runs across this Peninsula and empties into York River at Yorktown. They were on one side of this creek and we were on the other. We charged across this creek and tried to drive them from their position but we couldn't. So we commenced there a regular siege conducted on scientific principles. An immense line of breastworks was thrown up there so strong that it didn't seem as if all the artillery in the world could take it. We were digging ditches and throwing up breastwork for about a month. The morning dawned when we were to make the attack when lo and behold there was no enemy there. We felt a little jubilant marching right up by where the enemy had their breastworks partly concealed behind the trees and where we had hardly dared to look before. We didn't know whether to be glad or sorry. We knew we must meet them sometime. We marched all that day and part of the next before we came up to them. The rain was pouring all day. We were on a steep hillside or rather under a high bluff covered with trees and underbrush. In front of us, perhaps a mile and a half away, was the enemy's Fort Magruder. The fight was going on all day long. Occasionally a shell from the enemy would come screeching over our heads. We could hear the splutter of the musketry. Heavy fighting was going on. Now I don't suppose these boys ever heard any musketry firing in actual battle. Well, I will tell you just how it sounds. It sounds, when it is a good ways off so that you can just hear it, like popping corn. If you have a large popper full of pop corn over a good fire so that it will pop good, it will sound just like that. Of course when the musketry is right close by it sounds much louder than popping corn. It would almost deafen you then. We took no part in this. We were waiting for the order to come and expecting any moment to be ordered in. So we were just sitting there on our knapsacks with our rubber blankets drawn up over our heads and looking like a flock of half drowned turkeys. Here and there was a fire which some of the boys had kept agoing in spite of the rain, and every once in a while a soldier would pour some water from his canteen into his coffee cup and hold it over this fire until it boiled, or one would take a piece of meat and stick it on the end of a long stick and hold it in the fire until it was cooked. The boys did this not so much because they were hungry or were needing a cup of coffee just then but it helped to pass away the time. But we weren't ordered in to the fight that day. Just before night it stopped raining and a comrade and myself went onto the battlefield where we had heard so much musketry firing to see what had been done. We found them burying the dead. Here I saw one grave in to which were put 12 men all from one Company. They only dug it about 18 inches deep and the men were laid side by side. I don't remember the number of the regiment but I know it was Company B. and it was a New Jersey regiment. They were just laid in there with their clothes on, the cape of their overcoats thrown over their faces. A piece of a cracker box was stuck up at the head on which was the name, Company and Regiment, and then it was covered over with dirt. Unless those bodies were taken up and removed soon I don't see how they could be identified. Away out there in the woods where cattle and hogs were roaming about it would seem as if it must be impossible to ever find half of those that were buried there with any certainty.

We went back to our Company. We were ordered back from this bluff where we had been all day and when the line was reformed our place was in a cornfield. It began to rain again. The water was standing between the rows of corn, but here we must make our camp for the night and be ready at a moment's notice to fall in for active service. The prospect for the night wasn't very pleasant. There was a pile of rails not far off and I managed to secure three of them for a bed. But I found I couldn't sleep on a bed of three rails. That third rail was right in the way. So I took the two largest ones and put them together, put my woolen blanket on them and with my rubber blanket over me tried to get a little sleep. If any of these boys are ever soldiers, and ever have to sleep in a muddy cornfield and there is a pile of rails to make a bed of, don't try to use three rails. That third rail will make you say some bad words unless you are an unusually good boy. You will find two a great deal better. Well, I laid myself down there and I thought of my father and mother at the old home in Vermont. I thought of my sister at work in Lowell, Massachusetts. I thought of my wife—she wasn't my wife then, but I used to think of her once in a while just the same, and I thought of what was going to take place on the morrow. For those boys who had fought so bravely and had lost so many, had not beaten the enemy nor captured that fort. But the next morning was bright and clear. We had one sharp fight with what proved to be their rear guard and then the way was clear for entering into Williamsburg.

I started to speak of the willingness of the country to make sacrifices when called upon and I think the army illustrated it here.

But I am reminded also upon this day that there were other dangers to which a soldier was exposed besides the danger of sickness and death. There are moral dangers in the camp that are to be dreaded and the true soldier had to guard against. We were away from home and away from the restraints of society and in regard to many things could do as we pleased without any fear of public opinion. No man knows how much he is dependent upon others for the moral uprightness upon which he may pride himself. A man may be tempted to do a great many things in such circumstances that he would never think of doing at home and would never think he wants to do when he was with his friends. Men that at home do not drink and do not want to, feel a sort of mania when they are in a camp to know how it seems to be a little intoxicated. And they like to try a little gambling and the thousand little dissipating things that they would look down upon at home seem to have a wonderful attraction for them in camp. And then they are away from the privileges of woman's society. Someone has said that Woman carried civilization in her heart. A man that lives in a community where he has the privileges of woman's society becomes more refined than he is aware of, but when he is away from that the very best of men will degenerate or at least they will feel the deprivation. Then there is the entirely different way in which we live. The soldiers are their own cooks and seamstresses and washerwomen. They do not sit down to table and social intercourse as they did at home. I don't know how much religious influence there may be in clean clothes and a clean face but I am sure there is a very strong moral influence there. Cleanliness is next to godliness, and when all these things are neglected they beget carelessness and rudeness and a man drifts towards barbarism unless he has a settled purpose to resist these and counteract them. And in the fact that in the army sometimes tremendous exertions must be put forth for a short space of time followed by long intervals in which there is not much to do, makes army life susceptible of moral dangers. Along the wharves in our large cities where vessels are unloaded and where men can find employment only at intervals, you will find those who are the most demoralized and dangerous. We may sometimes rebel against the idea of being tied constantly to our business but continuous labor is the best thing for us. Satan finds some mischief still for idle hands to do. And then war is a place of physical violence. Sherman very truly says it is hell on earth. We must constantly see men killed, see men wounded and dying. To look upon these things and not be hardened into indifference by them is a difficult thing but I think men can do it and have done it. Those soldiers who had stamina of character, purpose and will to stand against all these influences came out of the army morally stronger than when [they] went in. I suppose it is true that some were morally wrecked by going into the army. They lacked the will power to resist the demoralizing tendencies to which they were exposed. They carried no heart, no faith into the work and they were swept down by the current. But there were others and by far the greater number who were made more manly, had a greater hatred of cruelty, more tenderness toward suffering and were every way more of a man after going into the army than before. When I hear anybody say the old soldiers are only a set of bummers, that they left their principles down on the southern soil if they ever had any, he is only picking out here and there an exceptional case and trying to make it appear to be the rule. No, when I hear a man say that a soldier has lost anything of his manhood, is any less of a man any way for his service in the army, I feel like turning to him and saying, "Sir, you talk exactly as I do when I am trying to lie about somebody."

Once more I am reminded by these soldiers' graves that war is sometimes right. It seems ridiculous that men in civilized [countries] can find no other way to settle their disputes only by standing up and shooting at one another. Here is one party in line of battle and there is another in another line of battle and because they cannot settle their differences any other way they must shoot at one another until one side or the other cries Enough. Certainly Christian people ought to settle their disputes some other way. When they have done their killing there remains the question to be settled the same as before. They might as well have settled it before the shooting as afterwards. I hope the time will come when war shall be among the things that are past, when men shall beat swords into plowshares and their spears into pruning hooks and learn war no more. For that I am willing to labor and preach and pray. I believe that time will come sometime but it hasn't come yet. When the old flag was fired upon it was the duty of every patriot to see that its authority was restored. To have done otherwise would have been cowardice. Had we allowed the rebellion to have succeeded the government would have been split into two sections. Soon the East and West would have disagreed and further dismemberment would have taken place. Instead of one nation there would have been several different nations with their mutual rivalries and jealousies, and disagreement and hostility would have been the result. The glory of this Republic would have gone forever and with it the hope of other nations besides our own, for other nations are being inspired by our example to seek for the same popular liberty we enjoy.

But there was one fellow in our Company that thought it wrong to fight under any circumstances. The command was "Thou shalt not kill" and it admitted of no exceptions. He was a Quaker; he had been drafted. He came to our regiment just before that terrible battle in the Wilderness. He said he should go in with the rest and be shot at but he would not shoot back. If he fired at all it would be over the heads of the enemy so as to be sure and not hurt them. I tried to reason with him but it was of no use. He was conscientious and thoroughly fixed in his principles. Well, he went into battle with us. It was a terribly destructive one for us. We fought for three hours and they seemed to me to be the longest three hours I ever experienced. I believe there must have been some fighting Joshua somewhere that had commanded the Sun to stand still and it had obeyed him. Both armies seemed to have been advancing at the same time and the collision was unexpected to both. We lost our Colonel and Lieutenant Colonel and Captain. My own tentmate was shot through the head there. I had drunk from the same canteen with him many a time and slept under the same blanket hundreds of times. I had a cap shot off my head which I have still preserved—about the only relic of the war I have. I fired my 60 rounds of cartridges. I fired my old Springfield until I could not get the ball down onto the powder and then I exchanged it for another. We all felt that we must do our best to hold that ground. But where was my peaceful friend all this while? I suppose he was there, but if he fired at all he fired over the heads of the enemy. He did not hurt any of them. He was a good conscientious Christian man but I was glad there [weren't] any more like him on our side. If he would have gone over on to the other side and done some missionary work there converting the rebels to his way of thinking I could have wished him Godspeed in his work. No, the war was on us and it was right. It was duty to fight until the enemy of the flag should lay down their arms. It would have been a great wrong to have submitted to this Government broken into fragments with its prestige destroyed. Its honor would have perished with it.

I am reminded too that these Grand Army reunions will soon be things of the past. The number of the soldiers' graves will be increased and the number of the old soldiers will be diminished. The Grand Army from the very nature of its organization cannot long survive. The qualifications for becoming a member of it cannot be acquired now. It is not self-perpetuating like other organizations. Its term of life is limited to the life time of its present members. But as long as there are any of us left we are going to get to-gether and talk over those old times which we can never forget.

If there is any man here that thinks our Government is doing too much in the way of pensions, I have a word of comfort for him. The pensioners are dropping from the list very fast. Now and then there is a man dissatisfied because so much money is being taken from the U.S. Treasury to pay pensions. I know the amount is enormous. It runs high up into the millions. The entire credit of the Government when the war broke out would not pay one year's pensions now. No other Government ever dealt so bountifully with their soldiers as our Government is doing. One reason for this is no doubt because no other government could ever afford to do as well as ours can. I don't think the climax of expenditure is reached quite yet. The new law brought in thousands of fresh claimants. Whoever is laboring under a physical disability does not now have to prove that it originated in the army. If he is disabled in any way except by his own vicious habits he gets help. This takes an enormous amount of money. But the highest point of expense will soon be attained and then the annual amount paid will decrease very fast. Over 20,000 old pensioners were dropped from the list last year, mustered out by death. More will probably go next year. So it isn't very long so large a sum will have to be paid.

———————

Oration delivered at
Alden, Minnesota, Decoration Day,
May 30, 1894

Mr. President, Comrades, Ladies and Gentlemen—

Our Post made a bad mistake in the arrangements for to-day. I was opposed to it so my skirts are clear. Decoration Day doesn't come only once in a year and I was in favor of having some speaker from abroad who could speak of the themes suggested by the day with eloquence, force and impressiveness. But the boys thought we could get along with home talent all right and they outvoted me. The fact is times are hard. It costs something to get a regular speaker and they thought we had better do the talking ourselves and save expense. It was a bad mistake but inasmuch as they gave me the honor to lead off and have all the time, I won't be too hard in my criticisms.

Our thoughts naturally go back to-day to those other days that we can never forget. It hardly seems possible that 30 odd years have rolled over our heads since the war cloud was upon us, that a whole generation have been born, grown to manhood and womanhood since the states were engaged in that mortal struggle with each other. Time flies. When the graves of the soldiers are decorated we are reminded that the number is increasing and soon there will be none of the old soldiers remaining to carry the flowers to the graves of their departed comrades.

I have been thinking of the winter of '60 and '61. It seems only a short time ago. I remember well the gloom and uncertainty of that period. State after state was seceding, a provisional government was formed at Montgomery, Alabama, afterwards removed to Richmond. Another government was being formed within our government, our nation was falling to pieces and there seemed to be no help for it. If they wanted to go what right had we to compel them to stay and of what use would they be to us if their sympathies were not with us. If I talk here to-day I shall probably have much to say of myself. I do this not because I imagine I had a remarkable experience. I think my experience was a tame one. I never tried to make a display of my bravery; I had no bravery to display. I did what I had to do; I didn't try to do any more. I shall allude to my experience, to things which came under my own personal observation because it is easier to talk about things you have seen and are familiar with than it is to talk about things you don't know about although the things you don't know about may be a great deal more important than the things you do know about.

Our interest during the winter of '61 centered particularly around the little fort in Charleston harbor, South Carolina. November 25, 1860, Major Robert Anderson had been appointed by Secretary Floyd commander of the defences of Charleston. He was appointed because he was supposed to be in sympathy with the southern movement or at least would not hinder it. He was a Kentuckyian by birth, a pro-slavery man, and Buchanan's Secretary of War thought he could depend upon him, but he was a United States officer and he felt it his duty to obey the instructions of the general government. He occupied at first Fort Moultrie but he found himself so surrounded by secessionists that his situation not only became unpleasant but dangerous. They had more guard duty than they could attend to, so much so that General Doubleday in his account says that his wife and Captain Seymour had upon one or two occasions to relieve them. All they had to do was to give the alarm if any hostile demonstration was made against them. On the 26th of December, just at dusk, Major Anderson changed his position from Fort Moultrie to Fort Sumter. Here the sea was all around him and he could better protect himself against the enemy. The change was made very quietly. The citizens did not know it till morning. When they found out what Major Anderson had done and knew that he had done it to protect the interests of the U.S. Government, they were furious, but there was no help for it.

Major Anderson had taken with him but little in the way of provisions for his company of 75 men including the band. Supplies would have to be sent or he would soon be compelled to evacuate. The U.S. hesitated to send relief because they knew it would irritate the people and precipitate the war. But on the 9th of January, a vessel was sent to their relief. It had been fitted out secretly but the South got wind of it and when the *Star of the West*, an unarmed merchant vessel, sailed by Fort Moultrie, it was fired upon. Fort Sumter did not reply. Major Anderson was reluctant to do anything that [would] bring on war. He was hoping all the time that some compromise would be made so that war might [be prevented]. He did not believe the South could ever be conquered. The *Star of the West*, finding that she was not defended and having no guns of her own, could not do otherwise than to put out to sea. So Fort Sumter got no relief. On the morning when the fort was attacked the garrison had for their breakfast only salt pork and water. Their supplies of bread of every kind was exhausted. The gun that was fired upon the *Star of the West* was really the first gun of the war but was not so considered. January wore away. February came and went, the cloud of war growing darker all the while. The 4th of March came and in spite of conspiracies to prevent it Abraham Lincoln was inaugurated President of the United States. The 12th day of April came and upon that morning at half past four o'clock General Beauregard opened fire upon Fort Sumter. He had notified Major Anderson that unless he evacuated he should commence action at that time. Fort Sumter did not reply till half past seven that morning. All day the cannonading was kept up and during the night. The next day the fort took fire from the red hot shot that was fired upon them. The magazine was endangered, the flag had been shot down but was immediately raised again. At noon, the men being out of provisions, out of ammunition as the magazine had to be closed, the fire raging in the fort, Major Anderson surrendered. On the 14th the flag was taken down after being saluted with 50 guns and the garrison were permitted to withdraw. It is a singular fact that though the flag was rent and torn by shot and shell not one star was shot out of it.

I remember when the news of that fighting came to the little town where I lived in Vermont. I was in the Post Office with some other young men to inquire for the news. The postmaster, an aged man appointed under Buchanan's administration and fully in sympathy with it, said almost with tears in his eyes, "The war has begun. I was in hopes something could have been done to have prevented it," and he spoke as if he felt there was an awful calamity brooding over the nation. We boys who loved excitement did not take it so seriously as he did. We were ready to shout hurrah because now there would be a chance to teach the South a lesson but we didn't realize how much it would cost us to teach it.

I had a Cousin Edgar. His father's farm joined my father's. We were about the same age, I being a little the oldest. We played together when we were just big enough to toddle around. We quarreled together, pulled one another's hair I don't know how many times, we blacked one another's eyes more than once. I know that upon one occasion I should have got a whipping from my father for getting into a fight with Edgar after he had told me not to if I hadn't been so badly punished that he thought I'd had enough of it. Well, I liked him all the better after that, had more respect for him than I did before, just as I believe the South has more respect for the North since the drubbing we gave them than they had before. My cousin enlisted immediately after the fall of Sumter with the three months men [and] was at Bull Run. After his return I remember how decided he was in the belief that you can never conquer the South. They were so united, so determined, so bitter in their hatred of the North he believed they would never yield to them. They would fight till the last man was killed; they would never give up. When their armies were scattered they would fight behind trees and stumps, keep up a guerilla warfare forever. My cousin was a brave man and was ready to do his part. It wasn't cowardice that made him think the South could not be beaten. He enlisted after this in another regiment, was color bearer, and fell in that ill-fated campaign under Burnside on Fredericksburg Heights. His widowed mother tried to recover his body but could not succeed. She sent three delegations down there, using nearly all the little means she had, to recover the body but the difficulties in the way of getting him through the lines were so great that they could not get him though they found the body and identified [it]. So the mother never had the sad satisfaction of knowing where he was buried or of being permitted to visit the grave of her boy. I hope somebody to-day will place a wreath of flowers on that grave for he was worthy of it.

I enlisted September 5th, 1861. The captain of the company that went from our town in the First Regiment and served three months, then came back and [was] reorganized into the Second Regiment, had come from the front to get more recruits for his company. My brother was attending school and could not well leave. I was working out by the month on a farm and could leave just as well as not. I had no excuse that I felt would justify and I thought in after years I should regret it if I did not listen to the country's call and become one of her defenders. A young man working on the farm adjoining the man's farm where I was working said he would put down his name if I would. We did so along with some 20 others and were soon on the way to Washington. We went into camp for the winter about 12 miles from Washington. Here we put up our A tents and spent the winter comfortably. These little tents were about 6 feet square and made room enough for four soldiers. We dug down about 18 inches, banked the dirt all around the tent to keep out the cold. Two of us had our bunks raised from the ground. They were made of poles and slats and made us a place to sit during the day. The other two made their beds on the [ground] between these two. We had also a fireplace dug out of the middle of one side with a chimney made of sticks laid up cob house fashion and plastered with mud on the inside. Here we ate and slept, read newspapers, told stories, wrote letters to the girls we left behind us and had a good time. We had our guard duties, our regular drills, and we were rapidly becoming inured to military life. On the 10th of March,

1862, we broke camp to advance on the enemy. It was a little too early, but the North was getting impatient. The newspapers were speaking derisively of General McClellan's masterly inactivity. "All quiet on the Potomac." It was too quiet to suit the Northern newspaper press so the order came to move. The things for our comfort that we had accumulated at Camp Griffin, much of it sent from home, we made bonfires of. Only those things that we could carry in our knapsacks could we take with us. It was a cold raw day when we started out. We marched towards Manassas, travelling all day long. We went across the old battlefield of Bull Run. I don't know how many miles we made but I know my shoulders ached under my knapsack. It was about 60 pounds we had to carry. It was a raw disagreeable night when we went into camp. We had our shelter tents, little pieces of cloth five feet square with a row of buttons and button holes all around it. Two or more of us could join together and make a tent larger or smaller as it suited us. I lay down and tried to sleep but I couldn't. It was too cold. I slept awhile then got up and walked around. I went to the camp fires that were burning all around and tried to warm myself there, then back again to get some more sleep. Before morning I had to get up the second time. I was chilled through. I began to think I wasn't going to make much of a soldier. If I couldn't stand that what would I do before the war was over. I began to think I was too far away from home. Well, there is no use for me to stand here and lie about it. If I could have got away I would have gone home that morning and let the country go to the dogs.

But going home was out of the question. The next day we marched to Manassas and saw the wooden guns that had frightened us all winter and then came the order to go to Alexandria and take boats for Fortress Monroe, and we were to advance on the enemy by the way of the Peninsula. As Mr. Lincoln said, it was only shifting the difficulty—it was not overcoming it. The difficulty he referred to being Lee's army. We started towards Alexandria and I remember just a few nights after this how it rained. It rained all the afternoon and the greater part of the night. We think it rains here in Minnesota but if we want to find a place where it can keep pouring till it creates a flood you will find it in the Atlantic states, especially in Virginia. That night we pitched our tent on a side hill and after we had got fairly laid down we discovered a brook was running directly through our tent. The little ditches around the tent were full. Of course sleeping was out of the question but what could we do? There were no camp fires for the rain had put them all out. The outlook wasn't pleasant. There happened to be a pile of brush near the tent and we piled our tent full of that and climbed upon it and it kept us out of the water in pretty good shape. In the morning we had to start on our march again but I was too stiff and wet and cross to know or care where we were going. Well, I was earning $13 a month and my board and was under a contract with Uncle Sam to serve him three years on those terms but if I could have thrown up my contract then I would and hunted me up a job somewhere where I could have had better lodgings. We went to Alexandria, thence to Fortress Monroe, advanced up the Peninsula to within 5 miles of Richmond. We crossed the Chickahominy, fought the battle of Fair Oaks. Afterwards we had the seven days fighting when we fell back to Harrison's Landing. Afterwards we came to Alexandria again. Then came the 2nd Bull Run, then South Mountain and Antietam and that finished up the campaign for that summer. In the winter was the fruitless advance under Burnside at Fredericksburg. The next summer we had Chancellorsville and Gettysburg. The next, Wilderness, Spottsylvania, Cold Harbor, Petersburg, Shenandoah Valley, Appomattox. Then the regiment came home. We had 220 killed in our regiment by rebel balls, 613 wounded, 866 in the regiment in the first place.

Well, the war is over and we rejoice. To-day we place the flowers upon the soldiers' graves. This is not to be a funeral occasion exactly. With reverent hands we place a wreath of flowers upon the graves of those who gave their lives into their country's hands in her time of need. To-day there will be large demonstrations in our national cemeteries where are buried thousands that were slain by the enemy's hand. But we are not to consider those who fell in the service as being the most unfortunate ones. Perhaps in the eternal ages of the future it may be found that their lives served a better purpose than those of us who survived. One who is the best authority in these things and in fact is the only one who could speak with authority has said that he that loveth his life shall lose it but he that hateth his life shall keep it unto life eternal. The idea is if we love this life, the pleasures of this life and give all our strength to securing them, it will be found in the end that we have missed the true end of life while those who regard principle and duty more than life and would be willing to sacrifice their lives that the principles may prevail or the duties be done, such ones will find in the end that they have truly saved their lives. I think we can see an exemplification of this in the case of our soldiers. There are the thousands who lost their lives in bravely defending the country's flag. This year and next year the story of their lives will be told. As long as we are a nation and have history so long will their deeds be mentioned and their lives held up for a pattern. Their memories will never be allowed to perish. While those of us who hid behind stumps and trees and came off with a whole skin will die by and by and be forgotten. We may find out we didn't so really and truly save our lives as those who gave them up in the defense of their country.

We may make this a glad day. We have many things to be thankful for. First, we may be thankful that there was so much patriotism latent in the country. We didn't know that it existed until the occasion called it out. When the states were seceding the ablest minds could see no way of preventing them, but when the flag was fired upon, instantly the objections cleared up. The shot and shell that were showered around the flag on that fort had more of persuasiveness in it, more convincing logic about it than the finest theories which the best minds North or South could devise. Constitutional objections vanished into thin air then, the Constitution itself was in danger and thank God there was patriotism enough to meet the shock and enough to carry the war through. And then we may thank God we had such leaders as were given us. Lincoln, a man of the people, conscientious, far-sighted, sagacious man. Grant, who never complained that he was not properly supported, never feared the enemy outnumbered him, always did the best he could with the forces at his command and never was defeated. Then there were Sherman, Thomas, Sheridan, Hancock and hosts of others. It took some time to find the true men. At first it seemed as if our leaders were thinking of their future political prospects rather than saving the country. They were too careful not to exasperate the enemy and the war dallied but the right men were found, men of iron, men who had but two words in their creed, *victory* or *annihilation*, men who saw that slavery was the cause of the war, the seat of the whole disease and who were ready to handle it without gloves. Then success came. Then we may be thankful too that the South held out as tenaciously as she did. Had the South made any concessions toward peace during the first three years of the war, she could have had almost [any] terms she might have asked short of going out of the Union. Slavery itself might have been restored on condition of their laying down their arms. The concessions we would have made them would have been a source of embarrassment to us for all time to come. How near we came to it we have only to consult the popular vote when Mr. Lincoln was elected the second time. There was a large party that wanted to stop the effusion of blood and McClellan was nominated on what was called a peace platform. We say he was overwhelmingly defeated and so he was so far as the electoral vote was concerned but the popular vote was not so large against him. He got 45 percent of the vote, 45 to Mr. Lincoln's 55 and this after the victories of the Wilderness, after the fall of Atlanta, after Sheridan had driven Early out of the Shenandoah Valley. But the South would accept no terms, they were determined to fight it out to the end. So slavery was swept away, and with their military strength destroyed the South was obliged to accept such terms as the North saw fit to give them.

There are important lessons that we are to learn from this conflict. First, that whatsoever a man sows that must he reap and he not only reaps what he sows but he must reap all he sows. When we plant a seed of good or of evil we are hardly aware how large a tree may grow from it or how much fruit it may bear. When I stand before a [Sunday School Convocation] I love to speak of the little seed sown by Robert Raikes more than a hundred years [ago]. He little knew how mighty a plant would grow from it or how great its influence would be. When Francis E. Clark, pastor of the Williston church in Portland, Maine, organized his young people into a society for Christian Endeavor he little realized to what an extent it would grow. When the Pilgrims landed on the coast of New England in 1620 they did not realize how much their coming there meant for this country. They had suffered oppression in the old country. They would plant the tree of liberty here. They were austere, too strict and severe perhaps but they were a conscientious God-fearing people and if they erred at all it was on the safe side. Their church parish was the town and from their parish meetings we get our town meeting. The Reverend Thomas Hooker of Hartford maintained that the people not only had a right to elect their rulers but also to limit their powers. His hearers put this into the state constitution in 1629. Other states copied after it. What the people could do for a state it was afterwards proposed to do for a nation and Thomas Jefferson got his idea of a national constitution from one of these early Pilgrim churches.

But at the same time the Pilgrims were sowing the seed from which we have reaped such a bountiful harvest there was being sowed a seed, an entirely different sort, further south. A slave trading vessel went up the James River with a cargo of slaves and sold them to the planters there about the same time the Pilgrims came over with their Bibles. So slavery was planted and it bore an altogether different kind of fruit. No one dreamed of the harvest there would be. No one looked upon it with approval. When the Constitution of the U.S. was framed it was carefully worded as to slavery. While it protected those who then held slaves it was so framed that when slavery passed away as everybody expected it would have to, no change [was] made in its terms. But slavery didn't die out, it grew. In 1820 the Slave Power wanted more territory and they told the nation that if they would let them have Missouri they wouldn't ask for any more slave states north of 36° 30' but they broke the compromise when they made it for nearly all of Missouri is north of that line. In 1845 they wanted Texas and the war with Mexico was fought. In 1850 they wanted the North to hunt their slaves for them and the Fugitive Slave Law was passed. So it became a crime to harbor any poor slave who was guilty of no crime only that he loved liberty and guided by the north star towards the Queen's dominions he was trying to find a place where he might enjoy his inalienable right of life, liberty and pursuit of happiness. Then in 1854 they wanted Kansas and Nebraska and the Missouri Compromise was repealed. So this seed had made such stalwart growth that it seemed to possess the nation. Everything yielded to it. And I think it would have continued to grow if it hadn't been for the war. The slave trade would have been established again before this. Why not? If I had been a slaveholder in Mississippi or Louisiana I am sure I would have wanted the slave trade. It cost a thousand dollars apiece on the average to get them from the more northern states when they could be brought from Africa for $300 apiece. And it would be just as humane to bring them from the wilds of Africa and domesticate them on the plantations of the Gulf as to bring them from the more northern of the southern states. And then instead of being the leading nation in liberty we should have taken first rank in oppression. How arrogant the Slave Power became. It was their right and they would stand up for their God given right and sneer at any conscientious scruples against it. It makes me think of the farmer in Maine who had never been in one of our big cities. He was going to Boston. "Why, Uncle Jonathan you will get run over in those narrow, crooked, crowded streets." "Oh, I can take care of myself." And if there was one virtue that he possessed more than another it was self confidence and pertinacity. He went and came back. " Well, did you get run over?" "You bet I didn't. I wasn't afraid. I noticed everybody else was afraid of the teams and kept on the side walks but I walked right down in the middle of the street. I had just as good right there as any of them. I saw one of those electric cars come bobbing along but I didn't care for it when they got most to where I was they pounded the gong and shouted get off the track but I didn't budge an inch and before it got to where I was the blamed thing stopped. They didn't dare to run over me. All you have to do when you go to Boston is to stand up for your rights." Well, that is what these slave holders were doing—they were standing up for their rights and the car of human progress and liberty had to stop.

We learn too that sin and wrong doing are costly things. Who can tell how much the war cost? Whole states were devastated and nearly half of the assessable property of the country was destroyed. But that doesn't tell it all. Go into the homes of those who fell and see the sorrow occasioned there and you know something. (Story of Charley Smith's death in the Wilderness). He was the only son and the only child of his parents. Multiply that by thousands of others when you are counting the cost. Sin and wrong are always costly things in the end and it seems to be ordained that full and exact payments have to be made. Every drop of blood taken from the back of a black man as Mr. Lincoln intimated in his inaugural had to be paid back by one drawn by the sword from the white man and all that was accumulated by those years of unrequited toil on the part of the slave was more than squandered during the war. And the suffering doesn't always come on the guilty ones. It seems to be ordained that the innocent shall not only suffer with the guilty but often suffer for them.

We learn too that war [is] unnatural. After the fight near Bank's Ford we had driven the enemy from the crest of the hill and repulsed their charge. Lieutenant Hayward says to me let's go and take a look of the field. We went some 40 rods from our position when we came to a good-looking wounded rebel soldier. We gave him a drink. "Will you do me a favor?" "Yes," says the Lieutenant. "I will do anything for you I can." "You are probably the last man I shall have a chance to speak to." He gave the Lieutenant his name and the name of his wife and her address. It was in Alabama. He gave him his pocket book and some letters. I don't remember what they all were. He gave him a locket in which was the portrait of his wife and two children. He wanted the Lieutenant to write the circumstances of his death. We shook hands with him and left. The line was moving to left—their right, and we would probably have to go into action again so we had no time to tarry. A few moments before that if I could have seen a shell fall into the rebel ranks and burst I would have swung my hat and shouted hurrah but I felt different then. To finish my story. Those things were sent to a Vermont Member of Congress and the Lieutenant got word back that they would be forwarded to destination under flag of truce the first opportunity. By the way that was Senator Morrill. He is in Congress now, has been there ever since. You see Vermont is one of those good old states that keep right on. She doesn't change her politics everytime the wind changes. When she has the right man in the right place she knows enough to keep him there. I always considered it one of the luckiest things that ever happened to me that I was born in that state of grand and noble men. Of course everybody couldn't be born there. You are not to blame, you have my sympathies, but I was one of the lucky ones that could.

The war is teaching us to look at things from the stand point of the other side. It is a little humiliating to take up a political paper and read what any party says of the opposite party. One would think all integrity and political honor was gone. The South didn't understand the North nor the North the South. The North thought it a monstrous thing to have property in flesh and blood, to separate families and keep a whole race in ignorance and subjection. The South was brought up in the midst of it. Many a humane master had a genuine attachment for a faithful and devoted slave. He cared for him and supplied his wants. The slave was proud to be called by the master's name and was contented and happy. The master thought the relation a heaven ordained one and felt that the North was meddling with what was none of their business when they tried to interfere. To the South it was a piece of impertinence that they could not tolerate. They thought the North were a set of fanatics that didn't know what they were trying to do. At City Point after the battles of the Wilderness one who had been a member of our company came into my tent and wanted to know if I knew a man by the name of Knox. I told him I did. "Well, there is a lady out here a few miles that would like to talk with you. Her husband is in the Army. His name is Knox and she says he has a brother in Vermont." I went out there. She talked about the war. It was awful. Not a family but had lost someone in those terrible battles under Grant in the Wilderness. She was a typical southern lady living on a large plantation. She thought it strange that intelligent men from the North should enlist in such a war against the South. "What did you come down here to fight us for? What will you do with the Negroes when you get them?" Oh, if we could only learn to see things from the other's stand point how much it would help us. I hope the time will come when if we cannot we will call in a third party and arbitrate.

First lesson of the war—faith. A country that has had the baptism we have is not going to ruin at once. The clouds will brighten. The powers that be are not all evil and the true and right will surely prevail. Let us each strive for it. A reformer was speaking upon the condition of the country, corruption of politicians, heartlessness of corporations, greed of millionaires, oppression of monopolies, &c. And now he says we will speak of reform and where shall I begin. A voice in the audience says, "begin at home."

Picnic Talk, G.A.R., at A. M. Johnson's Place
near Albert Lea, Minnesota,
August 22, 1894

Mr. President, Comrades, Ladies & Gentlemen—

I am not going to make a speech to-day I will just tell a soldier's story and let it go at that. We are all enjoying ourselves first rate. If I may be allowed to use an army phrase (and I guess this is a proper occasion to use army phrases) I would say we are having a *bully* good time. I can speak for the Alden Post. I know we enjoy the greetings given us by our comrades from the Albert Lea Post and the Glenville Post. We thought you were first rate comrades before and now we know it. We rejoice in this fellowship and greeting and the greeting too which comes to us from citizens who have honored us with their presence. We old soldiers on the platform, too, feel pretty good because we have a chance to spin some of our soldier yarns.

Well, I have been pumping my brains to fish up some thrilling adventure I had passed through, some hair breadth escape, some deed of bravery, that would make your hair stand on end, but for the life of me I can't think of anything of the sort. I guess I shall have to tell you how my comrade and I made a charge on a pig and captured him. It wasn't an event of quite as much national importance as the taking of Lee's army but it afforded us about as much satisfaction for the time being as that did. Some things are suggested by contraries. We have just had a bountiful picnic dinner. We have had every variety of food one could ask for but, boys, we remember times when we didn't have quite such a variety and yet we had a good meal. A comrade and I paid 12 1/2 cents apiece to a lady for making us some griddle cakes.

They were made of flour and water and salt, no other ingredient, wet up like paste and fried very thin—just as thin as she could make them stick together and she was pretty skilful at it and we had nothing to eat on them, but I have been to wedding feasts when they didn't seem half so good. It was a short time after the battle of Chancellorsville and before the battle of Gettysburg. We had been out to Chancellorsville and got neatly whipped, had come back this side of the Rappahannock and after resting a few weeks, there began to be considerable uneasiness as to the whereabouts of Lee's army. The authorities at Washington were fearful he had or would slip by us and move up through Maryland into Pennsylvania and tear up things generally in those places. Our division of the army was sent out through Dranesville and Leesburg and across the Shenandoah River into the Shenandoah Valley to see if he was there. We saw nothing of Lee and were ordered back. In crossing back through the river which was not very deep, my comrade and myself, partly through carelessness, got into a deep place and we got our haversacks all wet. The contents, principally hard tack, were thoroughly soaked. Well, what were we going to do for rations. We were a good way from our supplies. I don't know just how many days rations we had but our haversacks were stuffed full and there was no prospect of our having more for some time. Well, what were we going to do for supper and breakfast. You know boys how soon hardtack will lose its good flavor—if it ever had any, by being soaked in water. That night we were on picket and towards morning somebody started up a pig. Now there are some that think that about all the soldiers at the front did was to kill chickens and pigs and sheep and have a good time foraging generally but it is a fact I never captured nor helped to capture half dozen chickens during all the war. My disposition was good enough for it but the fact was there were more soldiers than there were chickens on the Potomac and it wasn't long before they were all gobbled up before the Potomac Army had been there a year. Occasionally we captured a big rabbit—sometimes with wool and sometimes with bristles. McClellan had forbidden foraging on our own hook for sheep or pigs. It was early in the morning in the short nights of June when this pig was discovered. The whole of the picket reserve took after him. We chased him and we chased him. You needn't tell of it but I suspect we ran faster after that pig than we ever did towards the enemy. How fast we may have run the other way we will discuss some other time. But the pig seemed to be too much for us. Nearly all the boys gave it up but my comrade wouldn't give up. He was determined to have the pig. Like the Irishman that was going to commit suicide he would hang himself or perish in the attempt, so my comrade would have that pig or perish in the attempt. He was a short-legged fellow and when he stepped on one foot he swayed his body over to that side and when he stepped on to the other foot he would sway his body over on the other side. He waddled along like a fat duck. You would have died laughing to have seen him run. The boys always made fun of him whenever he attempted to go on a double quick. But he made out to get that pig all right. His legs were good enough for that. I had about given it up but he made a success of it. I thought I ought not to make fun of him any more. Speaking of his short legs reminds me of an old joke they tried to get off on Abraham Lincoln. It was in '58 when he and Stephen Douglas stumped the state of Illinois for the Senatorship. Mr. Douglas was a very short man and was known as the Little Giant while Mr. Lincoln as everybody knows was tall and lank. A couple of men come into Mr. Lincoln's law office and they say to him, "Mr. Lincoln, we have got into a dispute and we want your opinion to help us settle. My friend here thinks your legs are too long and that Mr. Douglas's are about right but I think your legs are the right length but Mr. Douglas's are too short. Now we would like your opinion upon it." "Well," said Mr. Lincoln, "I hadn't given the matter much thought but for an off hand opinion I would say that I think a man's legs are about right when they are long enough to reach from his body to the ground." Well, my comrade's legs were long enough to get him where that pig was and I should have felt ashamed to have made fun of him after that.

Well, we had the pig and until we were relieved from picket we had a precious treasure to guard. We were much more afraid that pig would be spirited away as such things sometimes happened than we were of being caught ourselves by the rebel army. When the relief came we carried that pig into camp. It was a pretty heavy load. My comrade would carry him for awhile and I would take his gun and knapsack and then I would take him and he would carry mine. I don't know how much he would weigh—a hundred pounds or so. We got him into camp and now what was to be done? No conveniences for scalding and dressing, or anything of that kind. But soldiers are not long hindered by such trifles. We skinned the hog in tolerable good shape and there we had a No. 1 dressed porker and we two boys just about starved. We had the whole monopoly of the fresh pork business in that part of the camp that morning. We could have sold that pork for a dollar a pound! We were a ring. We had the monopoly and we could have put up the price as high as we pleased. That was the only time I was ever a monopolist and I have to admit I enjoyed it. I presume the reason Providence never allowed me to become a monopolist on a large scale is because I should have loved it too well. And I expect these monopolists we hear so much about, they are just like the rest of us. We would do just as they do if we were in their places. When I hear a politician denouncing the monopolists, ransacking the English language for epithets sufficiently expressive to give vent to their indignation, I have thought the real trouble with them is *somebody else got the pig and they didn't*. We had the pig this time. I said we could have sold it for a dollar a pound. But we didn't sell it, we wouldn't be so mean as that, we wanted it all ourselves. We had each of us a tin plate and we fried a plate full of it and [ate] it, and then we fried another and another and it all went the same way. If I should tell you how much clear pork we [ate], nothing with it whatever except salt, you wouldn't believe me. I told some of the comrades afterwards that we had eaten that pig all up and they wouldn't believe it. And if soldiers accustomed to swallow big stories wouldn't take that there is no use to tell it to you. But it is a fact just the same. We didn't leave so much of that pork as the boy left of the pears his mother told him he mustn't eat. She had a dozen very choice pears and as she was going away she says, "Johnny, you mustn't touch those pears." Of course then that would be the very thing Johnny would want to do. Tell a boy not to do a thing and he never will be easy until he does it. When she came back she found her pears all gone except one little gnarly sour one. She suspected Johnny. But Johnny denied promptly. He had never touched one of them, he said. The mother searched around and soon found unmistakable evidence that Johnny had eaten the pears. "Now Johnny, I didn't care anything about the pears but you have told me a lie and I must whip you for lying to me." "Oh no, mother, don't whip me. I didn't tell you a lie. I said I never touched one of them and that little gnarly one is the very one I never touched." But we didn't leave so much as that. We skinned it clean. There was nothing left.

I told my comrade it would kill us to eat so much. I was getting alarmed. Kill us! Of course it will but who cares. Nobody is going to get out of this infernal war alive and I had just as soon die eating pork as any other way. So we finished up our pig and went and lay down under a shade to die. Of course we expected to die. I never knew of one's eating so much fresh pork and living. I have felt ashamed to look a pig in the face ever since. But we didn't die. The order came to march and we had to tramp on towards Gettysburg.

Well, boys, the war is over. I don't believe there will ever be another war in this country. We have had enough of it. There was a war cloud [Pullman Strike] a few weeks ago but it was soon dispelled. As soon as the U.S. troops were on the ground at the scene of disturbance everything was quiet: We are finding out that we are a nation—that we have a central government with a strong arm to force obedience to laws whenever lawlessness breaks out. That editor of a Vicksburg paper told the law breakers they had better not get into collision with the U.S. troops. They would be severely punished if they did. "*We have been there*," he says.

I told you I wasn't going to make a speech, boys, and I won't. There are others here that will come forward and give you a good sensible speech. I didn't have time to get up a speech. I have been too busy, l-a-z-y busy. But I wanted to tell you this story. I thought it was important it should be told. You see comrades if I didn't get up here and tell about [it] nobody would ever know the fate of that pig. I haven't heard from my comrade for years and he may be dead before this time and if I had been taken away before I had told this story there would have been so much valuable U.S. history lost to the world forever. So comrades of the Grand Army of the Republic I want to have you know that Mr. Nelson Fassett of Jericho, Vermont, and your humble servant of Tunbridge, Vermont, both enlisted men in Company E, 2d Regiment, Vermont Volunteers 2d Brigade 2d Division, 6th Corps, on or about the 20th of June in the year of our Lord one thousand eight hundred and sixty-three did wilfully charge upon a defenseless rebel pig with intent to kill and that Fisk and Fassett did inflict upon the said pig injuries which resulted in its death, and furthermore the said Fisk & Fassett did in violation of the U.S. sanitary regulations did cook and eat said pig all at one meal. Well, we weren't court-martialled but I was just thinking how it would have sounded if we had been. I am not sure but that we ought to have been. If they had court-martialled us I imagine they would have sentenced us to wear a placard on our backs that would have been a warning to all the pigs in that country to keep out of our way.

Well, boys, if I am not going to make a speech I suppose the proper way for me to wind up this talk in good shape is to give some good advice and then quit. You know boys we did do some naughty things down south when we were in the army and we might just as well own it up as to lie about it. The ladies have found us out and we can't cheat them any more. But I think we did some good things there too. We did our duty. We didn't do any more but if we hadn't half done our duty these citizens honoring us by coming to our picnic the way they do and saying so many good words for us would make us believe we had done it. Let us be worthy of all the good things that are said about us, be true men everywhere, just as true for the right everywhere as we were true to the old flag in the war. We want to be true as citizens, as neighbors, as members of one great family. We don't want to go wrong at any place. We don't want to be like the good Bishop that was made Colonel of a regiment and like a good many others was swept away by the current of immorality and especially profanity. One day a member of his diocese who had heard him swear and felt shocked came to him and said, "Bishop, I am surprised to hear you use such language." "Well," said the Colonel, "when I swear it is as the Colonel but when I was praying I was the Bishop." "Yes, but when the devil comes and calls for the Colonel what will become of our Bishop?" No, we want to be true in every place. I believe in the good book, I believe every word it says. And you know what it says. Be faithful unto death and I will give you a crown of life. We knew what it was to be faithful during our service in the army. We want to be faithful everywhere. I don't know what a crown of life means but I believe it means as much as we think it does. We got an honorable discharge when the war ended, we want another honorable discharge when the war of life shall end.

NOTES

Introduction

1. "History of Co. E, 2d Regt., Vt. Vols." This "History" was among the papers given to the Tunbridge Historical Society.

2. All the quotations credited to Pliny Fisk are from a paper he prepared concerning the life of his brother, Wilbur Fisk, which was read by Edith Fisk Peters at the dedication of a boulder monument in Wilbur Fisk's memory. This ceremony took place at the church in Freeborn, Minnesota, in 1932. At the time, Pliny Fisk was a minister in Sharon, Vermont. Mildred A. Christianson of Albert Lea, Minnesota, the daughter of Edith Fisk Peters, sent us this material.

December 11, 1861

3. The Second Vermont Regiment was composed of ten companies of soldiers from the towns of Bennington, Brattleboro, Burlington, Castleton, Fletcher, Ludlow, Montpelier, Tunbridge, Vergennes and Waterbury.

4. In October, 1861, Camp Griffin was established near Lewinsville, Virginia, on the road from Chain Bridge to Lewinsville. "The Confederate outposts were five or six miles away, and the mass of the Confederate army, under General Joe Johnston, lay at Centreville and Manassas, fifteen miles to the southwest." (Benedict, G.G. *Vermont in the Civil War. A History of the Part Taken by the Vermont Soldiers and Sailors in the War for the Union, 1861-5.* Burlington, Vt.: The Free Press Association. 1886. Volume 1. p.237) Here the Second Vermont remained for five months.

5. The Union offensive at Bull Run ended in a Union retreat and the Second Regiment was part of this retreat. Wilbur Fisk, who enlisted in September, 1861, was not part of this action, but many of the men around him were with the Second Regiment at Bull Run in July, 1861, in battle just a month after they had been sworn in on June 2, 1861.

March 8, 1862

6. Henry Whiting of Michigan was commissioned as colonel by Governor Fairbanks on June 6, 1861. As a non-Vermonter, his command of a Vermont regiment led to dissatisfaction. But by March, 1862, the rank and file

indicated their respect and confidence by presenting him with this "sword and accoutrements."

April 6, 1862

7. General McClellan believed that Richmond, the political and industrial capital of the southern states, was more vulnerable and more accessible through the peninsula than from Manassas and Fredericksburg. The movement of Wilbur Fisk's unit from Camp Griffin to Fortress Monroe was part of this strategy.

June 7, 1862

8. Sylvester Graham (1794-1851), a reformer and Presbyterian minister from Connecticut, encouraged the use of coarsely ground whole wheat flour. He recommended a vegetable diet as a cure for intemperance.

January 15, 1863

9. After Mount Pleasant Hospital and the Convalescent Camp, Wilbur Fisk was sent to a rest camp in Brattleboro, Vermont, where he arrived on January 18, 1863. On March 10, 1863, he rejoined his regiment. During this furlough, on February 27, 1863, Wilbur Fisk and Angelina Drew were married at Nashua, New Hampshire. Wilbur Fisk's diary recorded these dates.

10. In his diary, Wilbur Fisk referred to a Mr. and Mrs Roberts in Washington, D.C., with whom he corresponded regularly and whom he visited when in or near Washington. Mrs. Roberts may be the "sister of charity" referred to here.

April 6, 1863

11. Colonel J.H. Walbridge of Bennington, Vermont, who was with the Second Regiment from its beginning in June, 1861, succeeded Colonel Whiting as commander in February, 1862. Colonel Walbridge resigned April 1, 1864, and was succeeded by Lieutenant-Colonel Newton I. Stone.

April 19, 1863

12. As Mayor of New York City in 1861, Fernando Wood, before the firing on Fort Sumter, had proposed that New York establish itself as an independent city. Despite a half-hearted gesture to raise a regiment later, he continued throughout the Civil War to be a leader of the Peace Democrats, the Copperheads, opposing President Lincoln's war effort. In 1862, he was elected to Congress where he became a leading spokesman for the Copper-

heads and a close colleague of the anti-Lincoln Congressman from Ohio, Clement Vallandigham.

May 2, 1863

13. In his diary on March 27, 1863, Wilbur Fisk recognized that "Major Tyler does not look like a fellow out of his teens but he fills his position with dignity and self-restraint." He added about Major Tyler's recent promotion that he "bears his promotion without giddiness." As Lieutenant-Colonel, J.S. Tyler of Brattleboro, Vermont, was commander of the Second Regiment in the Vermont Brigade for less than one day. Wilbur Fisk in his letters of May and June, 1864, described the Battle of the Wilderness and its awful mortality, and mentioned his "Lieutenant Colonel. . . wounded" on May 5, a wound that led to Lieutenant-Colonel Tyler's death on May 21, 1864, in the Metropolitan Hotel in New York City. (*Vermont in the Civil War,* Volume 1, p. 114)

May 24, 1863

14. Colonel Lewis Addison Grant succeeded Colonel Whiting as commander of the First Vermont Brigade in February, 1863. In Wilbur Fisk's diary for May 19, 1863, he wrote of Colonel Grant's careful preliminary Brigade review before a Division review planned for the next day. "He is anxious to have us appear in the best trim, perhaps the stars he is trying to get on his shoulder have something to do with it."

September 1, 1863

15. Under the Union Conscription Act of March 3, 1863, all able-bodied males between the ages of 20 and 45 were liable to military service. However, a drafted man who provided an acceptable substitute or paid the government $300 was excused. This unpopular law provoked nationwide resistance and protest. Disturbances were most serious in New York City, where for four days, from July 13 through July 16, 1863, rioters plundered, burned and murdered. Five regiments of the Union Army were sent to New York City.

16. Wilbur Fisk suggested that New York troops were not part of the controlling military after the Draft Riots, but the famous Seventh Regiment New York, which had been in the Gettysburg campaign, was sent back to New York City to help restore order.

17, Under the heading, "Summer Vacation in New York," *Vermont in the Civil War* relates that "A novel piece of service now fell to the lot of the brigade. . . detached from the Army of the Potomac, and ordered to New York. To this force the government decided to add several thousand of the best volunteer troops in the army — selecting for the purpose troops of tried courage and steadfast loyalty, who could be depended on in any emergency, and who would set an example of order, sobriety, and general good conduct. For this service, the Vermont brigade was the first volunteer organization selected. . . the order. . . was received by Colonel Grant on the 10th of August. . . and on the 13th and 14th the regiments went by rail to Alexandria, embarked on the transports Illinois and Ericsson, and were taken to New York, arriving there on the 20th. Here Colonel Grant. . . was ordered to land his brigade and march, without special parade, to Tompkins Square, and to establish there his headquarters, stationing three of his regiments there, one in Washington Square, and one in Madison Square. The regiments landed and went into camp in the squares named on the 21st and 22d. Two regiments of regulars that had been already stationed in Tompkins Square — which was near 'Mackerelville,' one of the worst parts of the city, swarming with rioters and criminals — were also placed under the command of Colonel Grant. The ammunition supplied to the troops included no blank cartridges. The officers were resolute and the men perfectly ready to obey orders; and there would have been no trifling about the business, if they had been called on to face a mob. The law-abiding people of the metropolis slept more soundly after the arrival of the troops; and the city was never more quiet, since its first settlement, than during the draft which soon followed. . . The respect of the New York mob for the uniform and the authority of the United States was noticeably strengthened by this little campaign in the north. About the time of the departure of the troops an order was issued by General Canby, complimenting them in high terms for their good behavior. . . On the other hand the troops were well treated by the people of New York and the other cities where they were stationed; and the brief return to civilization, the scenes and pleasures of the city, and the opportunities to see friends, hundreds of whom went down from Vermont to visit the soldiers, made this episode in their army life as agreeable as it was unwonted. Though the opportunities for desertion were almost unlimited, the desertions from the Vermont regiments were very few during their northern vacation." (Volume 1, pp.396-399)

18. The Sanitary Commission, which attempted to improve the hygienic conditions in the camps and hospitals, was modeled on the British Sanitary Commission of the Crimean War.

December 8, 1863

19. Lee's Mill was "the first assault on an entrenched line made by the army of the Potomac." It was "one of the bloodiest actions, in proportion to

numbers engaged, in which the Vermont troops took part during the war. It was also one of the most useless wastes of life and most lamentable of unimproved opportunities recorded in this history." (*Vermont in the Civil War.* Volume 1, p.249)

March 17, 1864

20. Colonel Newton I. Stone of Readsboro, Vermont, enlisted when he was twenty-three years old, and he was killed on May 5, 1864, in the Wilderness. He had succeeded Colonel Walbridge as commander of the Second Regiment in April, 1864.

June 19, 1864

21. General Nathan Bedford Forrest overwhelmed Fort Pillow on the Mississippi River on April 12, 1864, killing many Black soldiers in the effort. Although General Forrest claimed that the soldiers were trying to escape, most historians label the action a deliberate massacre.

22. In June of 1864, Wilbur Fisk knew that the Enlistment Act of July 17, 1862, provided that White privates should receive $13.00 a month plus $3.50 for clothing, while Negro privates were to receive only $7.00 and $3.00, and he argued for social and economic fairness. Responding to protests, the War Department in 1864 began to pay Black soldiers as much as White soldiers.

August 1, 1864

23. This letter written August 1, 1864, was not in the Vermont State Library at Montpelier, but it was available in this form at the Library of Congress. We assume the missing sentences would have explained Wilbur Fisk's return to the site of Camp Griffin.

October 12, 1864

24. This was the Chicago Proposition for peace: Resolved, that this Convention does explicitly declare, as the sense of the American people, that after four years of failure to restore the Union by the experiment of war, during which, under the pretence of military necessity, or war power higher then the Constitution, the Constitution itself has been disregarded in every part, and public liberty and private right alike trodden down, and the material prosperity of the country essentially impaired, justice, humanity, liberty, and the public welfare demand that immediate efforts be made for the cessation of hostilities, with a view to an ultimate convention of the States or other peaceable means, to the end that at the earliest practicable moment peace may be restored on the basis

of the Federal Union of the States.'' This platform plank was adopted at the Democratic convention in August, 1864, when General McClellan was nominated to run against President Lincoln.

October 30, 1864

25. All the other Anti-Rebel letters are addressed to the Editor of the *Freeman.*

December 15, 1864

26. General Grant needed these additional troops in his efforts to capture Petersburg and move on to Richmond.

February 8, 1865

27. Fort Hell is a reference to the Petersburg Mine Assault on July 30, 1864, by miners of the 48th Pennsylvania.

February 25, 1865

28. Mrs. Baxter was the wife of the Hon. Portus Baxter of Derby, Vermont, and the mother of Surgeon Jed J. Baxter.

29. Senator Henry Wilson of Massachusetts had strong anti-slavery views.

March 13, 1865

30. It is possible that ''Mr. Moody'' was Dwight Moody, the prominent evangelist, who served on the Christian Commission and was active in mission work in Chicago.

May 19, 1865

31. Jefferson Davis was captured on May 10, 1865, at Irwinsville, Georgia. General Grant, aware of the popular image described by Wilbur Fisk, wrote in Volume II of his *Memoirs,* ''Much was said at the time about the garb Mr. Davis was wearing when he was captured. I cannot settle this question from personal knowledge of the facts, but I have been under the belief from information given by General Wilson shortly after the event that when Mr. Davis learned that he was surrounded by our cavalry he was in his tent dressed in a gentleman's dressing gown. . . Naturally enough, Mr. Davis wanted to escape and would not reflect much how this should be accomplished provided it might be done successfully.'' (Grant, U.S. *Personal Memoirs of U.S. Grant.* New York: Charles L. Webster, 1886. Vol. II, p.524)

INDEX